Forbidden Science

Volume Two

Also by Jacques Vallee

In English:

Anatomy of a Phenomenon (Regnery, Ace, Ballantine)
Challenge to Science (Regnery, Ace, Ballantine)
Passport to Magonia (Regnery, Contemporary)
The Invisible College (E. P. Dutton)
Messengers of Deception (And/or, Bantam)
The Edge of Reality (with Dr. J. A. Hynek, Contemporary)
Dimensions (Contemporary, Ballantine)
Confrontations (Ballantine)
Revelations (Ballantine)
The Network Revolution (And/or, Penguin, Google)
Electronic Meetings (co-author, Addison-Wesley)
Computer Message Systems (McGraw-Hill)
A Cosmic Samizdat (Ballantine)
Forbidden Science, Vol. One (Documatica Research)
The Four Elements of Financial Alchemy (TenSpeed)
FastWalker, novel (Frog, Ltd.)
The Heart of the Internet (Hampton Roads, Google)
Stratagem, novel (Documatica Research)
Wonders in the Sky (with C. Aubeck, Tarcher-Penguin)

In French:

Le Sub-Espace, novel (Hachette – Jules Verne Prize)
Le Satellite Sombre, novel (Denoël, Présence du Futur)
Alintel, novel (Le Mercure de France)
La Mémoire de Markov, novel (Le Mercure de France)
Les Enjeux du Millénaire, essay (Hachette Littératures)
Au Coeur d'Internet (Balland, Google)
Stratagème (L'Archipel)
Français d'Ailleurs (Documatica Research)

Jacques Vallee

Forbidden Science

Volume Two

Journals 1970-1979
California Hermetica

Published by Documatica Research, LLC.

The author can be contacted at:
P.O.Box 641650
San Francisco, CA. 94164

Website: www.jacquesvallee.com

Fifth American edition

Cover graphics: Dark matter or dust ring, courtesy NASA/ESA

ISBN: 978-0-578-03231-3

Printed in the United States of America.

January 2017 edition

Contents

Figures

Introduction

Smiling faces, smiling faces sometimes
They don't tell the truth
Smiling faces, smiling faces
Tell lies and I got proof.

Smiling Faces Sometimes
The Undisputed Truth, 1971

Some twenty years ago an admirable friend told me his goal was "to live fully the life of a man, and having lived it, to share it with others," words I never forgot, hoping I would have the opportunity, some day, to fulfill a similar mission. Publication of the first volume of *Forbidden Science* partially satisfied that ambition, but the record halted in 1969. (**1**)

This second volume covers the decade of the Seventies, a troubled time everywhere. If you lived in Northern California you faced exciting challenges. These journals may help to understand some of the irreversible changes that followed.

An article in *New Scientist* magazine, addressing the problem of "capturing the flavor of research," has noted that "a rather skewed and unsatisfactory picture of the dynamics and progress of contemporary science would emerge if it came only from the remembrances of the Great and the Good." (**2**) This remark applies particularly to those neglected fields on the margins of science, and to new disciplines about to be born or refuted.

There was much birth and refutation during the Seventies. Technology accelerated, invading novel areas; robotics and artificial intelligence grew into serious topics; the exploration of the solar system became a practical endeavor; the first computer networks, forerunners of Internet were invented. I was not among the Great and the Good, but I did witness these changes. Some of my colleagues became wealthy, are cited by journalists and hailed by historians. Many among the most influential have remained humble; obscure; unnoticed.

Innovation in California was not confined to the proper world of the laboratory. The air was filled with arguments. Campuses burst in confrontation among factions and power groups. The sizzling spirit I experienced at institutions like Stanford University and SRI was a reflection of the years of Nixon, clashes in the Middle East and economic turmoil in the United States. The atmosphere was vibrant. There was a sense of imminence and danger in every sunrise. America even ran out of gasoline.

With such events as the end game in Vietnam and the turpitudes of Watergate in the background, the major topic of this Diary is paranormal research, which saw remarkable development even as lessons were forgotten or perverted in the ensuing chaos. It is in Northern California that the Human Potential Movement emerged; parapsychology entered the physics laboratory; as for "the problem" of unidentified flying objects, it came back into the news, although the establishment had dismissed it through the combined might of the Air force, the *New York Times* and the Academy of Sciences.

The negative conclusions of the University of Colorado report, published in 1969, had settled nothing. The pioneers of ufology resumed their work. Some of the figures the reader may remember from my first volume - researchers like Aimé Michel, Pierre Guérin, Jim McDonald - continued to play a prominent role. They were joined by others: scientists like Peter Sturrock and Claude Poher or independent investigators like Charles Bowen and John Keel, contributed to changing our view of the phenomenon. The genius of Steven Spielberg exploded it. But it is the memory of J. Allen Hynek that continued to dominate the ongoing mystery. As Timothy F. Murphy wrote, "testimony is witness in front of an indifferent world about the worth and merit of persons. And thus one writes, for the world unconvinced, that someone was here and that, death notwithstanding, a presence remains." For those who were close to him, Hynek's memory does remain.

It is during the years covered by this volume that I began to gain greater insight into the theater of the paranormal. The more I analyzed the conundrum of ufology, the more the link to older mysteries became clear. Drawn by nature to direct experience, I explored the esoteric groups and was surprised at what I found beyond the obvious charlatanism and delusion. I was fortunate in catching a glimpse of the chessboard and identifying some of those who moved the pawns.

Interaction with them left me intellectually puzzled and emotionally bruised. Along with the scientists and businessmen with whom I spent my professional time, I met elusive figures from what I came to recognize as the "undercurrent" of technical espionage, as well as disturbing characters like occultists Israel Regardie and Anton LaVey, and radical thinker Ira Einhorn, a youth leader turned management guru whose destiny would include an ugly accusation for murder that propelled him to the FBI list of most wanted criminals, and a life sentence.

Some day a perceptive historian may be able to document how and why Intelligence agencies of the major countries took such a messy interest in parapsychology and aerial phenomena during the Seventies. The argument that the Soviet adversary was researching the field provides only a tiny excuse for an answer.

I have never forgotten the harsh lessons of the *Pentacle Memorandum* (**3**) revealed in Volume One. This previously-secret document showed that scientific debate about the phenomenon had been cynically manipulated by the military and the CIA. A panel of Nobel-level scientists assembled in 1953 to analyze the problem had never received full disclosure of the data. Although official interest by classified agencies may have been legitimate, it opened the door to abuse. It flew in the face of the oft-repeated statement that the government was not interested.

There is more to ufology than stories of gray Aliens flying around in spaceships. And there is more to computer networks than e-mail and cyberspace. Some of the events this book relates may amuse you or shock you. All I can say is that these things happened. It is too late to go back and change them: they have shaped the world in which we live. Yet I would have withheld my testimony were it not for the publication of two books that call for clarification of the record. I am talking about Jim Schnabel's elegant *Remote Viewers* (**4**), which exposed the efforts of the Pentagon in paranormal research and made public the role played by the SRI methodology team of which I was a part; and *Where Wizards Stay up Late* by Hafner and Lyon **(5)**, which gave a slanted view of the early days of Arpanet.

Both books were written by outsiders. Contributing to the debate about the early history of both subjects is more than an interesting exercise for a first-hand participant, it is a genuine duty because, as my astrophysics professor Vladimir Kourganoff wrote in 1958: "Dogmatism and skepticism are the two monsters between which any truth must pass to enter the kingdom of science." **(6)**

I did pass between these two monsters and lived to see what was beyond, but found no ultimate answer. I can only offer this volume as a contribution to a marginal issue that continues to puzzle and inspire us, because the search for non-human intelligence is one of the most important scientific quests of all time. In the words of Andrew H. Knoll, chairman of the evolutionary department at Harvard, "it is our remarkable good fortune to be part of the first generation in history that has a chance of finding the answer."

The period reviewed here was not only marked by intellectual and social turmoil: it was also one of the most liberated in history. These aspects should not be separated. It is in the Seventies that the experiments of the previous decade blossomed, engulfing the nation until the new-found pleasures became inseparable from the scourge of drug abuse. The hopeful movement became a monster.

I was neither tempted nor repelled by those who indulged in drugs. Our family was very fortunate in not being touched by them. I never started using tobacco, let alone grass, LSD or hashish. More through cowardice than moral rectitude I avoided these substances, encouraged in my resolve by the fate of close friends who were physically and mentally destroyed by their habits. My personal goal was always to extract as much lucidity as I could from the all-too limited mind that nature had given me. Everything I saw in the drug culture seemed to go in the opposite direction. I would not use any drugs today even if they were decriminalized - as they should be.

By the end of the decade America was eager for a return to a familiar pattern - its cruel but predictable hypocrisy of yore. The

Moral Majority swept into the White House in 1979. Greed and egotism became virtues. In the eyes of many Americans, mystical experimentation and sensual pleasure were suspect again. The pendulum of public mores returned to the depth of conformity.

Everything could have been so simple!

When the Air Force closed down Project Blue Book in 1969 it could have left the door open to scientific investigation of the UFO phenomenon, no longer as a military or strategic threat but as a legitimate topic for wide-ranging research. In its review of the Condon Report, the U.S. Academy of Sciences could have noted that one third of all the cases investigated by the official panel at the University of Colorado had remained unexplained: thus a dispassionate program of small budget, competitive calls for proposals would have been justified to further elucidate the patterns behind the sightings.

This is the way normal science is done, with peer review, milestones and clearly-defined endpoints, in a dispassionate atmosphere. As the reader will see in this volume, there was plenty of material that could be studied, in the field and the laboratory, with the existing tools of science. Rationalism had nothing to fear.

But none of that happened. In one of its most shameful hours, the Academy summarily put its mighty stamp on Condon's rejection of all the reports, assuming that would kill the phenomenon forever. It did not, of course, but in the process the public had been taught that science was not only biased but impotent.

Our own research had to be conducted privately, in near-secrecy with almost no resources. Although remarkable progress was made during the decade, the field remained mired in confusion. As the reader will discover, I suspect that the intelligence community decided that the belief in UFOs could be used as a convenient shield for some of its own, very terrestrial flying devices, and for experiments with the dissemination of rumors, including the suggestion that America was in control of advanced technologies the Soviets could not approximate. The field was sinking in false mysteries, but Washington liked it that way.

I must add a word about my reasons for keeping this book as a diary. When the first volume of *Forbidden Science* was published in 1992, I was told by knowledgeable friends in publishing that I would reach more people if I rewrote my Journal as a Memoir. "That would be easier to read," they pointed out, "more accessible for the public." Serious reviewers don't bother with diaries and journals.

In preparing the second volume I decided against such rewriting for three reasons. First, I rather like the notion of only being read by those few people who are truly interested in digging out and analyzing scarce data. The UFO phenomenon raises some very deep scientific problems that are best studied away from the media. I don't feel a need to mass-market what I have to say. In an age of disposable consumer goods and evanescent digital communication I am not bothered by the idea of selling only a few hundred copies of a durable book. This is not elitism, it is good information science: What is most valuable must remain parsimonious, even in the days of the Internet.

Second, historians of science tell us that "what is known" is less important than "who knew what, at what time?" Only a diary or well-preserved correspondence can nail down evolving ideas.

The third reason has to do with my own private enjoyment of the art of the Diary, a craft distinct from any other literary genre, which I continue to acquire slowly as I get older. Transposing the facts into an ordinary narrative would make their special flavor evaporate. "In May of the following year I went to Montségur" is not the same thing as "*Monday 15 May -- I am standing here, on the crumbling wall of Montségur, with the wind in my face...*"

The art of the Diary rests in a unique way of addressing Time itself, by holding on to a particular instant, suspending it briefly in the light of the mind, underlining it, and throwing it back into the stream. In the process it acquires a special meaning, a kind of salvation from the universal drowning that sweeps our acts and thoughts - and everything we have ever loved -- into the gray horrors of entropy.

Jacques Vallee, San Francisco – August 2008

Part Five

COMPUTER CONFESSIONS

1

Brunville-par-Bayeux. Monday 15 June 1970.

In the blue bedroom with white open beams, I just finished typing my old diary (**1**). I wonder if I should resume these journals at the start of another decade. After a long gap, half a year without a single entry, can I find the thread again?

When rain falls over this Norman village, in a manner so steady and obstinate, every day feels like a slow dreary Sunday. The *pièces* (in local dialect, the pastures, the parcels, the *pieces of land*) are fat with mud and studded with raindrops. I listen to the hum of showers on the slate roof. A power failure has darkened the region. Janine's sister Annick and their resourceful mother cooked a whole shoulder of lamb in the huge fireplace, with a wonderful smokey smell. I watch the flames lick the blackened stones, the light reflecting on the somber wood of bookcases.

I find my imagination traveling back to a time when there was no electricity, no radio, no television, and no direct news of Paris or New York. In that slow purposeful time people were forced to think and live along with the rhythms of nature. For most of history this is the way mankind has existed, I forced myself to realize. There are people alive today who remember that era. The thought was pleasant. I felt safer than I had in a long time.

This house belongs to Annick. One could survive indefinitely here, even if electrical power never came back, even if the "outside world" faded away. It is an old farm structure built like a fortress in 1642 -- a long stone rectangle with a high pitch roof and lofty *mansardes*. The walls, two feet in thickness, keep the heat of the hearth. From the narrow country road one enters the courtyard through a gate between the main house and a stone cottage. Opposite the main structure are a large barn, as big as the house itself, and shelters for the poultry and rabbits. There is a special building with an oven where farmers in a bygone time baked their bread; a functioning well with a hand-operated pump stands near the front door, although the house has been modernized and enjoys running water.

Over the next few days a select group of researchers will be assembling here: I have organized a discreet conference involving a few British, French and American investigators of the mystery of unidentified flying objects. We'll try to map out a common philosophy, a strategy.

Later the same day.

California has caught us in its whirlwind, that's the problem. In the last six months, along with the joy of our new home, I have gone through the toughest crisis. What happens to me is happening to many others in the inebriation of the high-tech world.

When we moved to Stanford I hadn't understood to what extent the West Coast was in upheaval. There are two major centers of system development in computer science today: The Multics project at MIT and the Stanford computation center, the organization I joined last September. It is a team of accomplished craftsmen to which I am proud to belong. Our leader, a bearded red-haired tyrant named Rod Fredrickson, hired me into his inner circle when it became obvious to everyone that the University's multi-million dollar information retrieval project, named *Spires*, along with a related library automation effort, was in trouble (**2**). A short man with an even shorter temper, Fredrickson gave me six months to come up with radical solutions. I started from the tools I had developed at Northwestern University and improved at Shell, to create a database system I call *Dirac*. It ran successfully within three months - a thrilling period. We began using it as the nucleus of a Stanford information network applied to science. Rod and I made plans to move from *Dirac* to the design of an information machine that would surpass existing computers.

"I can optimize it," I told Fredrickson as we sat in his darkened office, the hum of glowing terminals filling the place. "We can isolate the *primitives* of the use of computers to process text, as opposed to processing numbers. That's never been done."

He thought for a moment: "You know what would be really

exciting? That'd be to go another step further - turn them into hardware. How would you like to have a machine in which text-processing functions were represented with actual circuits? Working at lightning speed... I'll bet even IBM doesn't have anything like that on the drawing board."

No such machine has been built or even designed. Yet it will be much more important, in the future, to manipulate information than to operate on numbers.

There's a problem at Stanford. It isn't technical but basely bureaucratic, bogged down in political muck. The titular head of all computing is Paul Armer, who finds it hard to manage eminent scholars like Ed Feigenbaum, a pioneer in artificial intelligence (**3**), and wizards like Fredrickson. So he procrastinates and ends up hiring consultants. The latest one was a character who looked at this world-class facility through the eyes of an accountant. He interviewed the bureaucrats and concluded: "Too many ambitious developments conflict with Faculty projects. Cut; stop; neutralize."

"Why did they hire us in the first place, if they don't want innovation?" grumbled John Borgelt, the jolly bearded fellow who had built our text processor. Predictably, the staff exploded, a hand-picked team of cathedral builders reassigned as museum curators. Fredrickson flew into a rage and resigned. The head of the physics computer facility followed. In my work with databases Rod's departure has left me facing a saturnine professor of communications who is building an empire around the floundering *Spires* project. "Smiling Ed" is the way his students call him. I should have foreseen that he'd feel threatened when articles published about our work began circulating (**4**).

This would be a mere anecdote if the rest of the world wasn't in turmoil. Larger events wash over our technical island, highlighting conflicts. Nixon has ordered the invasion of Cambodia, triggering uproar. Rebelling students blocked the computing center. The most radical ones called for blowing up our seven-million dollar mainframe as an Establishment symbol. Molotov cocktails did minor damage to our offices.

My assistant and I made an attempt to spinoff the database effort.

We sought outside funding; we bravely started demonstrating *Dirac* to executives from various companies. That was before the summer holidays, before I came to Normandy, hoping for a rest. Now a letter from California has reached me in Bayeux. Paul Armer is going to take a leave of absence, a year at Harvard researching the technical obsolescence of managers. “Paul has found his true field of expertise,” Fredrickson quipped.

Bayeux. Tuesday 16 June 1970.

What I've witnessed in the last few months is the scuttling of one of the finest computer teams in the world. Faculty members keep publishing reports that hide their failure under phrases like “This year again we have successfully identified new obstacles to scientific information processing...” They calmly request another million dollars, to identify more obstacles! Why should Washington spend millions a year in taxpayers’ money (including the fat overhead which lines academic pockets) if my two-man team on the computing staff has solved the problem they were supposed to “research”? Five user groups from geology to cardiology are already retrieving complex information on our computer using *Dirac*.

I must draw the lessons from this. Any idea of long-term stability in this capital of high tech is an illusion. The sooner I adapt to the boiling upheaval of Silicon Valley, the better. Every day I can see how hard it will be for Europe to learn this lesson. Europeans are still searching for an Absolute, while the future will be a world of permanent turmoil. In a society where information moves at the speed of light, *absolutes are obsolete*. The mistake the French made, when De Gaulle offered a choice between Himself and Chaos, was to choose him. California would have gladly embraced Chaos.

Aimé Michel, with whom I have discussed all this, believes that under President Pompidou, with Jacques Chaban-Delmas as prime minister, France is entering an era of grave uncertainty, after last year's monetary devaluation. Between the lack of good communications, high taxes on the middle class and the failure of technical education, our old country is in trouble.

Bayeux. Wednesday 17 June 1970.

We spent the last few days of May in Paris, where leftist demonstrators were fighting the police (**5**), then went on to Berlin for another Standards meeting. An eye-opening incident took place there, revealing differences in the way technology was perceived. I served as chairman of the software terminology group, an easy job because English and French definitions had already been prepared. Yet trouble developed as soon as we tackled the first definition. The Germans had an unexpected proposal for a carefully-crafted alternative. Their leader spoke up, a distinguished professor from Munich, a follower of Wittgenstein. He felt strongly that any technological definition must differentiate between the *physical unit* and the *functional unit* for every part of a system: The steering column of a car can be defined by how it's built, or by what happens when you turn the wheel (**6**). The two principles, he said, must be clearly separated in any good definition.

The French threw their hands up: we had 200 terms to review that day. Yet the Germans had a valid point. I had been taught in Europe that a scientist must have a philosophical framework for what he does before he can apply his knowledge. On the other hand, my experience with computers came from pragmatic America, where nobody gives a damn about philosophy as long as a gadget works: Deeper understanding is left for future generations to fathom. Philosophy follows practice in America, it precedes it in Europe. I felt torn between the two cultures, in a way I'd never experienced.

Our frustration was all the more exasperating because the words we were defining were well-known, common computer terms like *storage, memory, address*. I hit upon a test of our differences: I asked the German professor how he would distinguish between physical unit and functional unit in the definition of *virtual memory*, a scheme that enables a modern computer to manipulate a much larger set of data than it actually holds in its “real” memory. Here was a typical American invention that had simply grown out of everyday experience. There was no simple answer. The meeting was adjourned for lunch, and the professor, who had a weak heart, didn't return in the afternoon. I never found out what Wittgenstein would have said about virtual memory. What I did learn was that computers were forcing us into an age in which we may have to take action before we understand the consequences of our action, and I find that lesson disturbing.

We also had fun in Berlin. My former RCA colleague Pete Ingerman went out with the Italian delegates. He discovered that only one of them spoke a little English. In an attempt to be polite, he told them, *Machina ipsam culturam non habet*, Latin for "the computer has no culture of its own." The sole English-speaker replied, "Pete, there's nothing wrong with your Italian, except that you use all those archaic words!"

Janine and I went into East Berlin for a few hours, an impression of dread, far worse than anything we had expected. I felt ashamed to be standing on a street corner, displaying the luxury of my freedom inside that horrible jail. The inmates looked at me, reproach and envy in hopeless eyes. There was so much despair in those faces that I recoiled in sorrow. I never want to see those eyes again.

Later the same day.

Back in Paris I was able to buy a rare edition of Paracelsus and renew old acquaintances. Unesco offered me a job that I declined. Visiting Pierre Guérin at the Astrophysical Institute to discuss UFOs I found the same dirty walls I knew in 1961, the same trash in the hallways, a dark office basement, and photos of Mars pinned to the plaster. One of the consequences of the failed May 68 "revolution" has been the setting up of two bureaucracies rather than a single one, so monstrous that researchers relinquish lab space to make room for offices. Work has ground to a slow pace while the conventions of French academia collapsed.

"It's the carnal side that counts in life," Pierre told me. Was this the same scientist who had just discovered the fourth ring of Saturn? **(7)**

Now I'm waiting for Guérin, Aimé Michel and other members of our private seminar at the farmhouse owned by Janine's sister, watching the rain fall over Normandy. Charles Bowen, editor of the

Flying Saucer Review will come from London, and Fernand Lagarde, a founder of *Lumières dans la Nuit*, the best French magazine on UFOs, will come from the South of France. A man named Mike Jaffe will report on U.S. cases, along with Janine and me. It is through my friend Don Hanlon that I met Mike and his research group, *Datanet*, based in Silicon Valley. Their newsletter is full of timely news and incisive humor.

Mike, an electronics technician, works on the simulator for the F-111 aircraft. He's also a biker, an active radio ham, an optimist, jack of all trades, autodidact, seeker of magical truth. He was born in a poor family in Brittany. We've become close friends. Janine and I enjoy weekend excursions with him and his wife Christine, our two kids, their two kids. We talk endlessly of hermetic traditions, electronics and hippiedom, invisible colleges, computers and rockets.

Bayeux. Friday 19 June 1970.

Our conference has gotten off to a bad start. Charles Bowen arrived last night with the firm intention of getting me to reveal Hynek's secrets. He complained at once about the location we picked in Normandy: "Why not Paris?" he asked bitterly. Well, we don't have any facilities and we can't feed seven people for three days in Paris. He also complained about Mike Jaffe, not a "recognized authority." As if there were recognized authorities in this strange field. Bowen is a tall man with thick eyebrows, fifty-two years old, obsessed with the fate of his *Flying Saucer Review*. His wife detests the subject. He also suffers in his work at the South African embassy in London, in the accounting department.

"I have been passed over for promotion seven times," he told us sadly. "My employers disapprove of my outside interests."

We discussed psychic surgeons, in which he believes uncritically, and we got back to the subject of Allen Hynek whom he regards as sly, secretive and conceited. I had no intention to tell him about the still-secret *Pentacle* letter. Instead we debated the ideas of a writer named John Keel (**8**), because Charles had just read his latest work, *Operation Trojan Horse*.

Guérin drove in today. Characteristically, he started fighting with Bowen as soon as he stepped out of his car. The argument had to do with a pompous editorial by Bowen praising Guérin's discovery of Saturn's fourth ring, calling him "the great French astronomer" and hailing him for publicly joining the ranks of FSR supporters.

"What do my planetary photographs have to do with ufology? You're mixing up everything; you're not operating in good faith."

Bowen looked downcast: "I must cling to every straw," he said somberly. I tried to defuse the argument but Charles became bitter. I suggested a coffee break. Annick did her best to put everyone at ease but Bowen kept pouting like a child with a bruised ego. The discussion turned to a review of near-landings.

"When something comes close to a house at night, like a thief, and hovers over the sleeping occupants, it can only be motivated by evil," said Charles. Good, evil, what did it mean, in this context?

"My mind is spinning," Charles said. "I can't think any more... terrible headache."

Pierre and I went outside to play with the children. Aimé Michel arrived with Lagarde on the evening train. A good surprise: Raymond Veillith was with them: quiet, a seeker of absolutes, and a vegetarian, he makes it a point to tolerate every opinion and to give a chance to every idea. His associate Fernand Lagarde is a clear-thinking man, sure of himself. A retired worker from the French railroads, he is clever as an old farmer. In the car coming back from the station he told me, in his friendly, no-nonsense style: "We're here to tell you what we think and to find out what you think." We had a big family-style dinner with Janine's parents. Guérin noticed Annick's beauty and started courting her. She was amused.

Bayeux. Saturday 20 June 1970.

Mike Jaffe arrived, just in time for breakfast. The rain had stopped. Our children, who had been intimidated by Charles Bowen and Guérin, rushed out happily to greet Mike as he emerged from his rented Fiat. We began our talks in the main room around a large table covered with green felt. We only broke up for meals, a marvel of French country-style cooking, Norman specialties, veal in white sauce, grain-fed poultry, Camembert and cider.

Lagarde had a three-page agenda that emphasized the need for scientific analysis. Using slightly different words Guérin, Aimé and I pointed out that scientists didn't have any magical solution. The lists of expert consultants that amateur groups proudly mention in support of their activities have no meaning; they rarely do any work. This innocuous beginning elicited another reaction in Charles: He launched into an apology.

"At the death of Waveney Girvan, our first editor," he said tearfully, "there was nothing left of the *Flying Saucer Review*. The archives, the files, even the collection had disappeared. Girvan's wife disposed of them. She hated the whole subject... Just like my wife. That's why I have to rely on the names of our scientific consultants."

After lunch Lagarde gave us a demonstration of his skills in dowsing. He had brought a pendulum he used to find water, minerals and caves in the Southwest of France.

"How did you learn to use a pendulum?" I asked him.

"When I was a young man," he said, "I had just joined the French rail company. My boss taught me how to do it. He used it to locate our coils of copper wire."

Lagarde had also brought the original tapes of his investigation into the Aveyron case, to which we listened with rapt attention (**9**). The main witness is a young illiterate farmer. Since his observation of small wandering spheres of light, he keeps seeing nine men who come to the foot of his bed and instruct him to write a book.

Next, I brought up the American situation in general and John Keel in particular. Project Blue Book, which was, for better or worse, the world's only official UFO investigation has been disbanded by the Air Force. This hasn't helped independent researchers. The Apro group is in difficulty, Nicap is moribund (**10**).

The circulation of FSR, Bowen told us, has dropped from 3,300 copies in November 1968 to 2,950 today. Now comes John Keel with stories of disks in the sky and monsters in the countryside. I enjoy his refreshing style, but few of his reports check out.

Take, for instance, the incident on 16 August 1966 when hundreds of witnesses in the U.S. saw strange objects rushing towards them in mid-air. I pulled out the file at the time. The Air Force explained the object as the star Capella. This was ridiculous and discredited their consultant Allen Hynek: we plotted numerous independent witnesses in regions as remote as Wisconsin, Minnesota and Michigan! Just because it wasn't Capella, however, didn't mean that it was a UFO, so we resumed the investigation. Allen's chief engineer Bill Powers discovered the truth: a double barium cloud experiment had been carried out from a rocket above Canada (**11**). I passed on the solution to John Keel as soon as I learned he was going to publish the sightings, but he insisted to call it a mystery.

Charles looked miserable again. He mumbled that he felt as if he had been dragged before a tribunal, the work of his whole life questioned. Dinnertime came. A wonderful smell drifted from the kitchen. Aimé and Pierre tried to cheer up Bowen, but he retired to the bathroom, clutching a tube of medication.

Bayeux. Sunday 21 June 1970.

Aimé Michel shared the blue bedroom with Charles last night. He woke up two or three times and heard him tossing and turning. In the morning he saw Charles staring at him.

"You're already awake?" said Aimé.

"I didn't sleep at all. You see, I now understand what a terrible mistake my life has been. All these sacrifices, only to get to this point at the end!"

"This guy's a masochist," joked Guérin. "Like all those Englishmen."

Lagarde and Veillith arrived on foot from Bayeux. We sat around the table again; discussed plans, practical steps. The meeting became constructive. We managed to agree on a range of issues, including the open sharing of future research papers and sighting reports. None of us knows what UFOs are, but the observations need to be documented.

Aimé took Charles to see the Bayeux tapestry, "so he would understand how the French had conquered England," as he put it wistfully. Charles invited Janine and me to come and visit his home on our way back next week.

Tonight only Aimé, Guérin and Jaffe are still here. Pierre and Mike are competing for Annick's favors. As for me, I am apprehensive about what we'll find when we get back to Silicon Valley.

Bayeux. Monday 22 June 1970.

Our conference is over. Aimé and Guérin are gone. Janine and I are happy with our reunited family. Mike is having breakfast downstairs; I hear the kids laugh with him. The revelation of the seminar for me was Lagarde, a solid, stable thinker with common sense and an open mind. It is good to see that there are still people like him in France.

On the flight back to California. Thursday 25 June 1970.

We left for England after delays in Cherbourg, crossed the Channel on the ferry and slept in Southampton. The train stopped at every charming little town: we passed Farnborough and reached Woking. At Charles' house on Woodham lane we finally met Mrs. Bowen, a proper English housewife preoccupied with raising her daughters and over-cooking veal cutlets dripping with cranberry sauce.

A distinguished man in a gray suit was waiting for us at Charles' house. He quietly introduced himself as Gordon Creighton, and I shook his hand with genuine respect and pleasure. We had been corresponding for a long time: six years ago he produced the first translation of my work into English. We began our conversation in a small sitting room that opened on a garden. On the street side the tall trees formed a beautiful scene that reminded me of Saint-Germain, more open, minus stone walls and ugly French dogs.

Where did Allen Hynek and Fred Beckman get the idea that Gordon was too old to do valuable work? He's a brilliant man, full of wit, very sharp indeed. He may have exercised more influence over this research than anyone in Europe, aside from Aimé Michel. A master linguist, he started contributing to FSR with the earliest issues, using a pen name to translate foreign case reports from Latin

America, Russia, and China, to give readers the impression that the Review had a large international staff. He also serves as president of Bufora, the British civilian research organization. A former Intelligence specialist, he lived in China for a long time. After much anxious debate he decided not to spend the rest of his life there. He was sent to the United States (New Orleans) and to Brazil (Belo Horizonte) as British consul, and then spent seven years at the Joint Intelligence Bureau in London where he worked alongside CIA men, following Chinese affairs. There was an office in the same building, he said, from which official UFO "explanations" emanated.

"The higher-up people were in the hierarchy, the more interested they were in the subject," he told us.

"How come you never tried to approach them to discuss the sightings?" I asked. He did not evade the question.

"There was never any opportunity. There might be a chance now with Lord Mountbatten, who's just retired. The Duke of Edinburgh would never discuss the topic."

"Perhaps they're afraid of leaks," I said. "Why not get someone at a high level to sponsor a small, quiet study group?"

He seemed intrigued with the idea, but I had to confess that when Aimé Michel and I had tried to get the French to take an interest in the problem, they had gone straight to the Americans, who had served up to them the oft-reheated meal of Major Quintanilla's bogus Air Force statistics. Would the same thing happen in England? Very likely, Creighton said.

Our talks with Charles Bowen and Brian Winder (another FSR team member) were warm: the tension of Normandy was forgotten. But it is Gordon who should have come to Bayeux. He stood head and shoulders above the others, a master of the subject, while Charles and Brian could only talk about the tedious day-to-day stuff of recruiting, editing the magazine, answering mail, no research.

Gordon told us that the Red Chinese were fascinated with the problem. He knows two Australian businessmen who travel in mainland China. On every trip they hear of sightings, and Chinese officials often ask them if there are similar reports in the rest of the world, *or if the phenomenon is peculiar to China!*

Fig. 1: The June 1970 Bayeux conference: Mike Jaffe, Fernand Lagarde, Jacques Vallée, Pierre Guérin, Raymond Veillith.

Fig. 2: At the Stanford radio-astronomy array, 1970

Brian and Gordon drove us to King's Cross where we boarded the bus to Stansted for the long journey home. We took off at midnight, with a stop in Ottawa eight hours later, with mechanical problems.

Belmont. Saturday 27 June 1970.

Turmoil. We had only been in the house for ten minutes when the phone rang: My assistant was on the line telling me that the president of Stanford had resigned -- the campus was in disarray. Paul Armer has written me a note postponing any decision on my project.

The phone again: A recruiter wanted to know if Janine was interested in a new job. It turns out the Raychem Corporation, for which she has been working, has fallen on hard times and is laying off the whole team! We believe we can solve these problems, but we wonder how others are coping in this storm: older employees, people without technical skills...

There are emotional upheavals all around us: Mike's wife just called. She was itching to buy a motorcycle, she said, to take up skin diving, looking for an escape: "I want to live," she said with a hoary, sexy tone. She is running away from reality, like the rest of California. I can't say I blame her.

Later the same day.

It was true. Raychem just laid off 250 people. A financial crisis is reverberating through aerospace companies. Now that the moon landing has been accomplished, budgets are cut by Congress without regard for those who made this achievement possible. Washington doesn't see the long-term value of its investment.

It is because I believe that the most important facts of our age are paranormal phenomena that I keep this diary. The simplistic approaches are bankrupt: on one side, hard scientists are waiting for a ghost or a UFO to manifest in plain view of their recording gadgets, not a very likely event. On the other side, dreamers throw themselves into speculation, rather than looking at facts. Neither approach can work. There is no other science than instrumental science, but the instrument has to be the scientist himself. French writer Maeterlinck was right when he criticized a turn-of-the-century psychic researcher named Dr. Osty:

> He fails to give us, as he should, the detail of his experiments, his controls, his proofs *in extenso*. I know it would be a tiring, difficult task demanding a large volume, made almost unreadable by numerous childish incidents and unavoidable repetitions. It would have to take the form of an indiscreet autobiography, of a public confession, and this is not easy to face. But one has to go through with it. In a science in the process of being founded it is not sufficient to show the end product and to affirm one's conviction. It is essential to describe the paths along the itinerary, and to allow everyone to draw his own conclusions … (**12**).

Belmont. Monday 29 June 1970.

I went to see Rod Fredrickson with my assistant. We told him he had our loyalty. He said the battle was lost. His advice was for us to stay at Stanford, publish as much as we could. Now optimism is returning: Janine has received several job offers. And a psychologist named Arthur Hastings has invited me to speak before a science-fiction seminar on campus.

Belmont. Wednesday 1 July 1970.

Every day I enjoy driving my green Jeep through clusters of eucalyptus trees on my way to Stanford, but the landscape is changing fast under the pressure of encroaching development. From San Francisco Bay to the charming coves of Santa Cruz, luscious hills unfold in the majesty of redwoods. A mystical fascination has always been felt here, but it is getting harder to find amidst all the greed and the rush toward power that has seized the new inhabitants.

Stanford bureaucrats have “approved” my system. There's a catch: they want to turn it over to their programmers and rewrite it! They have new money from Washington; they need my software at all cost, but I feel no respect for them.

There are still some good moments on Campus. At 11 this morning a fellow with sparkling eyes and a black beard arrived in my office, asked if I was the author of *Anatomy of a Phenomenon* and introduced himself as a biblical scholar with Stanford's Humanities Department. He told me about his research into a landing in New Jersey, and then we went on to other profound topics: Ezekiel's wheels and Merkhaba mysticism. His name is David Halperin.

Mike's wife, who wants to "live, live, live," did go out and buy herself a motorcycle. She has not returned all day. The poor fellow is devastated. Mike cared for their two kids, prepared the meals. At work an argument with a supervisor almost cost him his job.

The weather is hot. It's holiday time; students lazily stroll around. I am getting ready for a short trip to the Midwest for a computer conference, a welcome opportunity to see Allen again.

Wednesday 8 July 1970. On a flight returning from Chicago.

Allen's house was full of kids, including Carl Henize's four children. Their father is now in training as a scientist-astronaut. He may fly with Spacelab as early as 1973.

As an appetizer, while we had lunch with Fred, Allen pulled out color pictures of a mutilated horse named Snippy (**13**), found in Colorado with all the flesh of the head removed. Nobody knows what it means, or if it's related to UFOs.

Allen spoke effusively about his latest trip to the Southwest, from which he had brought back magnetic tapes and some crystals that had fallen from the sky into the yard of a man in San Antonio. Two official-looking fellows came to the man's door and requested the object, a bright amalgam with shining colors. They claimed to be with military intelligence. He declined to look at their papers. He said that if God had wanted it to fall on his land rather than the Pentagon, that was His business, not theirs.

In my view there are two UFO mysteries, not one. The primary enigma has to do with the objects themselves: what they are, who or what is causing the phenomena. But there is a second enigma. I call it "the undercurrent": the covert behavior of authorities, the censorship, and the games being played.

My research, the last few years, into the link between folklore and what we now perceive as UFO phenomena has taught me that the historical connections are very deep, and poorly-recognized by the ufologists who are entirely focused on extraterrestrial visitors. The next logical step in my investigations should be to build a bridge to older traditions – from mysticism to witchcraft – that may have preserved some vital bits of information. The other lingering question is that of government censorship and secrecy: what does the government know, if anything?

Allen agreed with my assessment and said he was now determined to find out which secrets were being kept from us, to look under the bed. He showed us a letter from the Air Force: the Air Defense Command is still responsible for all non-military UFO reports. So much for the oft-stated pronouncement that they are no longer interested in the subject.

Project Blue Book unclassified files are now located inside the Air Force Archives, which cannot be accessed without proper clearance!

Fred Beckman is convinced there's a secret group. He took me to the Orrington hotel in his Volkswagen, which he drives like a Lamborghini. Over lunch we discussed recent sightings from other countries, Keel's articles, and the general confusion of the field.

"What about this fellow Jerome Clark?" Fred said, "He really went off the deep end!"

"I don't think so," I replied, "He made sense when I saw him last night here in Chicago, and we discussed his experiences."

It was Don Hanlon who introduced me to Jerry Clark, a young, dynamic researcher of the paranormal who shares an apartment with several people on the North Side. They live on a treeless avenue bordered by brick buildings, tiny lawns yellowed by the heat of summer. A good smell of mutton emanated from a nearby kitchen. Kids played and laughed on the sidewalk.

A small group of us went on to Old Town for drinks while Jerry regaled us with tidbits from the lives of writers like James Moseley and Gray Barker (**14**). I was disappointed to find the group more interested in the private peccadilloes of ufologists than in the findings of their research. This led us into a discussion of the possible relationship between sightings and the perceptions of witnesses. Don asked Jerry about his own sighting: he once saw a horrifying shape at dusk, and ran away in utter dread.

We drifted into a local bar, ordered beer and turned to UFO history, a subject Jerry Clark knows well. He has researched the 1897 wave in detail and with real talent. I urged him to co-author a book with Don, and to invite some folklore authority to write a foreword. The conversation turned back to Jerry's own sighting.

"What was your first impression when you saw that creature?" I asked him.

"I thought: 'What? Is that all it is?" he replied, apparently puzzled by a reaction that evidently was profound and genuine. But why the terror? We never clarified that point, because a young woman joined our discussion and led us into a debate about the hippie revolution.

"What changes has it made in the world at large?" I asked foolishly.

"What do you mean?" she jumped up, as if I had questioned the virginity of the Blessed Mother of Christ at a Vatican seminar. My damned critical sense got me in trouble. "Are there visible signs that a genuine revolution has actually occurred?" I asked, "other than some beautiful posters and some great music?"

"Obviously, you don't understand," the girl said sternly, adding: "And you never will, until you go through it. Acid. Grass. The whole trip. Get rid of the bullshit in your head."

She lectured me: thanks to their trips of exploration the hippies were kings, they had nothing more to learn, they ruled the future.

I laughed at this. I don't buy the idea of mystical truths attained through drugs. It isn't a moral judgment on my part: if it makes them feel good it's all right with me. It's even valuable experimentation, under the right circumstances. For those who've had no other way to become aware of the potential for higher consciousness, drugs may well open valuable insights. But they're a lousy tool for exploration.

When I told the girl I didn't believe that any chemical substance was going to turn a stoned hippie into a mystical initiate, she got mad, ranted about "the revolution" and what she called the shit in my brain. I said the idea that higher consciousness could be achieved by randomly disturbing the chemical balance of the mind seemed the height of absurdity to me.

"You've just met what's called a *head*," Don said as he took Sheridan road North towards Evanston. "Her habit has become a system. She doesn't need to think any more."

"You don't seem too impressed," I noted.

"I'm not. Drugs are a lot of fun, but she's missing the point. Chicks like her, they've cut themselves off from the world. She told you herself: she thinks she doesn't have anything to learn, from anyone. But she's right about the youth revolution. Mark my words, indeed Crowley's Time of the Child hath come!"

"And you, Don? What are you going to do now?"

"I have a choice to make. I can stay in Chicago with a lucrative career in photography, or start all over again in California. I could also move to England, even if Ken Anger fails me. He's quarrelling with his producer again."

Kenneth Anger is a gifted artist and cinematographer and, like Don himself, a devoted follower of late occultist Aleister Crowley. This scares off many people. Don's correspondence with John Keel, whom he greatly admires, deteriorated when Keel accused him of being "a member of an international conspiracy of black magicians."

Don concludes that Keel and Clark are sensitive fellows who lash out at the occult precisely because they can't tolerate the fear of the unknown. I encouraged him to work with Jerry, because his dedication is obvious. Don knows my reservations about Crowley.

Now I fly back to the Coast, carrying the draft of a paper on scientific networking co-authored with Allen Hynek. Following Fredrickson's advice, we drafted a proposal for an astronomical computer network. I also bring back recordings of a discussion in Boulder, reviewing our database experiments, and those of Hynek's investigations with Fred in Iowa, which the three of us spent hours discussing (**15**). The landings there have convinced them I was right about *Magonia* after all -- that we were dealing with an alternate reality rather than mere space visitors.

Belmont. Sunday 26 July 1970.

Dave Halperin, the biblical scholar with the sparkling eyes, has made the excellent remark that I neglected the Djinns. I should study Arab folklore, he said, in search of parallels with ufonauts.

Janine's brother Alain has come from Chicago to stay with us. We work together in the yard, terracing the hillside, planting bushes and flowers that we hope will grow even in this tough soil. We spend our evenings playing with the kids, sharing jokes. I am determined to build a strong base in Belmont, no matter what level my frustration reaches at Stanford. There is joy here, a real future.

Putt putt putt... a motorcycle stops in our driveway. Christine and Mike are walking up the stairs, dressed up like Martians in their matching bike outfits, laughing again like carefree lovers.

Belmont. Tuesday 28 July 1970.

Life must be sculpted with care. In France the basic material of existence has gone bad, like cheap concrete peeling off. Yet I am equally baffled by the substance of California, those iridescent dream bubbles so unpredictable they explode in your face when stroked with a mere feather. Mike and I are victims of such illusions. He lost his job yesterday. The managers of the electronics firm where he worked gathered the employees in the cafeteria and gave them the bad news. Only last week they had urged them to speed up the work, to come to the factory on weekends for overtime.

The same kind of management duplicity is at work at Stanford. A consultant they've hired wanted to see me; just an informal meeting. He was primarily concerned with cost-efficiency, they said. Yet he came into the room with systems programmers from the Spires project led by Smiling Ed and Paul Armer himself, who sat down with a supply of pipe tobacco and surrounded himself with smoke. Everybody was tense. My demonstration went well, updating medical databases, handling complex queries. I thought things were going smoothly: if I could impress them, maybe they'd let me go on with development.

"Well now, why don't you tell us how your system works -- in detail?" asked the consultant. This was the trap, then. The demonstration had only been an excuse. This was the best brain-picking operation I'd ever seen. They looked at me. Buy some time.

"It's not an easy system to describe," I said, gesturing towards the terminal, implying truthfully that there was a huge program behind what they had seen. "This was supposed to be a discussion of my future role..."

"We can't discuss your future until we fully evaluate your ideas. In complete detail."

For a fraction of a second I tasted atrocious loneliness, saw the plot. And decided to keep my mouth shut and my brain unpicked, whatever the consequences. The meeting lasted another interminable 40 minutes, a torture. Nothing technical was discussed. Now I worry. What I regarded as important in life suddenly seems impossible.

Belmont. Friday 31 July 1970.

A group of professors are plotting to patent the Center's software without regard for the programmers who built it. That's why they want my system. These are the same people who lecture smartly about the purity of academic traditions and the ethics of science. I want no part of their game.

For intellectual diversion I had lunch with my biblical scholar friend who introduced me to his professor, a distinguished Stanford Arabist named Lawrence Berman. To my surprise, he was seeking information about the UFO phenomenon. I mentioned Cardan's *De Subtilitate*, in which he says his magician father once saw seven Sylphs who came dressed in shiny garments. Cardan asked them about the nature of the universe. The two leaders of the Sylphs disagreed, one taking the position that God had created the world from all eternity, the other that each instant was entirely different from the previous one.

"That's the position of *Occasionalism*," Berman observed. He told me about this remarkable Arabic philosophy of the tenth and eleventh century, which states that the universe is being created from a higher plane from moment to moment: The pen I am using now is not the pen I was using earlier, only another *occasion* of it (**16**).

Dr. Berman promised to show me the Arabic texts. His own project centers on Averroes' commentaries on Aristotle, specifically his *Ethics*. When I left them two hours later I was amazed to realize that we had discussed computers, flying saucers and quantum mechanics without once leaving the perspective of Middle-Eastern mysticism.

Belmont. Sunday 2 August 1970.

All day we've been shopping for fabrics, vases and lamps. Our children are a delight. It is my great pleasure, the privilege of my life, to watch them grow up, to shelter them from an absurd world, and to play with them for those luminous hours that go away so fast.

Olivier and I have become Lego experts.

I've spent over an hour computing statistics from a catalogue of Spanish UFO landings I develop with Vicente-Juan Ballester-Olmos, a young Spanish researcher with whom I correspond regularly. Tonight I'll do more translations from the data he's sent me.

Belmont. Tuesday 11 August 1970.

Friends on the Stanford staff tell me people are busy trying to reverse-engineer my system, but there was a palace revolution today. Paul Armer was permanently pushed out. One of the new managers lost no time in summoning me. The Dirac system had to be taken down, he said. Heartbroken, I walked back to the main computer and sat behind one of the consoles to delete the files. "The wonders of software," I thought, "All this hard work and not a trace left... They can be happy, my little system is gone."

Belmont. Saturday 15 August 1970.

Sheer curiosity keeps me on campus now. The bureaucrats have bigger problems than me. It is of full-scale student rioting that they are scared. They've installed a plate of expensive bulletproof glass in front of the computer, as if Stanford students carried machine guns. I transferred my users' databases to the medical school computer where I have good friends and no one will be looking for them. The bitterness I feel is hard on my family: I often get angry, impatient.

In *The Crazy Ape* (**17**) Hungarian scientist Szent-Gyorgyi writes:

> The spirit of science is a spirit of goodwill, of mutual respect and of human solidarity... scientists form a single community that knows no border in space or time. The essential thing in the scientific method is that it tackles problems as problems and seeks the best solution, without bothering with prejudices and chauvinism. We do not ask who is right, we ask for truth.

Perhaps all that was true once, but I have never experienced it either in France or here. Scientists are crazy apes too. Did the scientific community raise a storm of protests when the first men on the moon unfurled the flag of one small nation, instead of a symbol for mankind? How was that for "prejudice and chauvinism?"

In computer science today the "community" boils down to a handful of American teams capable of developing the potential of the emerging technique of "time-sharing," where many users can access the same machine and even the same program. These teams are concentrated at MIT and here at Stanford, as well as Carnegie-Mellon and a few industrial centers. In France, recent editorials in technical magazines argue that "time-sharing is technically undesirable and financially unwise!"

Fredrickson has requested copies of my papers. He has just become computing center director at the Rand Corporation. He suggests moving my work over to the Arpanet (**18**), the world's first computer network, in the development of which he's now involved. He could hire me at Rand, if I didn't mind moving to Los Angeles.

Belmont. Wednesday 19 August 1970.

The Stanford summer institute on science-fiction, where psychologist Arthur Hastings has invited me to speak about UFOs, is taught jointly by William Tenn, author of novels under the pen name of Philip Klass, notably *Wooden Star* and *The Seven Sexes of Venus* (**19**). Tenn told the students of an interesting episode. He recalled driving in Pennsylvania with his wife, when they saw an unidentified light moving through the sky. He stopped the car and got out. The weather was clear, cold. Finally he noticed a high-flying aircraft whose wings had caught the sun, reflecting it onto ice crystals.

"Thank heavens we have an explanation," he told his wife. "As a science-fiction writer I can't afford to see something unexplainable!"

Fantasy writers and sci-fi buffs are among the most vocal skeptics about the paranormal. It seems they must constantly re-establish their credentials as hard-boiled, rational, down-to-earth fellows. Only at that price can they go on producing fanciful tales of other times and places. I find this cowardice curious, frightening and a little sad.

Belmont. Thursday 20 August 1970.

John McCarthy heads up the artificial intelligence department at Stanford. He's a participant in our science-fiction seminar (**20**). He cultivates the image of the smart and crazy prof, ties a black bandana over his longish hair and walks like a mutant bothered by the earth's unfamiliar gravitational field. He took us to his lab in the hills, a half-circular building once designed for the research department of the phone company. The hills that surround it are brown, arid, with few shadowy spots along the tree-lined roads. One can feel the unsatisfied seismic forces, the unfulfilled potential of the earth, pent-up demand ready to erupt, a good spot for robot builders. There is wild grass in the empty fields and a line of blue-green hills towards the Pacific. The skyline turns hazy and purple in the late afternoon. I do love this land. I feel at home here.

Inside the building we were greeted by a similar feeling of imminent upheaval. Secretaries in hot pants, the latest sexy fashion, and long-haired programmers who looked like zombies played among millions of dollars worth of high-tech toys. The staff affected an artsy look that bordered on the kind of chaos one might find in a nursery for hyperactive toddlers. The robots were waiting for us in a large room in the back. There is an orange road sign outside which reads *Caution: Robot vehicle!* Its true purpose is to impress potential sponsors from Washington, who dream of intelligent tanks.

Stanford. Thursday 27 August 1970.

The bullet-proof glass has been deemed insufficient, so this great University is now wasting $26,000 erecting a wire mesh barrier around our computing center. The atmosphere is somber.

Don Hanlon flew in from Chicago on Sunday. We gave him our pink bedroom, as honored guest. He'll stay with us until he gets a place of his own, in a couple of weeks. Don and I want to find out if the esoteric groups of California have any insight into UFOs. We'll team up to search for traces of the undercurrent in the occult world.

2

Belmont. Saturday 29 August 1970.

"Look at all that yellow haze," said my programmer friend as we reached a curve on Mount Hamilton Road from which we had a plunging view on Palo Alto and the rest of Silicon Valley. He had promised to introduce me to the astronomers at Lick Observatory. Through the smog we saw rows of rectangular buildings, semiconductor fabs, foundries, electronic assembly facilities. At Moffett Field the hangars and runways stood out. One large building, which used to shelter dirigibles, looked like a giant turtle.

While my Jeep negotiated the 365 turns in the road above San Jose we spoke of the human transformation taking place, the ecological peril. At the top we were met by the observatory's engineer, whose home was decorated with Navy signal flags. He told us the work was increasingly affected by smog from the industrial metropolis:

"We used to re-silver our mirrors once every five years, and to wash them every year," he said. "Now we have to wash them every six months and re-silver them every two years, because of the increasing smoke and acidity in the air. Light pollution is getting worse, too. Our spectra show emission lines of mercury, sodium, neon -- all the street lights reflected in the air. Much of our research will have to move elsewhere: Hawaii, Australia."

We walked over to the main dome to see the instruments, debating the issues of the day: the preservation of the environment, the hippie commune experiments, artificial intelligence and the sexual "revolution." As revolutions go, this one is pathetic. America struggles with an emotional heritage heavy with puritanical repression. The connection between free sex and open societies isn't obvious at all. History is full of examples of morally permissive political dictatorships. One should fight the type of society that strangles creativity in any form. I see the U.S. moving in a short time from hypocritical puritanism to hypocritical promiscuity.

Even Don Hanlon is curiously narrow-minded for an accomplished occultist. I enjoy challenging his preconceptions.

"In your Age of Horus, what'll happen to gay men or so-called 'deviants'?" I asked.

"There won't be any," he replied flatly. "They don't fit within the magical outlook."

We've heard that argument from followers of Hitler and Stalin. I had to remind Don that Crowley laid down a law of "Do Thy Will," about which his disciples make a big deal. Actually, all he did was to translate into English the Law of the Abbey of Thelema stated by Rabelais centuries ago: *Fays ce que Vouldras...*

The truth is that the old master's magick is disintegrating among his disciples. Most hippies, fortunately, would disagree with Don.

New York Hilton. Monday 31 August 1970.

Don drove me to San Francisco airport this morning, on my way to the conference of the Association for Computing Machinery to present applications of Dirac. On the plane I read *The Eye in the Triangle* (**21**), an interpretation of Crowley by his former secretary Israel Regardie who now lives in the Los Angeles area. Regardie reports that Crowley's magical order, the *Ordo Templis Orienti* or "O.T.O." was based on a contact Mathers alleges to have had with three men in the *Bois de Boulogne* who stated they were materialized "Adepts of the Third Order," an obvious link to contactee lore.

New York Hilton. Tuesday 1 September 1970.

I need to catch up on sleep, after walking all over Manhattan last night. Hynek was in town. He invited me to a Créole dinner with some friends in a West Side apartment: a young woman named Sheila and three couples who were eating gumbo. Allen had just flown back from London where he'd seen Charles Bowen, fully recovered from his arguments with Guérin. Our discussion turned to parapsychology. A joint was produced and passed around. I declined. I have no compulsion to conform to the current fascination with "altered states." Allen agreed that the mind was capable of reaching the same levels through other natural means, but he happily indulged in the weed, and the conversation slowly disintegrated.

New York in summer: unbearably dirty. On Fifth Avenue a generator belches out thick black smoke between the skyscrapers. A jackhammer thunders on. A brown sky hangs low over us.

New York Hilton. Wednesday 2 September 1970.

Allen came over to see me at 11 this morning. We spoke of his trip to England, changing morality, and drugs. Borrowing from ancient wisdom, the new credo holds that consciousness can reach higher states beyond normal awareness, which seems obvious to both of us, but when Tim Leary and his disciples advocate psychedelics to explore it, I only see muddled thinking. There are better ways to reach those states reliably. The fact that people who use LSD or hash experience extraordinary visions is true but irrelevant in the absence of calibration or reliable framework. Aleister Crowley, to his credit, tried to erect such a framework and failed.

"Sorry I had to leave before the orgy," I told Allen to tease him.

"There was no orgy," he replied. "Everybody had to get up early."

Nonetheless he was tired, so he slept on the sofa in my suite while I prepared my lecture. In typical fashion, just half an hour before the appointed time he suddenly woke up and announced that he had to go buy a model of a Batmobile for one of his boys, so he dragged me over to the giant toy store of FAO Schwartz.

Circling above Chicago. Thursday 3 September 1970.

Like it or not, New York is the perfect city. It is perfect *by construction*, as one says in geometry. New York is what people do when they are given infinite resources, infinite space, and infinite money. Every decrepit house, every rusty car, every fine statue, every trash can, every piece of garbage, every park has been put there by someone who had a choice to put it somewhere else. Everything one sees in New York is the result of a deliberate act. Therefore it is the optimal city, an operational definition of urban perfection. That thought is truly depressing.

Last night I called Janine, who laughed about Don the Terrible. For an adept of the Great Beast my friend Don, at 25, is far too enamored of the bourgeois comforts he professes to despise: a warm house, a supply of good food and cold beer.

The only long-term solution to the turmoil of the world, it seems to me, is a massive educational effort. Neither Don nor Crowley believes that the masses can be educated. They say "the kings of the Earth will be kings forever; the slaves shall serve." In the meantime, as Janine observes, Don's lifestyle is only possible because there are people who work every day to grow the food he eats, maintain the "pads" where he can "crash" and pay for the cars in which he hitches rides with such free abandon. Among occult philosophies I find the "King of the Earth" notion particularly repulsive.

In New York last Monday I heard a University of Illinois researcher, Dr. Bitzer, a pioneer in computer-aided instruction, talk about a system called *Plato*. He argued that mass education was now well within the range of possibility. He proposed an initial network of a thousand terminals. He projected the cost of their use dropping below 50 cents per student hour in a few years.

Belmont. Sunday 6 September 1970.

On the way back I spent the night at Allen's house. The book he prepares will contain a systematic presentation of important UFO cases (**22**). I promised to contribute a selection of occupant sightings: He now agrees with me that they hold a key to the mystery.

Fred Beckman has become his closest confidant although they frequently get on each other's nerves: "He keeps telling me what I should do! He drives over here, sits in this big stuffed chair, demands to read my files, and then he shrugs in that haughty manner of his; he takes me to task for not following up. So I tell him, Fred, why don't you do it, since you're so smart?"

We reviewed old documents, notably his October 1968 letter to the Air Force on the status of Blue Book. I urged him to publish it as an appendix. He showed me his mail, including a fat brown envelope full of papers spewing out wild pseudo-scientific discourses. He hadn't noticed that the sender, Carl Allen, a "retired Colonel", was none other than the notorious Carlos Allende, the vagrant who was the evil genius of researcher Morris Jessup (**23**). I told him about my own correspondence with him.

Allen said he would soon be in Los Angeles and offered to introduce me to his Rosicrucian friends, at Manly Hall's Philosophical Research Society.

Extending his esoteric circle, Don has made an appointment for us to see Colonel McMurtry, a retired U.S. Army officer who is the titular head of the American Branch of the O.T.O. Don believes in operative magic with its rituals, initiations and visions. We agree about the value of these experiences for the exploration of consciousness; where we differ is in their enhancement through hashish, Crowley's old favorite. If mysticism has relevance it can't be limited to a particular school -- it must override them all. From Crowley I take his keen insights, not necessarily his theories, certainly not his rules. In that respect it is important to know the history of the magical movements that are now emerging from the vortex of the "Age of Aquarius." The O.T.O. was founded in 1902, allegedly in Germany. Reorganized in England by Crowley a few years later, it sometimes claims a relationship to other groups of Rosicrucian origin, notably the San Jose-based Amorc that has a French branch in Villeneuve-Saint-Georges, with Raymond Bernard as Grand Master and my friend Serge Hutin as prominent adept.

Belmont. Monday 7 September 1970.

Colonel McMurtry, better known in occult circles as *Hymenaeus Alpha*, was in our living room today, accompanied by his wife Phyllis. He reminisced about the Normandy landing. His unit had been among the first U.S. Army forces to break out towards Paris.

"I may have saved the cathedral at Chartres," he said with a chuckle. "Our men had foolishly piled up all their ammunition a short distance from the church. As soon as I found this out I ordered them to move it out of the way. A single German bomb, or an accident, and everything would have gone up in smoke."

"When did you actually meet Aleister Crowley?" I asked him.

"In 1943, in London. He conferred upon me the Ninth Degree and made me his representative in the United States."

Don was obviously relishing the contact with a man who had known Crowley personally. I told the Colonel of my private doubts about the Great Beast: "As long as he was an underdog, a maverick fighting against the Establishment, he was a brilliant man, illuminating the faults of the system with his sharp, witty style. But it seems to me he wasn't much of a Great Beast," I began.

"What do you mean by that?" asked the Colonel, while Don frowned noticeably.

"Once he succeeded to the point where he could finally implement his ideas he collapsed into the quagmire of sex, money and drugs that defeats every would-be Master. He was surrounded by disciples basking in reflected light, but he couldn't manage his success, not to mention the cohort of well-heeled women in search of occult thrills.

His Thelema turned into a nightmare of false freedom, a confusion of contradictory rules. So I ask you, did the *Master Therion* fail?"

"Strange that you should put it this way," answered McMurtry after an awkward silence, "I once asked him the same question. In London during the war, evenings with the Old Man were always spent playing chess. He believed he was capable of divining his opponent's strategy. He even thought he could influence human beings through the game. One night, in the middle of a long match, I gathered up enough courage to ask him about his mystical errors. He puffed, produced a thick screen of blue smoke and said that given the chance, there were a few things he'd do differently."

McMurtry had brought his accreditation documents signed by Crowley's own hand. When the discussion turned to the Enochian system McMurtry became grave and recommended the strictest prudence in its use because, he said, Enochian words were truly the highest tools of Magick (**24**). The Colonel is a charming, witty man, a good conversationalist, a poet and a liberal. It is hard to believe he spent such a long time in the Army, a fact which is to the Army's credit. About Nixon's plan for sending American soldiers to the Middle East he said:

"That's an absurd notion, strategically speaking: to put our G.I.s in a place like Beyrouth, where we can't protect them unless we use nuclear weapons is suicidal" (**25**). He added:

"I'm not a militarist at heart; I am only a poet who happened to fight in two wars: World War Two and Korea. During the latter war I wrote a poem about a death machine that ravaged the earth, destroying men and villages. I ran behind, yelling "Stop!" I finally overtook it, ready to put a bullet through the head of the insane driver. But it had no driver! I couldn't halt its march of destruction."

We also discussed the early days of the American branch of the O.T.O. in Los Angeles when disciple Jack Parsons was one of the founders of the Jet Propulsion Laboratory. In Parsons' magical group were his girlfriend Betty and a young adventurer named Ron Hubbard who stole her away and took Parsons' money under the pretense of buying a boat for the group (**26**). There was a chase, an epic magical duel on the astral plane. Hubbard later founded

Dianetics, which became Scientology.

Parsons died prematurely in 1952, Don said, killed in his garage in Santa Monica. Did he really drop a load of explosives or was he involved in some "forbidden" alchemical operation? One version of his death states that he was blown away under a bathtub by a blast that cutoff his right hand. Parson's correspondence with his wife, a red-headed she-devil whom Anger used in his film *Inauguration of the Pleasure Dome*, shows him to be a brilliant man with insights into science and metaphysics. These letters were burnt by the woman, but not before an English occultist had saved the text, which is circulating among a select group. Don has given me a copy of it.

Belmont. Wednesday 9 September 1970.

All day I worked at the computation center, feeling silly behind the bullet-proof glass. I am finishing a statistical analysis of 400 cases of prostate cancer gathered by the Stanford radiology department, the last product from Dirac, forced to halt development just as such applications were coming to fruition throughout the campus.

Belmont. Thursday 10 September 1970.

McMurtry's masters thesis at Berkeley, a political science work entitled *The Millennial Glow*, was a curious parallel between the fundamental tenets of Marxism and those of Magic. At the height of the Summer of Love, McMurtry led a San Francisco commune built on O.T.O. doctrines. The group exploded in a violent conflict about which Don has no details, except that it is remembered by the initiated as "The Heresy of Frater Achad."

Until recently there was another small group in Los Angeles that claimed it continued the work of the O.T.O. Its temple was adorned with frescoes in the Crowley style, according to McMurtry. Among other figures, one could see a naked redhead leading the group's esbat on the astral plane.

Don and I may be able to learn more about this splinter group when we go to Hollywood this weekend to visit Regardie. The doctrine of this Southern California sect was dangerously close to Charles Manson's philosophy. They believed that the Blacks would soon rise up against the Whites and take over Los Angeles. Like Manson, they expected massacres; like him, they thought the time had come to seek salvation in the desert.

A tragic incident soon illustrated the horrible nature of such sects. The woman leader gave orders to keep a misbehaving child in a cage exposed to the desert sun. The red-headed priestess, who ran a number of restaurants and bookstores, exerted a Manson-like fascination over her followers. She even sent them out to ravage various private occult libraries. The group is suspected of stealing books from Regardie.

Studio City, near Los Angeles. Saturday 12 September 1970.

After the long drive from San Francisco, our exploration of mystical Los Angeles began under strange auspices. I was awakened early by knocking sounds. When the whole bed started shaking I realized we had an earthquake -- a curious form of greeting.

Sad first impression of Hollywood: colored facades over boxy buildings, sidewalks full of strange young men brandishing black Bibles who buttonhole the passersby with tales of Baby Jesus. They are the burned-out remnants of psychedelic experiments that went too far. Two years ago these same young men were strolling on this same pavement, dressed in flowing hippie garb, happily stoned. What happened to the dream?

This reminded Don of Allen Hynek's recent adventures. He'd corresponded with a ufologist who invited him to Baltimore. Over dinner the discussion took a strange turn, with the man increasingly agitated. He finally exploded:

"Admit it, Dr. Hynek! You're CIA! Everyone knows it, you're an agent!" Allen denied he had anything to do with the Agency, a fact obvious to anyone who knows him. But the hardcore UFO zealots find conspiracies everywhere. The evening ended with Allen dragging his suitcase at midnight to a secretly summoned taxi.

The rituals of the O.T.O. involve sex magic. Crowley claimed that the sexual force is one of the doorways to enlightenment, whether sublimated into mysticism as in the Catholic tradition of abstinence or channeled into the illuminations of Tantra as described by Serge Hutin in *Voyages vers Ailleurs* (**27**), when he asks: "Could the tantric attempt to free up the mind from the bonds of the senses be interpreted in scientific terms?" He gives this answer:

> The sexual tantric union is said to reverse aging. While genetic secretions have the reproduction of the species as their function, a special form of training makes it possible to interiorize them, turning their almost infinite potential inside the adept's body. In the ascetic tantra of the right hand path that uses no woman partner, a similar result is obtained by a gradual discipline of transmutation of sexual energy.

As Don and I explored the occult bookstores of Hollywood I was glad to find John Keel's interesting book *Jadoo*, published in 1952. We took pictures of the remarkable mural at the Aquarius cinema, flying saucers rising above the Sphinx. A long-haired troubadour dressed in white was climbing towards them.

"Aren't children taking over America under our eyes?" asked Don. That's not obvious to me. All I see is burned-out zombies handing out cheap Bibles on the sidewalk, their lives in tatters. A survey of the press conducted by Don has yielded new information about the group's activities in the desert (**28**). After leaving the Menlo house the Commune located itself between Blythe and Vidal.

Studio City. Sunday 13 September 1970.

The Magus Israel Regardie, whom we visited last night, lives in Studio City, in a plain one-storey house in Coldwater Canyon. We saw a lawn and a few trees in front and four cats inside, including an insane female kitten. The house is pleasant, the walls adorned with Egyptian scenes composed by the Doctor himself, using pieces of linoleum glued together (**29**). His office is full of books and notes, with a deep, warm sofa for the convenience of his patients.

Dr. Francis I. Regardie, D.C. calls himself a specialist in the "manipulative treatment of emotional disorders." He is not as flamboyant a man as this chosen title might indicate but a gentle fellow whom I liked immediately. However I couldn't understand Don's wild enthusiasm. If he has any remarkable feature it's a technical knowledge of Crowley's system. Regardie introduced us to his agreeably langorous woman friend, a Southern lady. Her intellectual curiosity and sense of humor were refreshing. The four of us had a simple, friendly dinner, good wine.

Regardie told us how McMurtry's group in San Francisco had exploded. One of his young disciples introduced him to LSD and *Hymenaeus Alpha* ended up ingesting the drug on a daily basis. The fellow took him to the beach during a "trip" and told him to stare at the sun. McMurtry was lucky not to go blind, insane or both.

Now that I've met two men who knew him personally, I am beginning to better understand Crowley. He wasn't the sinister character, the evil giant described in Symmonds' book (**30**). Regardie keeps the memory of a powerful man, intensely creative, always ready to interpret the facts and even his own "laws" in the ways that suited him best at the moment. Regardie never saw him do any real work during the six months of their association in Paris. Yet Crowley, in his inspired ravings, undoubtedly explored regions of the mind that are inaccessible to more sedate individuals. Perhaps he found, by brute force, some of those insights we all seek.

Crowley was clever enough to incarnate Evil in a Victorian society where the religions of the Good had made obvious mistakes. But his Beast of the Apocalypse was a pale simulation. It is laughable to see him being attacked as an agent of the Devil by good Christians, voluptuously tickled by any character who parades around with a couple of cardboard horns on his forehead.

Poor Aleister indeed, *poor Frater Perdurabo!* He couldn't cut the neck of a chicken without fainting, while Catholic Popes and Protestant ministers have allowed bloodbath, war, strife, pillage and rape in the name of religion, beyond the ability of historians to record the deeds!

Belmont. Tuesday 15 September 1970.

Sunday afternoon was spent roaming around Hollywood, a study in contrasts. At the terrace of our Sunset Strip café sat a teenage girl, her skin spotted with freckles, hair floating in the wind, the corners of her eyes upturned, her hips as narrow as those of a mannikin. And that face! A reflection in a mirror of liquid silver: floating, moving, waving. Her expressions changed constantly, from curiosity to astonishment, spite to pleasure, as if in response to some voice in her head or some strange inner trip, clouds seen in a pool of water. Something glittered on her forehead, a five-pointed star made of silver paper. Near us sat a distraught individual who had the short haircut of a businessman and the green trousers of a vacationing bureaucrat. His eyes were fixed and bloodshot, his face preoccupied. He got up, smiling, affecting self-control:

"I am Detective Harry James," he told me theatrically.

The sound of these words seemed to enchant him. He repeated them with assurance and flair. He walked around the tables, sat down, spoke into empty space:

"You know something?" he asked rhetorically. He answered his own question: "I don't." Three fierce-looking bikers arrived. The crazy man rushed towards them and started a speech while they parked their machines. They shook their heads, tried to understand.

"I am Detective Harry James," he said convincingly. "Know something? I don't." They patted him on the back.

Our next visit took us to the house of another occultist, an artist who once worked on *Easy Rider*. He looked like a young Christ with long blond hair and a beard, wore a red jersey with the number 13. We were supposed to discuss UFOs but he had nothing to say on the subject. He sent his kids to bed, pulled out a joint. Conversations became fragmented and dreamy. People posed questions, lost the thread, and never heard the answers.

The next day Los Angeles looked ugly, flat and dull. Don must have obtained some dope because he got up lightheaded, his eyes red. Cars that shone in the sun seemed gorgeous to him. I felt sad, disgusted: where was the joy of our earlier conversations?

I went to the Rand Corporation to visit Rod Fredrickson.
"It's good to see you, friend!"
He took me back to his office, a calm and stark room with little furniture -- none of the clutter that surrounded him at Stanford. A single computer terminal, a few papers. This magician has no need for Egyptian stelae, hashish or astral dances. In spite of Rod's expansive personality and obvious genius I found the Rand atmosphere weak, and didn't feel inclined to take a job there. Rand struggles with huge problems of database management that Fredrickson would like me to attack. But I am leery of the empty halls, the fragmentation of knowledge, and the little secrets behind those closed doors.

Belmont. Wednesday 16 September 1970.

It felt so good to come back to our clear, airy home overlooking the bay, sheltered by our big oak tree... At Stanford the managers, ever concerned with a possible attack from radical students, are sinking into paranoia. They have decided to "protect the scientists," this time by surrounding the entire computer complex with barbed wire.
Over dinner Janine and I heard a philosophical monologue from Don. He found the world to be quite simple: There were people who used others and people who got used. You just picked a few pals and you forgot everybody else.
"How do you recognize your true friends?" Janine asked. "Easy," he said. "True friends get stoned with you; and no one over thirty."
Not very nice for us. At least we know why we get used.
Don's fine mind is filling up with a garbage of astrological fragments, broken theories, faint shadows of Crowley's shattered visions. Concerning dope, he argues stubbornly that it cannot possibly hurt him, because "how could something that grows in nature be bad for human beings?"
Yet dozens of plants will kill you when you ingest their sap, suck their leaves or eat their fruit: "Haven't you ever heard of curare, for heaven's sake!" Such arguments are lost on him.

Belmont. Tuesday 22 September 1970.

Last night McMurtry added to our lively collection of hermetic surprises. *Hymenaeus Alpha* showed us original editions of Crowley's works, bundles of his letters, and a series of pictures of his own group, the Kaaba Clerkhouse; touching photographs of nice hippies with round glasses, little girls breast-feeding their babies, beautiful young golden gods who looked like Christ. Among them the fellow who took McMurtry to the beach, gave him a shitload of LSD and instructed him to keep staring at the sun.

One of the disciples once locked himself up in a cave with mirrors on every wall in order to "explore the astral realm." His newest project is to make baby homunculi.

Belmont. Wednesday 23 September 1970.

Don went to a new Commune. He came back stoned, with little red filaments in his eyes which certainly didn't come from extended reading of the mystic masters. He is increasingly dogmatic and bitter. His project is to become superhuman and to "do his Wilt." I think true magic doesn't work this way, in fleeting illusion of super-power. It comes with an ancient breath, a murmur, an echo like the song of a bird in the cloisters of Burgos swathed in gothic dust.

We visited McMurtry's "clerkhouse" on Balboa street, a long white building with a cleaner's store at one end, an art studio at the other, shields with the Templar Cross the only outside ornament we could see in the fog that rolled over from the Pacific.

With every letter from home, Don receives the prayers of his poor old mother, a devout Catholic from Chicago who calls upon him the forgiveness of the Lord. He is going to need them very badly, because I don't know how long we can continue to help him.

Belmont. Friday 25 September 1970.

"Well, I'm glad there's some beer on the table today!" said Don as he sat down for dinner. Yesterday he was reduced to drinking water with us. I had work to finish at the terminal while Janine, after a long day at the office, had to bathe the children, feed them and put them to bed. We didn't feel like going back to the store.

Every morning I am on the verge of telling him to leave, but Don, in spite of his silliness, has caught a flash of the spirit, even if poorly reflected in the broken mirror of Crowley's theories. Instead of searching for the true source he stumbles towards the false image, victim of his own fascination. There is still friendship between us, but our paths are sadly diverging.

Belmont. Tuesday 29 September 1970.

A young writer named Arthur Lyons has driven up from Palm Springs in a white Porsche to see Don and me. He researches a book entitled *The Second Coming* (**31**). We ate a pizza with him on El Camino while discussing esoteric subjects. Art told us the rare books stolen from Regardie and Mrs. Burlingame got burned in the fire that destroyed the Commune at Blythe. Don was affected and vain the whole evening, peppering sentences with precious hippie expressions like "he'll sure put your head in a far-out place," "it's a heavy trip," "where's he at?" He reminded me of my old student friends when they had just read their first Marxist book and could only talk of the "just struggle of the proletariat," the "dialectic contradictions of the private ownership of the means of production" and the "inescapable necessity of the dictatorship of the working class."

At a suitably late hour Art suggested we drive to San Francisco to visit his friend Anton LaVey, founder of the Church of Satan at 6114 California Street, a black house with permanently closed shutters. I went along as a lark. A black tailless cat greeted us on the front steps. Someone opened a round spy-hole, recognized Art and unlocked the heavy door. We met a pleasant, shapely blonde woman named Diane, LaVey's wife. With a flourish she introduced us into a purple parlor full of books, with a fireplace in one angle, a skeleton in a glass cabinet, a gravestone as coffee table.

We took our seats, avoiding the stately *chaise percée*. Of the High Priest there was no sign until the mantelpiece pivoted away, startling us. A bald head adorned with a pointed black beard appeared at ground level and a large man looking for all the world like Mephistopheles climbed out, idly twisting a five-pointed star. Wearing a green sweater, the jovial diabolist shook our hands and sat among us. While Diane served coffee, Anton assured us modestly, like a good pastor, that he sincerely believed in his religion, even if he did not trust his disciples farther than he could throw his massive Wurlitzer organ.

"How could I believe in them?" he said, "when they send me letters like this one: A young woman in San Diego wants to benefit from my Satanic knowledge in the procuring of forbidden enjoyment regarding a certain person... The man she loves, a well-known movie star, is a notorious homosexual; no Maleficient Powers will ever change that! The next letter is even more dramatic: This woman has a secret desire to be crucified like Jesus-Christ, actually nailed to a cross for eleven days. She can take a leave from her job after Easter, she says, offering me $400!"

As the laughter subsided Art asked Anton how sales of his book were doing. "Splendid," he answered. "Nice Christian kids have been caught sneaking into a church to burn copies of my *Satanic Bible*, hoping to exorcize me. Think of the publicity!"

Don engaged LaVey into a discussion about his published rituals. He inflated his occult accomplishments while the crafty Anton pretended to be impressed. He said he had received his rituals from Germany four years earlier. Don believes they are O.T.O. rituals, complete with sound and light instructions.

"And why did you publish truncated rituals in the *Satanic Bible*?" Don asked sharply.

The reply came, just as sharp: "What do these people expect, for 75 cents?" It was the answer of a true adept of the Carnival.

The discussion turned to Jack Parsons, a focus of Art Lyons' current investigations. Parsons, at JPL, is one of the few people who did active research on magic while keeping his status in the scientific community. He was linked to much early American science-fiction, from Jack Williamson to Van Vogt (**32**).

Belmont. Saturday 3 October 1970.

At my computer terminal, I watch the fog that slowly lifts over the Bay. The new president of Stanford has taken a stern "law and order" position, with a warning to students and their wealthy parents. Cameras have been installed at strategic points to identify troublemakers. Faculty, staff and "good" students are encouraged to report those who cause disturbances.

Stubbornly, I take refuge in my work with the oncology project. The doctors are looking for patterns in their file of prostate cancer patients. The computer is located in a dream landscape, a row of eucalyptus trees, a fine prairie, a swift brook running in the grass. But on three sides of the little redwood building rises a twelve-foot-high aluminum fence. To get into the machine room I have to knock on the bulletproof glass. The operator leaves the console to open the security door and let me in.

Yesterday the manager of the communications project drew an immense vista for me on the automation of the library. They have in mind "sociological" applications that will make use of a database of poor people. Cross-indexing has been done, from census data to criminal records. The only problem is that the new software that will run all this hasn't been designed. It would be nice on my part to turn my system over to them in return for their keeping me on the payroll. I'm scared: we do need two salaries to raise our kids and pay for this house but I'm too stubborn to go to work for people I don't respect. I renew my contacts with the astronomical community, demonstrating the stellar database and the file of supernovae.

In spite of the occasional frustration, only one thing is more fascinating than having lived in the Paris of the 1890s: it is to be in San Francisco in 1970, among magicians, artists and masters of technology. When I was invited over for lunch by the Berkeley astronomy department, I met a venerable man who conversed pleasantly with me. I thought he was a distinguished visitor, or perhaps someone's old father. It took me a while to realize I had shared professor Minkowski's table.

Belmont. Thursday 8 October 1970.

A clever saboteur has penetrated the central computer at Stanford. Ignoring fences and locks he logged in from a remote terminal and erased vital files. He managed to start a program that attacked system disks one at a time. He only made one mistake: he began with disk number zero which holds the operating system, so the computer stopped. If he had started from disk no. 21 and decremented his counter to zero he could have erased all our data units and brought the University to its knees. As it is, the machine was idle for eight hours while the operators backed it up.

I find a profound remark in one of Crowley's books. He asks what Buddha, Jesus and Muhammed have in common. The answer is: an omission. We don't know what Christ did between the ages of twelve and thirty. Muhammed disappeared into a cave. Buddha left his palace and went into the desert. All three started to preach a new faith as soon as they returned. What did they do during their retreat? Buddha gives convoluted explanations that explain nothing. Muhammed was visited by Angel Gabriel, who communicated some things to him "on instructions from God." Others had similar experiences. Moses came face-to-face with Yahveh. Saint-Paul was taken up into the heavens, where he saw and heard "things about which it is forbidden to speak."

Belmont. Monday 12 October 1970.

Everything has suddenly turned ugly, a nightmare. Janine and I have quarrelled. I let her cry alone: precious, irreplaceable hours. I barely slept three hours. Yesterday had started well, however. We had gone up to Mount Hamilton in the Jeep for a picnic. Then we quarrelled and I collapsed, sick with nausea. I told her that I couldn't stand Don's drug habits, that he had to leave, or I would. She replied through her tears that Don was our guest, even if he behaved like a damn fool. Don emerged from his room, blurry-eyes, stoned. I told him to go "do his Will" somewhere else.

Belmont. Tuesday 13 October 1970.

Janine is as radiant as all California in her pink dress, her long black hair that sweeps her shoulders. She is the free flow of a stream, the supple sway of a young tree. McMurtry says that the great trials and disappointments of life are initiations. Perhaps he is right. Perhaps Don has initiated me into the weird Seventies.

Some occult groups mix up occult philosophy with leftist political activity, but most esoteric movements are anti-democratic. Crowley and his disciples clearly state that slaves shall be slaves and kings shall rule, with the implication that they themselves belong among the latter. They relegate Blacks to mediocrity. Workers, too, are despised, as Don's attitude towards me and my research at Stanford clearly indicate. The world is a vast Disneyland where this little elite plays, while people like us toil.

Back to his field investigations, Mike Jaffe has met a forest ranger who had seen UFOs near Lake Tahoe. The man came close to talking openly, but finally said "I'd lose my job if I told you what I saw." This is the research to which I should return, instead of wasting my time with an exploration of the occult milieu that has turned up no clue, no data that might be relevant to the UFO question or to the undercurrent that feeds into it. These people know nothing.

Belmont. Monday 19 October 1970.

The first rain of the season came yesterday, washing off my anguish. On Saturday we went out for hot dogs at a beer joint on Alpine road, browsed through the San Jose flea market, bought colorful Mexican vases painted with dragons.

We spent Sunday on the beach in Half Moon Bay, playing games with the kids, jumping over the rocks sprayed by the waves of the Pacific. We bought a big pumpkin. Soon Halloween will be here, the true feast of the witches.

3

Stanford. Tuesday 20 October 1970.

Last night I returned from an astronomy conference in Santa Cruz, driving along Highway One, the thin ribbon of asphalt that marks the western edge of North America. The waves of the Pacific spilled white foam over the shoreline. To the right grew wildflowers and golden bushes, the sky a deep gray shade over a sea of mercury, a bluish tint in the squatting fields, a touch of green over the canyons. At the Santa Cruz conference I mentioned I was looking for a new position. At the Stanford computation center programmers still try to reverse-engineer my system (**33**).

My happier moments are the evening conversations around a cup of coffee with Janine, her luminous smile, the way she glows when the children run into her arms, and the special times: Olivier in Half Moon Bay, stumbling back to the Jeep under the weight of a huge pumpkin; my daughter on the redwood deck when she waves a joyous goodbye at me every morning; the quiet rhythm of the house.

I am still driven by magical dreams. They get crushed under the wheels of my moon chariots, leaving bright sparkling dust behind.

Belmont. Friday 23 October 1970.

Allen joyously tells me he's made progress on his manuscript and wants to discuss it. The work will be in two parts, the first one an exposition of the UFO problem, as I had recommended, the second part giving actual examples of observations. He also told me that the American Institute of Aeronautics and Astronautics (AIAA) was about to publish a communiqué on the subject. It was his impression that the problem was now being seriously studied by people within the Government. He's been asked to update our old research proposals. I will see him when I fly to Chicago next month.

Belmont. Saturday 24 October 1970.

The Age of Horus may be coming, but its manifestations turn out to be far different from Don's blissful predictions. Yesterday in Santa Cruz the police arrested an occultist who murdered the Ohta family. He left behind a burning house and five dead bodies in the pool, not counting the cat, also a card signed by the four kings of the Tarot, including a King of Pentacles prominent in Crowley's works.

Belmont. Sunday 22 November 1970.

Last Sunday I went back to Evanston, again feeling lost in an emotional desert until I reached Allen's house, a warm contrast to the superficiality of the town. He gave me his manuscript. We called Dr. Joachim Kuettner, chairman of the AIAA subcommittee that has just recommended that scientists "become better informed" on the UFO subject. Fred joined us and we started discussing Spanish landings. Allen worries about the dual nature of UFO sightings: sometimes they are physical and the next moment they are as evanescent as spirit manifestations.

"Who says spirits have to be evanescent?" I asked. "The parapsychology literature is full of *apports*, table rappings, and poltergeist. Those are material phenomena, aren't they?"

"It's not the same thing."

"Why not? If you could explain the Poltergeist, you could explain many UFOs." Allen was unconvinced. I continue to think that the universe must have a single set of laws, not one set for physical phenomena and another separate set for psychic effects.

I went out to dinner with Fred. We ended up in a nearly empty Skokie restaurant where a drunken old woman was ranting about a trip to Greece. Fred is gathering up data about the military-scientific complex. His theory of the undercurrent assumes there is a secret science hierarchy studying the far future.

The next day I met with Bill Powers, who settles into the life of a private inventor. He has developed a sophisticated ampmeter, a magnetic reading head for tapes and an engine that works along a

Moebius surface. Allen was supposed to join us but at the last moment he remembered an appointment with a wealthy lady from Oklahoma who was "just dying" to meet him. So I remained with Bill until my seminar at the computing center.

Allen Hynek met me for the drive back to his house where I would spend the night in the top floor bedroom. He sounded very serious:

"My lunch with this lady may well be the turning point of my life, Jacques. It will influence my whole career; maybe even make me leave Northwestern."

He told me that this woman was connected with Southern millionaires, had once seen a saucer and would finance a research institute if he agreed to head it up.

"The whole thing must remain our secret for now," he added sternly, "my wife has turned completely against the whole idea of UFOs, their possible reality. Mimi would be upset if she heard that I was thinking of leaving the Faculty to work on this."

On Tuesday I paid a courtesy visit to professor Mittman. He told me that my database compiler was still in general use at Northwestern, which made me happy. I went back to Hynek's house to finish reading his manuscript. Allen arrived after his class, and in great secrecy he finally spoke about the mystery woman.

When she arrived on Campus in her full-length mink coat Hynek had first taken her to LARC (**34**). She told him how one evening in 1957, between Leland and Orlando in Florida, she felt that she "had to stop her car" and saw a metallic object at ground level. She was able to watch it for a whole minute. It glowed a beautiful orange color, and changed to a greenish-yellow as it rose.

"I'd never seen such pretty colors," she said. "There was a dome on top and some sort of blades. It made no sound and was about the size of a Comanche."

"How do you know that?" Allen asked.

"I'm a pilot, I know damn well how big a Comanche is," she answered flatly. "Anyway the object rose and vanished in mid-air."

Hynek, who still thought she was just an excited woman of the type that commonly gravitates to the UFO problem, listened with grave reserve. However lunch time was approaching, he could not avoid taking her somewhere.

"I suggested we walk over to the nearby Garrett Theological Institute," he said.

Fred remarked with a snicker, "The worst cafeteria on campus!"

Allen ignored the interruption: "Anyway during this lunch..."

"Which must have set you back 73 cents..." I broke in, teasing our old friend.

"Not at all, it cost a dollar and a quarter. Anyway she insisted to pay for it."

We both exploded in laughter. Allen went on:

"That's when she started telling me about her plans for an Institute. She's a member of Nicap but doesn't trust them."

She could finance a research group, she said, but its members would have to be known scientists working full-time, with a long term goal. Allen told her that some years ago I had drafted a research proposal for computerization of UFO data.

"How much was the budget?"

"About $250,000 a year."

"Is that all?" she said in a pleasant drawl. "A quarter of a million?"

Allen seemed ready to spend money on computers, cameras, systems analysts and secretaries. Fred remained silent. He drove me back to O'Hare. All the way home I thought about Allen's impulse to leave the Faculty because of a rich heiress who knows nothing about science. Like many academics who make a point of despising wealth, Allen is fascinated with the aura of power that surrounds the rich. Yet as a human being he stands far above such people, but he relishes the thought of being vindicated.

Back in San Francisco Janine was waiting for me at the airport with our daughter. We drove back to Belmont in high spirits. Today the fog hides the mountains. Cold weather has arrived.

Belmont. Thursday 3 December 1970.

We are celebrating Olivier's 7th birthday. I just left a meeting of the Codasyl Committee, about to issue a report on standardization that will have repercussions throughout the industry. The heavyweights of database development, my former boss Bill Olle of RCA and Lefkovits of General Electric led the debate. Last night Janine and I went to a Codasyl dinner hosted by Bill McGee, the man who invented relational databases at IBM. The evening turned nostalgic when Bill Olle started singing old Yorkshire songs.

At Stanford the administration now thinks of selling the campus computer. My colleagues Elizabeth Michaels and John Borgelt have offered me to join in starting a company that would buy it. John is a warm, bearded giant, a formidable systems programmer who stands behind the implementation of the major tools at Stanford. Elizabeth is a frail middle-aged woman, her hair gathered up in a bun like a harmless grandmother, yet a real dynamo. Another member of our group, Susan Kolasa, is an intelligent lady with a background in law. But there is no indication that our company will get off the ground.

I emptied my office on Tuesday, piling up technical magazines and books into the Jeep under the eucalyptus trees. A recent storm has torn away much of their bark, spreading it in great smooth strips.

My plan is to quit the computation center, to leave the project to its own devices, without turning over my software. I can make an honest living by going back to science. During my visit to Santa Cruz an astronomer told me that professor Peter Sturrock, a Stanford physicist engaged in pulsar research, was looking for computational help. I decided to go see him.

Aimé Michel's latest letter resonates with me:

> I have known the last happy men. I still know a few: me, for instance. Materially, their life is the opposite of the hippie dream. They work sixteen hours a day. They impose lots of constraints upon themselves. They are happy even when they are ill, even when they get old, even when they have no money.

Henry Lefkovitz took me aside during a Codasyl meeting break, told me he'd read the Dirac documents circulating within his company. Clearly it is a feeler. But the laboratories of General Electric are in New Jersey, and I am not tempted to move back there.

Belmont. Tuesday 8 December 1970.

A few days of forced idleness. On Saturday I twisted my back; it still hurts so much I can't leave the house, so I rest and watch the hillside slowly turning green under the sweet rain. I have programmed some pulsar computations that Peter Sturrock had requested to test my skills. They revealed an intriguing periodicity in the frequency of three pulsars, and this could lead to determining their diameter. Peter Sturrock will talk about this result at an astronomy conference in Austin. We are thinking of co-authoring a note about this result (**35**).

Belmont. Monday 21 December 1970.

A French scientist named Claude Poher contacted me a week ago. He heads up the astronomy department at CNES (the French equivalent of NASA) at Brétigny, south of Paris. He wrote:

> I have recently become interested in the UFO problem, which I have discovered through conversations with some friends. This led me to quickly upgrade my documentation on this subject. I contacted scientists who consider the problem as a serious one.

He is now defining a research program, which he describes in its broad outline. His background includes a Ph.D. in engineering.

Belmont. Monday 28 December 1970.

I have moved to an office in the electronics laboratories, where I am now consulting for Peter Sturrock's Plasma Research Institute.

Last week I called Colorado University psychologist Dave Saunders in Boulder, where he has launched his own UFO statistical project. He gave me news of the Condon staff members. Rauch spends all his time in Hawaii on behalf of NASA. So does Roy Craig. Levine has moved to Misssouri. Bob Low has found an administrative job at Portland State College. Wadsworth has dropped everything, joined a Commune, and went up into the hills.

Marylou stayed in Boulder but had trouble finding a job, blackballed by the University as a trouble-maker because she is suspected of leaking the notorious memo in which Bob Low revealed that the Colorado project was a "trick" all along.

Lives scattered to an ugly wind: that is all that is left of Professor Condon's infamous "scientific" project, blessed by the Academy of Sciences, to its everlasting shame.

Belmont. Friday 1 January 1971.

The Provost discussed Stanford computing with me today in an office that looked shabby in spite of the stately view of the Stanford Church. He looked distracted. I told him why I was leaving.

"We ought to clarify our various options," he told me with a tone of utter boredom while he drew squares and diamonds on a bit of paper.

Last summer we had had a similar interview.

He'd scribbled things on a Styrofoam cup, then crushed it and threw it away, a symbol for what he might do with little people like me.

"We don't have much money," he went on apologetically. "We can't afford to develop a new system, as you proposed..."

"That doesn't matter, since I will be staying on Campus, only in another department."

It is nice, once in a while, to have the last laugh (**36**). Now it rains. The Telemann record has stopped playing. I do want to live here.

Belmont. Monday 4 January 1971.

Yesterday we went to Santa Cruz, had lunch and played on the beach. There is such joy around us that my concerns on campus mean nothing. I find that I can easily forget any slight I have suffered at the hand of bureaucrats when nature offers me her touching hospitality.

Peter Sturrock, a man I respect, offers me a full-time job. He has a long list of projects that require a computer specialist to attack the astrophysics problems. At the computation center my resignation is official. Fredrickson and I came close to realizing our dream of wide availability of information on this magnificent campus, but the old structures were too entrenched to allow the dream to blossom (**37**).

Belmont. Friday 15 January 1971.

Allen Hynek and I, flying together in a nearly-empty plane this week, discussed his book, which he now wants to call *UFOs: a New Horizon for Science.* His editors at Cowles push for a more sensational approach. Perhaps he should change publishers, I suggested. As for the flashy Oklahoma heiress, nothing concrete has come of the contact with her.

We had a quiet dinner at our home with Arthur Hastings, discussing parapsychology, the obvious pitfalls of the irresponsible new movement to hypnotize UFO witnesses, the subtleties of human testimony. I arranged for Allen to have lunch with Mike Jaffe.

Yesterday morning we flew to Los Angeles for a series of visits, devoting much of the day to our hermetic interests that included a private visit to Manly Hall.

The Philosophical Research Society stands proudly among the palm trees and the bushes along Los Feliz Boulevard, in a better section of the Los Angeles metropolis. It offers a striking contrast to the dilapidated occult centers I recently visited with Don Hanlon. We spent the afternoon in the library with Mr. Hall. There was polished wood everywhere, row upon row of esoteric books, and three gentlemen with white hair: Allen Hynek, Henry Drake and the Society's founder, who stood over six feet tall and wore a huge gray jacket majestically draped over his enormous abdomen.

In one of his books Jean-Paul Sartre speaks of "perfect" moments in life: I felt such perfection as I stood with Hynek among the books of hermetic scholarship, with the iron staircase going up to the gallery and the Chinese idols grimacing around us. We spent a private hour with Manly Hall. He showed us rare Babylonian tablets, Persian lamps with eight wicks. He told us about his admirable personal goal: *to live fully the life of a man, and having lived it, to share it with others.* "The books you see around you," he told us, "are all works I picked myself."

They do form a unique collection, but he has been forced to remove from the shelves the titles that dealt with witchcraft. Unkept fellows with a strangely haggard look kept borrowing them, handling them roughly, tearing out the illustrations or even stealing the books. Hall feels no respect for Crowley and the O.T.O.: “All this so-called modern occultism comes from one small region in Germany,” he said, “This isn't magic. Real esoteric research is much deeper.”

I walked along the shelves reading the spines, thinking of the people who had used these books -- from the lofty minds of scholars to the sick brain of Sirhan Sirhan ready to murder Robert Kennedy.

“Tell me one thing, Allen,” I asked him as we left, “is there a secret society under this overtly philosophical organization?”

“Not to my knowledge. And I've known them since 1930.”

“You surprise me. Manly Hall's best-known book hints at an occult order. It is entitled *Secret Teachings of all Ages* (**38**).

“That's the work that led me to them,” Allen went on. “At 16 I was a member of Heindel's Rosicrucian society; My friend Andy Howie showed me that book, which cost over a hundred dollars, a great deal of money at the time. I saved to buy it on instalment, paying his organization five dollars per month. All my student friends thought I was crazy: why didn't I buy a motorcycle instead, as they all did?”

We both laughed, and we went on talking until we reached the house of ufologist Idabel Epperson. Among her guests I was pleased to see researcher Ann Druffel and Dr. Kocher, who had visited me in Evanston in 1967. The topic of death and reincarnation came up. Allen had already brought it up with Arthur Hastings and it is clearly one of his major concerns, although he gives himself at least another ten years to live, since he is only sixty-one now.

I spent the evening with Rod and his wife Gloria, discussing science-fiction, UFOs and the Rand Corporation. I slept at their house in Marina Del Rey, as the waves crashed on the beach below.

Belmont. Monday 25 January 1971.

A reply has arrived from Brétigny, where Claude Poher works. He stated that the French had no money; he didn't even have a secretary, so it will be impossible to make serious progress on the subject of computer processing of the data:

> For the time being we do not plan to conduct research on information science at CNES. We have entered a period of lean cows, just like NASA.

In the next sentence, however, having made it clear that his organization did not want my help, he asked me in typical French way to turn over all my data to him:

> In a first phase I would be very interested in receiving a duplicate of the files you have accumulated in order to make a selection of French observations that could be used for statistical purposes. I am hoping to succeed shortly in obtaining a large set of witness reports controlled by the French Air Force, most of them coming from fighter pilots.

This afternoon I went back to Santa Cruz alone. I walked on the beach and around the harbor. On the way back I picked up a young Japanese hitchhiker, an environmentalist who was carrying some dead birds in a box. He told me that two tankers had collided. The resulting oil spill threatens marine life up and down the West Coast. Volunteers were counting the dead birds, and cleaning up those that were still alive, about five percent. And what about me? Can I still fly, or am I glued to my rock? I feel dirty from the intrigues at Stanford but I see no great guiding light anywhere else. I do enjoy working for Peter Sturrock, a man of high integrity who offers me a return to science. Allen's friendship remains a support but no sweeping inspiration accompanies his outlook on UFOs any more. A bold strike was possible five years ago, when the Michigan crisis swept the country. The opportunity will not come again.

Tonight Pnom Penh is falling into Communist hands. The grotesque machine of power is grinding on, with the slaughter of Indochina. I envy Aimé Michel perched high up in the Alps, living on goat milk. Soon I must start looking for my own retreat.

In the evening, after the children go to bed, we listen to Buxtehude, Vivaldi or Bach, Victoria, the songs of the Crusades, Sibelius. Time hovers in the darkness. The light of a candle throws our shadows over the soft fabric on the walls.

Belmont. Thursday 28 January 1971.

Joachim Kuettner has told Allen that Condon has given orders to destroy the UFO documents gathered by his team. Allen also told me about his latest talk with Winebrenner, the new commander at the Foreign Technology Division, who confessed to him after conferring with four-star general Brown that the Air Force was indeed still stuck with the UFO problem. Military sightings have started again.

Last night Janine and I had a quiet Chinese dinner at Ming's for her birthday. Conversation turned to our friends. A letter from my mother gives her impressions of Fred and his friend Sandra:

> He was nicer and more open than during his last stay. Perhaps that was due to his gastronomical excursions in Paris. He happily pointed out to me that he was gaining weight. I think he was very pleased with the evening. He enjoyed the dinner, the bottle of *Nuits Saint Georges* and the Champagne, while lamenting that some of the *Meursault* was left in the bottle...

It is a son like Fred that my mother should have had, rather than an intellectual such as me, with no talent for gluttony.

Belmont. Monday 8 February 1971.

Yesterday the weather was so nice that the staff of the weekend seminar on extrasensory perception served lunch outside at a long table on the campus of the University of California at Davis. The valley fog melted into a glorious blue ethereal light that was perfect for the occasion. Many leaders of parapsychology were there: Mylan Ryzl, former director of a psychic research institute in Prague, who left Czechoslovakia with his star subject when the secret police tried to abuse their talents; Arthur Hastings from Stanford; Ann Armstrong, a Sacramento clairvoyant; Dr. Jule Eisenbud who is Ted Serios' mentor in Colorado; Charles Tart, on the faculty here; Jose Arguelles, an art teacher who showed psychic paintings before the seminar, the first in the history of this University.

Arthur spoke eloquently of poltergeist investigations, giving precise references. I had a chance to speak privately to Ryzl about French research: He was amazed that Professor Rémy Chauvin had to publish under a false name. At Davis everything was joyously thrown in the open. Ann Armstrong spoke of Pompei, a place where she believes she spent an earlier life. Stanley Krippner, from the dream research laboratory at Maimonides in Brooklyn, is returning from a tour of communes: those that did survive emphasized work, discipline and structure.

Next, Jim Fadiman took the podium. All seemed relaxed, happy, liberated from ancient shackles.

The scientific establishment watches all this with amazement. Mainstream ufologists feel confused. Dr. James Harder, who teaches civil engineering at U.C. Berkeley, called me to warn me against the symposium: "These are people who believe in ghosts, even in occultism, for heaven's sake!" he said. "Why are you joining them, when our subject is a hard science? UFOs are extraterrestrial spaceships, the evidence is overwhelming, and we have nothing to learn from parapsychology..."

Such comments make me appreciate Allen, or Aimé Michel, who just wrote: "Ufology is not a science but a process of initiation. One starts with field investigations and ends up studying Arab mystics..."

This morning we woke up to dark news: overnight, the Pentagon had launched the South Vietnamese army across the border to Laos, triggering an invasion. Windows were broken at Stanford, including those of the president. Radicals tried to set fire to several buildings. The frustration that has built up since the summer approaches a peak.

On Saturday Janine and I went away to explore California, two lovers on a journey. Reality is simple enough: it is a matter of plain love, of spending my life at your knees, of watching this sparkle in your eyes, this glow on your skin.

Belmont. Tuesday 9 February 1971.

Television reports keep showing armored divisions crashing through Laotian jungles. Stanford students have published a pamphlet denouncing the computation center for illegally running a program called *Gamut-11*. It implements strategic simulations designed for the war by the Stanford Research Institute. SRI, largely supported by classified research, is supposed to be separate from the University, yet the students claim that our machine was used to plot troop landing techniques in Cambodia. Several professors, notably Dr. Bruce Franklin, support the mutiny. The fact is that SRI doesn't have a computer as powerful as our IBM 360/67. It would make sense for them to run simulations secretly. When Elizabeth Michaels checked among our operators, they told her some military programs had actually run on the Campus mainframe.

In our calm hillside home I gather magical books. When Larry Berman came over he was surprised to find himself surrounded with volumes he said would do honor to the rare book room at Stanford.

Blue sky: the beginning of our second spring in California. Tender green shoots on the trees. There was a total eclipse of the moon last night. I watched it with Olivier and made him draw its progress. Although many astronomers would laugh at this idea, I believe the earthquake in Los Angeles at 6 o'clock this morning may be related to this alignment.

Belmont. Wednesday 10 February 1971.

At one o'clock this afternoon the angry dragon put his foot down, disabling the computation center. A student meeting that started as an informal gathering complete with speeches and songs with guitar accompaniment degenerated into a sudden move to take over the Center. I got there after lunch with professor Berman. Students were sitting on the roofs around, and more students blocked the entrance to the Center. John Borgelt and Elizabeth were leaving the machine room, followed by the operators. The status panels were all dark.

"Did you stop the machine?" I asked them.

"Not us," they replied.

"Did someone pull the little red handle?"

"Not exactly. Someone pulled the big red handle, the main switch!"

"How did they get in? Did they break the bullet-proof glass?"

John laughed. "They just forced the lock. With a pocket knife."

"What about the security fence?" He shrugged: "They wheeled the big doors away. Some $50,000 worth of security around that machine, defeated in a few minutes!"

The intruders had removed a few circuit breakers. A fuse was taken out of a controller, thrown on the floor and crushed. A few disk circuits were torn away: inconsequential damages that can be easily fixed, even if the machine can't be used for the moment.

"We were lucky," said John Borgelt. "If they only knew what damage they could have done, simply by pouring a cup of coffee over the top of the mainframe..."

I saw the Provost in a gray jacket, pacing outside with a few gentlemen who looked like cops in street clothes. They hurriedly went inside the communications building. My former assistant has barricaded himself in the machine room. He yells that he will "break the face of any fucking radical who comes in."

Tonight the Vietcong flag waves lazily over the red tile roof of the Stanford computation center. Students in washed-out Levi shirts, girls wearing shorts and carrying babies are quietly drinking Coke around the idle machine. The scene is peaceful, disturbing, absurd.

Belmont. Thursday 11 February 1971.

The Center was evacuated last night. The administration called the riot police to do the dirty work. Half a dozen people are in jail. The computer has been fixed. I rushed in to complete my pulsar computations for Peter, just in case things got ugly again.

America is getting englued in its bloody adventure in Indochina. The Vietnam War has engulfed Cambodia and Laos. People die there while Washington goes on denying the obvious fact that this conflict is turning into a national disaster, a historical disgrace.

Belmont. Wednesday 17 February 1971.

It was a mixed group that took over the computation center. Contrary to what the administration claimed, they had no strategy. It's a miracle that the computer didn't go up in smoke. Among the group was a telephone worker who told Elizabeth she was there because she hated computers: "Soon they'll replace us." They did pull out a few wires from the drum controllers but the damage was minor. The truth is, they were seized with almost mystical awe once they found themselves alone with seven million dollars worth of gleaming, incredibly complex, utterly silent electronics.

It has become fashionable to talk of "counter-culture." Pompous social thinkers expound on this theme, but I see no substance in the movement. In Algeria, Tim Leary and his wife Rosemary were made prisoners by American Blacks. At Stanford, a few shots fired by provocateurs put an end to the mutiny. There's no counter-culture here. There's only one human culture, aimed at the control of man.

Belmont. Saturday 20 February 1971.

My goal is not to understand life; I am not equal to the task. "You should tell your experiences to help others, and yourself, make sense out of them later. That is part of the true magic," Manly Hall told me. There is a mystical identity in all beings.

Among the men who have studied the world and its control mechanisms in the most intense way are the kabalists who first appeared in Languedoc at the end of the twelth century. Tradition honors the name of Rabbi Abraham, who lived in Posquières, of his son Isaac the Blind, and of Abraham ben David, who lived about the year 1200. They followed prophet Elijah, in a line of mystical experiences that began with the earlier revelations of Moses and the Prophets, to continue with the story of the Holy Spirit speaking to the Psalmists, and to all those who claimed they could hear the celestial voice. To the Jewish mystics, hearing a voice was more important than seeing a light. Yet mystical experience, by itself, is amorphous. The physical forms described by beginners give way to peculiar configurations of lights and sounds. Eventually, in evolved practitioners, these structures dissolve into formless entities. The Kabala teaches that the mystic exerts an influence over history because he is privileged to receive the immediate experience of the Sacred -- a brush with ultimate reality?

Belmont. Thursday 4 March 1971.

Larry Berman is busy translating a 10th-century Arab manuscript. It presents a theory of language organized in formal levels, many centuries ahead of today's computational linguistic. He has lent to me the *Picatrix*, full of secret symbols, the Socorro design among them.

The *Picatrix* is a 12th century text attributed to mathematician Majriti, who lived in the 11th century and certainly didn't write the book. Although it is undoubtedly Arabic, it is based on Greek magical systems. Professor Berman has translated for me the part that shows the same sign described by a policeman in the classic UFO landing at Socorro, in 1964. It reads "here are the symbols used to designate the stars among those who are occupied with talismans..." The inverted V with the lines described to Hynek by the witness is clearly there, the character for Venus. Could there be a human factor rather than an extraterrestrial one behind UFOs?

At Hynek's request I have updated my proposal for a research center, *Project Capella*. He's still hoping to get it funded by the Oklahoma heiress. Fred Beckman is supposed to be writing the section about physics. In my own work I have achieved a breakthrough in the structure of the UFO database, a way to handle the observations not as a series of codes but in full English text. I can now extract at will any global statistics about witnesses, shapes of objects, weather conditions and so forth, even the type of terrain.

At Stanford I recently met Ron Bracewell, who heads up radio astronomy, as well as Nobel Prize winner Joshua Lederberg, the geneticist who was instrumental in the heavy use of computers in medical research here. I've also become friends with a geologist named Gerald Askevold, a big friendly bear of a fellow from Montana, the best user of my software for mineral applications.

On our hillside the other evening came six deer, like a sudden visit by envoys from the gods.

Belmont. Sunday 14 March 1971.

A curious, sad weekend is passing into the flow of time. The gray of a rainy Sunday softens my pain. I grasp for the recollection of happier days with Janine. "Evil is that which is finite," teaches the Kabala. I have done my best to reassure her. I was 19 when some higher force sent her into my arms. Men of far greater merit have exhausted their lives looking for a woman like her, running through crowds trying to find her, as I would run through crowds for the rest of my life calling out to her again if she ever went away.

Belmont. Monday 22 March 1971.

Gerald Askevold's slow, deliberate movements are deceptive. This big man with the deep mind is a ski champion, a downhill racer. Last Friday he joined us for dinner with Arthur and Sandy Hastings, and Larry Berman who is about to leave for a long research trip. I envy Larry's knowledge. He spoke of Scholem, the kabalistic expert, who explains that the powers of the divine level are manifested through ten entities called Sephiroth. It starts with Nothingness, the abyss inside the divine, the root of all roots.

Creation began from a "dark flame" that flashed in the abyss, say the Kabalists, resulting in a single point in ether, the seed of the world in the matrix of nature. From that point, strikingly similar to the idea of creation in modern science, genesis proceeds in stages.

Belmont. Thursday 25 March 1971.

It rains in San Francisco. I walk around, watching the city. Weak old people huddled in the lobbies of cheap hotels of the Tenderloin give this rain a somber meaning of loneliness. I love watching the faces; I savor the incidents on the sidewalk, from Market to the smart shops of Union Square and the gleaming auto dealerships and restaurants of Van Ness. I feel the need to be part of this life, to watch human crowds, kids playing innocently on the dangerous doorsteps among the drunks. I need to be with people before I return to my computer. Baudelaire, too, thought that "to enjoy crowds is an art":

> The solitary, reflective walker draws singular *ivresse* from such universal communion. He who marries easily with a crowd knows feverish enjoyments... What people call love is very small, narrow and weak, compared to this delicate orgy, this holy prostitution of the soul giving all of itself, its poetry and its charity, to the unpredictable sight...

Belmont. Tuesday 30 March 1971.

Gerry Askevold, John Borgelt, Elizabeth and I are putting together a business plan to restructure the Stanford computation center. We need half a million dollars to launch the venture. The professors have the ultimate power and no one knows what they'll do. Last night the campus was full of cops and fire trucks: someone expected bombs. There were uniformed guards at the computing center. In their blind rebellion students have stupidly vandalized the library, destroying thousands of cards, moving books around the shelves, pouring honey into the drawers that held the master index.

A businessman from Hong Kong who claims to be interested in flying saucers has called out of the blue to invite Janine and me to dinner in Chinatown. His name is Alex Pezzaro; he says he heads up a company which sells industrial machinery. He had a meeting with Allen Hynek which left him unimpressed, he told me.

Belmont. Thursday 1 April 1971.

Alex Pezzaro, Gerald and I were about to have lunch at Stanford when sirens sounded a bomb alert. Fire trucks arrived, policemen with walkie-talkies swarmed around us.

We ended up at the Faculty Club. We asked Pezzaro about UFOs in China. He said that he frequently travelled to Canton and that his contacts there had finally given up on the idea that flying saucers were capitalistic devices. Now they just don't know what to think.

Pezzaro asked me if I didn't "happen to have" a full listing of my UFO cases: he wanted to show them to his elusive correspondents. I turned down the strange request: who are they, really?

Belmont. Sunday 4 April 1971.

At home over the weekend I drafted the central section of our company business plan. Elizabeth picks up my text electronically on a terminal in her living room to integrate it with her own numbers. All this is accomplished over hard-wired, high-speed terminals connected to the Stanford computer.

In *Jerusalem* (f10:20) William Blake writes these beautiful lines:

> I must create a System
> Or be enslaved by another man's.
> I will not reason and compare:
> My business is to create.

Belmont. Monday 12 April 1971.

Violent demonstrations at Stanford. A black employee has been fired from the hospital staff. A crowd has confronted the director, who called the provost for help, and the cops again. The demonstrators locked themselves up inside the hospital and held the facility for 30 hours. Riot policemen broke down the doors. Their tear gas grenades proved ineffective against the fire hoses directed at them by demonstrators. The final assault ended in hand to hand combat. The violence of Vietnam, seen daily on the television news, spills over into the streets and the campuses of America.

Belmont. Tuesday 13 April 1971.

We called a meeting of the systems group to tell them about our proposal, which is now official. One of the senior men told me: "I knew this company was a serious project as soon as I saw your name associated with it." The cops have broken into the offices of the student newspaper. Doesn't anybody have any sense?

When I work at my terminal I can look up and see the Bay, pine trees in the blue sky, the vast landscape of the hills all the way to the domes of Lick Observatory. There are no limits to what can be achieved here. The secret is to keep on dreaming.

Belmont. Thursday 15 April 1971.

The provost is criticized for bringing the riot police to the hospital. The cure was worse than the illness. A photograph shows him reading aloud the demands of the radicals with a Black militant on one side, a leader of the *Alianza Latina* on the other.

The latest letter from Aimé Michel expands on the tribulations of Saint Vincent de Paul. In a document dated 24 July 1607 the Saint explains how he was abducted in Turin: he was sold as a slave to an old man, a kindly "spagyric physician, drawer of quintessence," who had worked for fifty years on the Philosophers' Stone. His adventure is supposed to have lasted from September 1605 to August 1606. But Saint Vincent's story is an obvious fabrication. He didn't speak a word of Arabic, and his statement plagiarizes an obscure Spanish novel called *Don Quijote* published in 1605, which described a similar abduction. When he borrowed from Cervantes, Vincent couldn't foresee that it would become one of the best-sellers of all time! The question remains: what did Saint Vincent do during that year? Where did he acquire his extensive hermetic knowledge?

Belmont. Friday 16 April 1971.

Waiting for me on my shelves are the twelve volumes of the *Archives of the Invisible College*, a few rare Rosicrucian books and the card index of thousands of UFO cases. I am trying unsuccessfully to concentrate on my work. It rains over my roof, a stream is happily babbling down the hill. Janine is up with friends in the mountains, where this storm will bring lots of fresh new snow.

Belmont. Saturday 24 April 1971.

A bomb has blown the red tiles away from the president's roof at Stanford, scattering the debris among the bushes. It wasn't a big bomb, but the fact is that it was planted in the attic just above the president's office, mocking the fact that the building has been under guard and surrounded with cameras for several months.

A new model of the solar corona, a favorite subject of Sturrock's work, is taking shape inside my computer. Olivier came home at three o'clock. I saw him climbing up the hill, stopping to pick some flowers. He knocked on the door, all out of breath, and he thrust the big bouquet towards me.

Belmont. Friday 7 May 1971.

Professor James McDonald of the University of Arizona, who has become such a prominent advocate of UFO reality since the late sixties, has shot himself in the head. Allen just told me the very sad news. He isn't dead but will remain blind for the rest of his life.

There is much speculation about the reasons for this failed suicide attempt. McDonald recently testified before the Senate, opposing the supersonic airplane. He stated that the water vapor in the plane's wake would decrease the density of our stratospheric ozone layer and would therefore lead to more skin cancer. Other experts claimed that his computations were wrong: The increased water vapor content would actually increase ozone density.

The media, gleefully, didn't fail to stress that this was the same professor McDonald who "believed in little green men." His colleagues shook their heads sadly, noting "you see, that's what happens when you get mixed up in all those stories."

Allen was shaken up in spite of his dislike for the man: "Let's promise each other, Jacques, that you and I will never do anything so stupid," he said somberly, "no matter how bad things get!"

I pointed out to him that we both had a solid sense of humor, a trait which had always been missing from Jim's personality.

4

Belmont. Saturday 8 May 1971.

Flowers ripple down the hill, the house perched high in the gray sky is celebrating spring. My spiritual exercizes in transcendence have given no lasting result. The rough edges of human pettiness have to be blunted for the spirit to rise. It is only when the night has grown tired, when the music has died, that one can taste perfection. Just one more breath, one more sigh, and it seems one could break through beyond the human level. How can the mind think rationally in the midst of such marvels?

Belmont. Friday 14 May 1971.

John and Elizabeth have gone to a key faculty member, seeking his support for our startup company. He was scared of me: “How do you think I'm gonna feel if I wake up some day and discover that Jacques' system is wildly successful, and replaces my project?” he asked. They countered with: “What changes should we make in our proposal for the Stanford Computing Company to obtain your backing before your Faculty colleagues?” The professor answered without hesitation: “I want 10 percent of your business.”

Belmont. Monday 17 May 1971.

I am recuperating from minor surgery, an eye operation. At the hospital, last Wednesday, I felt a needle in my veins and the next thing I heard was a nurse telling me the procedure was over. Chief surgeon Dr. Jampolsky removed my bandages and told me it would take a while to determine if I could develop binocular vision, after favoring the right eye all my life. Given my age, he doubted it. When I woke up again Janine was in the room, packing my suitcase. The car made me sick, but the house was a delight. Sounds and presences were heightened; there were fresh smells, faint perfumes. I kissed the soft skin of children. I heard laughter as they went back to play.

Now there is quiet around me. Janine has brought me paper and pencil so I could scribble down these notes. Through my taped eyelids I feel the white drapes fluttering in the warm breeze. The filtered sun caresses my face. This house has a soul, strong and sensitive. I feel so much delicate tenderness that I cannot sleep.

Belmont. Tuesday 18 May 1971.

Now I am well enough to sit up in bed and call up people on the phone, reconnecting with the world. In that short time the world has changed. Christine came on the line when I called Mike. “He doesn't live here any more.” She's asked for a divorce.

When I called Fred our discussion turned to his latest trip to France. He said he'd met with Poher, who had become absorbed in the study of what I regard as a deplorable hoax, the Ummo affair that continues to grow in Spain (**39**).

“I want to take a minute to tell you that Sandra and I went to Paris together,” Fred began. “We saw your mother and she was wonderful as usual, and gave us an excellent evening. And of course we saw Monsieur Poher. I believe he has written to you, hasn't he? Did he talk to you about what's going on in Spain?”

“Antonio Ribera, the local ufologist, told me about it.”

Poher is analyzing revelations by “Ummo,” a mysterious organization that claims to be extraterrestrial. Landings, physical samples and photographs, have been fabricated to support the tale. It fooled Ribera, who wrote a book about it (**40**). The affair may be part of our undercurrent, but Fred gives it an ominous meaning:

“I wonder if you know as much as you believe you know,” he continued in one of his loaded turns of phrase. “Perhaps I shouldn't reveal this to you over the phone, Poher checked the math, and he can't imagine that someone would go to the trouble of faking all this. Among these papers there's a sociology treatise, a textbook on astronomy and medicine, are we talking about the same thing?”

"Yes, obviously the knowledge of it has circulated fairly widely."
"This surprises me because Poher is a highly-placed scientist. The day I left Paris he was going to see the head of the French Air Force to pick up their UFO files. He clearly indicated to me he was well connected with everybody and knew the ropes."

Belmont. Thursday 20 May 1971.

This morning Janine drove me over to Stanford, because I still cannot see well enough to operate a car. I spent an hour with Peter Sturrock preparing a paper on pulsar fundamental frequencies.
"The radio-astronomers won't like this," he noted dryly with his British humor. "They'll say that theoreticians should stick to theory!"
The students claim "Stanford is a microcosm." Whoever wants to observe the future should look at Stanford today with its cryogenic accelerators, the computers under attack from confused guerilleros, the braless girls making vegetarian sandwiches at the coffee shop and the frustrated scientists, no longer acclaimed by loving crowds.
I have some wonderful treasures, these few friends, and my children. Catherine is 3 years old. In her tiny hands she holds a toy crystal ball and looks into it intensely, as if she saw palaces of untold glory rising in the purple glass.

Belmont. Tuesday 1 June 1971.

The catalogue of all the landing reports I have on file holds over 2,000 entries. Using my full-text technique the file represents 20,000 lines of information. At current rates the cost would be about $1,200 for database creation, with another $140 per month for storage (**41**).
A recent article in the *San Francisco Chronicle* is entitled: "Stanford nervous, a tottering campus." It quotes one of the administrators: "I count the buildings when I come to work every morning to make sure all of them are still there."
Last night I had a cosmological discussion with Olivier.
"When was it, the first day of the world?" he asked as I kissed him good night.

An innocent-sounding question. "No one really knows," I replied.
"Our teacher says it's someone who made it."
Now I was on the spot.
"People have two ideas. Some of them agree with your teacher, they say it's a higher being called God -- you know, that's why there are all those churches around..."
"Yeah... well?" He didn't seem to buy that at all.
"Well, they say he made everything right out of nothing."
"And where was he, all that time, eh? Flying around like a bird?"
He looked at me laughingly, as if I was pulling his leg, playing a trick as I often do.
"The other people say the world happened by itself."
He thought seriously about that.
"No, that's *even more* impossible," he said.
"I gave you the two explanations."
"And the Sun, how did it begin?"
That was an easier question, so I told him about hydrogen clouds and the birth of stars.
We drew up a comic strip of the solar system.

Belmont. Saturday 12 June 1971.

There is a manager at nearby NASA-Ames in Mountain View who likes the idea of building up a database of satellites. That might lead to an opportunity to build a parallel-processing database on the Illiac IV, and perhaps revive my idea of an astronomy network (**42**).
Vicente-Juan Ballester-Olmos is sure the Ummo story was invented by a secret group, but he doesn't think Spanish authorities are responsible. Hynek will see Poher in London in September. Claude is going ahead with a plan to build optical detectors, complete with gratings.
"That's ironic," Hynek told me. "We tried that in the early Fifties, and it didn't take us long to realize it was an expensive waste of time. We didn't get a single spectrum. But if the French want to spend money on it, it's their business. They didn't ask our advice."

Belmont. Wednesday 16 June 1971.

Jim McDonald has killed himself. His body was found in the Arizona desert. Janine and I can't shake the depression that this news has precipitated.

Belmont. Sunday 20 June 1971.

Yesterday I removed the canvas top of the Jeep and we drove out to the ocean. When we ran into the fog we cut towards the hills of La Honda. We followed a path along a little creek and we discovered a quiet clearing, ideal for a picnic. In that peaceful setting we remembered Jim, and others we've known, who have passed away.

Belmont. Monday 5 July 1971.

Mike Jaffe came over for lunch, bringing a list of California landings compiled by his friend Josephine Clark. We discussed our respective alchemical experiments, then: "I'm seriously thinking of leaving the United States," he told me.

"Where would you go?" I asked. "Canada. Québec. People speak French there. They have little towns like Bayeux."

My son and I spent most of our time in the hills with Mike, helping him setup a camp where he will stay to clear his head. We showed him the little creek we had discovered near La Honda. We fished dozens of crawdads out of the rocky stream.

Yesterday I completed the catalogue of Spanish cases in a format that allows me to process the English text of the reports with the names of witnesses, their ages, their occupations, the size of the object and other parameters. I brought the information to our little camp. Under the stately redwoods a black bird, wearing an *aigrette* like an elegant widow, stared at me with one eye. I was alone for a couple of hours, Mike and Olivier gone for a walk along the creek.

Destiny is always novel here, with thrilling energy. To live fully is to agree to be swept along. Our survival is challenged by the very machines we are creating. "Computers will have four times as much impact on our society as cars ever did," states a recent book by a sociologist, a stupid comparison: computers will compete with us at the level of human thought. Cars never did.

Last night Janine and I went to Sausalito for a quiet dinner. She is a *Soror Mystica* I discover again and again, in splendor and desire.

Belmont. Saturday 24 July 1971.

Janine's family has arrived from Normandy. We have turned the upstairs section over to them. They cook for us, we feel like their guests. We have moved to the large room downstairs. It makes a good meditation room, a magical chapel. I have moved our desks there, a Mexican vase, a water bed, new curtains, fabric on the walls. We play our favorite music: Sibelius, *Concerto in D* with David Oistrakh; Pablo Casals in Montserrat; Shostakovitch (*Trio no.2 in E minor* with Rostropovich); *Les Flutes Roumaines* with Ghoerghe Zamfir, the Moody Blues *Days of Future Passed*, and Corelli's *Concerto Grosso no.8*.

Last Thursday Janine and I returned to San Francisco for a fun evening of coffee, cheese and crackers over the tombstone in Anton LaVey's library. We spoke of Don, who has just spent several months at the Morningstar Commune.

"That boy is just collecting celebrities," commented LaVey. I now understand what Anger meant when he talked about his Elementals who vanished so quickly. This is a time of rapid change; character transformations that might have taken 10 or 15 years in another era happen before your eyes in a matter of weeks.

I am surprised to find that LaVey the Carnival man who played the organ in night clubs and the calliope on Fourth of July parades, the flashy psychic investigator who chased ghosts with busty actress Jayne Mansfield, has understood something profound about this century. Among the fakeness of the current "revolution" he is saving a little piece of weird creativity. Behind his charlatan's front, Anton has built a mind cathedral, not to an obsolete Satan as he wants his followers to believe, but to that major power of our time, the secret goddess of Absurdity.

Belmont. Sunday 25 July 1971.

There is more to Anton than meets the eye. I do not believe in the detached sociologist analyzing occult phenomena from the outside -- witness all the garbage written by modern academics about witchcraft. In my readings about Hitler and Admiral Canaris it's clear that historians have not come to grips with the deep nature of the dark forces. Neither are they concerned with a modern world where a young generation is subject to blatant manipulation of its ideals. I want to pierce that veil. In mysticism as in science what interests me is the underlying intellectual and emotional code. In Anton, surprisingly, I found neither the charlatan I expected nor an occult guru obsessed with his own persona. To the chagrin of his followers who worship a Halloween devil, Anton is an intelligent cynic who looks with detached humor at the fakery of pompous academe, the vacuity of politics, the silliness of the media, and the pretentiousness of the righteous.

Two kinds of seekers peer over the threshold. There are those who study it but never go through, like Fred Beckman. They observe, criticize, erect taxonomies, and argue about theories. They relish and document the contact with people who claim the ultimate experience, but they stay firmly on this side of the line. And there are those who do go through. Israel Regardie, Grady McMurtry and Kenneth Anger have jumped over the line of initiation with both feet, but not the kind I seek, to be known by its fruits.

Among the first group of seekers the man for whom I have the greatest respect is Camille Flammarion. Among the second? Hard to tell. Crowley is fascinating but his followers have no class. Anton fails because he has no interest in humanity in a broad sense, no empathy for the downtrodden, the real greatness of the Earth.

I am struck by the contrast between Anton and Aimé Michel. When Aimé suffered from polio at age seven, he remembers strangers coming over to his parents' house from the other side of the mountain to bring him some cheese, the only valuable thing they had. Aimé places such ordinary people and their humble values above everything else. It all goes back to the soul, an idea which is fast disappearing from official American marketing values just as it disappeared from Germany before World War Two. But as Admiral Canaris understood well, "Woe to the man who assigns limitations to the soul of man!"

Bill Powers was in town yesterday. We spent the evening with him in Livermore. He has grown a goatie like Hynek. Bill's book on behavior is now complete. When I pushed him on subjects like the survival of creativity, he said "The false notion of all of modern psychology is control. We don't teach people to control themselves. Instead, society forces them into models."

"What would you teach them?" I asked.

"I'd like people to realize they are actually in control of themselves at every instant. Once people know this they will be uncontrollable."

That statement begs the issue: Do people really want control? Or only the illusion of it? If they truly wanted to be in control, would they watch television six hours a day?

A design artist from Stanford has sent me a hand-drawn card with a nice message: "We hardly see you any more." That is so rare, a kind thought, a gentle word.

Belmont. Saturday 14 August 1971.

There could be two hidden goals in a group like Anton's: either an erotic one, with sex magic as a base, or a political one, with manipulation as its framework. But empty eroticism quickly turns into boredom; Anton understood this a long time ago. On the political plane he is consistent with occultists that came before him. Anton turns the appetite for power into the delusion of individual control - a repulsive illusion, darkly reminiscent of the early Nazi.

It is a subject I have been studying in books such as *Hitler and Secret Societies* by René Alleau (**43**) and *Nazism, a secret society* by Werner Gerson (**44**). The former argues that we are fooled by important events because we have the wrong idea about time:

> Mythical time flows in parallel with historical time, but at a different rhythm. What we call events may simply be

> multiple *advents*, obscure and inside, which suddenly trip massively and appear to the full light of day.

He goes on to argue that the essence of human beings cannot be transformed by man, except on the plane of physical, moral and intellectual appearances.

> However extensive his real powers may be, as "profane" science already shows without any mystery, they stop at a rigid border where the spiritual order takes over.

With that order, says Alleau, begin forces that are no longer human but universal. They can be compared to the force of gravitation. Whether we call them "love" and "the power of God," or "hate" and "the power of the devil" we use terms whose meaning is undefined.

> Man is spiritually free to open himself and to allow himself to be possessed by such non-human forces which alone can change his nature in *essential* ways, whether by allowing him to make progress towards light or by regressing him to an infra-human level.

Occult history is relevant here. On August 1918 Baron Rudolf von Sebottendorff founded the Thulé Society with the swastika as its symbol. This remarkable man was interested in lethal inventions and served as the financier behind engineer Friedrich Wilhelm, who invented the tank. An occult initiate himself, Sebottendorff sought to reveal a divination system based on self-hypnosis. This system, says Alleau, actually served to deliver his dupes to the neo-Nazi fantasy. The undercurrent at work -- already?

Alleau goes on to quote a Capucine father named Esprit Sabathier who wrote in his 1679 book *The Ideal Shadow of Universal Wisdom* that the power of Chimera was the most dangerous killer. Sebottendorff offered a Chimera to the Nazi; it would soon kill more people than all his tanks. In a fundamental passage Alleau says:

> The illusion that we are separated from earlier generations by a decisive transformation of our intelligence and our moral consciousness is unavoidable in a civilization which is marked by the extraordinary speed of technical evolution. This concept of history has been contradicted by enough overwhelming recent facts for its naivety to be obvious. The *mythical time* of the unconscious does not move at the same rate as the *historical time*. As long as we ignore the consequences of this observation (which would imply a complete revision of our insufficient political and cultural rationalism) all our attempts at societal transformation will fail because of the inertia of the collective unconscious.

The Thulé Society went to Bavaria, reputed for its mediums, and picked the half brother of one of their members, a war veteran with no work and no friends, to train him in the support of their activities, using his exceptional gift of eloquence. His name was Adolf Hitler.

Could a similar vision arise now? At the Altamont feast of hippiedom, three hundred thousand lovers of rock music stoned on grass, acid and testosterone were mesmerized and controlled by a handful of disciplined Hell's Angels. One kid was murdered in full view of the apathetic crowd. Mick Jagger was on stage singing *Sympathy for the Devil...* Anton LaVey, carnival expert, treads on dangerous ground when he rides on such imagery to shock his middle-class audience.

Belmont. Thursday 19 August 1971.

Last night we drove Janine's mother back to the airport, along with Annick and her son Eric. In a couple of weeks it will be my mother's turn to come and visit us. The world is in the throes of major economic turmoil. Nixon has blocked all prices and wages; he lets the dollar "float." It has become impossible to change francs into dollars. We gave money to Mamie for the trip home.

Mike came over to return my books. He spoke of investigating Jim McDonald's suicide, of buying a boat to sail around the world. His fantasy is to find an island where he can sleep at the foot of a banana tree without having to work another day in his life, which sounds utterly boring to me. Other people are coming into our life. A pleasantly eccentric middle-aged woman, Madame Mathey has just flown into town. She had read my books and wanted to talk. We met at a classy old San Francisco Victorian, its walls covered in pearl gray fabric, with an illuminated stained glass ceiling, deeply cushioned sofas and an ancient stove. The ladies wore long formal dresses. A gifted young psychic, the main attraction of the evening, told us of a recent meeting with Dr. Rhine and astronaut Edgar Mitchell (**45**) at a haunted house.

Madame Mathey invited me to spend a weekend with friends of hers at a ranch in the hills of Malibu, to continue these discussions. I suggested bringing Arthur Hasting and Professor Jeffery Smith.

The next night Janine and I were invited back for coffee and conversation with Anton. The black house was under siege, shielded by a newly-installed eight-foot wire fence. Diane came down the stairs to open the padlock. At the curb was their large black Oldsmobile Toronado with its VAMPYR license plate. Our talks kept being interrupted by Christians who evidently thought they could save Anton's soul by throwing heavy objects against his house.

Two magazines have just devoted articles to him. He is on the cover of *Look* while *Newsweek* displays the Satanic baptism of his daughter Zeena, with a naked woman on the high altar.

We had barely begun a discussion about hauntings when we heard the crash of glass breaking against the house. Anton and I rushed to the front. Diane was already there, gun in hand. Two men had tried to climb the fence. We returned to the small purple room where large stuffed rats crawled along the bookshelves. Anton gave some orders while Diane grabbed a broom. She returned, holding a napkin with the remains of a bottle of Orange Fanta, a cheap soft drink.

"These people have no taste," I pointed out. Anton concurred: "Unfortunately they rarely throw *Chateau-Lafite* at us. I'm a threat to their mediocrity. The police will lift off the fingerprints."

He used to be a police photographer and has evidently kept a close relationship to the force. Does he also serve as a channel of information about occult groups? As for my criticisms that his Church plays to a neo-Nazi sentiment, he finds them absurd: He claims as evidence his friendly relationship with Sammy Davis Jr. and people of all races and creeds.

Anton mocks would-be "satanists" who feel obligated to display hatred for everyone. "These people are not occultists," he says, "they're just sick." He introduced us to his favorite books: *God's Man*, with its dramatic woodcuts that remind him of the movie Metropolis (**46**). Or *The King in Yellow*, guaranteed to drive its reader insane (**47**). Or *The Circus of Doctor Lao*, from which he read to us the harsh predictions of the Sage Apollonius to the old widow who came to consult him about her future riches and loves (**48**):

> Tomorrow will be like today and the day after tomorrow will be like the day before yesterday. You will think no new thoughts. You will experience no new passion...

Such is the fate of most humans, alas. When Anton puts down the book and sits at the keyboard of the electronic organ he turns into one of the primeval forces of nature. Although I disagree with his philosophy, I see why I needed that excursion into his underworld.

5

Stanford. Friday 20 August 1971.

Our house on the hillside is peaceful now; steadily, research goes on. Cases accumulate and are followed up with phone calls, letters and site visits. I give priority to little-known incidents, privately reported by readers. We'll never get anywhere by chasing the witnesses of the latest sighting publicized by the media. The truth is elsewhere, hidden away. Occultists, I am now convinced, have no answers, so I must follow the undercurrent elsewhere, paying attention to the political context. A 1946 book by Husson called *Political Synarchy* mentions three groups. At the lowest level are the "legal" societies like Freemasonry, "nice people with an ideal." At the next level are the more discreet societies whose leaders remain unknown to the membership itself. People cannot apply to such groups, where joining is by invitation only. But Husson argues that it is in the hands of the leaders of the third level that real power rests -- an international elite which follows the rules of the *Bhagavat Gita*:

> Pay attention to the Work, never to its fruits. Do not accomplish the work for its fruits. Remain constant in your own self. Accomplish the work and banish all desire. Remain equal in success and in failure.

That is easier said than done. Gerson, who quotes the above, was inspired by Raymond Abellio's book *Towards a new Prophetism* (**49**). He predicted that the world was headed towards political apocalypse. He mentioned the *Golden Dawn* and the *Hermetic Brotherhood of Luxor*, of which he claimed (without proof) that Abraham Lincoln was a member, as outer forms of "initiatory sorcery." As I look into these sources for a possible link with the notion of alien contact, I find it interesting that one of the tenets of the Golden Dawn was the existence of "Elder Brothers" beyond the Earth, supervising the evolution of the planet. Crowley didn't know their names. He claimed to have rarely seen them in their physical bodies. In their presence he claimed he had trouble breathing and felt a force he compared to a lightning bolt.

Later the same day.

Last night we met Anton's inner circle, a remarkable group: A frail woman in her sixties, Countess de Plessen, wearing a fine em-broidened shawl; a young man in a red jacket flaunting an inverted crucifix at the end of a chain; in the purple room, a tall man in a classic suit and tie, who wore an inverted pentagram. He turned out to be a great humorist, an excellent musician, an expert on papal

Fig. 3: With my children in Belmont, 1971.

Fig. 4. Aimé Michel, a philosopher of transcendence
(photo by J.L. Seigner)

history. With him were a plump young woman artist, an editor with *Western Collector* magazine, priestess Loni, a voluptuous blonde, and a woman in her forties, her red hair in long tresses. While the women showed a great deal of thigh, the men were in formal dark suits. Diane and Anton wore black velvet for the evening's *Electric Prelude* where a pentagram of mirrors projects a ritual image to infinity in all directions, supposedly filling the universe.

Afterwards the group assembled in the kitchen with its glossy black walls and purple curtains, decorated by Anton with grotesque monsters out of Hieronymus Bosch. We ate cakes, told silly jokes and drank three bottles of Champagne.

It was 3 A.M. when we stepped out into the cold fog of California Street. Not a car in sight, and we might have thought that Anton's incantations had worked so well that he had emptied the Earth, which Jacques Bergier once defined for us as "a rather nice planet infected with humans." We could barely see to the end of the block. The Alcatraz foghorn, hoary and alarming, was the only music we heard. I thought of that old warning (**50**):

> O puny man, seek not to break open the gates to Beyond! For the Dwellers in the Abyss hunt souls like unto thine to hold in their thrall...

Belmont. Sunday 29 August 1971.

Last night Anton showed me his red room, the walls covered with masks. He quoted to us from *The Hounds of Tindalos*:

> You cannot conceive of an entity that does not depend for its existence on force and matter. But did it ever occur to you, my friend, that force and matter are merely the barriers to perception imposed by time and space? When one knows, as I do, that time and space are identical and that they are both deceptive because they are merely imperfect manifestations of a higher reality, one no longer seeks in the visible world for an explanation of the mystery and terror of being.

Anton also read to us parts of a new manuscript that contained the rudiments of his theory of Erotic Crystallization Inertia or ECI. He thinks of consulting Roger Peyrefitte who owns a fine collection of erotic art in Paris and has devoted a whole chapter to LaVey in his book *Les Américains*.

Peyrefitte saw the deeper mind in him, not merely another colorful California eccentric.

Belmont. Monday 6 September 1971 (Labor Day)

Two days of rest. My mother arrived on Friday night, showing few signs of tiredness in spite of her 71 years. Her suitcases were filled with toys, books, and Aimé Michel's latest package of notes about the Ummo affair. We went out to fish crawdads in the creeks beyond La Honda, and ate them on Sunday with Gerald Askevold.

Summer may have emptied the beautiful Stanford campus but it didn't prevent rioting in Palo Alto. A page has been turned. The days of non-violence and flower children are over.

Now I study a book by French historian Brissaud to try to understand the occult roots of the Nazi era, which seems relevant to the sectarian undercurrent in the UFO movement. Hitler once said an extraordinary thing: a new dogma was at hand in which the Führer "comes to relieve the masses from the burden of freedom!" A few years later he used this formula to become the master of Europe, and nearly conquered the world.

Could it be that an Alien myth is similarly knocking on our door, ready to relieve us from the burden of freedom? And does it relate to actual, physical things in the sky? Brissaud says that Hitler's occult master was Dietrich Eckart (1868-1923) who initiated him to the Thulé legend:

> The Hyperborean region is the motherland where angels coming out of the celestial kingdom, like extraterrestrials from the cosmos, had settled a long time before the Flood.

He cites the Book of Enoch:

> The Sons of God taught their hyperborean children, the sons of the "Outside Intelligences," all the enchantments and the arts of observing the stars, the signs, astronomy, the movements of the moon and the sun...

Herodotus speaks of "an island of ice in the far North, where transparent men live" while Nordic people have legends about Thulé as a true Eden, equivalent to "the country of the other world" in the Quest of the Holy Grail. The initiates of the *Thulé Society* reportedly taught Hitler, Rudolf Hess and Rosenberg the same belief mentioned by René Guénon in his 1927 book *The King of the World*, namely that the sons of the "Outside intelligences" broke off into two groups, one following the right hand path of the golden sun, the others the wheel of the black sun, the Swastika.

In my analysis of secret societies I find three distinct currents:

(1) *Magicians*. Leaving aside authentic Rosicrucians, whose tradition may or may not have survived, we find an undeniable belief in Thulé and the OTO.

(2) *Politicians*. This category encompasses secret elitist groups, racists of the KKK, white supremacists, the Synarchy, the inner circle of the communist movement.

(3) *Cryptocrats*. A scientific class concerned with space exploration, the development of computers, artificial intelligence, new drugs. Although not organized as a secret society, it shares many of its attributes.

When the three currents intersect the public suddenly becomes aware of a "historical mystery." Let us look at four such events:

The Nazi power structure was an intersection of type Magician-Politician in which the mystical current turned into a historical reality. There was a cryptocratic component (von Braun) that came too late to save the Nazi.

The Robert Kennedy assassination was an intersection of type Political-Magician in which a historical goal was achieved through the manipulation of occult sects. Sirhan, like Hitler, was a gifted medium. Both may have been picked and controlled by others.

The trip to the moon was an historical intersection of type

Cryptocratic-Political, with technology serving a government structure. It was a direct product of the von Braun heritage, itself derived from breakthroughs achieved by Germany.

Esoteric mysteries are either of Magical-Political type or of Magical-Cryptocratic type. The former are exemplified by the trend towards police states, the latter is found in artificial intelligence.

I mention all this because I wonder if the UFO problem shouldn't be seen as an esoteric mystery combining all three aspects.

The chilly realization is that some structures of the pre-Nazi era could have transcended Hitler and survived the Third Reich. Brissaud is one of the rare historians who have seriously pondered such questions. One of the most sensitive areas he analyzes is the existence of the *Ahnenerbe* (literally Legacy, Ancestral Heritage) whose label covered a horrible reality. Created in 1935 by Himmler, the founder of the Black Order, it had Wolfram Sievers as General Secretary and Walther Wust, the rector of Munich University, as scientific director. Its documents were destroyed before they could be seized by Allied forces and its members either fled or stubbornly maintained silence when they were unmasked.

Sievers himself, however, was captured and tried. He told his judges that the *Ahnenerbe* had fifty-two scientific sections, several of them classified top secret. One group worked on a death ray. Another particularly intriguing section was dedicated to the study of occult influences on human behavior. Among its staff was Frederick Hielscher, a close friend of Swedish explorer Sven Hedin, of Karl Haushofer, Ernst Junger and of Jewish philosopher Martin Buber.

At his trial, Sievers listened to the list of his crimes with detachment and reacted with indifference when sentenced to death. Hielscher was granted permission to accompany him to the gallows. Together, they said “peculiar prayers to an unknown cult.” Sievers' diary was seized and certain quotes were published at Nuremberg. Brissaud writes that he was able to read the document but Sievers himself had torn off certain pages.

What happened to the leaders of the Black Order and to the experts of the *Ahnenerbe*? Brissaud hit a thick “wall of silence” when he tried to answer this question. He believes that a secret society still exists today, with a few members in various countries who continue in the "Blood Myth" tradition. The Vril Society, to which Karl Haushofer belonged, had links with the Golden Dawn in London. Some leaders of the Thulé Society left Berlin as early as 1934 and 1935, settling in Oxford. Hess established links with such English aristocrats as the Duke of Hamilton, the Duke of Bedford and Sir Ivone Kirkpatrick, a former British diplomat in Berlin. But Brissaud cautions that the Luciferian quality of the Blood Myth isn't really satanic: "This Lucifer strangely resembles his sister Lilith who, according to an old Jewish legend, was supposed to be Adam's first companion before our mother Eve."

Belmont. Tuesday 14 September 1971.

A group of local entrepreneurs are starting a computer company called Amdahl, after Gene Amdahl, the visionary designer for IBM's advanced computers. And today I attended a NASA seminar dedicated to the new Illiac IV supercomputer. Unfortunately it got lost in trivia after a mere two hours. At Stanford I had one last opportunity to say farewell to my friend and colleague Dr. Peter Fung, a good physicist and an even better aquarellist who has decided to return to his native Hong Kong.

"Are there hippies in Asia, too?" I asked him. "Do you have a counter-culture with drugs and flower children, as we do here?"

"Hardly," he replied with a thin smile, "except for a few snobs. Young Americans are just beginning to discover drugs, but you must remember that opium has been around for thousands of years in China; altered states of consciousness are hardly a novelty there. Every kid has had his fill of traditions about yoga and meditation. Personally, by the time I had reached the age of 12, I was as bored with that stuff as the average American kid is bored with Sunday school!" I had never thought about it that way.

Last week we discussed UFOs. The subject fascinated him, so I gave him one of my last original copies of *Passport to Magonia*. He wanted to give me the price of the book; I would not hear of it. He paid me with a great compliment. He looked at me solemnly and said, “Jacques, you are like a Chinese man.”

For the last couple of days the weather has been warm, a heat wave not seen since 1912. The region is drowning in smog. I take the Jeep with the top down to pick up Olivier every day after school. He runs towards me, clutching his lunch box. We drive up the hill, joking and laughing together.

Belmont. Saturday 18 September 1971.

In bed with a cold, I have time to complete an article (co-authored with Ballester-Olmos) about the sociology of Spanish landings (**51**). Upstairs the children are playing on the redwood deck, Maman is busy in the kitchen, and Alain is talking with Janine.

Over lunch with a friend from Stanford a few days ago, she told me she felt “inadequate” in this world, a remark typical of a whole generation of Americans. Why are they so ashamed to be human, so unable to take flight, so guilty to be alive?

“You really live for the present moment, don't you?” she asked as if this was a big discovery. What else is there? The present moment is our only link to all the past and all the future.

Belmont. Saturday 25 September 1971.

Yesterday was my 32nd birthday. This place is a paradise but many things around us are collapsing. The international financial system is in shock, and China is in the grips of bloody wars of which the world knows nothing as it staggers ahead precariously.

Today I had breakfast with Ray Williams, ex-financial executive with IBM, co-founder of Amdahl. He had checked up on me in conversations with his Stanford friends. He said I had a reputation as one of the best scientific programmers in Silicon Valley.

Belmont. Sunday 26 September 1971.

You don't have to go far to find links between the early contactees and murky political figures. Thus André Brissaud comments on the

Thulé legend, which was taught to Hitler by Dietrich Eckart:

> In December 1923, before his agony in Munich, Dietrich Eckart said a very personal prayer in front of a black meteorite of which he said, "It's my stone of Kaaba." He left it to one of the founders of astronautics, Herman Oberth.

This offers an interesting link between the man who said "Hitler will dance, but I'm the one who wrote the music" and the visionary scientist who regularly presides over gatherings of saucer contactees. In 1954 he even stated publicly that UFOs were piloted by plant-like crews from Uranus!

I have been reading Carl Jung's remarkable book *Memories, Dreams, Reflections*, with the feeling that such autobiographies, as fine as they are, take too high a perspective from which to view the landscape of life: they miss the true nature of everyday events, the fine grain of existence with its contradictions and contrasts.

Would I still recall with precision the time when the Condon committee seemed to be open-minded and honest if I had not recorded my impressions, as well as our own mistakes? Would I still appreciate Allen as deeply as I do if I hadn't also recorded his weaknesses, a picture of a complete human being? Carl Jung is too Olympian to be completely believable when he states things like "My life is a history of the self-realization of the unconscious."

Dear Doctor Jung, when we say words like "my life" we should hold back our tears, as the poet says (**52**). In a passage dealing with spiritualism and psychic phenomena I note that Jung mentions an author named Passavant who was a spiritual thinker in the context of Eschenmayer and Gorres (**53**). He must have been a remote ancestor on my mother's side, since there is only one family bearing the Passavant name.

Stanford. Thursday 30 September 1971.

Allen Hynek has just called me at the office, returning from England where he gave a lecture at the Theoretical Astronomy Institute in

Cambridge. Unfortunately Hoyle wasn't there. Allen had dinner with Poher who told him that two French observatory directors now supported his work. "Poher spent most of the time pestering me again with that silly Ummo material," said Allen. "What a waste! Why does he pay attention to all this poppycock?"

At Stanford the students are back from summer holidays. The main physics lecture hall has been turned into a courtroom where a jury of six professors hears the administration's complaint against professor Bruce Franklin. The Provost wants him expelled as a troublemaker, for inciting the students to violence against our computer. Both sides are turning this outstanding University into a sick joke.

Belmont. Monday 11 October 1971.

Last Friday we went to San Jose with the kids for a fun visit to the extraordinary "spirit house" of Sarah Winchester, the late widow of the inventor of the celebrated rifle (**54**).

Today, after lunch with professor Berman, as I walked back towards the Humanities Department, I saw groups of students converging on the physics lecture hall to attend Bruce Franklin's academic trial.

The University wants to draw him out to blunt his message and provide the rope that will be used to hang him. They also want to make sure no one can ever say he was censored. Franklin himself is eager to display his eloquence and his militancy, so the campus is in for a long and verbose confrontation.

Professor Berman has introduced me to a man who has custody of Evans-Wentz manuscript on *Cuchama and Secret Mountains*. He believes the book is unpublishable and he doesn't want his name or that of Stanford associated with it. I volunteered to read the manuscript and to suggest ways to bring it out. Evans-Wentz is one of the towering minds in the field of modern folklore (**55**).

Over San Francisco floats the smell of kerosene: Men are fouling their own environment. I read the quaint thoughts of Souvestre's *Attic Philosopher* (**56**). I must trust the universe, learn patience.

Belmont. Wednesday 13 October 1971.

"Patience:" This is a new word for me. I had to come all the way to California to learn it! Here I no longer feel the rage or the sadness that took me so often in France or Chicago. The potential trapped in every moment is so obvious that I no longer complain of wasted days or useless efforts. Yesterday Janine told me she was puzzled by our own actions: "Why do we put so much energy into this big house? You and I could be so happy in a simple maid's garret again."

I do feel the need to create a framework for us and our children. There is pleasure in building a place of excellence in a world that denies beauty with such stubborn application. We don't have much money but it doesn't take a fortune to buy Mexican vases and warm fabrics, to drive over to the nursery and bring back some flowers.

Belmont. Monday 18 October 1971.

At Stanford I have just heard Willis Harman, one of the founders of the Human Potential Movement, defining a familiar theme: in a couple of generations, technology will make possible certain changes that used to take centuries. The nature of future transformations is unknown, however: "Imagine a pregnant woman in a world where no one understands the process of childbirth. They would think she was gravely ill. Can you picture her pains, her anxiety, and her anguish? Such is the case for modern humanity."

Mike Duggin, Australian scientist and UFO expert, came to see me at the Electronics Labs on Friday. I demonstrated my full-text landing catalogue to him. Duggin has just completed a tour of the U.S. during which he met with the leaders of both Nicap and Apro. The last time I saw Duggin was in Chicago. Olavo Fontès was with us that day: so many passing faces, and hopes that led nowhere...

I had a dream in which Janine and I visited Israel Regardie. He opened a trapdoor that led to a basement where a great ape-like monster spoke to us. It turned out to be an animated statue of Aleister Crowley. We went down to an underground library that communicated with the subway! On the way we met two Chinese men. As we went back upstairs I realized that somebody had stolen from me *Le Musée des Sorciers*, a rare book I had intended to show Regardie. This caused me so much grief that I woke up.

Dawn was coming to a bittersweet world, absent the early sunshine of summer that burned off the fog. But there is your warm presence, a treasure from Heaven. If only we could be sure to live another twenty years without any grave illness, any accident... if only we could give our children a good start in life and a few sane principles, we would have been blessed by destiny beyond the level most humans achieve in this miserable existence. The long-term challenge is to preserve the twin secrets of hard work and true compassion: secrets not described in books, or taught in classrooms.

Belmont. Saturday 23 October 1971.

Last night we attended a reception at the home of a Stanford professor, given in honor of Severny, the director of the Crimean observatory and a member of the Soviet Academy of Sciences. Peter Sturrock and Ron Bracewell were there. People spoke of galaxies and radiotelescopes. Janine and I escaped the gathering and enjoyed a quiet dinner with an artist friend.

Belmont. Thursday 28 October 1971.

A furious wind has been blowing all night long. At Stanford, Elizabeth testified at the trial of Bruce Franklin. Very professionally, she detailed the events that surrounded the siege of our computation center. Stanford is a nerve center.

The other morning Maman found an excuse to join me outside, at the top of the stairs. We looked at the flowers we had planted together. She started crying. The previous evening she had told us she would never come back to America. Now she reproaches herself for making me feel bad: "I will come back, you know," she said, "I will come back, if you ask me to."

I kissed her, aware of her distress in this land of sunshine and untold anguish.

Belmont. Sunday 31 October 1971 (Halloween)

We drove up to the top of Mount Diablo yesterday. We had a picnic with my mother in the shelter of a large rock. Later Janine and I went shopping like two kids, buying Halloween trinkets.

In *The Magus,* John Fowles points out that the Nazi did not come to power because they brought order over chaos, but on the contrary because they imposed chaos. They claimed it was all right to persecute the weak and the poor. They offered up all temptations to mankind: "Nothing is true, therefore everything is permitted." LaVey says something similar.

We haven't gone back to California Street. Anton is an original thinker in a world of copycats, a musical genius, a living encyclopaedia of many arts, a great performer, but his plans don't lead to genuine knowledge. I've enjoyed his non-conformity and our discussions of the paranormal, his explanations on how its effects were used in occult practice and how they could be faked by clever hoaxers. But I have left that behind.

What ancient alchemy is this? A cluster of Djinns swirl around with howls of joy. I love our laughter, the trust in your eyes.

Belmont. Wednesday 3 November 1971.

On Monday night I had a conference call with Allen Hynek, Dave Saunders and Fred Beckman, who called together from Chicago. The conversation consisted primarily in Allen and Dave arguing about the arrangements of a forthcoming meeting in Denver, where Allen says he is anxious for us to hold what he calls a serious summit meeting. But the conversation soon degenerated into trivia.

Long session with Peter Sturrock this morning in the office of Hans Mark, the new director of the NASA-Ames research center. We discussed the future of computing and the role of the Illiac IV supercomputer. Mark said that space science was in trouble, there was no more money, and the Illiac was only justified on the basis of aerodynamics. It may be used to design new airplanes, not to reach the planets.

Mike Jaffe came by to say goodbye. We lit up a log in the fireplace for old time's sake. We gave him coffee and cake. He told us in a sane and troubled way that he was leaving to see the world, driving at random.

Vicente-Juan Ballester-Olmos writes from Spain that he has met a captain Omar Pagani who is conducting an official study of UFOs for the Argentine Navy. He is convinced of the reality of the phenomenon, having assembled a mass of documents. However his government is not interested in the subject.

Pagani revealed that many publicized cases in Latin America were well-designed hoaxes, and that the CIA is definitely involved, playing its usual games. It keeps a sharp eye on everything that is done on this subject in Argentina.

At Stanford the Bruce Franklin hearings are still going on. A high administrator has been forced to testify. Under oath, he said that he had never said anything about keeping secret the connection with *Gamut-11*. He never ordered to close the SRI accounts.

"The women in accounting are the ones who closed down those files. Their bosses told them to stay quiet," states Elizabeth, who knows the true state of affairs, and can see through the lies.

Boney Mountain. Saturday 6 November 1971.

You drive for an hour north of Los Angeles, and then you turn into the hills. My companion's Mustang spits gravel into the turns of the mountain road that climbs into a rugged, deserted landscape. She points ahead to Boney Mountain, a jumble of orange and pink rocky towers rising like a fortified city over a conical base of brown and green. Ann Chamberlain, who had invited me to visit, greeted us at the ranch: stone walls, large rooms with tapestries, a fireplace, cowhide on the tile floor, windows with small square glass panes.

We drank tea on the terrace, watching the mountain above us with its cliffs and canyons that descend precipitously to the West towards the coastal town of Oxnard and the Pacific Ocean. In the caves the Indians have left paintings of magicians wearing feathers, of frog-like figures in a sexual dance, of strange concentric circles.

The clever Chumash obtained color by mixing powdered clay with the sap of a local bush. A peaceful people, they sailed out to fish near coastal islands, notably Catalina. Crude oil oozed up naturally on the beaches, so they used it to coat their reed baskets. They filled them with water, dumping hot stones into them to prepare their meals.

We walked back to the ranch at nightfall as a delicate haze drifted up from the canyon. After dinner we sat around the fireplace. I read to them from Evans-Wentz' unpublished *Cuchama*. My room had a small window opening out on the fog and a door towards the barn. The beams of the roof were high above, the cool wind blew around.

Pepe Sanchez came over. The son of the former ranch manager, he now lives on a nearby farm with his wife and five wonderful kids. I sat next to him in the truck. He told me about his mountain as he drove up on the road he had cut all the way to the top, where we could see the Los Padres ridge and the city of Thousand Oaks. We walked into the caves, sliding through tunnels. We came to a high rock where one lady, pretending to be a priestess, asked each of us what we wished most to have in our lives. Sanchez' youngest girl, who reminded me of my daughter, simply wanted "my daddy." I wished for "the path of the heart." Our wishes were turned into little stones ceremoniously placed among the rocks in the various sectors of a mandala, then we started walking down. Pepe Sanchez cut Spanish bayonets out of yucca canes for the children.

Boney Mountain. Sunday 7 November 1971.

Last night at Boney ranch I rode down the hillside sitting on the diesel tank of Pepe Sanchez' truck, next to one of his young daughters who asked me: "Do you like our mountain?" How could I not like it? We ate dinner while Pepe told us of his young years in California, and of his father who was a great expert on horses and women. He met Chamberlain in Mexico during the Revolution. At the time Panchos Villa and Zapata led their desperados and attacked anything that moved. Sanchez, his cowboys and a large herd of cattle were going up a canyon when they fell into an ambush. He was hit in the hip and fell from his horse. When the battle was over he had fourteen bullets in his body. He was 20. Everyone thought he would die. The women of the hacienda went up the canyon to retrieve him. They improvised a stretcher to carry him. His dogs licked his blood while insects buzzed around. The women stopped from time to time to give him warm milk to drink. He spoke about this milk for a long time afterwards -- “It was like drinking life,” he would tell his son Pepe. It took two days to get him to safety.

I think of Aimé Michel and his Alps and the joys of small village life as I hear Pepe (who can read but barely writes) discuss the future of computers with surprising insight. “I think about those things all the time,” he tells me.

Ann owns 168 acres of land here. Her taxes have been multipled by 40 since 1956, so she will soon have to sell part of the ranch. Will it fall into the hands of unscrupulous developers? Some Hollywood movie star? These fears are gnawing at the heart of this noble woman who wants to preserve the beauty of the land for new generations.

“Businessmen come here; they look at Boney as just another pile of rocks. They talk of building condos here, a road at the bottom, tracks for motorcycles, parking lots...”

The peace-loving Chumash Indians who painted their symbols in the caves of Boney were converted to Catholicism by force, after which they died quickly of alcoholism and the pox, but they died as Christians, which represented progress in the mind of their European conquerors. The mountain was silent for a long time, until the Los Angeles megalopolis started exploding, and the rumble of the suburbs began licking the foothills of Boney.

Denver Hilton. Thursday 11 November 1971.

We flew to Colorado for a computer science meeting. Denver, where the short sickly grass has already been yellowed by the first freezing nights of the year, is a city of crime and grime. This morning I had breakfast with other panelists. Former Air Force researcher Rowena Swanson was there, happy to be out of government service. She looked at Janine from head to toe: “So you're Jacques' wife,” she uttered, as if this was truly astonishing.

Rowena told me she was upset about current trends in computer science. Those agencies that give out money to universities have become so charged with politics that nothing makes rational sense any more: "Jacques, you may be upset after your bad experience at Stanford, but don't you think it upset me when the Air Force gave up a program to which I had devoted ten years of my life to build? You have to put these things behind you."

Belmont. Saturday 13 November 1971.

Yesterday morning we had breakfast with Allen in Denver. He was in great shape, as Janine remarked to me afterwards: "How can he continue to look so young, at 61?"

We could see the Colorado State Capitol through the window of his small hotel room. He gave us a big, unsorted pile of papers to read. His little tape recorder was lying on the bed. He insisted to play a bad rendition of *La Traviata*. He told us how delighted he was to have the whole afternoon with us and Dave Saunders, repeating that he had come all the way to Denver just to have this "summit meeting." Yet over the next ten minutes he was interrupted by a barrage of phone calls. Between two disconnected bits of conversation, Allen handed me the last two chapters of his book. Later we did meet with Saunders, a tall white-haired fellow.

I asked about McDonald's suicide. Allen said, "I'd seen Jim in Tucson a few months before he killed himself. Our conversation took the usual course, with a barrage of accusations, reproaches and recriminations on his part. We exchanged some bitter words, I'm afraid. I left without shaking his hand."

Allen and Dave took us to lunch at Catacombes. One of the waiters amused us by doing his best to seduce Janine, who was indeed ravishing. In the afternoon we went to Saunders' house. He told us about his new project, a catalogue he calls Ufocat. Begun under the auspices of the Colorado project, it started from thousands of cases from my old catalogue and the Condon project files, ranging from the verified to the utterly dubious. They are blurred by statistical codes of great complexity. He had 43,000 cases; soon there'll be

50,000, then 75,000. Yet there is no defined goal to the catalogue, no precise question it is designed to answer.

We never did have the long-awaited "summit meeting" that Allen had advocated. All we discussed was idle gossip.

Mary-Lou Armstrong had come to Dave's house accompanied by a bearded man named Richard Sigismond, a geologist. One rainy day in Montana, in 1966, he'd stopped his Jeep to look at the terrain when he heard a sound like a thousand bees. His mind became filled with mechanical sentences: *It is futile to look for the source of the sound you perceive...* A few hours later he was seized with nausea, as well as his assistant. They fell into a semi-comatose state that didn't pass until morning. In the afternoon they saw a lens-shaped object, huge, aluminum in color. Since that event Richard has been inspired to buy a copper and silver mine in the Caribou region. He expects to make a fortune and to finance a parapsychology institute.

At five o'clock we drove back to Denver in dense fog. We met Herb Roth, who leads an important program at United Airlines. He drove us to the airport. Allen, utterly exhausted, slumped over a bench seat in the bar. But as we left to catch our plane he had recovered. He was discussing John Keel's books and eating peanuts with a young fellow who had come out of nowhere to join his entourage.

Belmont. Friday 19 November 1971.

As I came home from work today Maman handed me a letter from my brother Gabriel with very sad news: my uncle Maurice has been found lifeless in his apartment of *Rue du Cherche-Midi*. My brother is a physician. He was called right away but could only verify the poor man's death. He was over 80 years old.

"He ended his life alone, the way he spent it," remarked Janine with great sadness. We both loved him, a soft-hearted man with an inquisitive mind. Although he had a keen technical intellect, he refused to tune it to a modern world he despised. It was Maurice who inspired my interest in science. I still own the telescope he gave me. He died a week ago exactly, on Friday 12 November, in the morning.

Belmont. Friday 26 November 1971.

Mike has travelled through the state of Utah and drove south to Arizona. He has attempted to meet with the Lorenzens. In typical clannish fashion they found an excuse not to receive him, regarding his tiny research group as competition to their own. It is becoming clear to me that the ufologists are irrelevant, and are incapable of setting up a genuine research program.

Last Tuesday Peter and Marilyn Sturrock came over for dinner with Larry Berman. Olivier "taught them" how to use binoculars. Peter encourages my work on UFOs, as Gérard de Vaucouleurs had done in Austin. I found out about his private interests when he asked me to computerize an index to his personal collection of reprints. It contained the keyword "ESP", which could have applied to such topics as Elementary Statistical Projections or Electron Spin Potential. When I inquired about the meaning he said, "Extra-Sensory Perception, of course!" It was my turn to tell him of my interests, which led to his requesting a copy of my books. *Challenge to Science* caught his attention. Now he keeps requesting more data.

Yesterday was Thanksgiving. Janine is in New Orleans with the Rasmussens, our friends from Chicago days. I spent the afternoon in Berkeley, visiting a park-like property that belongs to a wealthy old eccentric, Mr. Hopkins. Columns, greenery, foliage and marble pillars gave the place the forlorn feeling of great European ruins. Hippie groups live in cabins in the park, playing rock music on huge amplifiers. There is a large mansion, an abandoned fountain whose steps cracked during the 1906 earthquake and were never repaired, and a big hole that old Mr. Hopkins himself is digging in the hope of finding some gold the Martians are supposed to have buried. All this makes the place wonderfully surreal.

Belmont. Friday 3 December 1971.

Last Monday we had dinner guests: Arthur Hastings and his wife Sandy, and Richard Sigismond, the psychic prospector I met in Colorado. Gerry Askevold told me the man was sincere and knew about mining, but was far from getting his hands on the riches he envisioned: "It's one thing to know where the silver veins may be, it's another to get the metal out," said Askevold, himself a field geologist from Montana with vast experience as a mineral economist.

Olivier is 8 years old today. Among other presents he received his first scientific instrument, a minima and maxima thermometer we will install inside the lookout I have built for him.

Belmont. Tuesday 14 December 1971.

My mother is back in Paris and our life has fallen into a new rhythm. In the morning Janine takes the children to school. Olivier and I get home about 5 P.M. We go to the lookout to take a reading of daily temperatures, then we all have coffee with Alain and I get back to work at my terminal while Janine goes shopping, takes care of the children. Most evenings I play with them, building Lego castles, fancy cars. Alain goes off to a restaurant in Palo Alto where he works, coming home after midnight.

Janine's work under contract is subject to arbitrary changes: She's helping build an administrative computer system for Santa Clara County, one of America's fastest growing areas, heart of Silicon Valley. I try to shelter my family from uncertainty. In the last few years I have seen the evidence of an electronic industry in deep turmoil. Last week it was giant Memorex that was laying off workers. Pundits of the modern economy sing the praises of high-tech salvation, but what happens to those who get thrown into the street with two weeks' pay, kids to feed, a mortgage to face? Should we believe that they simply go on happily to the next job?

Mike who is young, smart and hard-working has taken his car and disappeared from Silicon Valley in a cloud of dust. What about older folks who have no safety net? What about the upset families, the dislocation? Is it any surprise if many turn to drugs?

The larger system, too, is in shambles. Christmas cards show happy faces and angels singing "Peace" but there's a war in Pakistan, devoid of white doves. That Asia whose inspiration was supposed to teach us wisdom is a stubborn warrior drenched with the blood of the poorest people on Earth. Israel and Egypt crave another war.

Jung's *Memoirs* summarize his theories on the collective unconscious. Because of the breakthroughs of science he is "seized with secret shudders and dark forebodings." At stake here, he says, is a long-forgotten thing, the soul of Man. Who is in charge of it? Is it not the religious malady which gives us endless conflicts among allegedly God-fearing people from Ireland to Palestine? Is it not in the name of the soul of man that "good" Christians, "good" Hindus and "good" Muslims are busy building atom bombs? The problem goes deeper than Carl Jung himself is willing to look.

Belmont. Tuesday 21 December 1971.

In the afternoon I came home vaguely nauseous. The sky is wrinkled like a sheet of gray satin; the fog drags it along rain-soaked roads. I have started to write some short stories. My working title is *Redeem here your ecstasy coupons!* (**57**)

As I contributed some sections in French for Anton's books (**58**), I was amused to see the changes he was bringing to the traditional Black Mass to make it palatable to his middle-class public. I laughed as an angry Black Pope complained: "Is nothing sacred for these people any more? How am I expected to achieve desecration and blasphemy in this materialistic culture? How can I shock these people who wallow in material riches?"

Ron Westrum, a Purdue sociologist wrote to me about the nature of the undercurrent, psychological warfare and camouflage.

Belmont. Monday 3 January 1972.

Mike Jaffe reached Betsy McDonald in Tucson; they had coffee together and compared their life stories. The truth is that it wasn't because of his eyes that Jim McDonald had been put in the hospital. His first suicide attempt had left him blind, and there was nothing the doctors could do about it. Instead he was hospitalized for psychiatric treatment, to try and prevent a new phase of depression. The doctors were taking him to the campus every day to make him talk to his students, to get him used to his professional environment again.

He tricked them. He told them he was going to teach again some day. He spoke about his future. That fateful Saturday he was alone as he left for the University. He met a colleague on campus and spoke to him. He called a cab. He had planned the thing well. He had money hidden away in various places. He managed to go to a pawn shop and bought a .38 gun for fifty-four dollars. He called another cab to be driven to the desert, near a little bridge. There he simply blew his brains out.

The note he left for Betsy said he was sorry he hadn't found her at home when he came to pick up the money. He left instructions to gather the rest of the cash and dispose of the gun. Jim killed himself out of frustration and love. His wife had gone headlong into politics. She belonged to a radical leftist group, not unlike the Venceremos at Stanford. They gave out weapons to Black revolutionaries.

Jim plunged into his research: UFOs, effects of supersonic transports on the atmosphere, the possible destruction of the ozone layer... He did it out of despair, with no humor, no ability to distance himself from what he was studying. Jim had even researched his own case very scientifically, as he did everything: He had gathered detailed statistics about suicide.

Belmont. Friday 28 January 1972.

Life at Stanford University is becoming absurd. Bruce Franklin's wife got herself photographed brandishing a rifle. Both sides are childish. I am tempted to go work elsewhere, in spite of my great respect for Peter and his research. At heart, I am an information scientist, not an astrophysicist any more.

This week Gerry Askevold and I made a joint presentation on geological databases at a computer conference in San Jose. Willis Harman, influential SRI thinker and friend of professor Jeffery Smith, was the keynote speaker. He discussed the impact of technology on society: catastrophe or golden age? he asked. Willis Harman and Jeffery Smith are among the founders of the Human

Potential Movement -- a generous, expansive philosophical current that seeks to transcend science to focus on the unfulfilled aspirations and powers of human beings. This takes the form of a new awareness of psychic functioning and a demand for technologies that are more "appropriate," in the words of Buckminster Fuller, less polluting and destructive. This comes at a time when Timothy Leary encourages young people to reject their parents' bigotry and seek instant enlightenment; at a time when the works of Alan Watts have revived interest in eastern meditation, when an occult awakening has brought Aleister Crowley and paganism into the limelight.

Harman quotes from Huxley's *Perennial Philosophy* and integrates these movements into a single thrust. But he also inspires his high-level clients, leaders of industry, government and academia. The human potential movement is the latest idea from California, at a time when the U.S. is still mired in the Vietnam mess.

Later the same day.

A group of computer scientists at SRI have offered me an intriguing job. They work under a Department of Defense contract to develop radically new software for what they call the "augmentation of human intellect." Rowena had told me about their leader Doug Engelbart, whom she called a genius and an inveterate dreamer.

During my first interview, Doug explained to me how he launched his project: at the end of World War Two, he found himself sitting on the sand of a Pacific island, thinking of all his dead comrades, surveying the smoldering remains of civilization. Why were people engaged in such wanton destruction? he asked. Was technology the root or the tool of war? The atom bomb, the aircraft, the radar, all had been developed to serve the high priests of Mars.

"With my training in engineering," said Engelbart, who had a Ph.D. in control systems, "I knew there must be a way to help people communicate without conflict. There must be a method through which humans could understand their neighbors, and if it took a machine to do it, then by God, I was going to build that machine."

Other scientists had shared that frustration. Vannevar Bush, in a magnificent flight of inspiration, had already proposed to create computers that would act like personal assistants to scientists, thinkers, leaders in important decisions. The machine he proposed would be called the Memex, for "memory extension." Engelbart embraced the concept and took it one step further, designing a structure that would do nothing less than enhance the human intellect. Now he has gathered a team of programmers and wizards to help him build the technology. **(59)**

On Saturday Janine and I drove off to the Sierra with the children to visit the little towns of Volcano and Daffodil Hill, which rekindled our dream of finding a retreat away from the noisy city.

Belmont. Monday 7 February 1972.

When Allen Hynek came over on Wednesday I introduced him to Peter Sturrock. The two men offer an interesting contrast because Peter is intensely focused, a theoretical physicist, a British academic to the tip of his fingernails.

We had arranged for Allen to lecture at Stanford. He presented his usual combination of intriguing seriousness and flippant humor. Even in this serious setting before senior Stanford faculty he could not resist cracking jokes and displaying cartoons. He even showed a slide of a half-naked girl and a tabloid headline: "A Flying Saucer saved my virginity!"

Allen informs and entertains but he has missed the opportunity to build a consensus among scientists. In contrast, it is precisely such a movement that Peter Sturrock tells me he intends to form, a true scientific society dedicated to frontier topics.

I have concluded my explorations of esoteric groups with the realization that they did not hold any key to the mysteries we are pursuing, although they may well have a hand at manipulating the beliefs that go with the expectation of alien entities. The time has come to move on with our research. I have in mind new experiments, based on the notion that the phenomenon may react to a manipulation of entropy.

On Friday night Allen had dinner here with Jeffery Smith and his wife. Several friends arrived in time for dessert, along with Arthur Hastings and Sandy, Peter Sturrock and Larry Berman. Jeffery, a founder of the Parapsychology Research Group, invited us to their next meeting. The speaker will be Czech experimenter Milan Ryzl.

Last night I woke up several times, overwhelmed by dreams where the night was yielding some final secret, showing how days followed days and turned into inexplicable memories. Soon we will be only memories too, even though we love with such force. Abstractions, scattered ashes... Was that us?

At the edge of tears I want to hold you. But you sleep softly, as you do everything else, your breast touched with sweet darkness. I am a silent creature in the warmth of your shadow. You are the infinity I adore.

Part Six

PSYCHIC UNDERGROUND

6

Belmont. Wednesday 9 February 1972.

Europe braces for economic crisis and the agony of unemployment. In a rare flash of accountability, French pundits speak of the "eroded outlook" of their forecast. In contrast with the troubled world below, times are quiet on the hill of Belmont while I wait for the job Doug Engelbart has promised. Next month I will start work at the Augmentation Research Center. They need someone with database expertise to complement their group of systems programmers and network hackers. And I will go on with my private research.

"When Doug started work at SRI," his staff explained to me as we walked from one work station to another in the lab, "the type of computer terminal we have today just wasn't available, so he had to improvise. He invented a way to display text on small oscilloscopes, where it gets picked up by a TV camera and relayed in black and white, like a page of newsprint, on the consoles you see here. Doug and a fellow named Bill English built something they called a *mouse*, this little device on the right of every keyboard. You move it in any direction; an arrow on the screen moves until you have found the right place. A simple keyset is used to type out characters."

"Whatever happened to Bill English?" I asked.

"Bill has moved to Xerox. He and Doug couldn't get along. He took the technology, so it may get out into the real world."

That seems to be a major problem with this group: people just don't stay around. Most of the early programmers have left, replaced by products of the stormy sixties: long-haired students with a strong counter-culture bent and well-defined views about an Establishment they regard as utterly discredited. They walk around in tattered jeans, apparently unaware that their salaries are paid by the same Masters of War that Engelbart wanted to make obsolete: the project is funded by Arpa, the Advanced Research Projects Agency of the Pentagon, the technological cutting edge of the industrial world.

Joining Engelbart's project is not only a chance to get back to the forefront of technical development, but also to see a new type of social system: this group is a microcosm of a future world, anticipating networked communities to come.

Last night Janine and I drove Peter Sturrock to Jeffery Smith's house for a meeting of the Parapsychology Research Group, one of the few active psychic research associations in the U.S. I counted 38 people in Jeffery's magnificent house. Built by a Stanford professor of architecture in defiance of nature, it stood squarely on top of the San Andreas Fault. A large fireplace warmed up the place.

Czech refugee Mylan Ryzl directed the evening's experiment. He created a state of mild hypnosis "to enhance our abilities." Four subjects who volunteered for a card-guessing session were given four identical envelopes, two black cards and two white ones. The person closest to each subject was told to mix up the cards and to present them one at a time in an envelope. The answer would be noted and verified. Mylan stood up in the middle of the room: "Listen to my voice and relax," he instructed the group, "your thoughts are slowing down."

The room became quiet; my neighbor fell asleep. The experiment got under way in the cathedral-like atmosphere. One heard nothing but the fire crackling and the creek giggling. Subjects were given their first card and provided their answer in a low voice. After forty minutes the results were duly tabulated. They showed 105 right answers out of 210 trials, precisely fifty percent, as expected by pure chance! During the first half there were 53 correct answers and only 52 in the second half, so there was not even the merest suggestion of any "learning." We had verified the laws of statistics.

"We could have stayed home flipping coins," I told Janine.

Belmont. Sunday 13 February 1972.

Our first foray north of San Francisco in search of a place where I could build an observatory and run my own experiments led us into

Sonoma County, to the Russian River and the redwood and pine forests of Mendocino. Our base of operations was the small town of Ukiah, where we visited real estate agents.

"We're looking for a piece of land, a retreat for a family of harassed folks from Silicon Valley," we told them. "We'd like the property to come with some existing structure..."

"Even if it's not in the best condition," Janine would add.

One agent proposed a 40-acre parcel with a small lake. We took a road that led among pear orchards and sunny vineyards, with a splendid view of the valley, but the property was a dump: two old trailers connected by a spiderweb of illegal wires, with rusty appliances and broken chairs strewn around. The lake was little more than a stinking pond. We were astonished to find that people who had the good fortune to live in such a gorgeous landscape would not respect the place enough to keep it clean.

Next stop: a creek gurgling happily, sulphur springs, a lake complete with wild ducks, a backdrop of hills. A geyser sprang up periodically in the valley below. To the South was a dark and foreboding mass of trees. We disturbed a group of deer who bounded away. In the pasture two rabbits hopped in circles, watching Olivier in surprise. He was just as astonished. I drank from the clear stream. Had we found Magonia? Not quite: we don't have the money to build on this land. We came back to Ukiah for an early dinner. The kids watched television, a luxury we deny them at home. In color, too!

The next day we headed to the coast. We had driven in the fog for a long time when the clouds parted and the forest became illuminated like the nave of a cathedral. We stopped and watched with reverence at the edge of a wooded canyon. Olivier went looking for sticks and pebbles. The site seemed carved out of the darkest Celtic legend.

In Fort Bragg, on the Pacific shore, another agent took us to see two properties I liked but Janine was not impressed: too many ugly trailers. Route One turned and twisted along the ocean, from dizzying cliff to plunging precipice, to that ultimate vision: a wooden cabin at the edge of the world, a garden suspended over a thick mattress of white fog. And down there, at the very bottom, a rugged circular hole of intense savagery, a horrible funnel of vertiginous swirls filled with the crashing foam of the tide.

"I wonder what it's like on stormy days," I told our guide.

He straightened himself up, his arms spread wide against the wind: "On stormy days, Sir, all this is just one huge boiling cauldron!"

He fixed his one good eye on me like a vulture and described the apocalypse as he stood on a rock, his back to an abyss that changed every second under the angry battering of the trapped waves.

We passed Point Arena in the wet wind. We saw yet another property, a postcard scene, a yellow acacia tree in bloom and pines framing the Pacific. It sported a witchy name: Koven's Neck. We drove on to Bodega Bay, sheep eating grass on the edge of the precipice, the blue line of the horizon dotted with fishing trawlers returning to port. Nothing had prepared us for such beauty. We passed the Golden Gate again and got home in peace and splendor.

Belmont. Monday 21 February 1972. Washington's Birthday.

Last night I asked the children to draw monsters for me. Olivier produced "the Devil at his desk." The Prince of Darkness was looking for his chair: his neck was eerily thin, his face red, and he had green paws. In another drawing he was ready to go to bed. Equipped with cloven hooves, he was "looking for his blanket." Olivier's devils are the smiling, beatific kind; my daughter has an elf-like companion called the *Meu*. She said she'd seen the Red Meu.

"Can you draw it for me?" I asked.

"I don't want to," she said firmly.

"Does he have feet?"

"No, he doesn't have feet."

"Does he come into the room?"

She shrugged impatiently: "He has no feet the Meu, so he can't come into the room!"

There is a lesser species of Meu called the Black Meu, *Le Meu Noir*: "I saw him through the television." This one does have eyes, a mouth. She is willing to draw his pointed head sporting a big eye and a big mouth. But *Le Meu Rouge* is only a small red blur she refuses to make any bigger or more precise for us.

Doug Engelbart has confirmed his offer, asking me to join his computer research group at SRI. We agreed my work wouldn't start right away, so I'm free to resume my search for Magonia.

Ukiah. Sunday 27 February 1972.

Eager to leave crowds behind, we reached our Ukiah base and spent the rest of the afternoon driving around the lakes in a romantic landscape that Chateaubriand would have loved. We visited a parcel near Willits, ravaged by a crazy owner with the delusion to develop the land with a bulldozer. The result was a heroic pattern of dirt roads in all directions, turned to mud, overrun, ravaged by the latest rains. We told the agent we'd look elsewhere. He recommended the area of Covelo, and gave us a contact there.

The mountain roads of Mendocino are magnificent and lonely. We had lunch in a little café full of Indians. Seeing the totem out front, a large dark wooden bird, Olivier commented: “He cries because he'd like to fly, and he can't.”

Garberville. Monday 28 February 1972.

We were late in leaving the motel and didn't reach Covelo until mid-morning. The real estate man had assumed that we had given up. “Many city folks make an appointment like you did, but they get scared as soon as they see the mountain road; they change their minds and turn around,” he said as he drove us to an old ranch, clearly unsuitable. On the way back we saw a bright double rainbow in the fog below us, like a sign calling us back. We reached the big trees and stopped at a place pompously called Sherwood Forest, which did have a medieval feel. We played with the children, took long warm baths, visited the local shops, and sipped hot coffee.

Crescent City. Tuesday 29 February 1972.

We drove down the Avenue of the Giants this morning. Rain was still falling but the high branches of the redwoods filtered it. Second breakfast in Eureka; showers stopped. In Crescent City we ran along a beach strewn with driftwood, played billiards with Olivier in a local café. I love my son very much, he's my great treasure.

Belmont. Sunday 5 March 1972.

The road we wanted to take was covered with snow, so we drove north into Oregon and cut over to interstate 5, the major artery that serves the west coast. We found snow again after Ashland, but we managed to get up to the saddle point and down the other side without using chains. Several trucks had gone off into the embankment; cars had spun out. We passed Mount Shasta, the sacred mountain, a legendary volcano covered with eternal snows. The landscape was magnificent as the storm turned savage. On the way back we drove through Redding and Red Bluff, a region I only knew from the UFO literature.

There is nothing but a monotonous, flat plain between Red Bluff and Berkeley, where we stopped for lunch among long-haired students, the storm howling behind us. Highway 101 was closed to trucks. The radio reported landslides. Eleven people have died in Oregon.

We managed to quarrel about the future. Janine reproached my uncertainty: "You don't know what you really want."

Belmont. Sunday 26 March 1972.

An illustrator who had done some dustjacket designs for *Redeem Here Your Ecstasy Coupons* came over last Thursday. "Such pain in your book," she said, "such pain I didn't know..."

My SRI work would be fascinating if the project wasn't caught up in human turmoil. Is it the destiny of technology to attract crises and power plays? The system Engelbart's team is developing, known as NLS (for "on-line system!") is one of the most advanced software projects in the Valley, but Engelbart is not a consistent manager.

In Silicon Valley, technical obscurity is a mortal sin. NLS may have been meant to bring harmony to mankind, but Engelbart has never clearly explained what his invention was and what it did. Like many brilliant inventors, he thinks in images and motions, structures, “plexes” and frames. The only people who have taken his ideas seriously are the military. His concept, born in an effort to eliminate the basis of war, is now funded by the Pentagon. No wonder it has suffered from an identity crisis throughout its stormy history.

In 1968, when it was publicly demonstrated for the first time in San Francisco, Engelbart's system was already capable of processing text, structuring it into paragraphs and sentences that could be moved around at astonishing rates, and of merging the blocks of words into larger entries. Engelbart, sitting at the console on the stage before 1,500 information science specialists, took “mouse” in hand and launched into a sensational, history-making demonstration.

Linked to his staff by microwaves, Doug projected on a giant screen both the text on his terminal and the contents of the computer files 30 miles away. But he went beyond mere digital prowess: His remote assistants were on screen, editing sentences and memoranda, formatting books, even drawing up graphs they could change on the spur of the moment. Superimposed on those graphs were the faces of staff members discussing the issues. The work was stunning, but instead of blossoming into a major industrial effort, Engelbart's vision got into trouble with the information community and his own sponsors. The pundits of computer science are hostile. Engelbart is seen as a loner, a heretic. The project is in danger of becoming another island in the turbulent flow of computer culture. Engelbart runs the project by subtle emotional blackmail: “See how much I am suffering, my children,” he seems to be complaining.

Later the same day.

When I tell Janine how secure I am in my love for her, how “pure” a feeling that is, she laughs and challenges me: “Try and define a pure feeling!” She says we are always alone. I disagree. There's a level of reality where information is common to all beings. Perhaps that level has singularities -- points that stick out of the information fabric. Each of these singularities becomes the root of an individual being.

When we plunge inside ourselves it is the beauty of others that we find. By offering our hearts to others we gain knowledge of ourselves. The man who is concerned with his own power and well-being only achieves a hardening of his unconscious, the sclerosis of his dreams. That is why I reject Anton's philosophy of self-love.

Belmont. Monday 27 March 1972.

The French papers speak of rising unemployment among the young, social violence in the air. It is here in California that the future is being built. The problems I experience every day at SRI would be just an anecdote, to be quickly told and forgotten, were it only a case of a small group of technicians preserving their livelihood. But this project is a microcosm of a future world. It prefigures a network-based society which will not be attained by the rest of the population for another ten, twenty or thirty years.

Our system generates communities that can work in many different places at once, yet participate in a single creation process. The idea is revolutionary in a world where the morning commute still dominates life, and much of one's existence is spent in offices, looking across a desk at other desks, through glass doors at other doors...

Engelbart's vision is of instantaneous exchanges over wires of intelligence, of a vast pool of information available to everyone. The technology is ahead of the transformation implied by electronic interconnection. Like most engineers, Engelbart underestimates the human factor. And the human factor is coming back to take revenge.

Belmont. Wednesday 29 March 1972.

I have found a mentor in Paul Rech, a former Shell manager I first met in Paris after the 1968 riots (**1**). He just joined our project with two of his colleagues, Dick Watson and Mike Kudlick. Ironically, they are the men who interviewed me for a job in Emeryville three years ago when I decided to join Stanford instead. As distressing as that experience was, my decision proved to be right: Shell went through even worse ordeals. The company moved to Houston. Paul had a rough time. Now we are both members of Engelbart's Augmentation project, increasingly puzzled by what we find there.

The Center occupies an entire wing on the second floor of Building 30 which overlooks the city park. On the same floor as Engelbart's lab are scientists doing advanced research on the physics of the atmosphere and a team of artificial intelligence folks who work on robotics with Charlie Rosen (**2**). Paul was hired by Doug to do research on group dynamics but his assignments, like mine, keep changing. Our team includes a tattered band of confirmed idealists, radical thinkers, professional hackers and bearded hippies who think of the group as a Commune, with Doug as visionary father figure. The group sinks into a social experiment where we serve as our own guinea pigs.

Belmont. Sunday 2 April 1972.

Last night Janine and I went to hear Berlioz' *Requiem* with a friend. We were swept away by the torrents of the music played by the San Francisco orchestra under Seiji Osawa: "Sanctus, Sanctus, Sanctus deus Sabaoth..." Many Catholic texts are inspired and beautiful. But what a stupid prayer is this *Requiem*! Under the magnificent music, what a debasing, masochistic manifesto for petty bourgeois wallowing in guilt! Stripped of the mystery of the Latin verses it reveals a shameful testimony to everything that is wrong with humanity, crawling in self-pity: "Save me, Holy Jesus, I am the reason for your pilgrimage, Do not let me down today..."

It goes on to an abject wail: "In the bottomless pit save me from the jaws of the lion. Prevent me from falling into the blackness. Make sure the dark abyss doesn't close around me." There isn't an ounce of dignity in this grovelling plea. Whoever wails before his God in this way deserves every bit of Hell's torments!

Belmont. Monday 3 April 1972.

When I called Allen Hynek today I found him filled with his new celebrity status, disappointed in Regnery who did nothing to promote his book. "I'm disgusted with the *National Enquirer*," he added. "In fact I regret joining their UFO panel."

"Well..." I began. The silence lingered.

"I know, Jacques, you'd warned me against it. So did Fred Beckman. You were both right, dammit: they've opened their campaign with great fanfare, calling for evidence and all that, but all we're getting are letters from religious nuts, and no science."

He did get some satisfaction from the Air Force: the head of the Foreign Technology Division, whom he now serves as a personal consultant, sends him to do an inspection of the Blue Book archives.

Belmont. Sunday 9 April 1972.

Madame Mathey, who just jetted back from Australia and New Zealand in her search for the Absolute, has made me spend a depressing afternoon. Her chauffeur scraped the bottom of her Cadillac limousine on our steep driveway. She has allowed herself to be led by random signs she assumed to be mystical simply because they were a little strange. In New Zealand she visited Bruce Cathie, who fantasizes Ufonauts have set up a world-wide grid of antennas. She learned that his sick daughter had been treated by "Doctor Toni," the Filipino psychic surgeon whose exploits we had seen, a long time ago, on a film that had astonished Allen Hynek (**3**). So she flew off, lodged herself in a Manila palace, got to Toni in time to see him extract some fibrous substance from a patient, and dropping it into the toilet before any evidence could be recovered.

When one is guided by "The Cosmic" without critical selection or standard, things necessarily end up spinning in a circle of New Age tricksters and promoters. She consults a long-deceased Hindu sage through a medium. He has already revealed to her, for a handful of twenty-dollar bills, that UFOs were "thought-forms." I could have told her this at no expense, but of course she wouldn't have believed it. "The only remaining question," I said over coffee and chocolate cake as Janine was fighting giggles, "is whose thought, and whose form?" So far the Hindu sage has no answer.

Belmont. Saturday 15 April 1972.

I spent the morning working hard on the hillside, fighting the weeds, and the afternoon in bed with Janine. Corelli is playing in the background. All the flowers are in bloom. My little girl has given us a definition of a gardener as "a gentleman who makes flowers quickly."

Back in Vietnam, American forces are caught in a massive attack. Thousands are dying. Washington retaliates, bombing Haiphong harbor. Crazy times.

Claude Poher, whose visit we are expecting soon, has sent me a thick study of UFOs he has conducted at Brétigny. Aimé Michel will also come over soon. And I have been contacted by Stuart Nixon, the new head of Nicap. He wants to discuss information systems techniques that could be applied to his files.

Belmont. Friday 21 April 1972.

The celebrated attorney Maurice Garçon made a profound remark in his book about Vintras, a 19th century French cult leader:

> The illuminated hold an important place in the history of societies... It seems that in order to get an idea accepted, even if it is a reasonable one, it must first be presented in an excessive form. Thus a study of the character of those who are generally called "illuminated" (or delusionary) is often a prerequisite to understand the mores of a given era. It is through them that one reaches an adequate knowledge of the evolution of ideas, and even that of the institutions. (**4**)

If I had Maurice Garçon's psychological talent I would write a fine book about the illuminations of Doug Engelbart, Silicon Valley martyr and visionary. Development is stagnating, so this morning Doug herded us into a meeting room to form a "spontaneous" new committee he had dreamed up, called the POD Committee for "Personal and Organizational Development." He had hired a consultant who spoke in lofty generalities. When Dick Watson and Mike Kudlick, tempered in the world of business, asked precise questions, he answered with verbiage. They walked out in disgust.

Later, over lunch at *Pot-au-Feu*, where Alain was working his magic in the kitchen, Paul Rech remarked: "Doug's consultant said he was conducting a study of managers to find out the secret of the good ones. Well, the answer is simple: The good ones know what they want, and the bad ones don't."

Engelbart has built himself an artificial business immune to external storms, populated with hand-picked individuals molded to suit his dream. But the chief engineer has resigned, Bill English is long gone, and many systems programmers have left, replaced by students with a counterculture bent and well-defined views about an Establishment they regard as bankrupt. Even grass and LSD are connected to the dream of an information world that is part of the consciousness explosion.

I see something altogether different here. I see a society in which the chemical control of personal moods will parallel the supertechnology for the manipulation of information. Yet research grants are vanishing, and Doug can find no other source of support than the Establishment, and its extreme expression, Arpa itself.

Arpa is the Advanced Research Projects Agency of the Department of Defense, created in the late fifties to react swiftly to the Russian threat in space. It is now deploying the first network of computers to span a continent. Arpanet is revolutionary in design, linking together machines of different makes in a bold strike that will soon force computing centers and universities across the nation to connect their computers together or forego Washington dollars. This is the kind of community Engelbart had predicted, but in order to connect his own machine to it he had to downgrade its capabilities and give up many special features of his own system.

We must say this about Doug: he was able to rise above all such problems. In his prophetic "right-brain" way (**5**), he sees the day coming when computers will no longer be used just by scientists but will be available to many people. He foresees entire communities working through them.

It is the suspension of time and space by the computer that excites me. On a good day, we come close to making it real, even if Doug is now dreaming of "knowledge workers" and office automation, two notions he has picked up from management expert Peter Drucker.

Belmont. Sunday 23 April 1972.

Janine had a curious dream last night. She was visiting a kindergarten. In the library was a large, beautiful book by Aleister Crowley entitled *Yarden Yarder*. "I understand why you feel it's important to expose the children to Crowley's philosophy," she told the teacher, "but do you realize they don't know how to read?"

Anton has expressed a profound thought, that truth has never made man free: "Truth is the most dangerous thing man has ever had to handle," he said. "Knowing the truth will get you killed!"

We both admire the statement by Lovecraft:

> The most merciful thing in the world is the inability of the human mind to correlate all its contents. We live on a placid island of ignorance in the midst of black seas of infinity, and it was not meant that we should voyage far. **(6)**

Belmont. Monday 1 May 1972.

An O.T.O. member from Virginia writes to me, berating Anton for using a "corrupted form" of John Dee's Enochian language **(7)**. Corrupted or not, that didn't stop a celebration of the Night of Walpurgis at Anton's house. Rex and John F. were there in a gay mood. Faithful Loni was in attendance, as well as Ann the dentist's pretty wife, who left early when he started drinking a bit too hard. Rosalind, as plump, loyal and pleasant as ever, completed the intimate group. Anton was relaxed.

One of the assistants, who is completing a Ph.D. in sociology in Berkeley and, like me, is a participant-observer at such events, requested that he play the organ. Soon the night resounded with masterful renditions of national anthems, from the *Deutschland über*

Alles to *L'Internationale* and *La Marseillaise*, after which he reverted to classical improvisations until three o'clock in the morning.

When he sits at the keyboard, Anton is a true magician, deliberate and smart under pretense of overt buffoonery. His group isn't a real church or sect, although he relishes scaring everyone with that notion. Its real purpose is to provide entertainment for himself and a steady supply of stimulating people to relieve his boredom.

On Tuesday night Claude Poher and his wife came over. Poher is a young man with clear ideas and the build of a rugby player, a French technocrat, methodical and disciplined. His wife is pleasant and smart. We took them to *Pot-au-Feu* for dinner. A musician was playing the accordion.

"Did you find out what was in the French military files?" I asked as we sat down.

"Yes, I went over to our Air Force," he said, sounding important. "They agreed to cooperate as soon as they heard that my boss at CNES was supporting my project. They gave me their file, which is not very big..." He spread his thumb and forefinger. This must be the same file I studied eleven years ago. He went on: "That's only about 300 pages. Most reports are vague, not interesting."

"Do you conduct your own investigations now?"

"Not really. Since January we've had four or five good sightings in France, about which I have done some research. I send them on to GEPA (**8**) and they publish them."

"Which agencies are doing the actual field investigations, then?"

"The Army, sometimes the Air Force, most often the Gendarmes."

"Is that all? The newspapers often report that some mysterious gentlemen dressed in civilian clothes have come over from Paris or Marseilles... I am thinking of the case of Vins-sur-Caramy, for instance... they took samples..."

"Well, those were from the *Renseignements Généraux*," he said.

"So they must have their own files, right?" Poher evaded my question: "That would surprise me. All they do is to collect the information and forward it to others. They are a political outfit, they report to the Interior Ministry. In each *Préfecture* there are five or six fellows like that, following current events. They may pick up a few pebbles, but that doesn't mean they do any analysis."

"In other words, the poor farmer who sees a flying saucer in his field has every chance to be visited by the cops, the *Barbouzes*, the amateurs, the CNES, the journalists..."

Poher laughed, put his hand on my arm: "No, Jacques, you got it all wrong! The journalists get there first!"

The owner offered us a drink on the house. The accordion began another tune.

"What will you do next?"

"Every year the scientific board of CNES considers a few hundred proposals for experiments. Some of them get financed and actually built. My boss has suggested that I submit a proposal for an automated detection station. As soon as any anomaly happens, all possible physical measurements would be run. With space technology we've got the sensors under control. For the photos we would use the same camera as the astronauts."

"Where would you put these stations?"

"At some observatory like Haute Provence, where it could run unattended. Nobody needs to know about it. As far as the public is concerned it's better to be discreet. But scientific opinion has been changing in France. Even your old boss Muller, from Paris observatory, now concedes there may be something up there!"

I recommended building a transportable version of his station, so that it could be setup at the site of recurrent events. There is no indication, I told him, that UFOs would necessarily choose to concentrate around Haute Provence.

Poher remains fascinated by the weird story of Ummo. He is curious about the stories that surround a cave at La Javie where the "Ummites" allegedly stayed.

We went up to Belmont. I gave him a demonstration of the interactive catalogue of landings.

Belmont. Sunday 7 May 1972.

A strange episode took place yesterday. I had woken up in the middle of the night after a disturbing nightmare. I had killed someone in a bloody scene. The whole day seemed weighed down by this nightmare. I acted uncertain, awkward, starting one project only to drop it and half-heartedly start another. Olivier was playing outside with the neighbors' kids while I tested new software that required two terminals simultaneously. I set up a heavy unit on top of the round dining room table, where it didn't fit well. There were phone lines and electrical wires all over. To add to the confusion my program didn't work right and I couldn't find the "bug."

Suddenly I heard sharp cries, turning to howls of terror. The door burst open and my son rushed in, his arm dripping with bright red blood. The neighbor's usually quiet dog had jumped at him and tore deeply at the flesh. "I'm gonna DIE!" I'm gonna DIE!" the boy was yelling as he trembled and shook.

Everything fell into place. I poured cold water over his arm. Janine rushed to join me. We controlled the bleeding and covered the wound. The doctor was called. Five minutes later we were racing along El Camino on the way to the emergency room.

"You're lucky," I told him, deliberately minimizing the episode; "The neighbors could have kept a crocodile as a pet!" My son gave me a pale, skeptical smile. Yet it was hard to escape the fact that my bloody nightmare had been a vivid premonition. The stream of the day had somehow been wrong, as if everything had been waiting for a violent episode to snap it out of its falseness. In such events, what happens to reality? Should we even look for cause and effect? Had my brain perceived the accident that would occur a few hours later? Had my dream of a bloody mess, with its heavy load of absurd guilt, actually precipitated the accident? If I'd kept Olivier inside, would the energy have manifested in other ways? Is there simply a premonitory aura around significant dramas where blood is involved, as in primitive rituals? Should I have been able to decipher my dream as a premonition, and predicted the event?

Later the same day.

Our lofty project for the Augmentation of the Human Intellect is still plodding along. In spite of my skepticism I remain interested: this is, after all, our future, whether we like it or not. Sociologists may write complicated scenarios about the computerized world to come, but we're already living its conflicts here, I thought as I looked at the rectangular room with its computer consoles equipped with keyboards and mice. I felt like the little kid of the wonderfully horrible movie by Dr. Seuss, held prisoner in the big hall of Dr. T's castle, waiting for 5,000 fingers to come and press the keys of the Big Piano Machine that would control the future. (**9**)

Having wired up his audience Doug went to the blackboard, a spotlight on his white hair. In black pants and a black sweater, he started speaking about himself, detailing the persecution of his genius. Ten million dollars have been invested in his technology and the man complains that he is being persecuted! Doug uses us to bear witness to his suffering. He has even put one of his programmers in charge of monitoring our "beliefs and attitudes." I'm fascinated by these totalitarian measures in a project aiming at an egalitarian community, where blue jeans and long hair are *de rigueur*.

Belmont. Saturday 13 May 1972.

Aimé Michel has just spent three days with us. He arrived on Tuesday, driven by his American cousins. We went to SRI, where he started explaining to Engelbart how Sextus Empiricus had invented a tree structure for all human knowledge a long time before the theory of plexes, and how Raymond Lull devised a logical machine to demonstrate Christian truth to the Arabs.

On Wednesday I took Aimé to Stanford for lunch in the midst of a half-hearted student demonstration against the Vietnam War.

"It's ironic," he told me, "the U.S. Army is devastating Indochina, so what do your young leftists do in protest? They get together in the sun to sing Joan Baez songs..."

The students were quietly selling bead necklaces and leather belts. Boys had taken off their T-shirts and rested on the lawn next to tanned girls in shorts. The area was strewn with books, tits, asses and beards. Bruce Franklin sat near us, surrounded by his faithful militants wearing red armbands. We listened in growing astonishment to a Christian revolutionary: "We must love the North Vietnamese, and we must love Nixon."

Aimé had heard enough, so we walked over to my old office at the electronics labs. I introduced him to Peter Sturrock, who started arguing about UFOs. I tried Poher's recent argument on Peter:

"If one assumes that these objects can bring their mass down to zero, don't you think a lot can be explained? No sonic boom, time relativity effects, ionization..."

Peter smiled. Next, Aimé tried Plantier's theory (**10**). Again, Peter shook his head skeptically.

"You're looking in the wrong direction," he said softly. "Antigravity, electromagnetism, relativity, magneto-hydrodynamics, all that is irrelevant. What's at stake is much more fundamental."

"More fundamental than relativity?" asked Aimé, looking around him to make sure he was actually speaking to a Stanford professor. He seemed reassured by the long shelves loaded with physics publications, the photographs of the solar corona on the walls. "That may be a shock for your physics colleagues," he continued.

"It won't be a shock," Peter said in his restrained English manner, "only a revolution."

In the pause that followed I could hear the rustle of the trees outside the window, the song of the birds, and Aimé's mind spinning.

On Thursday we had lunch with Arthur Hastings, who spoke of ghosts and poltergeists. Aimé told him the story of commandant Tizané, who investigated hauntings for the French gendarmerie. He was subjected to the ultimate affront when a spirit took away his cylindrical *képi* from his head and ran it through his body (**11**).

Hynek's book *The UFO Experience* has just been published (**12**). As we expected from the draft, it is honest, serious. But it passes unnoticed: the media are preoccupied with the elections and the Vietnam turmoil.

Belmont. Sunday 14 May 1972.

We are still in bed. Janine reads, the kids are playing on the redwood deck in the warmth of a fine spring morning. Yesterday we had as a guest the new director of Nicap, Stuart Nixon, a tall man with a long face. He came with an IBM engineer who said nothing. Hynek had recommended that they consult me about computer projects, so I gave them a demonstration of the full-text landing catalogue. (As far as industry is concerned, interactive interrogation of databases is still in the future, and full English interrogation is not on the horizon). I urged them to decentralize Nicap, give autonomy to their affiliates, and encourage members to publish their own work, with case summaries in English. They believe they have some 15,000 cases, 10% of them landings. But they keep a centralized structure, hoarding all the data.

I gave Aimé my early Journals. He reacted with emotion, stunned that I trusted him to such an extent. "It's a big responsibility, to read this," he told me after a few pages. We spoke about the role of sects in history, Christianity and the Apostles, "those *Poujadistes* of Tiberius' time!" as he calls them (**13**). He muses about writing an apocryphal *Gospel according to Pilatus*, in Latin, and to bury it secretly somewhere, in the hope that it will be discovered a hundred years from now, forcing scholars to think new thoughts.

Belmont. Sunday 21 May 1972.

When I took Aimé Michel to Anton's house last night he reclined happily in Rasputin's chair and prepared to be entertained. But once he saw the genuine depth of the man he had first regarded as just another amusing charlatan he changed his attitude and argued in earnest about psychic realities. After this, Anton in turn was inspired to sit at the keyboard and launched into pieces by Prokofief that took us into the hours of dawn while Anton's stupid dog Typhon ran in circles, hitting his head against the furniture.

Anton LaVey was happy to meet Aimé whom he knew only through some of his articles in Bergier's *Planète* (**14**). Aimé regaled him with descriptions of Provins, the "French Jerusalem" where a medieval church stands on top of an ancient temple of Isis. Anton told us that a trap door in his basement opened up into a secret passage to the coast, but he did not offer to show it to us, so perhaps it is just more bragging by the old carnival man.

The discussion turned to Aimé's psychic experiments. "You're using self-hypnosis?" Asked Anton. Aimé acknowledged it, adding: "I've stopped doing it. The entities behaved like those in the Tibetan Book of the Dead."

"You were in contact with *the mind that is held by no head*," remarked Anton, who laughed in a sardonic way that chilled us.

Rasputin's chair, allegedly a priceless antiquity, was happily rocking in the ritual chamber. Again using his carny tone, Anton claimed that it was cursed. Indeed a little carved demon in the back of the seat has a pointed nose that sticks out between one's vertebrae with the most disagreeable effect. Aimé left the black house pleased to have met LaVey, whom he found oddly vulnerable and an admirable musician.

On the way back Aimé told me he found himself moved by my Journals. "You're much more emotional than I thought," he said. "I had taken you for a dry intellectual."

On Thursday we had Mylan Ryzl and Donmaier for dinner with the Hastings, Larry Berman and Peter Sturrock. We discussed parapsychology and mathematical prodigies. My friendship with Aimé has deepened over those few days. He confided some of his private thoughts to me. In a serious conversation he even told me how, at several points during his own life, he felt he had actually experienced thought transference.

On one occasion he found himself in the body of a courtier coming out of an evening of gambling at the king's palace. He was urinating copiously into the darkened bushes as he told a companion in a roguish voice, rolling his French R's: "Well we emptied it this time, the King's cashbox (*la cassette du Roi*), didn't we?"

Aimé vividly recalls the boots he wore, his trousers, his ribbons.

On another occasion he was a Centurion, stealthily climbing up a hill with a sword in hand. It was only a flash, a snapshot, a single instant in the life of a soldier. Someone had made a noise, dislodged a stone. He raised his hand in warning, and that was all.

The most impressive memory was of another scene: He was crouching at the edge of a cliff. He watched a canyon overgrown with vegetation. A creek flowed at the bottom from right to left. He heard an animal scream, knew he would die.

That particular memory was Aimé's most terrifying impression in his whole life. "These episodes have convinced me that something survives death," he said, adding that "all the experiments in spiritism have led nowhere. Why not concentrate on the more physical manifestations instead? And on attributes of human consciousness?"

"I am disturbed by what you've shown me of artificial intelligence," Aimé went on, referring to our discussions at Stanford and SRI about Turing machines and later developments. "Obviously many of the effects of human consciousness can eventually be duplicated or surpassed by automata."

"Yet consciousness is unique, universal..." I pointed out.

"I disagree," he answered. "Consciousness is intensely individual. Think of pain, think of despair. Think of standing next to an open window as you suffer in silence. Look outside: Nobody cares! Nobody knows about it. Your pain affects nothing: the birds sing, people laugh... In such moments any notion of universal consciousness vanishes."

"You're tripping over your own carpet," I replied. "What about that terror you said you felt from the mind of a prehistoric savage crouching at the edge of a cliff? And the alarm in the gesture of the Centurion? Those were local, too, in space and in time, and yet you felt them yourself, in your own study, in 20th century France. And the spirit entities in your experiments? Do they exist between séances? Or are you their *locus*, the sole operator for their manifestations? Are you the modulator for that great spirit attached to no head that Anton mentioned to us? Let's draw the real hard lessons from the UFO phenomenon: there are other dimensions. They apply trivially to matter, but in the spiritual domain they open up incredible possibilities."

Aimé sees little hope for a France poorly managed by politicians who represent a mere continuation of mediocrity. Mediocrity is something they know how to manage. Aimé thinks the world is headed for a "soft apocalypse."

Monday night we had dinner at Engelbart's house in Atherton.

Aimé said that the only good strategy in life was to know and participate, to share in the knowledge, and then to retire in silence and denial to some faraway place, turning inside, refusing to adapt.

"In the information-rich world you've shown me, the only people who will survive will be the invisibles, the very poor, and those who cannot or will not communicate."

Last night, on the way to San Francisco, I asked him if he thought Janine was happy. "She is," he answered without hesitation," and the proof of that is that she asked me the same question, about you!"

Later the same evening.

We celebrate Catherine's 4th birthday. This evening Olivier and I drove Aimé Michel to the airport. He is now on a flight to Utah, where he will meet with Frank Salisbury. I hope to go there myself to conduct field research with Gerald Askevold in the Uintah Basin. The Indians in the area have observed a remarkable series of events, which Salisbury has documented (**15**). I have made discreet plans to follow up with him. Only Hynek is aware of our project.

Aimé Michel is gone. He has left a big hole here. I am bitter against the tyranny of time, the constraints of communication. Yet I have to smile when I see my daughter, bending over a cane-like stick, mimicking his gait as she climbs the stairs. Yes he went away, that good *Meussieu Missel*, as she calls him. He has gone back to the Alps and the fields of Haute Provence that smell so sweetly of lavender and honey. I told him, "I have to stay in the U.S. because it's the only place where I can escape from Americanism."

Belmont. Friday 2 June 1972.

A fine letter has arrived from Aimé, now back in the Alps, contemplating our coarse world below:

> Children, may *Le Diable* keep you in His Holy care! I arrived back home yesterday. I have been meditating on everything I saw and especially on our discussions. I am disappointed in

> the failure of language to communicate essential things. On one hand your Diary is slowly maturing in my unconscious, making its own place in a way I cannot tell clearly...on the other hand I realize that I have searched in vain for that which I regard as the heart of all our problems, namely a certain way to reach the Essential through the path of solitude.

Later he recounts the various visits he made on his way back. His pictures of our friends stand like little vignettes:

> Salisbury is a funny guy full of talent (...) Saunders is a *solitaire* full of confused intuition, with unlimited patience and obstination.
>
> Hynek carries your departure from Evanston like a wound. He loves you like a son, that excellent man. Powers is an impatient genius...

Belmont. Friday 9 June 1972.

Aimé has sent me more details of his reactions, following his return to France:

> What is certain is, first of all, that the information science and biological revolution will lead to a new being and, second, that there is a body of occult knowledge to be saved. You and I have an essential part of that knowledge, which is ignored by most people.

About Anton, he wrote:

> Either he has no powers, other than those of his strong personality, in which case he is not interesting except as a distant friend; or he does have powers and they are maleficient for those he touches, because he puts strength and personal realization above everything else. His system

> anticipates nothing except using others for his own profit. I tend to believe he does have such powers or rather, he knows how to trigger some of them, without controlling them. According to my own experiments the powers in question practice the same morality as LaVey himself: they use those who think they can use them.

He urged me to be careful, adding that one cannot imagine what the Devil can be, such as an entity he says he once met, leaving him terrified and upset. Yet he concedes that the "Bearded One," Jehovah, is just as evil as his Adversary. What do good and evil mean, anyway? Nothing, said Aimé, except that "the love of your wife and your children is good, and if you think about it, you can understand the whole universe based on that idea."

At SRI, later the same day.

In Engelbart's lab I now spend frustrating hours. Doug proposes to replace the English language with a fantastic computer vocabulary of his own composition. He views it as the means to have men finally understand one another. Gerald and I are at work on a joint article about geological databases for the upcoming Gordon conference, an exclusive invitation-only affair that will gather the luminaries of the field behind the gates of an East Coast college in a few weeks.

I am going through an awkward crisis. From now on, our only source of security and stability will be the knowledge that nothing is secure or stable. I haven't adapted to that reality yet. When Janine frowns I feel broken and distressed. All day at work in this lab I feel a furious urge to punch mirages in the nose.

Perhaps my mind was simply sensing the coming violence. Day before yesterday a two-hour arson fire destroyed an entire wing of the Stanford administration building. Gerald described the scene to me: Students were sitting around, drinking beer and indifferently watching the structure burn while twelve big fire trucks poured water over the flames. Evidently I am not the only one feeling angry, or living through a crisis.

Belmont. Saturday 17 June 1972.

A beautiful day. We have laughed, dreamed, listened to the Songs of the Crusades. I'm reading *Stranger in a Strange Land* by Robert Heinlein. I spent the day with Olivier, assembling a plastic skeleton.

Two publishers have rejected *Redeem*, so I read the manuscript with a new eye and suddenly I don't like it either. Perhaps I should publish some of the good chapters as separate texts (**16**). Do I still know how to love, how to listen to others? Janine makes sure I do. "But you are so extreme!" she points out. "With your friends, with everyone. You're always ready to give them your heart, your soul; then you think you catch a glimpse of some little weakness in them and suddenly you banish them away, it's all over, you take everything back. Can't you take them as they are?"

Belmont. Saturday 24 June 1972.

Allen will never change. He just called me to say he was late leaving Los Angeles, where he gave eight interviews today. He griped against his publisher because he had only arranged for him to appear on a single television show during his stay in San Francisco.

I don't like being around Allen when he's a celebrity. He will be here in the morning with Salisbury, with whom I'll make final plans for my research trip to Utah.

Belmont. Sunday 25 June 1972.

I've finally met Salisbury, a member the Mormon Church. As a bishop he felt obligated to turn down our excellent *Saint Emilion*, but he neatly polished off a cup of ice cream swimming in Cointreau and asked Janine for more. Allen and Frank are on the *National Enquirer* UFO panel which will supervise the award of $50,000 for proof of UFO reality. It has not escaped my notice that organizing such a panel would be an excellent way for a secret "undercurrent" agency to gather fresh data. Allen denies he might be used in this fashion (**17**). So far the tabloid's money has only been spent in flying this small group around the country, chasing chimeras.

After lunch Allen went to lie down in our guest bedroom while I discussed our proposed investigation trip to the Uintah basin with Salisbury. Numerous objects have been seen there, he reported, in a semi-desert area bordering northern Utah. For two years (1966 and 1967) there were many low-level sightings. A local teacher, Junior Hicks, has compiled an impressive catalogue. Curiously, not a single incident involved occupants. The population there is half Mormon and half Indian. Would they talk if they saw such beings?

I spent the afternoon with Allen, bitterly disappointed with Northwestern. He'd hoped to attract Karl Henize back to the Faculty, since he hasn't been selected for the Skylab flight. Karl was willing to come back to Evanston to run a two million dollar project but Northwestern played so many games that he ended up in Texas.

"You did the right thing in leaving Evanston, Jacques," he added with sadness. "The administrators are only looking at the short term, the bottom line; they ignore the quality of the science. Bill Powers has moved on. Soon we'll only have a few astronomers left."

Allen and I walked up to the heights of Belmont. It was a gorgeous evening. Cascades of white fog flowed beyond the coastal ridge; the moon was rising over the Bay. We spoke about the fact that science was increasingly secret; we discussed the work still to be done on our subject. Allen hopes to live long: "I come from a line of people who died in their nineties," he told me. "In six years I will retire, and then I want to devote all my time to this question. No more publicity, Jacques, I promise you, no more books, no more of these stupid interviews, no more dealing with ufologists, always fighting among themselves like cats and dogs! I want to do quiet research on UFOs in the same way serious research is done in astronomy."

We walked back slowly, talking about mysticism. Janine was waiting for us, the children already in bed, dinner on the table.

Belmont. Wednesday 28 June 1972.

On Monday night Janine and I had dinner with Hynek at *Pot-au-Feu*. Conversation came back to the Rosicrucians. I had not known that

Allen had followed a vegetarian diet for twelve years of his life, and had done his best to attain sexual ascetism.

"That experience wasn't for me," he told us with a twinkle in his eye. He has five kids to prove it, and his mood changes measurably whenever a pretty girl walks by.

"Besides," he added with a sigh, "I've seen most of those who followed these guidelines end up as sick people, hopeless drifters or idle dreamers."

Belmont. Monday 3 July 1972.

There were only four programmers in the office today, so we started gossipping about the vagaries of human intelligence and its augmentation through computers.

"The human potential movement started as a serious philosophy here at SRI, with Willis Harman and thinkers from Stanford," someone said. "Doug and Willis even had an official project to find out if LSD could enhance problem-solving. Then Timothy Leary started preaching, all hell broke loose."

The office next to mine is occupied by a cheerful woman named Mil. She is our administrative assistant and something of a mystic. She knows everything about the history of the project, so we share confidences whenever the main computer crashes and interrupts our work, a situation that is fairly common.

Colby College. Thursday 13 July 1972.

Gerald Askevold and I have come to this small New England College at the invitation of the Gordon conference on information storage and retrieval, an exclusive academic affair that gathers the leaders in the field without fanfare. We were given two little cots in a small room of this old building, a girls' school deserted for the summer. My friendship for Gerald gets deeper as I know him better. We discussed philosophy. I quoted to him James Thompson's poem *The City of Dreadful Night*, the grand diatribe, the most magnificent indictment of divine creation ever conceived:

As if a being, God or Fiend, could reign,
At once so wicked, foolish and insane,
As to create Man, when He might refrain!

Yesterday we made a well-received presentation, after which Gerry and I drove up to the White Mountains of New Hampshire to visit the site of the Betty and Barney Hill abduction. We went from Ashland to Indian Head, absorbing the remoteness of the landscape, stopping periodically to take photographs.

Belmont. Sunday 16 July 1972.

Bushes are growing fast around the lookout I built for the kids; the green of rosemary branches crawls all over the hillside. A warm wind brings the smell of eucalyptus trees, laurels and acacias. The east coast was the exact opposite of all this beauty. Gerald and I had an appointment to discuss software and real estate management at an insurance company. The only thing they could talk about was money. A car was on fire on the turnpike. Downtown Boston smelled of pollution. Traffic was bad, the Mystic tunnel clogged up like a sewer, so I missed my plane. When I finally landed in New York I collapsed, tired and frustrated, in the downtown bus.

After I checked in at my hotel, and changed into formal clothes, I had dinner at *La Grenouille* with my old uncle Jacques Passavant and his wife Gabrielle, nearly blind.

I had seen them last in Paris when I was only 12. They had reached the end of a fascinating life of business and pleasure: he made a fortune in pelts and leathers, lost it, made it again. Their life had been consumed with collecting.

Later the same day.

I feel hurt because of something stupid Allen has done. He rang up Janine on Monday: “Guess where I'm calling from? Utah!” He exulted. “In the Uintah basin, with Mimi and the kids. I'm gonna talk to all the witnesses. Junior Hicks is here, I'll let him speak to you.”

Janine didn't have much to say to Junior Hicks, so they both hung up after a few awkward exchanges.

This is sheer one-upmanship on Allen's part. He has destroyed my trust in our work together. We had agreed to careful plans to "discreetly" investigate a delicate series of events in the Uintah basin. Whatever we did would be kept quiet. Salisbury himself had warned us that witnesses were taciturn Indians whose trust must be earned by a dignified approach. This was going to inaugurate our new policy of serious research... But Allen couldn't resist rushing ahead with his camera, his little tape recorder, his family in tow. The local people will shut up. All that remains for me to do is to cancel my trip.

The new issue of *Time* features the occult revival and "42-year old Anton LaVey", calling his *Compleat Witch* sordid, blaming him for trying to "seize the materialistic values of an affluent society."

Naturally Anton is delighted at such valuable promotion. "Since when is *Time* dedicated to anything but the materialistic values of an affluent society?" he asks with a chuckle, "just look at their ads!"

Belmont. Saturday 22 July 1972.

Janine has gone to visit friends in Florida. I had an early dinner at the *Pot-au-Feu*, where Alain was celebrating his 30th birthday. It was still light when I picked up my little girl at the sitter's. We took care of the garden and watered the flowers. We shared a dessert of pears in syrup. The large airy house breathed softly around us.

Belmont. Thursday 27 July 1972.

Doug beamed when he found me at a terminal, keyset and mouse in hand, earphones around my head, transcribing a tape of a recent meeting. The scene reminded him of Mao-Tse-Tung, who wrote that intellectuals must be able to do any kind of work. Personally I think it would be smarter to have the secretaries transcribe the tapes, and for me to go on writing software; not because transcribing is menial, but because they would be so much better at it.

Doug Engelbart may find it hard to solve his project's identity crisis, but Arpa, back in Washington, has a similar problem. Its managers have trouble justifying to Congress their continued involvement in network research. At an annual budget review, a Defense subcommittee recently called Dr. Larry Roberts on the carpet to ask why the Pentagon was dabbling in office automation when IBM and Xerox, for starters, each had multi-million dollar projects to do the same thing? Arpa's computer budget was cut. It became anathema to mention office automation. Projects are re-absorbed into Defense missions.

To recapture his vanishing grip on his staff, Engelbart is using the latest fad to sweep California, a new spiritual movement called EST, Erhardt Seminar Training. It supersedes polarity therapy, rolfing, Esalen, even psychic healing. All the people who have been wandering from group to cult, looking for cosmic truth, the veterans of the great drug explosion of the late sixties, the seekers who were forever joining new movements, have finally been engulfed in what is claimed to be the end of the search. They have seen the light at last. Now Doug and his disciples are among them.

Belmont. Saturday 29 July 1972.

The lofty claims of progress through computers leave me cold. Smiling Ed has just published an article in *Science Magazine*, calling for the building of television networks that are supposed to lead to equality in education: This is pompous drivel. Such networks could just as easily lead to the standardizing of thought, the suppression of original ideas in the name of better control of the public mind.

Belmont. Thursday 3 August 1972.

For the last two days, my tiredness borders on laziness. The augmentation of human intelligence bores me to death. Engelbart has put the project through what he called an "Arcathon," another weird word to patch over our problems. He rented an old Franciscan convent for a lengthy seminar that turned into a poorly-managed encounter group. One of the unspoken goals was to force Mike, Paul and me to conform to the group's thinking. On the first day we formed boy-girl couples, sat on the grass, looked deeply into each other's eyes and spoke of our aspirations. On the second day the meeting droned on in empty verbiage. By then I had dug up a breviary from an old wooden chest. I sat in a corner and read the *Mass of the Martyrs*, in Engelbart's honor.

Belmont. Tuesday 8 August 1972.

Tonight we attended another parapsychology research group meeting at Jeffery Smith's house. Engelbart, his daughters and his wife attended, while Arthur Hastings spoke about "the psychology of extrasensory perception." Afterwards a woman named Jean Millay demonstrated a machine to visualize brainwaves, and Jeffery announced to the assembly that I would give a talk about UFOs at the next session. Upon hearing this, an intense-looking man sought me out. His name was Elmer Burns. He insisted I must give him an evening, because he was receiving messages from a "space source."

Belmont. Wednesday 9 August 1972.

Mil, my friendly neighbor, is a white witch in her late forties, a former National Security Agency employee. Instead of computer reference manuals and compiler printouts her office is filled with astrology books and dissertations on the Kabala. I often drink herb tea with her between two computer runs. She has formed an exaggerated opinion of my magical abilities. Today Mil introduced me to a young Rosicrucian who is helping her decipher ancient texts. The three of us had lunch at Tokaj. He looked like an accountant, short hair, and clean narrow tie. He never once looked me in the eye, but what he told us about the Order was interesting. Half a dozen old men who had inherited the organization from Spencer Lewis were about to retire from AMORC, he said.

Glad to have an initiate before me, I probed his knowledge of the UFO subject. The result was the same I had found among Pagans:

neither knew much about it. The topic was never mentioned among the Order, they said. They have not even grasped the obvious connection between UFO occupants and the Sylphs and Elementals of their own tradition. “I have to go back to my plastic sphinxes,” the man said after lunch, as we shook hands at the door. “If you ever need me, just summon Scribe XYZ!”

Belmont. Sunday 13 August 1972.

Aimé Michel has sent me a letter full of ideas about psychic gifts:

> One does not use the Gifts. It is them which manipulate you if you set them free. The clever ones, or rather the Wise ones are those who, having watched the Gifts at work and having recognized their nature, study them without attempting to use them.

Such an idea, of course, runs contrary to our time of unbridled, greedy exploitation of every phenomenon science uncovers.

> In order to dominate the Gifts one must die first, either in actuality or through ascetism, that is, having nothing to lose in this world. This price is too high for me. Our friend Anton probably does have some powers, like the King's horse, who has the power to kick you in the jaw with impunity. But he has no choice but to carry the King and he never knows where he is going next. So, I implore you, look around, watch carefully, but don't put your hand into all that.

Aimé has no need to be afraid: I have reached an even more rash conclusion about Anton. He goes on to our main subject:

> Like you I believe that the realm of flying saucers is magical: it is what lies beyond man, the trans-human, the fairies and the enchanters, except that enchanters only enchant themselves. The dream of operating magic is a dangerous utopia.

He ends with another warning:

> Ah *merde*, I sense that I will never succeed in convincing you, and that scares me. For you to really see what I mean, you would have to touch it with your finger, but without burning yourself. In truth, I have been insanely lucky. Or rather, I have been protected. Could it be that you are protected, too?

It's a serious mistake to talk about magic in terms of complex ceremonies and elaborate rituals. Nothing can compare to everyday life in terms of magical opportunities. No combination of personality and phenomena can possibly be more open to the application of human will. This is the basis of my own conduct: everything must begin with small, ordinary acts in the real world.

French ufology was recently shaken by the death of René Hardy, a Defense engineer, co-founder of Fouéré's GEPA group. He held a doctorate in science.

According to Aimé, he announced that he had found the solution to the whole problem, the way to catch these "Gentlemen from Elsewhere" once and for all. He gave some details to Jean-Claude Dufour, with whom he made an appointment in Draguignan to explain his plan.

Dufour and his friends waited but he never showed up: he was dead. At home the previous day he allegedly blew his brains out. Hardy's relatives swear that he had given no indication of such imminent action. Aimé wonders if it was really a suicide. Hardy was involved in heat-seeking rockets, infrared detectors, technical military matters.

In the mail I was happy to find a book by Commandant Tizané, with a handwritten dedication. He is the man who supervised the paranormal investigations of the French Gendarmerie for 32 years. Many of his cases involved hard-core ghosts and poltergeist cases, clearly observed by officers.

A new book about the Hindenburg dirigible acknowledges Anton's assistance. **(18)**

Belmont. Sunday 20 August 1972.

Janine is sewing a dress, resting from long hours of work on the huge computer programs she has been testing for Santa Clara County, bringing her flow-charts and listings home. She has a new job as a senior analyst on a massive computer system that links the Courts, the Public Defender's office, the Sheriff.

On Monday Elmer Burns came here with his voluminous files. His experience with automatic writing began in earnest in 1970 when he was a draftsman with an electronic firm. He drew lenticular objects, and then his hand wrote: "This is the floorplan of the craft," signed by an entity that sent him to a beach near Santa Cruz for a contact that never took place.

Elmer continued his exercises with Jeffery Smith, leading to pages of tedious dialogue with an entity he calls "Shiny Face." As we were discussing this at our house Elmer felt a trance coming. For the next hour he drew circles and ellipses. I pushed him to question his source but all we got was the silly message, "the meaning of such drawings will become available to you as the Higher Entities permit!"

Belmont. Thursday 24 August 1972.

Olivier has returned from France. I took him to SRI to watch Shakey, the robot invented by the artificial intelligence group of Charlie Rosen. The house has been joyful since my son came back, filled with new experiences. In France he went fishing, took a boat trip on the Seine, visited museums, and became fluent in *argot*, learning many bad words among the wicked country boys of Normandy.

He has brought me a new French edition of my own *Passport to Magonia* by Denoël. They have stupidly entitled it *Chronicles of Extraterrestrial Apparitions*, while the book centered on the thesis that UFOs were not necessarily extraterrestrial! The publishers hadn't sent me the translation, full of gross errors.

Yesterday I had lunch with Douglass Price-Williams, a professor with the psychiatry department at UCLA, who is embarking on a study of myths. He had begun by gathering up descriptions of little men such as I described in *Magonia*: he was surprised to find them not only in Celtic countries but in every culture. He also examined the following problem: when an aborigine observes a radically novel artifact, how does he describe it to others? And how is the report received? The answer is that the account of the new artifact often elicits no reaction whatsoever if the story is sufficiently incredible.

"That's the secret one should use to remain undetected, of course," he told me.

"Can you give me an example?"

"Sure. When aborigines on remote Pacific islands described to their leaders the first aeroplane they had ever seen, they were asked, 'Did it have eyes?' When they answered negatively the whole village simply lost interest. The plane was never mentioned again."

Belmont. Sunday 27 August 1972.

Janine and I have had a long talk about emotional freedom. I want to be a source of joy for her, never a burden. She kissed me; my anguish went away with my tiredness.

I have obtained some details about the death of French ufologist René Hardy, which happened on Monday 12 June at 7:45 a.m. He was 62 years old and lived with his wife Rita in a residential section of Toulon. He had just asked Rita for a cup of coffee. She was in the kitchen preparing it when she heard a noise and found him stretched out on the ground, a pistol in his hand, a small hole in his right temple. **(19)** Hardy had told his colleagues at *Ouranos* (a journal he had co-founded) that he had discovered something important about the Humanoids. He had asked them to meet with him two days later to perform an experiment. Even more curiously, all his notes vanished. A few days before his death he had told a friend that he had been burglarized.

"Someone came to my apartment," he said. "Nothing's disappeared but some documents; some photographs have been picked up and moved around."

Hardy had served as the director of an RCA electronics lab in France and he ran the French Air Force laboratory for guided missiles. He worked at Matra from 1950 to 1966, and then served as a consultant for the first French satellite. He remained a consultant for the French Navy until 1971. His name was attached to some 250 patents in electronics, optics, infrared, television, and ultrasound. He had been a member of the I.M.I. (Institut Métapsychique International), a French parapsychology research group, since 1946.

Belmont. Tuesday 29 August 1972.

This morning Catherine rushed into our bedroom. "The moon has melted inside the sun!" She announced with enthusiasm and a great deal of fear. It was the rising sun she was watching, all orange and twisted, through a thick layer of fog and smog. She will be a poet some day -- or an alchemist.

Belmont. Sunday 3 September 1972.

Janine is somber, tired. I am grouchy and tense, in a phase of feverish physical work, painting and fixing things, the perfect suburban homeowner. I miss a smile from her to make everything luminous. She brushes off the feelings I regard as sacred.

Commandant Tizané has pointed out in answer to my questions that haunting phenomena did not follow a pattern of waves, as UFOs did. He is going to send me a map of his investigations. The agents of poltergeist manifestations have no moral law, he pointed out. To him, they're crooks in the same class as pickpockets, arsonists or burglars. They know how to disintegrate and reintegrate matter. He also felt that generalizations about teenagers and the paranormal side-effects of puberty were hasty and wrong. There were many adults among those who seemed to act as "energy condensers."

Tizané stressed that the thing worked through organizing impulses and pushed its subjects to make impossible confessions, which people retracted once they regained control. Both in small hauntings and in great apparitions, such as those of the Virgin, the goal seems to be to leave us thirsting for an explanation: it is our free choice that is challenged.

Belmont. Friday 8 September 1972.

Peter Sturrock has written a proposal for the evaluation of UFO Phenomena. His idea is to gather a team of objective experts and to bring before them the few people who have something to say on the subject. I called Allen: "Will you cooperate?" I asked. "Peter is serious; his name carries a lot of weight."

"I have reservations about the whole approach," Allen answered. "Sturrock is setting himself up as a referee for the whole field..."

The truth is that Allen is fearful to see a scientist with greater clout emerge as a focus for the UFO community. This is a petty reaction, but Peter would have been well-advised to anticipate it, and to enlist Allen's help beforehand.

A woman from Berkeley has put an ad in a local paper, to talk to anyone who felt they were extraterrestrials. I called her.

"You can't imagine how many people believe they're from another planet," she told me. "They get upset when I challenge them. I ask them which day they were born; they tell me something like, April 14th. That's stupid, on another planet there would be no such thing as April 14th."

She once had an extraterrestrial lover, she claimed. He was a white man (she's black) who could change the color of his eyes; his skin turned to silver: he became transparent. She claims she's learned to control such phenomena as leaving her body. As a little girl a voice told her to look up at the sky. She found herself paralyzed while the sky came down and "filled her." She's often seen a gray, uniform smooth disk in the sky, replacing the sun, as in the Fatima miracle. The alien theme -- pretending she has extraterrestrial beings in her life -- enables her to give meaning to her condition, to function almost normally in spite of these classic delusions.

It is by taking the time to study such cases that I can learn to distinguish between genuine phenomena and their fanciful reflection in human imagination and in pathology.

7

Belmont. Saturday 23 September 1972.

Our affluent friend Madame Mathey has expressed her desire to "sponsor my research," because, as she puts it, "my astrologer says I should do something in the occult domain..."

I'm not looking for disciples and sponsors. I hold no personal "occult" truth. I am not waiting for any largesse, as kind as Mrs. Mathey's proposal is. Of greater significance is a conversation I had at SRI with Hal Puthoff, a laser physicist who works one floor below our computer project. I had met him at the lecture I gave at the Palo Alto Research Group, and he invited me to visit his lab. He told me about paranormal experiments he was starting under government sponsorship with a gifted New York psychic named Ingo Swann.

Belmont. Wednesday 27 September 1972.

I have just become a United States citizen. My two witnesses were Paul Rech and Mike Kudlick. Last night I attended a PRG meeting where Russell Targ, another SRI physicist, summarized current parapsychology research. His talk was based on a conference he recently attended in Europe. Many parapsychologists are redoing in a sloppy way some of the experiments that were done quite well in France and England in the 1890s, now forgotten. Their main contribution is to provide beautiful new words like "precognitive functioning"... Fortunately I was able to meet Ingo Swann there. We plan to get together with Hal at SRI tomorrow.

A sad phone call from my uncle Charles informs us that his brother, Jacques Passavant, died day before yesterday in a New York hospital, survived by his wife and two children.

Belmont. Thursday 28 September 1972.

Over lunch at SRI I found out that both Ingo and Hal were keenly interested in UFOs and the secrecy attached to the subject. Like me, both want to "look under the bed." Ingo himself saw a disk when he was a kid, in the Rockies.

I feel happy. Both children are adorable; we spend much time playing, laughing with them. My daughter throws both arms around my neck with such confidence when we say goodnight that I feel blessed with her love. She develops a cynical sense of humor, telling Janine with a playful wink, "I love you, because you feed me..."

Olivier detests measuring the outside temperature, as I try to teach him proper scientific discipline. The other day he didn't write down his readings, and he accused me of erasing them! These temperature readings, he tells us with passion, are the only dark point in his otherwise happy childhood.

Belmont. Saturday 7 October 1972.

Over lunch at *Pot-au-Feu* with Russell Targ, Hal told me about a former colleague of his at NSA (**20**) who has told him that a fresh study of UFOs was secretly under way in the government. Puthoff, who is currently reading *Challenge to Science*, mentioned my work to him.

In spite of the flu and a dull headache I have a strange feeling of happiness. It is as if I had reached a center, a heart of worlds where destinies could be grasped, exploits anticipated. One burning enigma is unsolved, however, the mystical nature of love - that equation whose solution escapes me.

Belmont. Sunday 15 October 1972.

Work goes on at SRI. Doug Engelbart has a new batch of converts led by a visionary named Walter with long hair and short ideas.

Hal Puthoff has finished reading *Challenge to Science*. I showed him my catalogue; we discussed his Washington contacts. The risk in approaching them is to get caught in weird games; I will have to stay on my guard. The potential benefit: understanding their role in the undercurrent, their view of the problem. I plan to stop in Chicago on the way, to see Allen and Fred.

On the flight to Chicago. Friday 20 October 1972.

In another two hours I will be with Fred Beckman. Earphones attached to my head, I am listening to the *Slavonic Dances* by Dvorak, of which he would approve.

Engelbart has forced upon us another exercise in group psychology in our continuing pursuit of “Personal and Organizational Development Activity,” newly called PODAC. My friends were praying for a miracle, an opportunity to express their views. Suddenly an ominous sound was heard. We all turned around; it emanated from Walter, Doug's newest fair-haired boy. We tried to solve our conflicts over the augmentation of human intellect but Walter, our new spiritual leader, was belching with abandon.

According to general opinion Walter is a bad programmer and a dead weight on the project. Perhaps for that reason, Doug has put him in charge of our spiritual development. His fat ass anchored to the crater he made among the cushions, legs apart, he dug into a bag of potato chips and popped them three at a time into his mouth. Once in a while he took a sip from his can of Coca-Cola and belched with contentment while the group went on trying to resolve its conflicts.

I described that scene to our friend Madame Mathey when she came over that evening, smelling of *muguet* like Paris in the Spring.

“I've watched three generations of American men during my long life,” she told us with a sigh. “First the innocent boys returning from World War One, all pink-skinned, gangly and scrubbed. Next came efficient businessmen with their square jaws, well fed, obsessed with money, utterly neurotic. They died wealthy and young. Now it's the Buddhas: young men with fat jowls, big stomachs. They come in two versions: one model is a fat rich fellow who yawns and plays golf, the other a fat hippie like your Walter, who pops potato chips into his mouth while discussing non-verbal sensitivity...”

Aboard a flight to New York. Saturday 21 October 1972.

Last night Sandra and Fred met me at O'Hare. Two rich fellows from Texas have come out of the blue with an offer to help Allen, said Fred. Here he goes again, entertaining the wealthy. These so-called tycoons have also contacted Stanton Friedman, a physicist who was part of the secret CIA/Douglas aircraft study a few years ago and now lectures about UFOs.

On the South side of Chicago lives an individual who claims to have built a flying saucer and flown off to Mars; he had found the natives friendly, coming back with a harem of extraterrestrial girls. He invited Allen, Frank Salisbury and Fred Beckman to meet him at a deserted strip mine in Coal City. His saucer would fly out of South America that night, he assured them, and pick them up on its way to Mars. Characteristically, Fred declined but Allen and Frank did go. Nothing happened, Fred said, but the man did show up with two attractive "Martian" girls.

"I asked Allen if he had detected anything alien about them and he had to confess that he had not," Fred told me in his driest tone.

"Perhaps they were from Venus instead?" I asked just as seriously.

He replied: "If you want to know the truth, I think they arrived on the bus from Skokie!"

It had started raining over Evanston. The town was black, shiny, and greasy. We finally reached the house on Ridge Avenue. Mimi had cooked an excellent dinner, with pancakes for dessert. We discussed Fred's latest plan to invite futurist Hermann Kahn to give strategic advice to "our team." Is there really a team any more?

A visit with an astronomer friend the next day enabled me to measure how much Northwestern had stagnated. "Dr. Hynek did a remarkable job of building up the assets of the department," he said. "He raised money from private donors for the new observatory and our two telescopes. But his book on UFOs has hurt him. It created antagonism among the Faculty and made him a controversial figure. In spite of a fair review in *Science Magazine*, many professors have felt that the reputation of the school was tainted. There's talk of merging our department with mechanical engineering."

Fred and I had planned serious conversations with Allen that afternoon but he was so volatile that all we did was trade anecdotes. Allen finally conceded nothing would come out of the *Enquirer* panel. Worse, when they finally publish the fact that no hard data has been found in spite of the tabloid's offer of monetary reward, this will support the skeptics. In Dayton, Colonel Winebrenner continues to shower Hynek with favors and compliments: "My wife has enjoyed your book very much, Allen!" he said recently.

We had this conversation in the attic bedroom where I had slept during my last stay. It has been converted into an office for Allen's UFO work. The three file cabinets I bought when I reorganized his files were still there, now yawning, unlocked, drawers half-open. On the floor piles of paper spelled out imminent disaster: Allen had lost control of his files again. This became obvious when he decided to show us a research report one of his students had compiled: it was already lost. The room was filled with boxes, letters, pictures, envelopes containing rocks, slides, unanalyzed soil samples, unsorted random trivia.

We had to listen to *The Magic Flute* played loudly on Allen's tinny-sounding little Sony, which made Fred furious. He walked over to the little window and opened it to dissipate the smell from Allen's heavily perfumed pipe tobacco. I welcomed the fresh air. We returned to our talk about research projects, endlessly proposed, never carried out. Fred understands there is a threshold beyond which one is irreversibly changed by the phenomenon, and he isn't ready to go through it. What he relishes is the vicarious thrill of hearing witnesses tell their stories. He still hopes that one of them will eventually describe some miraculous detail that will hint at a solution. Allen hasn't reached that stage. He is disturbed by the statements attributed to the alleged occupants. He has not overcome the logical block of their allegorical existence: so real, yet so absurd.

"What we really need in order to do UFO research is some money to cover telephone calls," he told us, filling his pipe one more time. I voiced agreement out of tiredness. We never discussed what, if anything, Allen had found in his famous trip through Utah.

Washington Hilton. Friday 27 October 1972.

This is a momentous event, the first public demonstration of the Arpanet to the press and the American public. For the last few days I have shared this room with Paul Rech. Arpa is paying for our travels with the Engelbart team, as it pays for most of the research currently being done on computer networking across the U.S. Tomorrow, I will meet Gerald Askevold at the airport and we'll fly down to Oak Ridge to discuss database retrieval with local experts.

The Arpanet demo has lasted three days, a historic turning point in the use of computer technology. Our main system was successfully installed in only 48 hours, with 30 terminals connected, a tour-de-force completed just in time to demonstrate network technology to a parade of visitors. We ran some 20 different programs, including the retrieval system I have created for the NIC, the newly-created Network Information Center.

The Arpanet is designed to grow organically and as such, it has no center. But if you had to point to an indispensable repository of data that is essential to run the whole net, it would be the NIC. The Center relies on a database system, so the task of building the first implementation went to me and to Elizabeth "Jake" Feinler, a library science specialist. The NIC provides an index of all computers and programs for any Arpanet site, and over the last couple of days my interactive retrieval system has become one of the most heavily-used pieces of software on the whole network.

At the conference I bumped into Fredrickson who reminded me that I could have a job at Rand any time I wanted, but I am not ready to move my family to L.A.

On Wednesday, having a little time on my hands, I called Stuart Nixon at Nicap. We had dinner at the Marriott. The food was bad but the view of the Potomac was spectacular. The next day he took me to meet his boss John L. Acuff, a management consultant with Grumman. While Stuart Nixon was a nice fellow, his boss was a man of little vision who spewed out redundancies. The Nicap offices shared space with his own consulting outfit in a round building located in Wheaton, Maryland. Acuff had a letter from Sturrock on his desk, so he asked if I knew him, which showed how uninformed he was. I urged him to cooperate with Peter's project. Acuff explained that the Board was at the point of declaring bankruptcy when he agreed to take over Nicap. He managed to pay the debts and to show a slight profit of $5,000 in 1971. This year he hopes to double this figure, which would be a real achievement.

At the Hilton desk I found a note from Puthoff with instructions to call a certain "locator number" and to ask for Howell McConnell. I was supposed to say I was referred to him by "R.T." I have just called the locator, which rings inside NSA, and left a message.

Later the same day.

A bizarre incident. I was awakened at 3 A.M. by a television set blaring in the next room. Voices were loudly arguing about UFOs and Hynek's book! It wasn't a dream: the voices continued when I got up. I leaned against the wall to listen. It was a television panel discussion. One voice said: "Dr. Hynek said he'd love to have a five-dollar bill for every Air Force captain who's seen a UFO..."

I called hotel security to complain, because I was much more interested in getting some sleep than in hearing about UFOs. I was told that my neighbor's name was "Soltis" and that his phone line was busy. Was it a coincidence that the program had just tackled this topic? Was someone testing me?

Washington. Dulles aiport. Saturday 28 October 1972.

Gerald's plane is two hours late. This gives me the opportunity to continue reading an excellent book by Rinn on psychical research (**21**) and to review the morning's events.

Howell McConnell does work at the National Security Agency, one of the most secretive components of the Intelligence community, whose initials are said to stand for "Never Say Anything" or "No Such Agency." He arrived looking like a jovial math teacher, a rotund character with spectacles and gray mustache, oddly sweet for a man in the spook business. We sat in the dining room, ordered a pot of coffee, and spent the whole morning there.

I was ready for almost anything, except for that discussion about mysticism, the nature of the universe, poetry, cosmic consciousness... I had prepared an introduction: "I want to talk to you on a confidential, personal basis, not as a member of any research group," I began. We seemed to be on trusting terms, but I remained on guard. Aren't these people trained to project an impression of trust? I explained why professional scientists rejected the idea of a phenomenon which threatened their mental structures.

"Bureaucrats are just like your scientists," he said. "I work for a bunch of bureaucrats whose tendency, too, is to deny. But an Agency like ours can take no risks. So we keep an eye on things. If something does happen, they'll be able to say they were aware of the situation, that one of their analysts was informed, his documentation up-to-date..."

He asked me if I'd ever heard of a group based at Wright-Patterson, which is supposed to do secret analyses on behalf of the Air Force. He's heard that the office in question confiscated UFO negatives in order to analyze them secretly.

"Perhaps we should continue this discussion in my room," I suggested, aware that a group of people had come in, sitting down at a table close to us. Howell laughed:

"In a hotel like this the rooms are equipped with listening devices. The security men need to find out about any improprieties. Who knows who may be paying them to get information? We're much more private here, right in the restaurant."

That remark threw me into a world of new questions. I thought back about the incident of the previous night. In the rest of our discussion we went deeply into the topics of psychic reality. I told him about my computer compilation.

"This catalogue of yours is more important in terms of the consciousness evolution it represents than as computer data..."

That remark led us towards psychic phenomena, where he knew a great deal, and mysticism, his favorite subject. "What an unfortunate word, mysticism!" he said. "I prefer to speak of contemplation. Nothing exists in itself, only in relationship to other entities, so if you think about it, everything goes back to the triad, the Trinity."

This turned our talk to religion. He belongs to the Charismatic Community, which strives to reach a higher level of consciousness through prayer, miraculous cures of the sick. He compared my catalog to prehistoric paintings of animals on cave walls, a magical representation of the hunter and the hunted, except that my own magic was that of the computer. He added: "If you ever need help, don't hesitate to call me." But I don't plan to require help from NSA.

Belmont. Tuesday 31 October 1972 (Halloween)

Gerald and I flew back from Oak Ridge this morning. In the once-secret city, old men with doctorates in physics from places like Budapest and Prague are still living in prefabricated houses that date from the heroic days of the Atom Bomb. Computer linguist François Kertecz took us to the Country Club. This delightful scholar taught me an important lesson when I expressed surprise at the fact his project in machine translation had not been affected by the great debacle of artificial intelligence that stopped better-funded researchers when the Air Force decided their claims of "imminent success" were without merit:

"I didn't have a budget!" He answered with good-natured laughter. "My work was part of an atomic lab; it didn't have any identification related to artificial intelligence research, so they never found me!" I will remember this lesson; bureaucrats can only attack a project that spends money. If I ever mount a UFO research project I will do it with my own resources, keeping the data away from accountants.

The next day we drove to the borders of the plant, after which we had to cover another 7 miles to reach the laboratories. The earth has rejected Oak Ridge. The secret city won the war but chased away the farms and polluted the rivers.

This morning I walked over to Puthoff's office as soon as I could find an excuse to leave my terminal. I told him about my talk with McConnell. He was with Russell Targ, preparing an experiment with a new subject named Uri Geller, a young Israeli who claims to have the ability to break metal rings just by looking at them, to fix watches, to make objects vanish and reappear. Hal showed me the device they will use: a metallic frame, a mirror at forty-five degrees, a glass plate, a transparent box with a ring inside. Several cameras will film the experiment.

We discussed the need for secrecy. I reminded him of what Condon said when Hynek asked him what he would do if his research reached a positive conclusion: "I'd stop everything and ask to see the President," he'd answered. Hal told me that in fact they already had a green light from a Nixon adviser. He wanted me to be available to keep watch on the sky above SRI. Strange objects are said to have manifested during Geller's psychic moments.

We had lunch at Tokaj. I asked Puthoff: "You've mentioned scientology several times, and so has Ingo Swann."

"I took the training," Hal answered. "I've reached the stage we call Clear. Ingo too."

We walked back to SRI, stopping at the East-West new-age bookstore along the way. "If Uri Geller can fix Von Braun's pocket calculator just by thinking about it, or if he can break a gold ring without touching it, he can just as easily trigger a nuclear device... That may be the real intent of those who finance your work."

"If we don't do this research here it will move elsewhere. We're already engaged in a bidding fight with Grumman." (*)

So, the same company that employs John Acuff, the new head of Nicap, is involved in psychic research, that new aspect of the chessboard. Behind it, there's also intense interest in the UFO problem. Someone is pulling those strings. But why do I find again an "intersign" at this place and time, as at Paris observatory when Aimé Michel's letter happened to arrive in 1961? I was reminded of the parting words of Howell McConnell: "I am surprised by such meetings, by the meaning of apparent coincidences," he said. "And I wonder who we are."

(*) Dr. Harold Puthoff remembers McDonnell Douglas being a potential competitor with SRI, but does not recall the involvement of Grumman, so one of us may have a faulty memory here.

Santa Monica. Monday 6 November 1972.

Between two job interviews I am sitting quietly in Rod Fredrickson's office at Rand. Janine and the children have spent the weekend with me at Ann's ranch. We climbed up to see the rocks with the ancient Chumash paintings. Olivier and I hiked even higher, exploring the top slopes of Boney.

It had rained in the morning; fog lingered in thick gray waves around the volcano. We ate lunch in a crack among the rocks. My son was happy and sweet. Time flows differently on the mountain. The sky, the earth, the distant Pacific beyond Oxnard formed a tapestry that held no urgency. Janine was relaxed. Our daughter made striking, magical statements: "She is a very old soul," our friends said.

Belmont. Saturday 11 November 1972.

It's been ten years since we reached New York harbor and stared anxiously at the foggy Manhattan dawn through the portholes of the Queen Mary. Do you remember our cab ride to Newark, Janine, that cab ride that felt like a trip to nowhere, then our flight to Austin in a noisy propeller plane?

Later we moved to Chicago, Bryn Mawr Avenue, anguish and victory, boredom and passion, tender moments, intense debates... We lived among friends, with a backdrop of scholarly fellows and slightly drunken acquaintances, fog over Lake Michigan, computers never free of bugs, and those stormy nights when the air itself seemed to turn to warm glue.

Now my days are spent at the cutting edge of network software with Doug Engelbart. Yesterday a potential sponsor from Washington pointed out that we were building a fragile world indeed: if information networks are not based on human trust they will surely collapse, he said. Our project, where dissent and rage are barely hidden under the surface, is an example of collective agony, which the computer fails to heal.

If the truth be known, it is Puthoff's friendship that keeps me at SRI now. On Thursday, a man passed in the hallway, popped his head into the office and asked the way to the coffee machine.

"That was Captain Edgar Mitchell," Hal said with a note of deference after he had turned the corner, adding: "the astronaut. He's here incognito, to attend our first series of experiments with Uri Geller, which begin on Monday. He's covering $15,000 and SRI contributes another $10,000. But we've had some leaks. Many people are asking what we're up to."

Puthoff, a serious scientist who doesn't want to take any chances, said again he wanted me to monitor the experiments from outside, without Uri's knowledge: he proposed that I scan the sky in case something unusual shows up. An old wooden tower rises over the building where the tests will take place. It has an unobstructed view over the roofs of Menlo Park.

Belmont. Sunday 12 November 1972.

Hal called me at home early this morning, greatly excited: "Geller is really good. We've got things appearing out of nowhere. It's time for some tests. We're going into the lab at 10 A.M. Can you cover us?"

I grabbed a compass and my camera, drove down to SRI and climbed up to my tower in time to see Hal and Russell arrive in the company of Geller, New Age researcher Andrija Puharich and their entourage, which included Ed Mitchell, a blonde woman and two other fellows. They crossed the parking lot without seeing me. I watched the cloud-covered sky. I only noted a few airplanes and birds, but no anomaly. Hal later told me his experiments had been inconclusive.

Belmont. Friday 17 November 1972.

Stomach flu. I was unable to sleep all night and nurtured gloomy thoughts. Life appeared so dark that Janine laughed at my despair:

"You keep deploring what you call our endless wanderings," she said, "but I rather enjoyed the way we packed our bags and left France, just the two of us; and the way we left again in '68. If I hadn't met you I'd have gone off to Saigon as a schoolteacher."

Today the rain stopped. I felt less bilious. I spent an interesting morning in Russell Targ's office. Uri Geller was there with Andrija Puharich and a girl, and Wilbur Franklin, a physicist from Kent State. Geller didn't make a convincing first impression. He is an intense young man with long wavy hair, very personable. I was told he kept producing extraordinary phenomena outside the lab, but none of the recordings made at SRI under controlled conditions show paranormal evidence. He makes rings disappear, bends spoons, closes his hand on a rose petal and opens it on a blooming flower. Since I have just read *Sixty Years of Psychical Research*, by Houdini's trusted associate Rinn, I am skeptical of any such effect. Puharich inspires even less confidence than Geller.

Uri told me he himself had no power, everything came from the saucers. What I find striking is the way in which blind belief is spreading among scientists who are ready to embrace it uncritically, just like Ted Serios' alleged psychic photos a few years ago (**22**).

I spoke to Wilbur Franklin for over an hour. He's a small fellow with short hair, a hearing aid behind his right ear. He wore a white shirt and a narrow tie. He said that Kent State had proposed to run the tests but that SRI had won. The girl told me later that during the experiments Franklin kept interfering, bumping the table at the precise time of a crucial test, or offering water to Uri just as he was concentrating the hardest.

SRI. Monday 20 November 1972.

"Evidently you inspired confidence to Uri right away," said Puthoff today as we went to lunch. "He has instructed me to tell you everything. So here it is: he's seen UFOs all right. He's been contacted by their occupants; he believes he's been chosen to demonstrate certain powers. In coming years they will contact us openly, he says. By then, either we'll have accepted their existence, in which case contact will be easy, or we'll have rejected it, in which case they will go away forever to avoid destroying our civilization..."

"Surely you realize none of this makes any sense," I told Hal. "At best Uri uses this as a way to rationalize some paranormal effects that are beyond him. At worst he and Andrija are making up the whole business."

So far Hal and Russell have witnessed some phenomena but they become increasingly fuzzy when strict controls are introduced.

"Look for the absurd," I recommended.

Puthoff told me that Geller's telepathic ability interfered with the science: "This guy warms up by writing numbers on a piece of paper and asking us to think of some digits. And the number we come up with generally happens to be the one he wrote down beforehand. Everything works as if he could force you to think what he wants."

Allegedly they did shoot a movie showing a spoon hanging in a glass cage with no force applied to it, but nothing is proven. The head of Hal's department, Bart Cox, thinks that Geller tricks everybody. Uri says he isn't sure that "his space contacts" do want him to provide scientific proof. If the phenomena remain magical effects, those who choose to believe are free to do so, while others always have a rational explanation they can hang onto. Uri is bright, very quick.

The geraniums we brought back from Boney Mountain are growing in dense red bushes; the world is beautiful again.

Belmont. Sunday 26 November 1972.

I don't write much any more, or else I write badly and end up tearing up every page. Last Tuesday we watched Uri perform at Jeffery Smith's house in Portola Valley. The SRI team was there, the room filled with PRG members. Even Bart Cox and Doug Engelbart had come over. Edgar Mitchell did the introductions, explaining how Puharich "discovered" Uri in Israel, how Geller left the army in 1968, went into show business. He needs a crowd to focus his powers. Uri proceeded to give a series of telepathic demonstrations. The first test consisted in reading a color, a three-digit number (I immediately wrote down 726 as I heard this) and a city name that a volunteer from the audience would write on a board.

A woman got up and wrote "Blue, 725, Washington." Uri only

missed the city name. He may have listened to the sound of the chalk on the board and recognized the words, but why had I written 726 beforehand? Had he "planted" a number into our minds?

After another successful test, he attempted psychokinesis and failed. His only achievement was to bend someone's spectacles, but it was obvious that he was exerting a force with his fingers. Even Elmer came away skeptical: Uri had changed the time on a watch but he had been holding it in his hands, clearly twisting it.

Aimé Michel is working on his *Gospel of Pontius Pilatus*:

> By itself, intelligence only creates courtiers and lawyers. Do not become a courtier or a lawyer, unless that is of use to you for hiding purposes. But try to hide in other ways. Keep in mind that all you will take with you beyond death is your passion (*ardeur*) and your acts, because intelligence and reason are of the body. And since they are of the body they can eventually be supplied by artifice. When you observe that they are beginning to be supplied by artifice you will know that the decadence of mankind has started.

Evidently he recalls our discussions about artificial intelligence.

SRI. Wednesday 29 November 1972.

Another massive computer failure took place today, so I had a cup of herb tea with kindly Mil and she told me the inside story of the Rosicrucian order in America, including Spencer Lewis' tale of his initiation in Toulouse. Was that initiation valid? His own master, an old Frenchman, had been initiated at home rather than in a formal temple as was the rule. He never told this to his Amorc disciples.

Mil told me about *Builders of the Adytum* (Bota), a group that derives from the teachings of Paul Case, a kabalistic expert. She showed me their application for membership, a typical American document where the first page discussed mysticism in lofty terms and the next three pages were requests for money.

SRI. Thursday 30 November 1972.

Hal is happy about the experiments with Geller, in spite of constant tensions within the project (**23**). Two days ago they were having dessert when half of a tie pin belonging to Ed Mitchell materialized in Uri's vanilla ice cream. During the afternoon the other half fell behind him in the lab. Things have just kept on falling. A watch that had been kept inside a sample case crashed to the floor. Puthoff tells everybody to apply what he calls *Vallee's Principle*: "Look for absurdity." He wants me to keep monitoring the skies above SRI, to test Uri's claim that UFOs have something to do with his powers.

In a book by Max Guilmot entitled *The Spiritual Message of Ancient Egypt* I find the notion that cosmic unity demands an initiation, "as if Truth only revealed herself to a tiny number. Why these priviledged few? Is it so that human history will continue its conquests, always spurred on among earthly fighting?" (**24**)

Belmont. Saturday 9 December 1972.

I spent the morning writing a review of Allen's book at the request of Dick Lewis, now the editor of the *Bulletin of Atomic Scientists.* Janine and I ate lunch in the kitchen, admiring the ever-changing landscape of the Bay, the hills covered with snow under the blue sky, green and red trees. The mail brought a copy of Musès and Young's book *Consciousness and Reality*, where a chapter is devoted to illustrations of ancient seals showing priests and flying disks.

Last Tuesday I had lunch with Uri Geller and Puthoff's group, which included SRI's legendary photo expert Zev Pressman. I told Uri about the Phoenician seals in Wallis Budge's treatise about *Amulets and Talismans* (**25**). In turn he told me about the two contacts he had experienced. The first one took place when he was with Puharich and a woman, driving in the desert near Tel Aviv. A craft came down. He doesn't know how he got in. He recalls finding himself in a hollow space. He came back semi-conscious, holding an object "they" had given him, an ordinary fountain pen.

"Last Sunday I succeeded in dematerializing it," he said, suddenly adding: "I want to do an experiment with you. Think of a target."

Russell Targ handed me a blank envelope containing a piece of paper folded in four. I saw a drawing of a whale. I began sending it mentally. I looked at the whale spouting and it reminded me of the fountain in the yard, so instead of scanning the target card I scanned the actual fountain, then the mental image of a fish. In other words, I changed the conditions of the test, sending two objects rather than one. Suddenly Uri was all business.

"Here's what I received," he said with great assurance, producing two separate drawings -- a fountain next to a fish! I was astonished to see that he had actually picked up what I had sent, rather than what was on the card.

"Think of a color," he said next. Instantly, blue came to my mind. It came so fast that I suspected Uri was trying to plant that color into my consciousness, so I deliberately picked another color, yellow.

"I'm getting the word yellow," said Uri after I had "sent" my selection three times. "But in one of the trials I got blue."

Now we were having dessert and Uri had finished his ice cream. "You know," he told me, "those things are little things. That's not what I really do. I do things with hard objects, like a teaspoon..."

For emphasis he touched the spoon he had left in his ice cream, and instantly he recoiled as if he had stepped on a snake. There was silence around the table as he slowly picked up the spoon by the handle and extracted it. It was literally folded in three, with the wider, round part bent against the handle. I had an identical spoon in my hand, so I tried to fold it and after some effort I succeeded, but all I got was a bent handle, folded at the narrow point. To bend the rounded part, as Uri had done, would have taken a tremendous force. Any instrument would have left a mark.

I was struck by an eerie coincidence, which Uri could not have known. In my 1962 novel *Dark Satellite*, published ten years ago, one of the main characters is Xarius Chimero, an eccentric inventor.

He warns a friend about the fickle nature of reality:

> "People regard the Known as a large and orderly domain that is well-lit and properly managed," he told me in his slow,

lecturing tone. "They believe there is no danger for their personal safety as long as they remain wisely within this perimeter of cleanliness, calm and quiet competence. They think it is the role of the scientists to push the circle of shadows farther and farther away... And the scientists answer, 'the known portion of an object is nothing but the part of it that is currently perceived. You must realize that the real object goes deeply into the unknown, just like the larger mass of an iceberg goes deeply into the sea'."

The narrator recalls that Xarius Chimero would illustrate his theory by talking about the extraordinary nature of ordinary objects:

> It was at that point that he took his teaspoon and pointed it at me like a sword, adding, "The limit of the Unknown is not a hundred billion light-years away, which is the range of our finest telescopes. The limit of the unknown passes within us. It is in our hearts, in our souls, in our eyes, in our loves, just as much as it is in the faraway star and inside the atom and even in this very teaspoon. For no physicist worth his salt will ever tell you, 'this teaspoon is real and it is made of aluminum and I understand it.' The physicist will tell you instead, 'here is a teaspoon whose existence I accept empirically because that is the best way to explain the image I receive through my eyes and the sensation my fingers are feeling as I touch it. As for its deeper reality, I must confess my ignorance. My knowledge does not go further than matter itself. For the rest of the story, please come back and see me in a century or two. In the meantime, don't think too much about it and keep stirring your coffee. But don't hold me responsible if the spoon turns into a dragon to bite you, into a girl to seduce you, or into a beam of radiation to pierce your body'."
>
> I was thinking of Xarius because my spoon was changing shape. It was getting larger and its silver color was taking on an ashen tone.

Prevailing academic opinion does not bother itself with philosophical or poetic considerations about spoons that change shape. Instead, the professors believe that Puthoff and Targ are crazy and that Uri is tricking them. However Puthoff now says he has photographic proof that Geller can bend metal psychically. He has not shown me the pictures, however.

On Thursday Hal called me up at Engelbart's lab.

"Can you come over for a few minutes?" he said with urgency.

"I'll be right down to your office," I replied. But he warned:

"No, we need to be careful. Let's meet by the elevators."

Intrigued, I grabbed paper and pencil and went down just as Hal was turning the corner. I felt foolish, as in a bad spy movie. Hal took me to a deserted electronic lab with a wall of measuring instruments that kept us hidden from passersby. Only then did he pull a large envelope from his pocket.

"Recently Uri flew from London to Germany," he began in hushed tones. "All of a sudden his camera floated up in the cabin. At least that's what he's told me. He grabbed it to snap pictures through the windows. He gave them to me to be developed, saying he felt sure saucers would turn up on those photographs. Well, here they are."

Indeed four of the prints clearly showed a formation of dark elongated objects.

"I don't like this," I said after examining the pictures. "The formation is rigid on all four exposures, yet the photographer clearly moved, as you can see from the angle of the window. Uri could have painted these things on the glass. Or they could be little pieces of paper stuck to the window. I'd have to analyze the geometry."

Belmont. Sunday 10 December 1972.

After we had eaten our cheese and crackers on top of the tombstone in the purple room, Anton took me to a private chamber in the basement where he keeps his best books. There we spoke of Patton, one of his heroes, and discussed the *Satanic Rituals* (**26**). He launched into a dazzling series of anecdotes, literary references, circus lore, movie trivia, unknown musical traditions, exploits of espionage. At midnight he retrieved various treasures from the crypt: James Thompson's poems, *The King in Yellow*, *The Circus of Dr.Lao*. He read aloud from his favorite texts, with obvious pleasure.

"People need someone to scare them." he commented. "That's why they love those UFOs of yours. All animals are conditioned by fear, humans included. Their God scares them, and the Devil scares them, and now ecology, too, and flying saucers. You and I are different. We know that there is nothing to fear, ever. That's the basis of initiation, the primary secret."

As I protested this view of things was too limited he added:

"Can't you see that you scare them, too? That fear you cause is power. Money is one measure of power, but a lifestyle that projects an image of power and freedom is enough. People are afraid of their own repressed side. That's why they love me, even the Christians, when they see an outrageous picture of me with my plastic horns on the cover of *Look Magazine.*" He laughed: "I supply them with that fear without which they wouldn't exist. That fear defines them, makes them real."

He went on: "I know well what you're capable of. To judge a man I always look at the women around him, I watch how they treat him. Only a small and scattered group will ever understand the deeper truths. We must continue this solitary work far away from one another, that's our dark destiny. That's always been the case, down through history. It's useless to reveal a secret to anyone who hasn't understood it already... but you, you have nothing to fear."

It was two in the morning, yet he insisted on showing me his new musical acquisition, a magnificent organ that emulated an orchestra. He'd even mounted a police siren on it.

Belmont. Wednesday 13 December 1972.

Uri leaves California today. When I joined Hal and Russ on Monday they quickly closed the door to their office to discuss my analysis of Uri's pictures. I told them:

"The worst thing that could happen would be for Uri to go public with this stuff."

"Well, these pictures belong to him," Hal said defensively. "We have no control over that. He can mail them to the *New York Times* tomorrow if he wants to, with a letter saying, 'I snapped these from an airliner'."

"That's not what I'm worried about," I said. "The *Times* gets 15 letters like that every day. But his letter might say, 'I snapped these from an airliner on the way to doing secret psychokinetic research at SRI'."

"I see what you mean." Now they were even more somber.

I went on: "Any bright 12-year old kid can see these pictures are staged."

"Do you really believe they are fakes?"

"Look at the geometry: these objects keep the same relative position, and they are in a single geometric plane, which happens to coincide with the plane of the window."

There was a knock on the door. Hal unlocked it after hurriedly concealing the pictures. Ingo Swann came in, outwardly jovial, a forced smile on his face. We were as uncomfortable as a bunch of kids caught looking at a girlie magazine, and it didn't take the world's greatest psychic to see that.

"What were you talking about?" He demanded to know. "*Behind closed doors?*"

"Nothing much. We were looking at some pictures," Hal said with obvious embarrassment.

"*Donnez-les moi, s'il vous plait.*"

"I don't understand French," replied Hal.

"Oh yes you do," Russell broke in. "Jacques understands perfectly, I got the general meaning, and you can guess what he said."

"Well, Ingo, can you keep a secret?"

"If you only knew all the secrets of which I am the depository!" sighed Ingo as if under a heavy burden.

"I warn you, it would be a disaster if our East Coast friends heard about this."

"You can count on my discretion. Besides, for every secret you don't tell me I will keep two from you."

Sheepishly, Hal produced the prints.

"Ah, those are Uri's celebrated flying saucer shots, aren't they?"

It was Hal's turn to be flabbergasted: "You've already seen them?"

"No."

"Someone must have told you about them. Who was it?"

"I won't tell you," said Ingo with a smile. "It's a *very big* secret."

"But you must tell us."

"My sources of information would dry up."

I decided to break into the conversation.

"Come on Ingo, we'll never get anywhere."

"All right then, if you have to know, your own photographer told me all about it. It's incredible the things people tell me here at SRI."

"That's a problem, a real problem," said Hal, visibly annoyed. "Zev knows damn well these pictures are top secret. And the negatives have vanished."

"Oh, I just can't stand the excitement!" cried Ingo with faked delight. "We are in the midst of true international intrigue now, aren't we, my little darlings?"

Later the same day.

On Tuesday I had lunch with Arthur Hastings who introduced me to another SRI consultant named Brendan O'Regan. They both work on a new project directed by Willis Harman on "The Images of Man."

The main topic was the psychic factor in UFO cases. Brendan is a lively Irishman who nearly died in a high-speed head-on collision a few years ago. At the time of the impact he saw his life in reverse, taking every sequence to the end, then jumping back to the previous one. He went back to a period of his childhood when he was in a blue room and had nightmares, finding himself in a space where he heard voices he could not understand and saw bright lights that scared him. He would find himself back in his body, screaming.

As a result of the accident he was no longer afraid of death. He saw how little contemporary physicians knew about death and dying. As personal secretary and research director for Buckminster Fuller, he lived in his geodesic dome. He avoided any study of UFOs until Hal told him he should read *Passport to Magonia*.

Belmont. Tuesday 19 December 1972.

Quiet talks with our children. Mixing French and English my daughter told me: "*Je suis contente quand c'est comme* today". Olivier was sweet and happy: "You know, when we got to New Jersey the days were passing just like that... (He snapped his fingers) My birthday, Christmas, and then we were in the plane to come here. At the end of the days we must think, 'already?' I can't believe that all that has happened, not yet!"

"That's not important," I said. "What's important is to have my boy with me, and my little girl, and Janine."

"Stay with me, I like it when we talk like that," he said quietly.

Over lunch Ingo predicted a major earthquake for January 3rd.

Aboard a PSA plane returning from Los Angeles. Wednesday 20 December 1972.

In the hot weather Los Angeles vibrates like a sperm cell under a microscope. It's a sexy city, its palm trees caressing the desperate brown sky, girls laughing in red convertibles as the shirtless, careless boys of Sunset boulevard whistle at them.

Rod Fredrickson took me to a staff meeting reviewing the social experiments monitored by Rand. The topic of the day was the dubious impact of a certain failed education program. Rand is looking for a director of database systems to handle massive files and to save a medical information project that is also in trouble. Would I consider moving? I declined again.

Belmont. Monday 25 December 1972 (Christmas Day).

Catherine plays with all her new toys at once, cowboy hat on her head, revolver at her belt, a doctor's stethoscope over her ears and a plastic syringe in her hand. Olivier is busy with a big toolbox. Alain is staying with us. I make stained glass windows out of colored paper for the downstairs room, a colorful scene of the Garden of Eden.

Last Friday I had an interesting evening when Elmer Burns took me to see a clairvoyant lady named Jan in the hills of La Honda. I met him at the bachelor's hideaway he rents in Palo Alto, a converted garage filled with books and records.

We took his Toyota through the tortured landscape of the wild ridge above Woodside, deep ravines and tall redwoods drowned in fog. This is where hippies hide to grow pot, where runaway kids find love, where new rock bands get organized, where white witches dance naked in the moonlight. This is also where the sheriff of San Mateo County occasionally finds severed fingers or the head of some hitchhiker murdered by a passing fool high on LSD.

Jan and her husband lived at the end of a quiet lane; a swollen creek had carried away the bridge. The house was full of color. She spread old playing cards.

"You don't depend heavily on women," she began quickly, without hesitation. "Only one has a strong influence on you. Are you often in an airplane? I hear jet engines around you. You will do a great deal of travel, I see you on an airfield with the wind in your hair and the noise of engines. I see your mother among trees, nature, a park. (*Le Jardin des Plantes*?) I see a woman close to you, with light-colored hair. She's not your wife. You like fine, beautiful things. I see you reclining, a beige pillow. I see a lot of warmth."

So far there was nothing remarkable in what she had told me, I thought. Everybody has a mother; men tend to have women in their lives. She could guess about me from my clothes, the way I combed my hair and shaved, other details. She went on:

"The cards are full of your love for others and of others' love for you. You have a brother. You should write to your mother (now she was on the edge of tears). I see you putting money into an envelope for her, to pay for her trip. I feel your wife very busy, with her own world. She works, right?" (I said yes) "You're going to buy a new house. I see you having two houses, that is clear. I see you moving to a large house, isolated."

She seemed to be looking at something else, just above the table.

"Every time I try to interpret something about you it's accompanied by intense emotion. I see an older man who comes to your house. He comes into your living room. He has a graying beard. He brings some good news. He's a professor, or a professional man."

Outside was silence, with only the bristling of the leaves around the house. "He's 65 years old," she went on. (Hynek, I noted silently, was 63.) "He wears a coat against the cold, carries a briefcase full of things he wants to show you. He rushes into your living room. There are steps up to your place; he takes them two at a time."

The session struck me, not only by the many correct images it contained but also by the emotional effect it seemed to produce on Jan. She didn't accept any payment. The vision of Allen climbing the stairs of Belmont with a briefcase full of papers was striking. Jan's only major miss was not seeing my children.

Belmont. Saturday 6 January 1973.

The other day I bought a money order for my mother, to reimburse her for books she'd sent me. Only then did I recall Jan seeing me place money into an envelope for her.

Hal Puthoff came here for coffee and cake last night with Russell Targ and his wife. They brought Ingo Swann (whose prediction of an earthquake this week had fortunately not come to pass) and an aerospace friend of Targ's. We spoke about the current SRI experiments, after which we watched a heavily-advertised program called *Ancient Astronauts* based on the books of Von Daniken (**27**).

My own research goes on quietly, fueled by plenty of data from my readers. Among the Christmas cards were paintings by a young artist named Megan who wrote she was influenced by *Magonia*. As for Janine, I wonder where she finds her reserves of wisdom. Certainly not in me: I'm often stormy, uncertain.

Belmont. Tuesday 9 January 1973.

Our department director came into my office last week. He closed the door, picked up the chalk and drew a scale on my blackboard.

"I need advice. I'd like to know what you think of the kind of research that's going on downstairs with Geller and Swann," he said.

"You've done work on controversial topics, and you've managed to keep your scientific credibility intact. That's a skill we need to master. I don't have to tell you that this psychic project is potentially one of the major contributions this Institute will make to the country. What's at stake is a reassessment of the nature of consciousness. In an operational sense, proof of these abilities could be central to national security. But we're in a quandary. On this side of the scale (he drew a large box on the right) we have industrial and government research revenue of the Institute - well over 150 million dollars a year. And on that side (he drew a tiny dot on the left) we have the potential return from Puthoff's project, at most a million or so. Does that justify putting the Institute in jeopardy?"

I answered that it was precisely because SRI had taken risks in the past that it had its exceptional reputation. Anybody can do mundane research. SRI specializes in reaching beyond the state of the art. He'd thought of that, but my argument wouldn't fly long if the Board of Trustees read in the morning paper that Uri Geller was busy bending spoons in our basement. So I have written a long memorandum to Targ and Puthoff, proposing a strategy for paranormal research (**28**).

I argued that some of the research should only be classified in initial years, to provide a quiet setting where all implications could be studied, and that a healthy exchange with the scientific community at large should be maintained by open publication.

Belmont. Sunday 14 January 1973.

A decision has come down from SRI president Charlie Anderson, barring Targ and Puthoff from a conference on psychical research at the University of California. He has no problem with me because my SRI software work is unrelated to the research on UFOs I'll be presenting. Engelbart himself encourages me to go on: "Ten years from now, you'll be proud to have taken these risks," he told me.

I spent the weekend studying the story of Vintras, the 19th century Norman contactee and cult leader. The brilliant attorney, Maurice Garçon, noted that Vintras was fooling his Catholic disciples by producing bleeding hosts by trickery. One can have no confidence at all in an individual who resorts to such fraud, he said, "even if all the other phenomena he produces appear genuine." This remark could well apply to Uri Geller. I want to understand the mechanism through which these people influence our culture.

Belmont. Sunday 21 January 1973.

A violent storm has damaged the roof I built over the patio, so I worked outside today to repair it. Over dinner in trendy Union Street we watched the upscale young people who are gradually replacing the hippies, dressing up in English fashion. We went to see *Discreet Charm of the Bourgeoisie*. Today I continued my research on the French magical revival of the nineteenth century, Boullan's dark deeds and Guaita's strange life.

Megan has taken me to Ghirardelli Square for a tour of the mobiles, the sculptures: she knows all the local artists who created them. On the way back, driving along the ridge between the Pacific and the Bay I had one of those esthetic shocks to which I thought I had become immune in California: an orange moon rose beyond the hills over thirty miles of diamonds spread around the valley.

Belmont. Sunday 28 January 1973.

Allen called me today, very excited: "Jacques, we finally have physical proof of UFOs, physical evidence! Yes, I'm talking about hardware. I know you don't think much of the *National Enquirer*, but we've received a metallic fragment picked up in Sweden. It's an alloy of gold and tungsten, with many holes made by micro-meteorites. Jim Harder has analyzed it at UC Berkeley. He's about to make a public announcement."

The next step, Allen said, might be for Peter Sturrock, Harder, himself and me to form a new corporation for UFO research. "I'm ready to devote all my time to it," he added, "even if that means leaving Northwestern."

Without throwing cold water on the project, I told Allen we needed better confirmation. I am not convinced that Jim Harder knows much about micro-meteorites.

The bookstores have been filled with Von Daniken's works since the "Ancient Astronaut" program on television, starting a futile movement of pseudo-archaeological curiosity.

Belmont. Thursday 1 February 1973.

I spent the morning at SRI, writing letters to friends, notably Bill Powers whom I congratulated for his well-deserved recognition in the pages of *Science*. In the afternoon Brendan O'Regan came to see me with Bill Whitehead, a senior editor at Doubleday, who expressed interest in my future writings.

Belmont. Monday 5 February 1973.

We came back from an excursion in Nevada sooner than we'd planned. Reno didn't deserve three days, and snow was coming.

We did enjoy Carson City with its Old West museum, its fine climate and rugged mountains. Unfortunately the landscape was littered with stomach-turning scenes of rusty trailers and old appliances groaning in the breeze among piles of old tires. Car engines in various states of agony were strewn about the glorious desert, giving the impression that modern man, left to himself with the near-infinite resources of technology, would erect garbage dumps as monuments for the future. You never know when you might need a sparkplug from a 1934 Studebaker.

Belmont. Sunday 11 February 1973.

Over lunch with Sturrock and Harder on Thursday I was finally able to see and touch the famous sample of tungsten silicate that got Allen so excited he wanted to start a new company. It does show evidence of cratering but that doesn't prove an extraterrestrial origin. Many ordinary materials exhibit fine cratering.

I gave a lecture attended by Ingo, Russell and Hal, Michael Murphy and people from Esalen who had invited me. In the audience was a woman named Trixie, dressed as a cowgirl, who told me about experiences with UFOs near her ranch above Petaluma.

My esoteric friends have told me that the Monographs of Amorc, the basis of their correspondence school all over the world, were not original material but were based on texts that Spencer Lewis received from the French group in Toulouse.

"Some of these monographs are mediocre, empty of real meaning. They correspond to periods when the Imperator was waiting for the next installment from France, and the mail was late!" my initiated friends told me, adding: "At headquarters we have a closet where the son of Spencer Lewis, who has succeeded him as Imperator, has hidden all the documents about ritual ceremonies! Lewis Junior is afraid of that material, perhaps because his own father had an accident after performing one of the advanced rites."

When I asked Mil about this, she would only tell me that "he entered into the famous circle and didn't have the strength to maintain it." He died two years later without being able to resume his activities. The fearful incident must have taken place about 1937.

SRI. Tuesday 13 February 1973.

Ingo tells me he had a similar experience to that of a French farmer in Aveyron who saw nine men around him in a dream. The first time, the bell rang and he found "them" on the landing. "What are you doing here? I'm not ready!" he told them, slamming the door shut. In the second dream he was with a woman when they rang. "Why don't you come back another day?" he said. They never did.

We went on to discuss astral travel. "When I leave my body," said Ingo, "it's not a part of my body that goes out, it's some sort of entity that has existed inside bodies for years or centuries, it has lost its memory of non-physical conditions. It has adapted to the machine that enables it to experience this reality and to optimize its local conditions in space and time. That's why testimony about the astral plane is so diverse and confusing."

My artist friend Megan has taken me through the Avery Brundage collections of Asian antiquities, marvels adorned with dragons chasing fine pearls all over the sky, reminiscent of the UFO quest.

Belmont. Saturday 17 February 1973.

Over tea during yet another computer failure, Mil freely admitted that she was not "finding the Light" at Amorc, in spite of Spencer Lewis' genius. As president of the Society for Psychical Studies in New York at 19, he won the confidence of Henry Ford and Vanderbilt. In his role as a psychic consultant to the latter he obtained the money he dedicated to the founding of Amorc. His associate, the Order's treasurer, fled with $20,000 and the founding charter of the organization. To the credit of Spencer Lewis, he resumed his consulting activities to return the missing sum.

The charter of the Order designated Spencer Lewis' heirs as his successors. This was a mistake, because Ralph Lewis turned out to be a typical middle-class man with no inner fire or understanding of spiritual issues. The Order is no longer properly managed, its French members caught in turmoil. Raymond Bernard, the French grand master, is expected to designate his son Christian as successor.

Mil believes she remembers a past life as a medieval Templar: she fled Paris on horseback the day of the arrest of the Knights, taking away precious crosses, documents and holy vessels. She reached a certain farmhouse on a plateau West of Toulouse. She drew the landscape for me. She spent the rest of her life at a place she described to me, a house the Order owned in the Pyrenées.

Such are the things that are quietly discussed around a cup of herb tea at SRI when the mighty computer network of the Advanced Research Projects Agency experiences a prolonged failure.

Belmont. Monday 19 February 1973.

Last night a group of our friends got together at our home to discuss how we might start a community in the Mendocino woods. Gerald was one of the instigators. We felt the hippies had the right idea but didn't execute it well: their Communes have been destroyed by survival issues, lack of food or income, organizational disputes, drug abuse. Those that survived preserved discipline, work ethics, privacy, but were too cultish for our tastes.

What we have in mind is different. We would pool our resources to purchase a large piece of land, enter into a collective agreement with rules for the preservation of the environment.

Gerald and another experienced geologist proposed guidelines: not too close to an expanding city, so it wouldn't be engulfed in some dreary suburb; not too far either, for access to civilization. It should have a pleasant climate and support a garden. It should have water and privacy, two items that will soon be in short supply.

Belmont. Wednesday 21 February 1973.

Hal Puthoff has come back from another trip to Washington. After our failure to get anywhere with well-intentioned McConnell, who evidently knew nothing, Hal has spoken to other "Government officials in a position to discover the true state of affairs" about UFOs. They told him that people who recently saw strange objects in the sky in the Southwest had only been watching classified prototypes. However they also conceded that there were "true" saucers. Hal said his high-level contacts walked around with UFO books in their briefcases, particularly mine. I found this depressing: Doesn't that imply that they know less than I do? (*)

Belmont. Monday 26 February 1973.

The long-awaited University of California conference has taken place, the first instance of a discussion of UFOs in the context of parapsychology. I spoke there in spite of Jim Harder's repeated admonitions against "those people who believe in ghosts!" Arthur Hastings was there as well as Stanley Krippner, a pioneer of dream research, and clairvoyant Ann Armstrong. We had a big dinner in San Francisco. Janine came with me. We climbed the hills happily, her black cape around her shoulders, her warm hand in mine.

(*) Much later (in 2014) I was dismayed to learn the contact in question was Sidney Gottlieb, the "dirty trickster" of MK-Ultra, who sponsored Hal's early work in remote viewing.

8

Belmont. Thursday 1 March 1973.

A computer science conference is in session, an opportunity to spend another full day in the City, although I find it hard to listen to technical gurus spewing out the jargon that makes them look important, all about bits, bytes and central processing units. The fact that I am regarded as an expert in all this doesn't make it any better.

I have had an interesting conversation with Paul Rech about economics. We're headed for a serious crisis, he warned. Nixon has devalued the dollar for the second time, the price of gold rises and the Dow Jones is falling after hovering above 1,000 for a short while.

Paul argues that real estate is the best refuge: "At Shell I conducted a strategic study that pointed to a crisis in the 1977 time frame. Political measures may mask economic problems for a while, but inflation will escalate before the end of the decade. Nixon can probably control the process until 1976, but the next President will be faced with an ugly mess."

Belmont. Wednesday 7 March 1973.

Croiset the Dutch clairvoyant is in Palo Alto today (**29**). When I ask Ingo how he leaves his body he never gives a clear description of the process. Now I understand the difficulty with my own moments of disconnectedness from the coarseness of the world. For the last few days I have felt psychically vibrant, an opportunity to direct my consciousness to a larger realm, but I couldn't describe a technique for others to do it. People tell me that drugs do the same thing, but I am not interested in any "trip" that cannot be calibrated.

In a noble move, the Board of Trustees of SRI has expressed support for Puthoff's and Targ's experiments, congratulating management for its courage in exploring uncharted regions. While such an attitude is helpful, I am bothered by the fact that many scientists are rejecting their overly-skeptical attitudes only to jump to the other extreme, suddenly embracing the most absurd beliefs about everything from spoon-bending to extraterrestrial contact. If I hadn't seen an unexplained object myself in 1955 I don't think I would attach any credence to the subject on the basis of current data (**30**).

Belmont. Sunday 11 March 1973.

Jim McCampbell, a private researcher I met after one of my lectures, came to pick me up on Friday at the wheel of a huge Lincoln Continental convertible. He insisted on explaining the mechanism of his car in detail before lunch. He's a dynamic man, about 50, an avid tennis player. His current income enables him to work full-time on UFOs, he claims. He is writing a book on the subject (**31**). McCampbell has rediscovered Plantier's theory of UFO propulsion, but he has refined it by taking apart my Magonia catalogue. He noticed that the colors and smells described by witnesses were consistent with ionization of the air. He hopes to be able to deduce the propulsive power of the objects from this.

"Many cases in my catalogue are vague or unverified, it's just an index," I cautioned him. "You should only consider the best ones."

"You're wrong, your catalogue is a gold mine," he replied. "I am taking all of it at face value. There's a margin of error, that's always true of any compilation, but every case is useful as long as it provides physical parameters. We should be able to understand how UFOs paralyze witnesses and stop cars. The military could use something like that."

Don Hanlon called unexpectedly, saying he had "gone through a lot." He was getting better, he said, "thanks to Doc," his code name for Regardie.

Belmont. Thursday 15 March 1973.

A teacher who had prompted me to give a lecture before the gifted kids at Aragon High in San Mateo insisted that I must do it again for their dropout special program. So I spoke for an hour to a roomful of kids who had left the normal curriculum. To my surprise it was an exhilarating experience. At the previous session the bright students kept trying to show off by displaying their knowledge of arcane science in complex sentences. They may well go on to be Mensa members (**32**). The dropouts were more interesting. Acknowledging the obvious fact that I was a straight establishment type, I showed up in a suit and tie: “I've become a scientist,” I said, “because I'm interested in what we don't know. Your teachers are telling you about all the things science has discovered, but science isn't only about what's in your books, or what Carl Sagan can explain on television. It's about the unknown.”

From then on I had their attention, so I gave an overview of common things people misidentified as saucers, then launched into a description of real UFOs. Hard questions fused, like “If this was all true, and they were really around, wouldn't people's first reaction be to shoot at them?” I'd never been asked that by adult audiences.

“That's exactly what people did,” I said. “There are dozens of incidents when witnesses grabbed a gun and shot at UFOs. The Air Force, too.”

At the end of the class they were given a multiple-choice assignment. They could answer prepared questions or write an essay. Later the teachers came around and grabbed my arm: “You have no idea what went on there!” they said. “We've never seen those kids sit still for 50 minutes. Why do you think there were three teachers here? Usually the kids start talking, yelling, jumping out the windows and throwing things at the speaker. The 16-year old girl who asked you about people shooting at UFOs has had an abortion. The fellow who wanted to know about evidence has been arrested for pushing drugs. I'm curious to see if they'll turn in any essays.”

Belmont. Saturday 24 March 1973.

Hal and Russ invited me to watch their film about Uri. Marvin Minsky, the artificial intelligence pioneer, was with us for the screening. We talked about funding. It turned out that Hal and Russ are currently financed in part by “NASA” (wink, wink) and in part by a woman named Judy Skutch. Puthoff's rich Texan friend, Bill Church, offered them independent funding but they need the credibility of academia.

Several colleagues have returned from the Werner Erhardt "est" experience more docile. Now Doug puts pressure on me to take the training. My response to this is to look for another job, leaving SRI.

Last night Elmer insisted to drag me to another parapsychology group in San Francisco, the Meta-Foundation, headed up by a psychiatrist. He also wants us to drive up to the Sierra to visit a contactee who gets daily news from the Aliens.

Belmont. Monday 26 March 1973.

Elmer and I did go to the Sierra; on the way we talked about an esoteric organization created in Berkeley by Claudio Naranjo, a Chilean who comes from a diplomatic family. His uncle was said to be among the founders of the United Nations. Naranjo's occult master was another Chilean, 40-year old Oscar Ichazo. Allegedly he perfected his esoteric knowledge in Afghanistan, at a center known only as "the Kingdom of the Bees."

The man we went to visit, Gayne Myers, was at the center of every spiritualistic and contactee activity in Los Angeles for many years. The "channel" for the group is a Detroit radio amateur. Their special belief is that the Aliens are already among us. Auburn is a charming town at the foot of the Sierra, another fine landscape where people had been unable to resist the urge to litter the emerald hillsides with old car parts and rusty trailers. Gayne Myers's living room was filled with the souvenirs of a lifetime. He told us about channeling, tensor beams and magnetic tubes, his complicated terms to describe trance communication. The revelations are as vacuous as ever. We left him in the early evening, a touching figure, a happy old man.

Belmont. Tuesday 27 March 1973.

The teachers at Aragon High have called me in a high state of excitement: their dropouts have submitted many essays following my lecture. Now the teachers wonder if they had given up too early on these kids, whose writings reveal a lot of hope buried at the bottom of all the anguish and despair.

Brendan O'Regan told me yesterday in a mysterious tone that he had met "high-level Intelligence people" who had confided to him "certain things he wasn't supposed to know." The Air Force is said to have picked up UFO fragments, but all the officers who had gotten close to the evidence were later dispersed, some in insane asylums. His informers claim to have names, addresses, documents.

Belmont. Thursday 29 March 1973.

This afternoon I am scheduled to meet with Paul Baran, the inventor of packet-switching and inspiration for the Arpanet, and managers from the Institute for the Future who are looking to fill a senior research management position.

IFTF is a low-profile thinktank, a spinoff of Rand and SRI, which specializes in medium-term forecasting for corporations, government agencies and private foundations. Its president is Roy Amara, the former SRI Vice-president who helped Doug get his very first proposal funded by the Air Force, in the good old days before Arpanet.

Yesterday I spoke to Fred Beckman. "There have been hundreds of sightings in Illinois in the last two months," he told me, and do you think anybody is doing anything about it? Of course not!"

"What about Allen?" I asked.

"He's never here, he's travelling. There's been no follow-up to the Ozark cases either."

Belmont. Sunday 1 April 1973.

Anton and Diane came over for dinner on Saturday. My daughter jumped on Diane's knees and demanded their names. "I'm Diane, and he's Anton," said the High Priestess.

"I don't like his name," she answered without any hesitation.

"You may call me Szandor," intoned the Black Pope in his deepest scary voice.

"Do you like that name, Szandor?" asked Diane. "No," said my little girl flatly.

"Then what would you like to call him?"

"Suzy," came the answer as we burst out laughing.

"There's a problem," said Anton, "I left my girdle at home."

Diane and Janine were ravishing. The dinner was equally sensual: fish *croustade* after a plate of mushrooms, tomatoes, peppers, olives, cucumbers, grated carrots and red cabbage in a vinaigrette sauce. After the fish came a pepper steak *flambé* with Cognac, fresh asparagus and *pommes Princesse*. Cheese, pastries and coffee completed the meal. We drank a Gray Riesling, a Châteauneuf-du-Pape and a Saint Julien 1967 with dessert.

Discussion centered on mysterious media personalities of the Forties who had led double lives as spies for either the Nazi or the Allied side. Some of them vanished, yet the public never wondered where they had gone. "People are so blind!" observed Anton. The American public is not curious, just as the French never wondered what happened to commentator Jean Grandmougin, to whom they had listened every night for years, when he was suddenly dismissed; or to General Ailleret who died in an unexplained plane crash, a week after he said he would break the official silence about UFOs.

We discussed my trip to Auburn, channeling, and his own ghost-chasing expeditions. "Many people have multiple personalities," he observed. "I used to have a caller with three personalities, an eerie experience. People don't like to have such mysteries explained."

Anton once explored a haunted house where ominous sounds were heard, only to notice a glass bottle sticking out of an attic partition, filling a hole in the wall. He took it down.

"Here is the source of all the howling you've been hearing on windy nights." The owner's disappointment was visible.

"Oh no, a simple bottle couldn't possibly make such sounds!"

Anton's only answer was to take the simple bottle, blowing across the opening, to produce a credible rendition of the *Marche Funèbre*.

"Well then, you'd better put this back where you found it," said the owner who enjoyed being visited by celebrities of the psychic world.

The mystery gave meaning to his life. "Yet there are true enigmas," added Anton. "I do believe we can contact higher beings."

Anton added that he no longer entertained visitors, except for close friends, perhaps as a result of conflicts in the group. (**33**)

A fine weekend is ending, the Bay had a deep bottomless blue tinge, and we can see every detail of the towns on the far shore. Our garden looks like a California tourist poster, full of purple flowers and pink bushes. I drove out with the kids to buy paint and plants. We worked and played all day. I helped Olivier assemble a plastic model of the human body. We busied ourselves under the lamp, mixing paint, handling blue lungs and yellow intestines.

Belmont. Sunday 8 April 1973.

We've returned from Mendocino tired after long walks through the woods. This time we visited Navarro, Comptche, Hopland and Willits, and ended up making an offer on a ranch with a lake. Our previous offers on other properties have all fallen through.

Tomorrow I will hand in my resignation from SRI. After another long interview with Paul Baran the Institute for the Future has given me a firm offer to take over two teleconferencing projects on Arpanet. It represents a chance to manage my own software development group, but also an opportunity to go beyond the mere technical level -- to deal with the top ranks of science policy at Arpa and NSF in Washington.

Belmont. Tuesday 10 April 1973.

Engelbart gathered the group yesterday to tell us that Dr. Larry Roberts, the source of our current funding at Arpa, was coming over from Washington. Characteristically, he announced that Roberts was coming over "to learn our system." We all know that his real intent is to look us over and decide whether or not he'll continue to fund us. We are a divided group, incompletely converted by Werner Erhardt.

Erhardt trains two or three hundred people at a time. His trainers lock the doors, physically cutting off access to the phone, candy machine and bathrooms, denying the students any materialistic comforts they count on. He proceeds to break down their defenses, using standard techniques designed to disorient the uninitiated.

For those like me who had not yet taken est (you said "I'm taking est" as you would say "I took the waters at Evian") the pressure to conform has become enormous. It comes from all the groupies who have gone through the ordeal and have a stake in the outcome.

I detect another reason for their plea: they had submitted to the humiliation, the stripping, the public flogging of their souls, the *animectomy*. Now others must do it or suffer rejection.

Quietly, I made it clear that I wouldn't go.

Others resisted the pressure: conflicts continued to deepen as the experience wore off.

At IFTF I just had my first series of technical reviews with Paul Baran (**34**) and my future staff. I find computer research exciting again, as the first large-scale network is built from the ground up.

Belmont. Thursday 12 April 1973.

The other day Olivier came down to my room, arrayed like an alchemical laboratory full of books and odd artefacts.

"That's funny, when I'm with you down here I get plenty of new ideas," he commented.

My son is fast becoming wiser, more mature.

We spent last evening with Brendan, who didn't leave until 3 A.M. Tantalizing ideas but few verifiable facts. His friend Jan claims to have an uncle who was one of the Air Force officers who analyzed a saucer that crashed in Aztec, New Mexico. Brendan is both fascinated and repelled by the Intelligence world.

He gave us as an example a certain research institute that is working for "them," and seriously considered eliminating Ingo Swann after his magnetometer experiments at Stanford: Ingo not only described the device through concrete, electric (Faraday) shielding, magnetic (mu metal) and superconducting shields, but was able to halt its output. Such a man, they said, represented a threat; he could just as easily detonate a nuclear weapon at a distance.

Belmont. Sunday 15 April 1973.

On Friday, as we were driving up towards Mendocino, I told Janine I would turn down Engelbart's last minute efforts to keep me at SRI. The est experiment has been useful, even if the results were not those Doug hoped for. It revealed the deeply hidden faults in his brilliant project. It gave us the special strength of knowing we could stand up alone if necessary, and preserve our own standards against the type of pressure the solid-state society is soon going to place on all of us.

The Augmentation Research Center may be a prototype for a world where advanced computer technology will combine with mind-control to enforce desired behaviors. Can we avoid going through such a phase before we discover a higher level of human freedom?

We discussed all this on the way north, Janine and I, having left the children under the care of a pleasant old woman from Redwood City. We were happy to be alone for a while. The next day we were sitting in a booth at a roadside café, lamenting our lack of progress in our search, when a local real estate agent rushed in:

"I've found what you're looking for!" she announced. We hopped into her Bronco. She took us to a large ranch near Willits, a beautiful place, with a big white house and a smaller cottage. But the most beautiful thing of all is the redwood grove that comes with it, beyond a three-acre pasture. There are two creeks and several magical spots with old madrones, dense manzanitas. Janine fell in love with the place. It is called Spring Hill, and is the door to invisible realms.

Belmont. Monday 23 April 1973.

Friday was my last day at SRI and our first visit to Spring Hill with our children. Fearlessly, they walked across a log bridge stretched over the canyon. We met the owners, the Daytons. We negotiated the deal through Doris, a clever blonde with all the shrewdness of an old farmer. The Daytons accepted our offer.

My plans for tonight: caviar and Champagne with Janine to celebrate Spring Hill *à deux*. We have found a philosopher's stone that transmutes common gestures into the gold of adventure.

9

Belmont. Tuesday 1 May 1973.

This was my first day at the Institute for the Future, heading up the network conferencing research. I hung up a painting of the *Unicorn in Captivity* on my wall and organized my files. I have a large office, California-style windows overlooking a wooden deck and the pine-covered hills on the other side of the linear accelerator and the San Andreas Fault.

The idea of "computer conferencing" goes all the way back to the Berlin Crisis of 1951, in many ways a prototype of the classic management emergency. All Western countries had to be consulted but there was no time to fly the leaders to a central location. A telephone conference call in 17 languages would have been an impossible enterprise.

The State Department had teletype channels to each country, so an attempt was made to splice together the wires to create a crude information network. The result was chaos, any character instantly duplicated on all the teletypes.

Some bright people in the Defense community suggested that it should be possible to put a computer in the middle and use its memory and logic to organize the flow of messages and data around the various sites. Such an idea was easier to propose than to implement. At the time there were no computer networks, no time-sharing systems to enable the machine to service several users simultaneously, and no convenient terminals. There wasn't even any notion of primitive electronic mail when the Institute for Defense Analyses, a think tank for the Intelligence community, began a research program into what started to be called tele-conferencing.

In the late Sixties other groups started experimenting at the Rand Corporation and at the U.S. Office of Emergency Preparedness in Washington. The man who started the program at Rand was a Polish-born genius named Paul Baran, the same brilliant engineer who was already responsible for inventing packet switching, the routing technique that made computer networking possible. Paul later was among the founders of the Institute for the Future, and he is turning over to me the network conferencing project. Given a group of people at different locations and a common need for information, computer conferencing is a new type of technical link enabling that group to interact either simultaneously (as in a phone conference call) or at different times (like a message center with unlimited memory). This technical link consists of terminals, a local telephone call to a computer that controls the process, and a program that gives members of the community the ability to enter information into a permanent record of group conversation.

I had been discussing all this with Roy Amara when Russell Targ called me, proposing lunch. Hal joined us at *Pot-au-Feu*. They asked me to take Mylan Ryzl's seat on the board of the Parapsychology Research Group. Rylz is leaving for Texas, where he'll work with Silva Mind Control, a psychic training organization.

Ingo Swann and I had a serious discussion about remote perception. He was looking for ideas to build a new model of psychic functioning, because old techniques inherited from Rhine and others have failed to bring about conclusive results. I told him to look at the concept of "addressing" for inspiration.

I've been struck by the evidence which exists throughout the literature of parapsychology, for various means of accessing data which is clearly beyond sensory grasp. I tried to impress Ingo with the fact that the notions of direct and indirect addressing, which are familiar to every programmer, would apply well here as useful metaphors. So would the concept of "virtual" addressing - reaching out for a piece of information that isn't there, in local storage. Ingo noted this with interest. (**35**)

Belmont. Thursday 3 May 1973.

Two letters have arrived, both touching on the topic of evil. One is from Aimé Michel and the other from Howell McConnell.

Fig. 5: Working on Arpanet's first Network Information Center, Stanford Research Institute, 1972.

Fig. 6. The Forum team at the Instotute for the Future with Hubert Lipinski, Bob Johansen, Ann McCown, Olaf Helmer, Rich Miller, 1973.

Aimé writes:

> I am not saying that evil or good exist. I say that I choose to develop within me, not the snail which is within me, not the crocodile which is within me, not the monkey which is within me, but that which is not yet within me -- namely my own limits away from the monkey, the crocodile and the snail... I have already been everything which precedes man, and I have emerged out of all that through the enormous effort of death. I have died of being a snail, a crocodile, a monkey and now I am dying of being a man. I agree readily that I do not know where this movement I have chosen leads me. All I know is that it will be more complicated, more difficult, and that the animal within me will vanish a little more.

Aimé finds that ignorance "delightful," adding "It is like being inebriated, like high speed, or a storm, or Columbus' long voyage, or the suspense that precedes a big war." And he adds, on the topic of occult powers:

> It is hard to say where and how that thing we call "love" will fit, except that it belongs on the same side. That's why our friend Anton leaves me baffled. I don't know what he does. I would have liked to have the time, or the intuition, to grasp it. If he is only after certain Powers, I do know one thing: *whoever seeks them finds them.* Perhaps Abellio is right when he predicts a psychic military technocracy. Except that those who seek such Powers only find a new master, and end up as slaves... It is to spare us this process that someone, or something, is controlling the Contact process so strictly, making the contact so stealthy, so clearly designed to remain undetectable.

Howell's letter revolves around a classified meeting he recently had with Geller, presumably in the Washington area.

> My conversation with him convinces me that we are about to cross the border to the new world mentioned in "the Future of Man." He forces us to confront the pitfalls we must meet when we lift the cover of Pandora's box.

Howell sends me some books by Christian novelist C. S. Lewis, who uses science-fiction as a vehicle for ideas about the grand cosmic fight. Then he asks for detailed biographies of Geller and Ingo Swann! I don't intend to play along. Doesn't NSA have its own channels to get that kind of information?

When I recently went back to SRI to meet with Brendan's spooky friend, Jan Brewer, we talked until one in the morning. Jan's family comes from the Aztec area where Scully claims that two saucers crashed in the 1948-49 time frame. His uncle worked at Wright-Patterson, in the technical section. Between 1953 and 1955 the man was withdrawn from his job and placed in an asylum, to the despair of his wife who kept claiming he wasn't insane at all. He was treated with electroshocks, lost all memory. His wife committed suicide after killing both of their kids, but there is no proof that any of this was connected to UFOs.

Now Elmer Burns has called to talk about his latest passion, pyramid power. I waste my time trying to tell him it's a delusion. Now his psychiatrist friend has invited me to a meeting at the home of a woman named Margot whom I've seen at sessions of the Meta-Foundation research group with her friend Sheila, a striking brunette.

Belmont. Saturday 5 May 1973.

At our evening meeting with the Meta-Foundation good old Mr. John Hopkins, the Berkeley contactee, sat down at a small Chinese table, entered his trance and started channeling in a bizarre alien tongue, all the time firmly holding on to the table: "I have to do that," he said, "otherwise I start levitating."

Personally I would have given anything to watch Hopkins levitate, with his girth and jolly countenance. I had to be content with his silly space song:

Galabazoo -- Gada - Rala - Mazoo
Pet pet pet pet pet pet
Radala - Meez - gara - Lamay - Zoo

"Ah..." intoned the psychiatrist who stretched down voluptuously on the carpet, overcome with delight.

"Ah..." echoed a hippie astrologer who was sitting there as hippies do, his eyes closed in the higher stages of ectsasy.

"Ah..." repeated a young man shod in silver slippers who sat in the lotus position, his hands on his knees, palms upturned to the sky.

I closed my eyes too, but only long enough to stem the flood of giggles welling up in my chest. When I opened them again briefly I saw Mr. Hopkins gesticulating with his free hand, the other hand still acting as an anchor to the earthly plane, as he sang his extraterrestrial litany like an overweight shepherd calling forth a herd of paranormal goats. I wanted to laugh so hard that it hurt, especially when I caught sight of the fair Sheila, who was in an agony equal to mine, bright little tears forming at the corners of her eyes, her shoulders shaking with tiny uncontrollable fits, ready to burst.

When the song thankfully came to an end Hopkins consented to give us a translation in common Earth language:

For Ye are children
Not of the past or the present or the future,
But the children of eternity.
In your mortal quest Ye shall never die
In your efforts to find perfection.

The words were as inspirational as the message was bland and pointless. The Great Master who had spoken through our guest concluded his sermon with:

I must now leave Ye
For I have much to do:
Others than Ye are expecting
My visit tonight.

Sheila rushed out of the room, pretending to look for the bathroom.

Feeling a little better now that the seance was over and general conversation had resumed, I looked around me and wondered what the doctor was really up to. Margot had received us magnificently in her fine apartment, furnished in Chinese style, a blue carpet stretched across the floor. She was majestic in her black dress, elegantly made up, creating a vortex of mystery and voluptuousness as she whirled around the room. Sheila too was dressed all in black. With her dark hair, her pale face, she looked like an enigmatic sorceress.

"*Jacques, reprenez-vous du Champagne?*" she asked in perfect French while the others chatted about various higher worlds they had recently visited. The stereo was playing sentimental songs. Elmer told everyone about his experiments: he was drying up little bits of pickle inside pyramids, he said. Every night he carefully weighed fragments of rotting strawberries and banana slices on the precision scales of the lab that employed him in Silicon Valley, to see if decay slowed down. Having concluded this report Elmer decided to lie down on the carpet and promptly went to sleep.

About midnight the psychiatrist must have felt that the time had come to talk about business. I discovered that, all along, the agenda for the evening was to coax the wealthy Mr. Hopkins into giving money to the project.

"What marvellous harmony arises from this group!" the doctor couldn't help but notice. "Wouldn't it be wonderful if we all decided to work together for the long term?"

It is at that point that Elmer woke up, stretched his long frame, yawned a couple of times and stated coldly that he hadn't felt any special convergence in the group at all. Elmer is a very great fool, but I could have kissed him at that point.

"Really?" reacted the doctor. "It's curious that you don't feel this harmony."

"As a matter of fact I wonder if all that stuff doesn't just come from sick brains," continued Elmer, compounding his *gaffe*. Clearly he resented the fact that Hopkins, not him, had been the center of attention all evening. But then Elmer doesn't have any money.

"What does that mean, 'sick brains'?" asked the psychiatrist.

"I know what that means," said Elmer, "I used to be paranoid. But don't mind me," he added,

"I'll just go back to sleep for a while."

Good old Mr. Hopkins then showed that he was far from stupid, even if he was rich and occasionally driven silly by all the extraterrestrial stuff he read.

He told the doctor that he had indeed felt great warmth within our group, and perhaps that would encourage the good doctor to join Hopkins' political organization, the Universal Party, which even now was working towards putting the United States on a platform dictated by the Space Brothers, and was in need of financial contributions from earthlings like him.

Inspired by whatever he had been smoking, the hippie with the silver slippers felt the moment had come to regale us with one of his long poetic tirades. Unfortunately he lost the complicated thread in mid-sentence, fell silent, gestured in mid-air and said graciously,

"I'll let the rest of it slip for the time being."

Elmer, as if he had heard enough nonsense, got up and left. As soon as he passed the door everyone started speaking at once as if a heavy weight had been lifted.

The doctor revealed to Sheila and Margot that they had known each other in a previous life. He gave Sheila the classic line, "I have seen you in Egypt dressed as a queen."

It's always the same thing when there is an attractive woman in these circles. They always turn out to be queens, or at least temple prostitutes of high rank.

"Look at her eyes, Jacques, just look at her eyes!"

Next we were instructed to "share" the visions we had seen while Hopkins sang his space song.

The doctor had felt "alone, but not lonely," whatever that means. We kissed the women and went home.

Belmont. Saturday 12 May 1973.

Bill Powers has come over from Chicago at the invitation of the Institute for Advanced Studies in the Social Sciences at Stanford, to present his anti-behaviorist theory. He had dinner with us.

Stimulus-response models, Bill claims with some justification, only described the environment, not the psychological system. They should be replaced by feedback models. At 47 our friend Bill seems happy, free and sincerely moved to see us again.

At the Institute for the Future my research project is starting to move ahead. Hal Puthoff, Russell Targ and Ingo have come over to see our group communication system, which I now call Forum. They brought Ken Showalter with them, a manager from the Office of Naval Research. I demonstrated the online database of landings. Showalter read with astonishment one abduction report after another.

Belmont. Monday 28 May 1973. (Memorial Day)

A hundred and forty acres, a large pasture, two running creeks and majestic redwoods: that is Spring Hill, nestled in the forest near Willits. At a turn in Black Bart road one finds an old white fence and a dirt path going up. A white cottage and a garage face a white stone wall that curves towards a studio with a roof of green asphalt shingles. The main house stretches along, with a swimming pool in the back. Blue flowers cascade over the slopes. There are roses in bloom, lilac trees, apple trees and pears, a big fig tree. The creek bubbles and giggles in a shaded canyon where huge ferns grow. An ideal place to build an observatory, assemble our research library, and begin my experimental program. I left Janine there with the kids and Alain, to take possession of the place. On Monday, as I had driven back to start my new work, Janine wrote:

> It's six in the evening. I am sitting on the front steps enjoying the rather cold air. It's incredible how slowly time flows here... I started the cleanup work and I wonder if I will ever see the end of it. In one whole afternoon I only did three walls of one bedroom... I love you. I'm anxious for you to come back. It's very beautiful and pleasant here except for the nights. The house is very dark, the floor is hard and the bed is too big.

She tells happy stories of walks around the ranch with her brother and the children.

Later the same day.

Last Saturday Russell Targ invited Uri and members of PRG to a “secret” experiment in the hills of Cupertino. Geller was supposed to summon a saucer and bring it down over the Ridge vineyard of which Hu Crane, an SRI engineer, is part owner. The sight was breathtaking, Silicon Valley sparkling below us in the crisp night air. The tenors of psychic science were there, from Lee Sanella to Jean Millay and Jeffery Smith. Uri never showed up, so we sat in a circle among the vine, looking at the sky. It all ended in confusion.

On Sunday I flew to Boston for an Arpa meeting of principal investigators. It was raining over the city, which I found dirty and sick. Boston is run by insurance companies that spend their time and our money erecting taller and taller skyscrapers. Ironically, the wind occasionally tears off large windows from the higher floors, dumping tons of glass over innocent bystanders, in danger of being guillotined as they walk peacefully to their jobs. One can only hope they carry a good life policy.

It rained a dirty rain over my motel in Fresh Pond and the offices of BBN -- Bolt, Beranek and Newman, the firm that is building our Arpanet infrastructure. For two days I spoke to potential network conferencing users and allies of our project. A fellow named Craig Fields, Dr. Licklider's heir apparent, dominated the proceedings.

“I intend to fund *N* projects among those you will submit, with *N* greater than or equal to zero,” he said in his jargon in response to a question about his management strategy. Paul Baran and I looked at each other in dismay.

On Tuesday I joined Roy Amara, the Institute's president, in Washington. We went to dinner *Chez Francis*. The city was filled with talk of the Watergate scandal, where both the FBI and the CIA are deeply compromised. We spent Wednesday with Ruth Davis' team at the Bureau of Standards and with sponsors of computer research at the National Science Foundation. I flew back that afternoon. On Friday morning, refreshed, I drove north in a burst of spring sunshine. Janine had settled in at the ranch. I started painting with her. We took a break for an escapade into the woods.

Belmont. Wednesday 30 May 1973.

Brendan tells me that Uri doesn't trust SRI.

"There's something tragic about Uri Geller," I pointed out.

"You noticed it too? We've had similar childhod experiences, Uri and I. Our parents would put us to bed and we'd wake up in empty space, or we would see an explosion of light. In Uri's case he felt he was actually inside the explosion. Also both of us used to hear voices. We felt that something, some force, was after our souls."

Belmont. Monday 4 June 1973.

We had a constructive weekend at Spring Hill. We found tenants for both houses, which we cannot afford to occupy for a few years. We will have to be content with enjoying the land on weekends. I climbed up to the waterfalls with Olivier.

On Saturday we were walking along Black Bart road when we heard a noise where Rowdy, the Daytons' dog, was rummaging among the bushes. It wasn't the dog we saw emerging from the underbrush, but a magnificent buck with tall horns that jumped to the middle of the road, landed next to Catherine, and bounded again beyond the fences, towards the Russian River. The dog followed, panting heavily. The girl staggered back, trembling with wonder.

Brendan tells me the government is setting up a secret psychic research center. They've offered a high salary to a friend of his: following his interview he will be leaving immediately for an unknown destination if he passes the tests.

Belmont. Sunday 17 June 1973.

While America becomes interested in parapsychology, the magazine of French science is giving an oddly-distorted rendition of it. *La*

Recherche is quoting unnamed "investigators" from the Defense Department as saying that the SRI experiments are not rigorous enough to be convincing. *Time Magazine*, they say, hired a magician who achieved the same tricks. At no time does the French author (who signs "Antiproton") suspect that perhaps his sources are motivated to downplay the SRI psychic breakthroughs while they are fully exploited by classified operational groups.

Yesterday I had some passing thoughts about writing a new UFO book. I chased them away: "That would be stupid," I reflected, "nobody would read it, the subject is dead, I would simply risk my reputation..." So I put down my pen. But today the thought came back. I decided to entitle the book *The Invisible College*. I drew up an outline, began work on several chapters.

Belmont. Friday 22 June 1973.

On Wednesday I flew to Los Angeles, where the air was filled with smog, to demonstrate the computer conferencing concept at the USC Information Systems Institute.

Brendan tells me that his friend did go to an interview in Oregon and has not been seen again. He believes the secret facilities are in the Southwest. Next I went to see Ed Mitchell and gave him my National Science Foundation report. He liked my idea of conducting psychic experiments using our "Forum" conferencing system, linking various sensitives together. I met his assistant John White.

Belmont. Tuesday 24 July 1973.

On Wednesday I was in Washington to defend our research proposals at Arpa and NSF, a million dollars worth. The weather was hot and muggy, traffic impossible. I went to the Office of Naval Research, and later to the Department of the Interior to visit Gerald's boss, then I spent Friday morning at NSF with another manager.

A big storm finally blew in the afternoon, bringing rain in buckets. I understood why French diplomats used to consider Washington as a hardship post in the early days of the Republic, when Paris sent off people in disgrace as ambassadors to the United States: Washington was a tropical marsh, with mosquitoes and provincial bureaucrats. It hasn't changed much, except that they have drained away the swamps and killed a few of the mosquitoes.

Roy Amara and I had dinner with teleconferencing pioneer Murray Turoff and his wife. On Monday, a depressing visit to Arpa. Washington was englued in its summer weather and the lingering crisis of Watergate. I'm reading *The Golem* and *Future Shock* (**36**).

Belmont. Saturday 25 August 1973.

The first draft of *Invisible College* is finished. It was another quiet weekend at home, working in the yard when I didn't feel like writing, and improving the library. I've installed my terminal downstairs, and now run Institute staff meetings interactively on the computer over phone lines. This enables me to work from home more often and extends my access to the project beyond normal working hours.

Belmont. Tuesday 28 August 1973.

On Sunday Janine and I went to see two movies produced by Edgar Mitchell, followed by a reception at his house in Atherton, with a sparkling pool and impeccable grounds. Mitchell and his friends are researching consciousness, which no two people define in the same way. He seeks the answer in laboratories where trembling plants are said to be influencing other plants, electrodes strapped to every leaf.

I will only take a brief vacation this summer. There is too much work at the Institute for me to be able to get away for long. We're developing various software levels that will support computer conferencing in the real world.

Ukiah. Friday 31 August 1973.

All day I worked hard at building redwood cabins over the frame I had erected on our last visit. An astonished hummingbird was my only companion. I drove up here through the fog of Mount

Tamalpais. Spring Hill was deserted. Our tenants' lonely sheep greeted me; the Jeep bumped its way into the woods.

I am proud of our experiments, even those that fail. I can't explain what I know. There's a link at the extreme limit of consciousness - that word again! - between destiny and the expression of love, when harnessed to the right symbols.

A spring is babbling near our fairy-tale clearing, surrounded by clusters of 200-foot redwoods and the stars above. How long has it been since I have watched the sky in its true beauty? Ten years at least, since my days at McDonald Observatory.

10

Belmont. Friday 7 September 1973.

Anton has read an occult monograph I wrote recently: "How did you ever find out the secret of Templar initiations?" he asked. This launched us into a deeper discussion than I'd had in a long time. Contrary to his popular "Black Pope" image, Anton's view of esoteric reality is that all cults and sects are bound to fail. Instead, he believes in isolated scholars living and thinking in splendid remoteness with a few trusted friends, in contempt of the insults from pedants and bigots.

Jim McCampbell has brought me a manuscript tentatively entitled *Understanding UFOs* (**37**), a vast compilation that started from my Magonia catalogue. He concludes that the effects of the saucers can be explained by microwave phenomena. He wants to start a research program, the first phase costing "only" four million dollars.

Belmont. Friday 28 September 1973.

Mil told me about an underground computer group called the "I-Colony" that operates in the shadows of Arpanet. That sub-culture deals in stories, magic, advanced systems, and occasionally dope as well, using the Arpa network facilities.

The members are among the operators of the major hosts, the systems programmers, and the hackers who spend the night implementing various features nobody had ever intended the network to possess, like the strange "worm" program that has the capability to project itself from one site to another across the country, and manifests as a little wiggle that crosses your screen when you least expect it. They call themselves the Midnight Irregulars.

Belmont. Sunday 30 September 1973.

Old Mr. Hopkins has given us precious details about his life as a proper Contactee: he always sleeps naked, with all the lights on. The various groups that form his Universal Party comprise nudists, illuminati, small-time crooks, and a fat fellow who runs around in a T-shirt that reads "I love Jesus." Occasionally he takes it off, as well as his pants, and runs through Berkeley calling for penance.

Rain is in the air. I hear the foghorn of the Redwood City harbor. The Forum project is going well, with good team spirit. My first article about Forum is about to be published in *Datamation* (**38**).

Belmont. Friday 5 October 1973.

Suddenly there are UFO sightings all over the U.S.: Georgia, Tennessee... There was an observation near Ukiah, and I got a phone call from a Colonel Floryan ("Call me Thaddeus") who said he was in contact with an engineer from Peru who had spent 18 days inside a flying saucer. I'll have lunch with them on Thursday.

Gordon Creighton has sent me a curious letter following his recent meeting with Allen Hynek, en route to Australia. "I have understood that you were now engaged in the same train of thought we ourselves are following, namely the ultraterrestrial theory... It is fairly obvious that Dr. Hynek shares this view. Is that what McDonald discovered suddenly, and is it because of this that he was killed?" As if the world wasn't strange enough as it is.

Tonight the sky was clear, I showed the moon and Jupiter to my children through the telescope. Why is it always so moving to show the sky to young people?

Belmont. Sunday 7 October 1973.

The mood has changed with the rains; we cannot even see the Bay down below. Our hill is now covered with blue flowering bushes and red berries in heavy clusters. This morning I finally read John Keel's earliest book, *Jadoo* (1957). His style is exciting, always ready to burst, like boiling milk on the stove.

Janine and I were planning a quiet day when phone calls started. Allen Hynek told me of a case in Missouri where a man driving a car had his glasses melted by a flash from a low-flying object.

Belmont. Tuesday 9 October 1973.

Yet another war in the Middle East. Israel was attacked by Syria and Egypt on the day of Yom Kippur. Hundreds of men have died.

We spent last evening with friends in San Francisco. The dinner they prepared was very complicated, done with utmost refinement and skill. Others arrived, pockets full of dope; everybody started tripping out; we left quietly. Today I had lunch with John White, psychic Allan Vaughan and a Swedish psychiatrist. They seemed ready to believe anyone who claims to get messages from space, no matter how silly.

Belmont. Saturday 13 October 1973.

Sociologist Bob Johansen, who has just joined my project, flew back with me last night from a conference on audiovisual techniques in education at Snowbird, in the mountains above Salt Lake City, a typical affluent ski town with all the boorishness that wealth implies, under a fake veneer of social pretension.

Fred Beckman called this morning: “Magonia has been unleashed!” He said happily. “Hynek left on Thursday for Dayton, and from there he went straight to Pascagoula in Mississippi. Two fishermen have been abducted and later released by aliens. Unfortunately I can't reach Allen: Mimi won't even give me his number!”

Fred also gave me details on the case of the driver with the melted glasses. The fellow saw a doctor who diagnosed sunburn on half of his face. He was examined at Barnes Hospital in Saint-Louis, where doctors found no clear cause for his blindness. When they ran an EEG, his evoked potentials in the occipital region were weak. Everything looks as if he'd had an experience so strong that his brain, rather than his eyes, had been affected.

I find this interesting because I've spent a good part of Thursday with Colonel Floryan's Peruvian friend, Manuel, a consultant in organizational psychology. He claims his experiences began in July 1961 when he heard a voice ordering him to go away from his companions, saw a craft on the ground, went inside and was transported into the jungle. He spent three hours there before a “teaching machine.” Curiously, he doesn't recall any beings. When he returned to civilization 18 days had elapsed. For the first six months afterwards he slept over 12 hours a day, now only needs two hours of sleep. He moved to California because “this is where the great changes of the future will take place.”

Belmont. Tuesday 16 October 1973.

The newest UFO wave continues to sweep America. Last night I spoke to an exhausted Hynek and to Fred who sounded bitter. Jim Harder has hypnotized the Pascagoula fishermen. He didn't get much out of Parker, the main witness, still under heavy trauma, who did describe three “monsters” with wrinkled skin, silver-colored, a big nose, a slit-like mouth and claw-like hands.

Hynek has heard that over 80 sightings had been reported in Ohio on Sunday night. The Air Force doesn't feel an investigation is warranted: "No imminent danger."

Yesterday I had lunch at SRI with Targ, Puthoff, Robert Monroe, George Leonard (author of *Education and Ecstasy*) and his wife, and Pat Price, a new psychic with the project who specializes in tracking people psychically. George says he feels a "cosmic wind" when he moves to that other level of reality he calls "Locale II."

Later the same day.

Today I had lunch with Hal Puthoff again, at my request. I had many things to discuss with him. The outcome was unexpected.

We had decided to have a sandwich at the *Perfect Recipe*, a coffee shop in the Stanford Shopping center where we could talk quietly. I told Hal about my frustration with NSA and McConnell, a nice guy with strong religious beliefs but no hard data. As far as I was concerned the undercurrent was elsewhere, I said, and I needed to make some moves. Should I do it alone, or continue to seek support? If there was a project actively investigating UFOs within the government I didn't want to step on their toes.

"Well, yes, there is such a project," Hal finally admitted. "In fact they call me from time to time to find out what my psychics have to say on the subject, and to do remote viewing of certain places where they think there may be UFO bases."

"All right, but do they understand the real scope of the problem?"

"They seem to know what's at stake. They have an official charter. In fact they have so many questions they are wondering if the time hasn't come to go see the President."

I had to shrug when I heard this. "You don't go to the President of the United States with a bunch of questions," I reminded Hal. "You need facts and options. Otherwise the President will ask, 'why have we been paying you guys all this time'?"

We had eaten our sandwich and drained our coffee but we hadn't finished our conversation, so we went out, crossing the parking lot to a green area with grass and shrubbery along the creek that separates Palo Alto from Menlo Park.

"Let me tell you what's bothering me," I told Hal, with the feeling that at last we were getting to the real issues. “Back in 1961 I published a science-fiction novel in which I imagined luminous spheres going through walls. Now Geller and Vaughan are seeing such spheres. The following year I published another novel in which the world became twisted when a young scientist watched his spoon bending in front of his eyes, now Uri is doing the same thing in your lab. Then I found myself in my boss's office just as Aimé Michel wrote a letter offering to turn over his UFO data to Paris observatory! I was there at the day, hour and minute when that letter was read.”

“Perhaps you're just causing these situations yourself, psychically?” asked Puthoff as we were still following the little twisting path among the trees.

“How would I know? If that's the case we could be causing many other things. Have you noticed how the UFO landings seem to be staged? Everything works as if the close encounters were theater, created by the UFOs themselves, not genuine happenings. But then... the history of ufology should be placed within an esoteric context. Throughout history there has been a tradition of higher knowledge, and the claim that it was accessible to us, if only we agreed to be tested, to work through certain spiritual problems... That's the meaning of the hermetic schools. The UFO problem, the question of parapsychology, are central to this business. Looking for the solution isn't just a scientific project; it's a quest, an initiation, an enigma like that of the Sphinx...”

We both froze on that word. We had come to the end of the trail, and our path was now blocked by a chain-link fence. Behind that fence stood two sphinxes on huge pedestals, staring down at us.

The weather was hot and sticky. We could smell the pollution in the air, wafting over from Silicon Valley. We walked over to the fence in silence and watched the statues. They were about eight feet long. The two beasts, on close examination, were more like winged gryphons than sphinxes. They stood absurdly amidst bushes and debris, Coke bottles and beer cans thrown there by strolling students. There was a low, undistinguished stucco building in the background.

“Is that our answer? If we can create gryphons,” I told Hal, “we can do anything..." He must have thought I had known about the statues all along and had maneuvered him to the spot deliberately.

As soon as we got back to the shopping center Hal went to a public phone and called someone in Washington. He wrote down a name on a piece of paper: David M...

"That's one of the men in charge. I'll call you tomorrow about it."

There was a large ashtray next to the phone. Something in it burst into flames. A woman who was walking by took off her shoe and beat down the fire until it was out. Hal staggered away towards his car. I felt elated: perhaps we were beginning to get the bigger picture. It's not about extraterrestrials visiting our planet, I thought. It's much bigger than that. It is yet another "intersign," bigger, and far more interesting.

Belmont. Saturday 27 October 1973.

No contact with David M. He told Hal that his unit was being disbanded "because of the current events" (Watergate?), but he remained "very interested in Vallee's long-term approach." (*)

Travel plans: a trip to Asilomar for a keynote speech on management information systems, and on to Washinghton to visit several federal agencies again, starting with Arpa where professor Licklider has now replaced Larry Roberts as head of the information processing technology office that runs Arpanet. Later I will see the Education Institute, the Institute of Mental Health, and the Department of Labor. The murderous war has just ended in the Middle East, Nixon threatens to send American troops to Suez.

On this trip I also plan to talk to Larry Roberts about business applications of our Forum system in his new role as president of Telenet. Next I'll see McGowan, head of MCI, and with Bill Whitehead's friend Ira Einhorn, a hippie leader in Philadelphia who works with people at NBC.

(*) In 2012, shortly after his death, I learned that David Mark was charged by the CIA with monitoring UFO and parapsychology research. Serving as a "domestic contact officer," he gathered information about Puthoff, Targ, Sarfatti and me, among others. He had informers within the UFO groups.

Hal Puthoff tells me about a session with Pat Price and Ingo in which they “visited” a super-secret facility, drew a plan of it by remote viewing and started reading the codes and the labels on files inside locked cabinets. “All hell broke loose,” he said. “They didn't know whether to shoot us or congratulate us!”

Belmont. Friday 2 November 1973.

Hynek is in New York today, a guest on the Dick Cavett show. Ralph Blum and Einhorn had called me to suggest I participate, but I declined and flew home instead. I did call Puthoff, who told me that he'd identified the “number one man” in the government who tracked the UFO field, with a passive attitude. “Mind you, it's a rather sophisticated passive attitude,” he said. “His group follows the sightings, but he says nothing can be done.”

On Thursday I took the Metroliner to Philadelphia for dinner with Ira Einhorn and his girlfriend Holly, at Brendan’s urging. The evening left me disappointed. Ira is a cheerful, energetic, buoyant fellow with long unkept hair, a bushy beard and sparkling eyes. We spent most of the time with his local friends. The women gave massages to each other while the guys smoked pot and talked about comets. The intellectual level was mediocre in spite of Ira's constant hints about his mystical relationship with Einstein's spirit. The pleasantness of the gathering was spoiled by his strong need to project his ego, to dominate others.

The reason for Blum and Ira's interest in talking to me is that they have a contract for a quick paperback on UFOs. They have four weeks to deliver it and no idea where to start. When I offered references about various cases they said: “It's a book for a popular audience; we can't allow it to deteriorate into a work of erudition!”

Belmont. Saturday 10 November 1973.

When I watched the Dick Cavett Show I congratulated myself for not going to New York to take part in it. Allen looks indecisive, timid and tired while Carl Sagan takes control of the discussion from beginning to end and ridicules UFO research.

We are leaving for France soon. Janine's father is in the hospital, in a terminal state. At the Institute I learn to manage a team of researchers, including communications specialist Rich Miller and sociologist Bob Johansen, who have strong ideas about the project's direction. I need to listen carefully to everyone, and I am losing sleep over it as we define the next version of our conferencing system.

Belmont. Saturday 17 November 1973.

In Los Angeles last Wednesday I visited Rand and the Information Science Institute at USC. Afterwards I had dinner with Don Hanlon and two girls. I hadn't seen Don since he had left my house. He hadn't changed much. He dresses well, a young tiger comfortable in any jungle. He keeps his friends by supplying them with various delicacies. His best clients are the rock groups. He lives in a picturesque garret, at the top of a rambling structure reached through a shaky lift encased in a tower.

The next day at Rand I spoke to Rudy Bretz, author of a taxonomy of communications, and had lunch with Rod Fredrickson again.

On Monday Janine and Alain will leave for France with the children. I'll fly to Washington first, and will meet them in Paris.

Spurred on by our conversation at the *Perfect Recipe*, Hal Puthoff tells me he has found the leader of the CIA group that monitors the UFO field. The team used to be under David "M", a middle-level manager who became overly excited when the recent wave struck. As I had anticipated, when he spoke of taking the problem to the President his managers told him they couldn't go to the White House with a bunch of anecdotes and unresolved issues, so he was pushed aside and another man, a biologist, was put in charge. Hal says the new man doesn't want to see me yet.

"He doesn't want to have to lie to you when he meets you."

"That's a funny reason. Doesn't he believe in psychic abilities?"

"He believes in it so much that he wants to finish his old project before he talks to you."

Belmont. Sunday 18 November 1973.

Allen called today. He was thinking of founding a formal group after all. He wanted me to join the new organization, the "Center for UFO Studies" or Cufos.

I suppose he feels a need to have people around him, disciples and admirers and supporters. Will they do any real work? Or will they simply use his name, steal his energy?

Washington. Tuesday 20 November 1973.

Pick Lee hotel. I flew to Washington yesterday morning, sitting next to an expert in tropical diseases who painted a depressing view of illnesses in Africa and our inability to get medication into the regions that most needed them, even if we did develop the right drugs. I found Washington as dirty as ever.

I went to Arpa this morning and met Connie McLindon, an astute administrator with a sense of humor who took the time to explain to me the meanders of the bureaucracy. Tomorrow I'll see her boss, Arpa's director (**39**).

Washington. Wednesday 21 November 1973.

The energy crisis is the main worry in Washington. The only visible result is mindless political agitation. The Arabs are blackmailing the rest of the world and the oil companies are profiting from the situation. The Japanese economy is slowing down. Europe is at the mercy of Big Oil. The National Science Foundation urges me to organize a national computer conference on the topic of energy.

I went back to Arlington for another meeting with Connie, who took me into Steve Lukasik's office. As Arpa Director he reports to the Secretary of Defense.

Afterwards I went out to dinner at the Provence, the dining room at the Madison, and then I walked around, vaguely depressed, anxious to leave the country.

Paris. Sunday 25 November 1973.

I walked through Paris, astonished to find the streets so noisy, worse than New York, and the air filled with fumes. I strolled around the *Arènes* with Maman and Olivier. The Fountain of the Innocents is being taken apart. I had lunch at my brother's apartment. He argued it was important to "do nothing." He's constructed a philosophical system around this idea. Our uncle Maurice has left us a tiny studio we must sell, and there's a mass of papers which Gabriel asked me to sort out, correspondence and postcards, letters from the time of World War I, and a "genealogy" with every birth announcement, every notice of someone's death in the family for the last century.

Some of it belongs in the fire, since we have already saved the important relics. But I cannot destroy this copy of the testament of Victor Lehodey, my worthy Norman ancestor and one-time mayor of Mesnil-Rogues. He wrote it at age 79, in June 1914:

> *To my children, after my death.*
> *My dearest children, these are my last wishes, my last advice, not to say my last orders which are more like a prayer.*
> *I find myself pursued by an illness which rarely spares anyone, and I must submit to the common law. I love each of you with the same deep affection. I hope that you will acknowledge that I have sought justice for all. Do not conduct a public auction after my death. Sell the cattle at the fair. Allocate the furniture among yourselves. Let no one hear one word spoken louder than another about the settling of this affair.*
> *Whatever may happen to French society, keep the fear of God, it is the beginning of wisdom and the safeguard of honor.*

My uncle left no document of the kind. He died alone, without children. He belonged to a generation that was too disoriented to bestow any last advice.

Bayeux. Tuesday 27 November 1973.

It only takes two hours nowadays to reach Bayeux by train. Olivier and I made the trip together after lunch at the station's restaurant. At the farmhouse we found the family gathered around Janine's father, who has returned from the hospital in a very weak state.

The barn is filled with Maurice's possessions. We must start sorting all this out. I began with his telescopes, identifying parts, re-assembling them. I will sell the largest one, a monster that has no equatorial mounting. All his life he dreamed of looking at the stars, but never had access to an open site. That is a lesson for me, to make certain I realize my dreams while I can.

Bayeux. Wednesday 28 November 1973.

Janine has gone off to Yvetot with our daughter and Alain, to visit her family. I closed the shutters to rest. Maurice's papers are quietly burning in the courtyard: Yellowed technical books, old copies of *Le Figaro*, May 68, the landing on the moon, the devaluation of the Franc. I feel as if I was giving his soul the last honors, as my brother did to his body. The barn still holds dozens of gadgets, transformers, fuses, measuring devices, all worthless except for the memories.

Gabriel has shown me the autopsy report. Maurice just became dizzy and died. A heart massage would have resuscitated him. He could have lived many more years. Something had stopped inside him, the will to live on. He must have been conscious to the end. Everything interested him: the genealogy of Greek Gods, particle theory, the gnomon of Saint Sulpice, the history of the United States. He kept a file on many subjects. He had volumes of naughty songs and every program of the *Opéra Comique* over many years.

I looked in vain for any useful philosophical observations among the moralizing platitudes he wrote. He was a good man with no inclination to risk-taking. The most interesting writings he left concerned the Liberation of Paris, which he witnessed. We had a good laugh when we found a collection of old Norman songs, which Janine's mother remembered and sang with gusto.

Janine shares my sad impression of Normandy, its tiny villages crushed by the boredom of the night, with only a few yellowish lamps in the dark landscape. Today the sun came back. Janine and Annick were happy again. We went shopping, laughed like kids.

Paris. Sunday 2 December 1973.

Leaving the children in Normandy, playing in the puddles left by the latest rain, Janine and I came back to Paris. We spent several hours with Aimé Michel, who looked exhausted. He has "friends" here who have given him a tiny unheated room under the rooftops. We urged him to leave such ascetism behind and move to a decent hotel. As always Aimé is doing interesting research on his own. He has succeeded in bringing the issue of mathematical prodigies before scientists. He is worried about Guérin who now accuses anyone who disagrees with him of being a paid agent of the Pentagon.

There are new players in French ufology, notably Jean-Claude Dufour, an inspector with the French equivalent of the FBI. Aimé is intrigued by Poher, who has the collaboration of the Army, the Gendarmerie and the Air Ministry. He believes that Poher, a member of a well-connected political family, has close contacts within the French secret service (**40**).

Aimé told me that at the age of eight he had seen a flying saucer himself. He was in a field close to his house when he saw a flat silvery disk flying overhead. At the same time he had a very strong idea: "I shall find a way to go to the stars some day."

Last night I had an absurd dream about a cow. I was desperately trying to move her by tempting her with apples. Today it turns out that Alain missed his train, the road between Bayeux and Caen blocked by a cow nobody could move out of the way.

Why is it that premonitory dreams are about silly incidents?

Aimé came over. We spoke all afternoon, of things one can only discuss in this way with Aimé Michel, of France and the French language, of Greece and the Greek language, of civilization.

Janine asked how he spent a typical day.

"I don't sleep well," Aimé answered, "so I am up early and I write letters until eleven, when the mailman comes. I read, I have lunch and at two I start writing until dinner time. After dinner I read some more, until eleven."

He is working on a book about Pythagoras, so he is reading Greek again. The only France he knows is that of the soul and the spirit. He

Fig. 7: In Belmont, studying UFO cases with Arthur Hastings and Allen Hynek.

Fig. 8: Paris: Janine and our children at my mother's *Rue de la Clef* apartment with Annick.

confessed he didn't have access to the real leaders and the *parvenus*.
"I don't want to know them, I hate them!" he said. But it is the promoters, the stinking rich, who run the country today under Pompidou, whether we like it or not.

Paris. Tuesday 4 December 1973.

Abellio is a clever, careful man. Aimé and I met him in his apartment on *Rue des Bauches*, where he lives alone. We saw a well-stocked library, but paint was peeling off the walls. He was dressed all in gray, with a turtleneck sweater. He told us about the therapeutic value of pyramids in ridiculous terms worthy of Elmer Burns, and urged us to read about Enel's four hemispheres. Abellio is a former member of Synarchy, a secret political society with connections to St.Yves d'Alveydre and the Vril movement (**41**).

It was snowing when we left Abellio's apartment. Visiting Louis Pauwels on the Champs-Elysées, we bumped into Bergier in the elevator. Pauwels, in his literary persona, is a fine and clever man, an optimist who believes in the happiness of the masses based on leisure afforded them by the capitalist system.

From Pauwels' office we went down the hall to see Bergier. The contrast was striking. His desk was piled so high with manuscripts, books, galleys and journals in every language that we could barely see his bald head beyond all the paper.

"So, how are you?" asked Aimé with concern. Jacques Bergier has recently been diagnosed with cancer.

"Very poorly, I am getting worse and worse," answered the bald head beyond the wall of books. The voice was uncharacteristically plaintive and weak. As we searched for something comforting to say, he went on: "You see, I am sinking deeper and deeper into paranoia." We started laughing with relief as he added: "What makes my case especially grave is that *I am paranoid in reverse*: I believe there is a conspiracy to help me!"

We all went downstairs for coffee. He was so pleased with the conversation that he took us to Beruga, his favorite Russian restaurant. I turned our talk to UFOs. It isn't every day that one has dinner with Jacques Bergier.

"What happens to official sighting reports in France?" I asked.

"Nothing. They are sent to me, or to Poher at Gepan. I'm in touch with government people who give me the files they don't know what to do with", he bragged.

"What do you think of Abellio?" asked Aimé

"We're enemies, of course. At the *Libération* he was arrested, but freed for lack of evidence. I'd love to know what secrets he'd learned in his collaboration with the Germans. Only four Frenchmen were among the people who went through Nazi initiations in the Black Order. Three are dead. The fourth one was Abellio."

"What did you find out about their monasteries?"

"Almost nothing. We'd sent an agent but all he learned was that during the celebration of the ritual of *L'Air Epais* (**42**) it was impossible to breathe in the vicinity. It was never established whether asphyxiating gases were involved."

"At the end of the war couldn't you inspect such places?"

"No such luck. At Mauthausen, the concentration camp when the Germans held me prisoner, there was a special commando called *Hartheim*. It was rumored that those who served in that commando were sent to do construction work at a Nazi initiation center. They never came back. At the end of the war the building had been razed, the German guards killed by their own SS masters."

This chilling conversation around a bowl of borscht naturally cast a new light on our own speculations about parapsychology and politics. After dinner we drove Bergier back to his apartment which he calls the *Folies Bergières*. In the cab he found the time to recite several theorems he claims to have discovered, notably the First Law of Cheops: "Workers have a tendency to accomplish less and less."

In contrast Joël de Rosnay, whom I met today, is a dynamic specialist in the creation of high-technology companies. He works under the aegis of the European Enterprise Development (EED) created by legendary venture capitalist General Doriot, the founder of Digital Equipment. We discussed my research. He understood Forum right away. Later Janine and I walked through Paris, buying books by Gustave Le Rouge and Gérard de Nerval. We ended up in

Les Halles and went over to *Le Capitole* for coffee. A light shines at the window in the tiny apartment where we lived when I worked at Paris observatory. Eleven years have passed; we are more in love than ever. Love always loses, as Pauwels says -- and always wins.

Paris. Wednesday 5 December 1973.

My brother and I went to see the estate agent this morning. He was a gray man, busy, correct, bored with our affairs and life in general. We gave him instructions for the sale of the tiny studio left by our uncle. The air was soft, sweet and wet. I had lunch with Aimé and the director of *France Catholique*. "What a mess this country is in!" Aimé remarked angrily. "The telephone doesn't work; the people we need to see are always in meetings..."

Janine and I went to visit my editors at Denoël. We arrived just as a courier was loading piles of my books to deliver them to bookstores.

"That was a shock," Janine remarked later, "to suddenly see copies of *Passport to Magonia* piled up on a sidewalk in Paris; like meeting an old friend unexpectedly."

Paris, Rue de la Clef. Friday 7 December 1973.

Guérin came to see us yesterday. Aimé Michel was already here. Pierre immediately launched into an unprovoked tirade, choking on his anger, arguing about the reaction of "the Masses" to the imminent Great Truth about Extraterrestrial Contact. I tried to change the subject by telling him about psychic research in California, but he was only interested in Aliens. When I spoke about Uri's alleged contacts he blurted out: "That guy should be shot!" by which he meant that no fraternization between humans and the entities should be tolerated -- else we were all doomed…

Things calmed down when Maman served the *apéritif*. The four of us went out to lunch at a Chinese restaurant on Place Monge. I reiterated my intent to spend more time studying abduction cases. I told Guérin that I was intrigued with the striking correlation between the 1973 wave and the proximity of Mars, which ufologists hasn't noticed. This finally got his serious attention. We walked over to the Astrophysical Institute, where he pulled down an astronomical table, and we verified that the two curves were in close, even eerie correlation. Is the phenomenon trying to tell us something? Or is it only another coincidence?

Visiting Guérin's office, which used to be occupied by De Vaucouleurs in the Forties, shocked and pained me. The walls were dirty, the hallway filthy; there were old boxes everywhere. Janine and I escaped into the night to meet a friend who had promised to guide us through the newest entertainments of Paris.

Today Joël de Rosnay introduced me to the head of SESA, a prominent Anglo-French software company that has the license for Arpanet technology in Europe. He was a typical French businessman, utterly stressed out, every minute filled with a thousand details. He explained to me very pompously why network-based communities of the type we're building for Arpa in California would never amount to anything.

Janine and I have met with publisher Jacques Sadoul of *J'Ai Lu*, a likeable man from the Landes region. He was in control of facts and figures about the French book business: “In mass paperback it's not the author that sells, it's the topic,” he observed cynically. “Our best seller is Lopsang Rampa, not Jacques Bergier. Sending our authors to a television show doesn't help. Jean Sendy, who talks to journalists all the time, sells fewer books than Churchard or Flammarion, who've been dead for decades! We do like your *Magonia*; it'll be out in February.”

London. Hotel St. James. Sunday 9 December 1973.

Janine waved at me gaily from the subway car that whisked her away to Saint Lazare and back to Normandy while I took the Silver Arrow to Victoria station, after which I dragged my suitcase to this hotel near Buckingham Palace. The first person I called up was Charles Bowen, who started complaining immediately, telling me about his problems with typesetters and printers. He has a plan for founding an Institute with Hynek. Institutes are in fashion.

Next I called Brendan O'Regan and caught him in the middle of a party. He raved about Uri Geller's recent successes with British scientists and the BBC, where sensitive pieces of electronic equipment are said to have gone crazy. Brendan has organized a lecture for me and promises to introduce me to Desmond Leslie (**43**). Uri's psychic demonstrations in France have all failed.

London. Hotel St. James. Monday 10 December 1973.

When I reached Woking a transformer blew up just as I got to Charles Bowen's house. As a result all train traffic was halted. Brian Winder and Gordon Creighton were kind enough to drive me back to the hotel. Hynek, too, had suffered a nearly tragic incident when he visited Charles: he had gotten off the train on the wrong side and had fallen onto the tracks, barely missing the electrified rail.

I spent an enjoyable evening with the three luminaries of British ufology. The convivial atmosphere was only marred by the fact that his family treated Charles like dirt in his own house. This man, who performs great work editing the *Review*, with subscribers worldwide, must suffer terribly in his personal life. There's little doubt, too, that the BBC censors the subject. Times are tough here. The weather is freezing, coal miners are on strike, electricians are unhappy.

At London University I visited researchers Ederyn Williams, of the Communications Studies Group, and Peter Kirstein, the computing center director. I demonstrated Forum to them, enlisted their help in our future research, and was able to send a report of my visit over the computer network to my team in California.

London. Hotel St. James. Tuesday 11 December 1973.

Gordon Creighton thinks that witnesses are out of their bodies at the time of the event, hence the similarity with occult traditions. I told him that *Passport to Magonia* was being misunderstood by Americans, who seem unable to grasp the mythic power of the phenomenon, beyond its physical reality.

"People misunderstand the word *myth*", he said. "They think of a myth as something that isn't true. They can't understand that, on to contrary, *a myth is that which is truer than truth.*"

I called Janine in Normandy. She told me that Olivier was saddened and shocked by his grandfather's illness. How I miss them all!

London. Kenilworth hotel. Wednesday 12 December 1973.

This morning I met with the research group of the British Post Office, who took me to lunch and demonstrated Confravision, an elegant but expensive version of video-conferencing that now serves seven British cities (**44**). In the afternoon I gave a lecture and the discussion went on for hours. There was a curious incident when the clock in the back of the room started to make loud hammering noises. A man finally had to get up and unplug it.

Also at the meeting was Sir John Whitmore, a former leftist radical who told me that Puharich hypnotized Uri three years ago, producing a tape where Geller's voice changed into that of a being who forecast a major change in earth history under the control of a superior entity called Spectra. Geller believes his mission is to become a celebrity to herald the arrival of the Saucers.

Desmond Leslie is a gangly devil of a man with a long face, long black hair, a deep voice, vibrating a bit off-key but always dramatic in its effect. I liked him immediately, in spite of the crazy things he believed. Leslie is a member of an esoteric society, the White Eagle Lodge, which studies such topics as mediumnity and healing through colors. He invited me to Castle Leslie, in County Monaghan, which I imagine to be a lonely place.

Paris, Rue de la Clef. Saturday 15 December 1973.

The streets are filled with sounds of affluence, expensive cars, and people on their way to the theater. The restaurants are decorated for Christmas festivities. Darkness comes at five o'clock in the streets of *Les Halles* where antique shops sell ashtrays with painted devils, fake swords and horny statues. Naughty women "whose virtue I am too late to save" glide out of medieval doorways, wearing lace bikinis under red leather capes or long fur coats. Near Saint-Merri church, a gallery sells the marvellous works of Clovis Trouille.

Jacques Bergier warned me about the secret role played in America by an Argentine named Lopez Rega, said to be the Gray Eminence of Peron and a firm promoter of the extraterrestrial theory. Bergier said there was a neo-Nazi conspiracy to promote belief in an Alien invasion among the Western public.

I had a long talk with Maman about psychic phenomena. She is aware of her own natural magnetism. People often tell her spontaneously that they feel better in her presence.

Paris, Rue de la Clef. Sunday 23 December 1973.

Janine and the children have returned from Normandy. We had a pleasant lunch with biologist Rémy Chauvin.

Taking time to visit Paris, I wandered near the old Temple. Next I went to the Catacombs, where mounds of skulls (eight million of them) tell the story of forgotten eras. Some of the passages bear romantic inscriptions among the bones. Aristocrats used to give gallant suppers there while musicians played the *Danse Macabre*. It is astonishing to emerge a mile later to the busy surface of Paris where people argue about the price of oil. Later Janine and I went to see a magnificent film, *The Master and Marguerite*. (**45**)

Paris, Rue de la Clef. Tuesday 25 December 1973.

It rained as we went out with Olivier to hear Pierre Cochereau's recital at Notre-Dame. I had the feeling something had been forgotten; the interaction of the organ with the stone and the space was all wrong. The music was studious but Cochereau was playing just a musical instrument - he wasn't playing the Cathedral.

We went home for a *Réveillon* with my mother, sweet and happy, who had spent a fortune on fine food and gifts. I feel the tiredness of the whole year in my bones. I can only lean on my pillow, making new crazy plans in my head, thinking of Spring Hill.

Part Seven

FUTURE NETWORKS

11

Belmont. Saturday 5 January 1974.

In time for the New Year a spectacular snowstorm has buried the hills. The road to the coast at Santa Cruz is closed, the mountains that overlook the Bay shiny with ice. In Woodside, Alain's restaurant does a brisk business with families whose kids have never seen snow on the coastal range. Janine and I have returned from Europe with sorrow at the distress we left behind but delight at the simple order of home, the rain in big drops falling down the metal pipe in pleasant musical contrast with the confused murmur of the town below. My research on networking has begun again at the Institute.

Allen's Center for UFO Studies now has a phone line and a part-time secretary who sorts out reports. Fred wisely insists there should be no hierarchy, organization chart or dignitaries. Saunders, Sturrock and I support Cufos. But as soon as they heard that Mufon would share its data the Lorenzens made it clear they wouldn't collaborate. I don't understand why ufologists detest one another with such passion. Hate is a foreign emotion to me. Allen has the media on his side, for what that's worth: the *National Enquirer* pays his half-secretary. But Northwestern pressures him to move. In angry retaliation he cancelled his annual lecture to the Alumni, always well-attended. He remains the most popular professor on campus.

Belmont. Sunday 6 January 1974.

Hal Puthoff likes my recent article in *Psychic Magazine* (**1**). His friend Bill Church might support my work if I created my own research center. But Janine wisely reminds me that my credibility comes from the fact that I have no axe to grind and don't get paid for my research.

When our conversation returned to the undercurrent and the

activities of the government, Hal insisted it was time for me to meet his spooky friends.

"I'm ready, if they mean business. Where are they hiding?"

"Right now they're drowning in sighting reports, assembling old files, trying to catch up," he answered in his most confidential tone.

"What can I contribute, if they've got so much information?"

"They're getting nowhere," Hal said in frustration... "They have no concept of the Magonia angle; they still see the topic in terms of extraterrestrial technology, propulsion systems, space hardware."

Belmont. Sunday 13 January 1974.

Every day, new ideas come up for the use of computer networks like Arpanet. At the Institute for the Future my conferencing project is taking shape. We are taking the concept of online communities beyond the situations Doug Engelbart and Turoff have explored.

On Tuesday I went over to Hal's house in Mountain View, which he shares with his girlfriend Adrienne and another woman. Psychic Pat Price and his wife were visiting as well (**2**). Hal, who suffered from a slipped disk, was lying on the sofa.

As a test of his contacts I had prepared a list of UFO cases for follow-up, including the Puerto-Rican wave and an Alabama incident where a chief of police has been plagued with strange events. I also wanted to follow-up on Bergier's confidential allegations about Lopez Rega and his role in the occult scene. Hal promised to "get some specialists involved in all this."

Belmont. Thursday 17 January 1974.

We are all sick with colds. Olivier stayed home from school today.

Hal called me at the Institute, extremely excited, but not about UFOs: "Where on Earth did you get that stuff about Lopez Rega?" he asked. "My friends in Washington went ballistic when I asked about him. Rega's daughter has just visited California!"

So Bergier was right about that. But I am disappointed Hal's friends had nothing to say about the UFO cases.

Fig. 9: Janine at her sister's house in Normandy.

Fig. 10: In a Paris café, arguing with Pierre Guérin and Aimé Michel.

Belmont. Sunday 20 January 1974.

A friend tells me that many scientology trainees recall past lives, some with impressions of coming from outer space and burying their spacecraft into the earth to hide them!

Yesterday we went to Spring Hill as another storm engulfed the area. In Ukiah most motel rooms were filled by utility company crews. Thousands of homes were without heat as a result of rains, landslides, overflowing rivers, but at the ranch the air was soft in the wake of the storm, the wind gentle; torrents were bubbling from every direction into the gorge. At the head of the canyon where I climbed to repair the pipes, waterfalls converged towards me from three sides at a magical spot where time melted away.

Belmont. Saturday 26 January 1974.

Foolishly I have agreed to speak at a celebration of comet Kohoutek, the latest in a series of New Age efforts culminating with a session which brings together 8,000 people. Kohoutek was supposed to fill the sky with eerie light and the soul of men with awe, but it has remained a mere speck, eluding all but the best-equipped observers. I find this funny, amidst all the hype from "leading astronomers" and telescope vendors, predictions from seers, and academic publishers reprinting Sagan's works and every book about comets. I had dinner with Puharich, Arthur Young, Tom Bearden and Ira Einhorn, and then drove Charles Musès back to his hotel. Among the whole group, I feel closest to him. (**3**)

Belmont. Sunday 27 January 1974.

When I walked to the auditorium against the cold wind, I asked directions from a young woman, a red flower in her hair, who noticed my accent and gaily answered in French. She turned out to be Jerry Rubin's girlfriend. Inside the hall I found psychic Alan Vaughan with John White. Contactee Allen Michael arrived in his red Messiah uniform, a rainbow over his heart, a cluster of flowers stitched on his béret. His "One World Family Commune" (**4**) ran the restaurant in a side room. Like his Berkeley shop, it was a model of order and cleanliness, if not *haute cuisine*. He was promoting his *Everlasting Gospel* in anticipation of an imminent Armageddon.

The program called for Einhorn, Bearden and me to speak after Jerry Rubin. In spite of the cold Ira only wore a T-shirt and blue jeans. With his long hair he was quite a contrast to Colonel Bearden in an Army brown suit and dark tie, but they had the same alarming willingness to believe unproven claims.

Psychic researchers Lee Sanella and Andrija Puharich were talking about Geller in a room furnished as a meditation center. Leaning against cushions, we listened to Andrija telling weird tales of space messages that vanished as soon as transcribed. Uri channels tensor equations that Andrija can't reveal... In another breathless tale, Uri left Puharich's house at Ossining and went shopping in Manhattan. As he left the shop he claims he was abducted by a flying saucer and projected to the house 30 miles away.

A yoga expert named Christopher Hills, founder of the University of the Trees joined our group, as well as a tall baby-faced fellow dressed in gray mechanics' overalls embroidened with peculiar symbols who drifted in, carrying a pot with live flowers. He had long blond hair and a big smiling head, which he had some difficulty keeping in a vertical position. Such human flotsam is found everywhere these days, unfortunate products of the absurd idea that overloading brain circuits with chemicals is good for the mind.

In this atmosphere of delusion and escapism I couldn't get Andrija to understand why we needed to analyze the UFO phenomenon, not embrace every rumor about it. It was his responsibility to reveal the imminent massive landing of flying saucers, he kept repeating. Doubleday was about to publish his book, which would usher in the era of open contact with extraterrestrials (**5**). The same themes were discussed in public with Charles Musès, Arthur Young, Einhorn, Puharich and Bearden. They saw human society poised at the edge of a chasm created by war, violence and the inequities of the social system. Their solution was to jump into the unknown: The government must announce that flying saucers are real! Then people would assemble in the expectation of a paradise of love. This seemed absurd to me. When Einhorn gave me the floor I said I disagreed with what had been said, these idealistic images hiding too many unsolved issues. I wanted to know more about my purported saviors before jumping. When we are asked to relinquish control, the result may not be new freedom but tyranny and exploitation. I expected to be heckled. To my relief, the audience burst into warm applause.

After the show a celebration got under way, songs were played in the auditorium; hundreds were dancing. We took a cable car and went off to the Cannery, the popular area near Fisherman's Wharf. A puppet master was doing a hilarious outdoor show with caustic political overtones. A diminutive Nixon in a red cape and gold crown was handing a jerrican over to Kissinger: “Henry, we're out of gas... Run to the Middle East!” he instructed as the crowd laughed.

Cambridge. Homestead Inn.
Thursday 31 January 1974. Midnight.

A raging wind is turning this Boston suburb into a little corner of hell. It cleans up the landscape by picking up debris on the road and throwing it against the walls of the motel. It plays horrible tunes with the angles and nooks of this awkward building that dares to stand in its path. It draws a sound resembling thunder out of a stack of metal plates that a construction company has left lying in a vacant lot.

This afternoon the technology of networking was discussed in big words among Arpa investigators who are building the next level in network architecture. My friend Paul Rech was there on behalf of SRI. Dick Watson (who has left Doug's project) represented Livermore. The meeting was run by Craig Fields, as cocky as when I first met him last May. Responding to a suggestion by a senior scientist, he snapped: “Doctor, your idea is feasible, undesirable and even superfluous!”

It is Licklider, head of Arpa's information processing office (**6**), who put Fields in charge, so there was no opportunity for rebuttal. Paul Baran remarked that he felt much too old for such games.

My mind drifts to images that are more dear to me than all of modern technology: Janine at the farm in Bayeux, speaking softly in the quiet evening; my children happily sprawled on the floor in a corner of my library, so absorbed in their reading that they forget their occasional quarrels, strands of their hair mixing over the pictures in the book; I think of my mother on *Rue de la Clef.*

I went to bed early and slept for three hours, woke up and went up to the window in time to see a car missing a turn and hitting a pole. The driver got out unhurt. Midnight. The wind is howling anew; curiously there's no cloud in the sky. The half moon glistens, the stars are pure. On my nightstand lies *The King in Yellow*:

> Strange is the night where black stars rise,
> And strange moons circle through the skies...

In this technocratic world, the future all too obvious, I feel sad for the generous ideas that die. In this awesome storm is a faint message: I will always be able to create, provided I never give up my ideals. I must never let anyone in a position of authority make me lose sight of my own standards, for the sake of money or the illusion of power.

Belmont. Saturday 2 February 1974.

Francois Meyer, professor at Aix University and friend of Aimé Michel, has sent me his data on trends of technology and population, with a remarkable theory on positive feedback. He suggests that we collaborate by pooling our observations. As for Hynek, he sends along a remarkable memo from a Hollywood production company, Sandler Institutional Films, setting up a meeting with Colonel Friend and Major Quintanilla, Al Chop and Robert Emenegger. They prepare an explosive documentary, he writes excitedly, designed to stir up public opinion, and financed by the Air Force!

Allen believes the military has decided to prepare the public for extraterrestrial contact. This almost sounds like the fulfilment of Kohoutek follies: could Puharich be right? "And could that future contact be a contrived event, a staged happening?" I asked Allen. He had no other answer than a confession of puzzlement.

Now, a call from France, very sad news: Janine's father, Jean Saley, has died in Cherbourg. He'll be buried at Yvetot, a brave man to whom life offered few opportunities.

Allen Hynek just called me from Los Angeles. His meeting with the producers was inconclusive. The military consultants were retired officers, so any Air Force involvement will be indirect, unofficial, deniable. Quintanilla agreed that UFOs were real, "a surprising situation," Allen said. He sounded relaxed and serene. I wish I could feel the same way. Instead I am still sick, tense; the children get on my nerves. I'm worried about the future, sad about Janine's father.

Paul Rech thinks this would be a good time to launch a company for office automation. I should discuss the idea with Ray Williams.

In a recent letter McConnell mentions a delightful story he found in a book by Thomas Merton about the Fathers of the Desert. A hermit was once visited by an Angel of Light who told him: "Behold, I am Archangel Gabriel and I have a message for thee!"

The humble man was unimpressed: "I have done nothing to deserve such a great honor," he told his celestial visitor. "Go and take your message to someone else!" Quite a lesson for our New Age gurus.

Belmont. Monday 11 February 1974.

From Wednesday to Friday I attended another meeting of Arpa Principal Investigators in San Francisco to present our Forum project. John McCarthy, Ed Feigenbaum, Paul Baran, and Keith Uncapher were there. I sat next to Saul Amarel, whom I hadn't seen since my visit to the Princeton RCA Labs years ago. Everybody ignored Engelbart, his research seen as too esoteric: Doug's insights are brilliant, but everyone is tired of his sermons.

The conference was held in a large square room in the basement of the Marriott. It was presided over by Licklider. The participants were seated around a huge circle of tables; we had to shout to be heard. What all these people had in common, besides being middle-aged white men with good minds, was an unquenchable thirst for government funding. On the Arpa side were young managers like Craig Fields speaking pompously of "transfering technology into the real world." What interests me is research that actually creates, rather than looking to Washington for budgets at the whim of bureaucrats.

We have had several recent house guests, including Allen Hynek, whom I picked up at the bus station, his four suitcases filled with papers, funny cartoons, tape recordings, sighting reports and various gadgets. As he climbed the stairs to the house I had a sudden impression of *déjà vu*, recalling the clairvoyant description I had been given over a year ago. Over a pleasant lunch on the patio he told us that the Center now was the major thing in his life, yet confessed that the information it was getting hadn't improved.

In the afternoon I invited Peter Sturrock and Jim McCampbell. I regretted this as soon as Jim came through the door. He jumped at Allen, pushing his self-published book, begging him to promote it. Allen was offended, Sturrock was shocked and I was embarrassed. Worse, this effort at unabashed promotion detracted from McCampbell's good research about technical factors in UFO events. While we were engaged in these discussions the telephone rang: Hal was calling to tell me that his main Intelligence contact was at his house. He proposed that I meet him that same evening.

In the next hours I learned that there was another approach to the question Allen and I had debated. Hal's contact is a boyish fellow, Dr. Christopher Green nicknamed Kit, a dynamic bespectacled young man of medium build with alert brown eyes. He holds a doctorate in biology, exudes optimism and refreshing humor.

Dr. Green wasted no time getting into our first topic of conversation, the Pascagoula case (7). He knew more about the details than the "experts" who had claimed to analyze it. Hynek had interviewed both witnesses with Jim Harder, who made a big show of hypnotizing them. But Dr. Green told me that a fortnight after the supposed abduction two other men fishing from a boat in the same river had seen an oblong, torpedo-like craft in the water. It was about one meter long and emitted a cone of light. They touched it with an oar: The light went off, and then came back, suggesting inner control. The Coast Guard was called up and confirmed the observation, after which everybody was debriefed by Naval Intelligence and all hell broke loose. Green was alerted by the Navy.

"Nobody has pointed out that Pascagoula is a strategic site," he said, "it's the place where most of the U.S. nuclear subs are built. So the Navy surmised the object was a soviet spying device. But why did it have a light, if it was designed to spy? Furthermore it's difficult to make a robot device that swims under water."

We went on to discuss computer catalogues. But when I asked if they had any data about the Lead Mask case in Brazil (**8**) he had never even heard of it. The most important thing I learned was that Green had counterparts in every branch of the Executive. Like Howell McConnell, they mainly operated "out of personal interest," with the blessing of higher-level managers. They occasionally exchanged data, but he claimed little was done with it.

"In my case, I have a perfect excuse for doing this, out of my office at the Central Intelligence Agency: if there are Aliens around, dead or alive, they come under the mission of my group, which is biological intelligence. I wouldn't be doing my job if I didn't keep my mind open to this possibility."

"Are you involved in longer-term research, looking for patterns?"

"Not the Agency. Not until there's clear proof that the problem is real. My bosses have read the same reports you have. They've even read your books, but they simply have never been scared by the problem to the point of setting up a serious project."

I pushed him a little more: "Don't you agree there must be a secret effort somewhere?"

He thought about it for a while. "Yes," he finally said, "I do agree with that statement. In my group we've wondered if it wasn't being run within private industry."

"I thought you guys had all the latest gadgets," I joked. He answered with a wink: "We do, but we have to go buy them somewhere, from people who are four or five years ahead of the Agency. Before we can procure an advanced system there has to be a working prototype somewhere, usually in your backyard, Silicon Valley. After all, that's why we're sponsoring the SRI psychic work."

So I'm back to square one. We do have two levels here: (1) a genuine unknown physical phenomenon with an apparent alien intelligence, (2) an undercurrent setup by groups capable of using decoys and false sightings, influencing public perception through the believers. We've only seen a small part of the chessboard.

I couldn't tell Allen about my meeting: Puthoff had placed me under strict secrecy. I made it clear that I was uncomfortable with this situation, hoping Hynek could be brought into our team.

Belmont. Saturday 23 February 1974.

Noted inventor Arthur Young, credited with key developments for the first helicopter, brought together the psychic elite of the Bay Area at his house in Berkeley last evening: writer Jeff Mishlove was there with theoretical physicist Saul-Paul Sirag, who came wearing a dyed shirt, his long hair extended into an Einsteinian look. Freda Morris arrived with her guitar. Elmer Burns sniffed around. Psychic Ray Stanford bragged about his exploits. He gathered a group around us and said the saucers were material, not psychic.

"We've established they originate on several worlds," he said, raising his voice. "Just the other day I was with Uri on a yacht in the Mediterranean. A hawk materialized in the bathroom, a golden bird, a big hawk flapping its wings! When Uri arrived he observed it like something sacred. The hawk is a symbol of Hoova." **(9)**

Everywhere there are such clusters of breathless believers with stories, real or imagined. Saul-Paul owns a small box that contains a key broken by Geller, a twisted spoon, various flattened utensils. A hush fell over the audience. People touched these relics one by one.

Jim Harder showed up late in a tight gray suit and the kind of narrow tie IBM men used to wear. He had deep furrows across his forehead, as if in the throes of some crisis. Then Trixie, who had told me of her sighting a year ago, called from her ranch in Petaluma. She'd just seen a strange light that turned into a mandala (**10**).

Belmont. Tuesday 26 February 1974.

Television reporter Jean-Claude Bourret called from Paris to interview me. He said Robert Galley, the French defense minister, had just stated it could no longer be denied that there were unexplained observations and radar trackings (**11**). Galley mentioned the consistency in reports from the Gendarmes and praised Poher's work. The Board of the CNES, the French equivalent of NASA, met in extraordinary session to discuss future options. Politics have entered into the equation with an editorial in the communist press criticizing those who, "under orders from the Government, mobilize the airwaves to turn the attention of the Workers away from their economic condition."

I had lunch with Pat Price and Hal Puthoff. A temporary clearance is being setup to enable me to visit Kit Green next month in hopes to better understand the chessboard. Oddly enough, in this situation, it is the individual researcher who is in the best position to gain an understanding. As I extend my contacts in Washington it is that precious freedom that I must preserve above everything else.

Belmont. Thursday 7 March 1974.

Ten researchers are now working with me on Forum. I've hired Thad Wilson, a former colleague of Janine at Santa Clara, as a research assistant. The work is exhilarating, to a great extent because of the quality of this group, with such smart computer scientists as Rich Miller and software genius Hubert Lipinski, Bob Johansen who is an astute sociologist with total integrity and an uncommonly clear viewpoint on futures research, and several good assistants.

The challenge is to bend network technology to the needs of group communications in many disciplines -- from policy experts to the humanities or the arts, people who have never seen a terminal. Another challenge is to convince our colleagues in computer science that network communications are as important as faster calculations or more elegant compilers, and that some day this field will play a critical role among electronic media. We are running the world's first conference done entirely by computer, discussing economic tradeoffs between transportation and communications, a timely subject in view of the gas shortage. The participants never met face-to-face. The transcript will be published under the sponsorship of Bell Canada.

In a week I will be travelling to a UFO meeting convened by a group of scientists in Boulder, then to New York to brief the Trustees of the Institute on our computer work, and to Washington to visit our sponsors and also Kit, who has just sent me a confidential translation of a book by Zigel on soviet UFOs. In the middle of all this John White just called. He said the Noetics Institute had financial problems, laying off its staff.

Boulder. The Sheraton Inn. Saturday 16 March 1974.

In an hour I'll have dinner with Poher, who has flown from Paris for the joint meeting of the AIAA's UFO Subcommittee (**12**) and Allen Hynek's Cufos. The former group is directed by Dr. Joachim Kuettner, a white-haired scientist with a German accent who currently does most of his research in Europe. With him are Vern Zurich, of the National Atmospheric Observatory, Jacob Birdwell of Woodward Environmental Consultants, Don Swingle of the Army Electronics Command, Glen Cato of the KVB firm in Los Angeles, and Bob Wood of McDonnell-Douglas. For the Center, with Hynek and me, are David Saunders, Fred Beckman, Ted Phillips, Douglass Price-Williams, Peter Sturrock, Dick Henry and Eugene Epstein.

Our meeting began yesterday with a conference call between Epstein and a soil analysis expert who had studied the Delphos traces (see figure 12 on page 250). He had estimated that the amount of energy coupled into the ground was of the order of 5 megawatts. Ted Phillips, a short, red-haired fellow, had all the information about the case. This is an episode in which a boy named Ronald Johnson saw an object on the ground in the yard of a Kansas farm. His dog was petrified, the sheep in an uproar.

The object gave off a blinding flash, and the next thing Ronald was able to see was the disk flying away. He dashed inside and told his parents, who saw the disk high in the sky. They noticed a glowing ring on the ground. A tree branch was broken off. In the following days the dog made a big scene every evening as he tried with desperation to get inside the house. The sheep remained scared and skittish. Ronald's mother, a nurse, lost feeling in her fingers for a few days after touching the whitish material.

Fig. 11: The "Invisible College," Boulder 1974. From left: Douglass Price-Williams, Dave Saunders and Leo Sprinkle, Dick Henry and J. Vallée, Allen Hynek, Claude Poher and Fred Beckman (courtesy Ted Phillips)

Fig.12: Investigating physical traces: Ted Phillips and Allen Hynek in Medford, Minnesota, November 1975 (courtesy Ted Phillips)

I asked Ted Phillips how the boy had slept since the incident. "Funny you should ask," he said. "He couldn't fall asleep at all for the first few nights. Later he started developing nightmares in which he saw little men staring at him through his bedroom window."

Kuettner took the leadership of our larger meeting. He said he followed a conservative approach "in order to maximize the impact on the scientific community," looking for facts that might refute the Condon report. In spite of these auspicious beginnings nothing much was accomplished. Sturrock suggested organizing a workshop of academics at Aspen. We spoke of international cooperation.

"What do we know about the Russians?" Kuettner asked.

"Nothing, zero," Poher answered immediately, to my surprise. Surely the French space agency has at least the same information I have. "We do know they're researching the subject," I interjected. At which point Allen said theatrically, "Gentlemen, let me make an announcement! At this very moment the CIA is translating for us a big document we have obtained from Moscow. It's full of sighting reports." Then Allen dropped the other shoe, saying he expected a financier to give him a million dollars a year to study UFOs.

This left the assembled scientists in a quandary: was Hynek just boasting? At the break I found myself in the elevator with Allen and Fred, so I asked about this much-advertised new funding: it was only a vague hope. I began to see why it was impossible to tell Allen about our new contacts. Any confidences I entrusted to him would have the same fate as the Soviet book he had just bragged about.

"What's going on with that Russian document?" I asked him. "That's all thanks to Sandler," he said. "The guy's terrific. He got turned down when he first applied for a clearance to see the Blue Book archives but he managed to see them anyway. He even flew off to the Foreign Technology Division, saw all the files he wanted."

"How does he do it?" Fred wondered. "Didn't you tell me that Winebrenner, the FTD chief, drove him everywhere, like a VIP?"

"Yeah, the three of us had lunch together, at the Officer's Club," Allen stressed proudly.

"Oh yes," said Fred with his sharp tongue, "and which wine did they serve you this time? *Mouton-Rothschild* again, from the

Colonel's personal cellar?" Fred continues to believe that the Air Force is pulling the wool over Allen's eyes.

Our science meeting took place at the National Center for Atmospheric Research, with a spendid view of the snow-covered Rockies. Ted Phillips presented the Delphos case. He passed around a sample of the soil that included an obvious white filamentous substance that no one has taken the trouble to identify in the seven years elapsed since the landing. I volunteered to get the work done and he gave me the vial. The rest of the time was devoted to a wide-ranging discussion about radar, magnetic fields, and statistical correlations that yielded nothing concrete.

We were eager to resume our talks after lunch, but two women whom Allen evidently had been expecting arrived from Denver and drove him away. Once Allen had gone we addressed the puzzling issue of cases with evidence of human manipulation, like the sighting in Georgia where a woman witnessed a robotic entity walking around her car. The vehicle became hot to the touch. The police told her they'd recorded two similar cases. The car was moved to a garage for study. The next day it wasn't there any more. She was told that the insurance company had taken it away, and she was supplied with a brand new car in record time. If the CIA is not involved in all this, someone else is doing a very thorough job.

Poher said he was investigating symbols painted on the side of various roads in France, but he was uncomfortable when asked for details (**13**). I invited him for dinner.

"You don't have to answer this next question," I told him, "but I'd like to know how you manage to get information out of the French government."

"That's quite simple," he said, "I carry a secret clearance. When I ask for documents I sign a receipt. That's how I got to see the military files. I even obtained some data from French Intelligence, a UFO report from an agent in Moscow. Would you believe the fellow was walking around Red Square carrying a theodolite?"

We discussed the causality principle and the relevance of the humanoid shape in landing reports. He was impressed, he said, with the increased cranial volume of the ufonauts. He saw that as representing the next step in man's evolution, and a proof they were indeed space beings -- a rather simplistic interpretation in my opinion. The theory that cranial size is correlated with intelligence has been blown away a long time ago.

I told him about Geller's contact claims and gave him the highlights of Puharich's forthcoming book. We discussed the Ummo affair, which still fascinates him. Poher is a good aerospace engineer who is just beginning to grasp the complexity of the problem but he doesn't yet understand the control system concept. Price-Williams is a step ahead of him in this regard. This afternoon he commented on my computer-derived graph, which shows the "wave" structure as a non-cyclical learning pattern. He said it looked like a reinforcement schedule which might lead to retention of imagery and to irreversible changes in mankind's mytho-poietic framework. But what is it that is being taught? What is the guiding principle?

New York. Gotham hotel. Tuesday 19 March 1974.

It is a pleasure to think about leaving tomorrow, yet I confess that I roamed around the city last night with fascination. The trustees of the Institute held a meeting where I presented network conferencing before George Vila, the CEO of Uniroyal, among other luminaries.

Today, over lunch at the *Clos Normand* editor Bill Whitehead (Brendan's friend) handed me a contract for *Invisible College*. Next I will meet Bob Johansen at an experimental video-conferencing studio. This evening I give a presentation on UFO research in the lecture hall of the United Nations.

Belmont. Saturday 23 March 1974.

Another long flight home: my thoughts oscillate between detachment and sadness. I feel a mystical oneness with people who labor in ignorance, in terror of their own follies, in crazy hope of happiness. Yet much of what we call "human" is contemptible; much of what we do is filled with stupefying self-satisfaction embedded in mediocrity. I had an example of this on Thursday when I spent the morning at the Langley "Campus" of CIA. At 9 A.M. I finally met the famous David M. and his colleague Mary S. at a supposedly secret building in Arlington, close to Arpa's Architects building. (The secrecy is a joke: everybody knows it houses Agency offices.) From there we took the Blue Bird bus to Virginia.

Although surrounded with high wire fences, the campus in the woods manages to give a feeling of openness with its well-kept lawns and large avenues connecting the various buildings. After signing the security log I followed my guides along the wide corridors. We met with Don M., a specialist in aerospace and biochemistry, and I gave the same briefing I'd given in Boulder, followed by a two-hour question and answer session that left me with the impression that these people actually knew very little. After lunch at the Agency cafeteria Mary drove me over to my next meeting at NASA.

I have drawn three observations: *First*, the paranormal chessboard is wider than private researchers imagine. *Second*, the people in the room knew less than I did. They certainly are not the people who switched a woman's car in Georgia, pretending to come from an insurance company... *Third* and most surprising, the major topic for them isn't the phenomenon itself, but what the military may be doing behind their back. They kept asking me if I knew anything about a "Black Air Force," which seemed to be off-limits to them.

Arlington, Virginia. Wednesday 3 April 1974.

Allen spent the weekend in Belmont to work with me on *The Edge of Reality*. Arthur Hastings was our facilitator. On Sunday night, after the others had gone, Allen relaxed and spoke to us from the heart, saying he felt like a member of our family. We spoke about the mystical sense of existence. And on Monday morning, when we took the Jeep for the drive over to the airport, I told him: "Perhaps UFOs represent the end of science as we know it?"

"I became a scientist out of a passionate desire to find its limits."

"I wonder how old you were when you saw your own UFO..." I said in jest.

To my surprise he answered me seriously: "I must have been eight years old. It wasn't a saucer, mind you, just something that passed in the sky. I saw it from my doorstep. It made a big impression on me, because of the absence of sound."

Thus Allen, like me, like Aimé, saw one of these objects when he was young. Now I fly over the Pentagon in the middle of a hellish node of expressways and overpasses. Ed Condon is dead. When Peter Sturrock visited him during our Boulder conference, Condon told him to burn everything, that UFOs were a waste of time. He died two days later.

Another significant death is that of Georges Pompidou, who passed away yesterday in Paris, of a rare form of leukemia (**14**). I never had a strong feeling for Pompidou, who presided over the partitioning of Paris real estate among greedy developers. They turned the capital into an assemblage of smoke-filled expressways, ugly towers and ill-planned suburbs where discontent and despair are brewing.

Belmont. Saturday 6 April 1974.

This latest Washington trip ended with an interesting visit to NSF with Roy Amara. The National Science Foundation understands the long-term potential of community interaction through computers, so it may pick up the support of my project to replace Arpa. The flight home was magnificent. It had snowed all over the Midwest. Rivers reflecting the full moon revealed an eerily diverse landscape that didn't look terrestrial. It seemed that drops of mercury glided in every direction over sheets of black velvet. Salt Lake City straddled gray hills at the edge of the lake, drowned in a supernatural glow.

Janine and I spent the evening with friends in the Woodside hills, and today I started seriously writing *Invisible College*. Over dinner with our kids, discussion unexpectedly turned to the state of the world, to nuclear war. My daughter, nearly six years old now, told us with great poise: "I'd take care of myself," she stated. "I'd take the Jeep, I'd go into the mountains, I'd build myself a cabin."

"What about this house?" asked Janine.

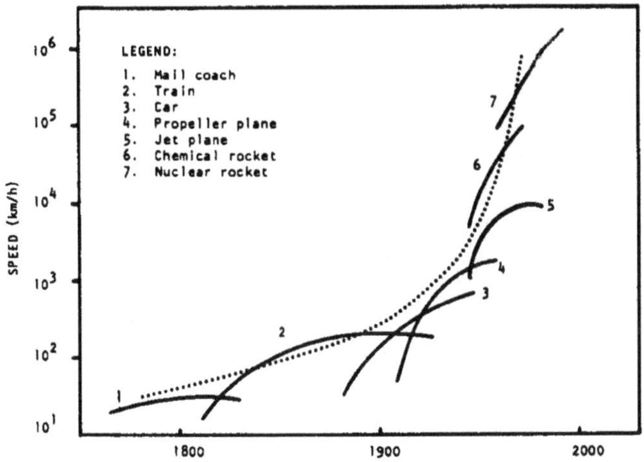

(A) Speed of vehicles: Although each technology follows its own S-shaped curve, the envelope of successive generations of innovation grows much faster.

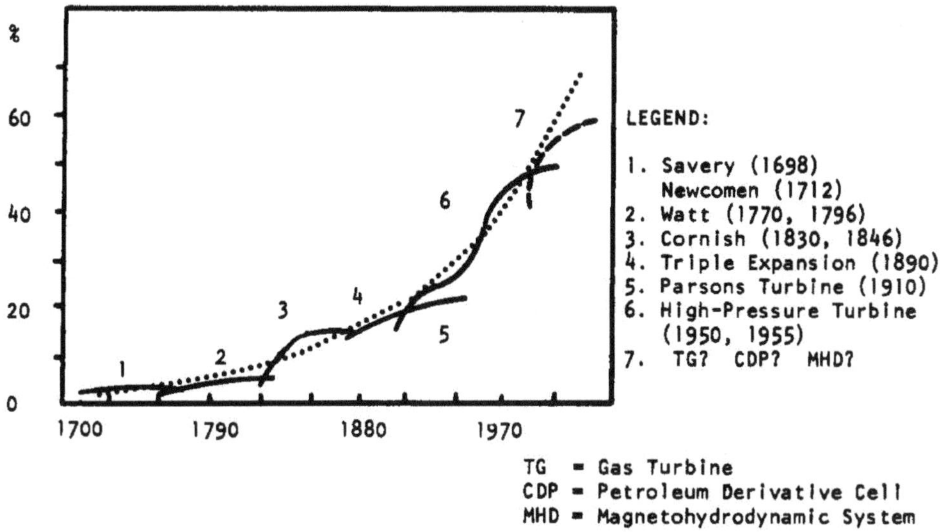

(B) Efficiency of external combustion engines: the same phenomenon applies.

Fig. 13. The dynamics of long-term growth: Prof. François Meyer and I showed in the *Journal of Technological Forescasting and Social Change* (1975) that growth was hyperbolic, pointing to a discontinuity in mankind's development about 2026.

"I'd leave it behind," she said. Then, as an afterthought: "No, I'd come back once, to take my marshmallows."

Belmont. Friday 12 April 1974.

On Monday I had lunch in Menlo Park with Australian researcher Mike Duggin, who gave me a well-documented picture of the UFO phenomenon there. They have a rich history of sightings, good investigations and some troubling photographs.

Olivier and I spent yesterday at the NASA-Ames research center, where communications manager Brad Gibbs gave us the grand tour, even getting Olivier into the cockpit of a U-2 for a look before it took off on a data-gathering mission (**15**). NASA has become one of the most active users of our Forum system, linking various projects among their centers (**16**). Until then, Brad Gibbs was bored with the bureaucracy. When I first went into his office, carrying a computer terminal, there was a single number written on his blackboard. He told me it was the number of days he still had to wait until retirement! A few weeks after he started using Forum, that fateful number disappeared from the blackboard.

Belmont. Saturday 4 May 1974.

The Institute project is in full development. This weekend we move to a new location across famed Sand Hill Road in Menlo Park, which is fast becoming synonymous with high-tech and venture capital.

I've been approached with an offer to join Mitre, one of the Beltway Bandits (**17**), where people have heard of my work, but I have just taken several trips to Washington and feel no affinity for the place. The truth is that my contacts there, including my visit at CIA, have led nowhere. I don't expect any breakthroughs from the government world. Instead I am busy transcribing *Edge of Reality*, now ready for review with Allen. He suggested Corralitos observatory in New Mexico as a suitably quiet place for us to finalize the manuscript, which still needs much editing.

Belmont. Wednesday 8 May 1974.

Hal Puthoff, Russ Targ and Pat Price are still laughing at Geller's exploits last night. He decided to "demonstrate telepathy" with a pretty girl from the audience. To achieve psychic contact with her he kept asking her to get closer, so that by the end of the "experiment" she was in his arms, whispering into his ear!

I had to smile: The girl in question was none other than my friend Trixie, who told me herself about this episode. Next, Uri was handed a Geiger counter.

"He manipulated it discreetly, to disconnect the high tension input. He kept saying, I feel it, I feel it!" Hal laughed, "Until the wire came loose, releasing 2,000 volts to his fingers. Then he really felt it!"

A specialized photography magazine has analyzed Uri's pictures, proving them to be fakes. In spite of this I continue to think that Uri has abilities, based on my own observations, but I could never prove it. As far as the scientific community is concerned he is discredited.

On Friday I leave for El Paso, where I will meet Allen Hynek for our two-day work session on our manuscript. We will be cut away from the world in the New Mexico desert. As an experiment, I told Pat Price that I was taking a trip, without any details. He will try to find us psychically, and then will track me from SRI.

A Russian correspondent recently wrote to us. I had left the letter on my desk at home, and now I cannot find it anywhere. That seems strange because I have a well-organized filing system, and rarely lose anything of significance.

Las Cruces. The Palms Motor Hotel. Saturday 11 May 1974.

In El Paso people socialize at the local Sambo coffee shop. I met Allen there for the long drive to Las Cruces, during which he told me the FBI had requested an article for their Bulletin: "We could help you," they volunteered, "we can isolate landing sites, preserve the physical data..." Allen is puzzled about their true intentions.

We drove over to Corralitos observatory, two small domes on a piece of land that rattlesnakes still consider their God-given property.

From the hilltop between the *Sleeping Lady* and the *Rough and Ready* mountains, all we can see is the empty blinding sky of New Mexico, resting on an orange and green desert that looks like a Martian plain. A dust devil made a cone of gray dust over the stocky bushes. Allen started reading our edited manuscript. He was relaxed and focused for a change, but the phone rang: some fellow from Maine had managed to track him down all the way to this desert. He kept him on the phone for twenty minutes to discuss some "mysterious" Florida balls. A man claims to have found metal spheres in a remote corner of his land, so he's trying to convince the *National Enquirer* that they've been dropped by a saucer. Harder tested them and concluded they had "unusual" properties.

While Allen was so occupied I read the script for Sandler's documentary and I was amazed at his claims, including the story of an alleged saucer landing at Holloman Air Force Base. Allen told me that Sandler had a project to go to Russia and shoot a movie about "their" UFOs in September. At night we watched galaxies at the console of the 24-inch telescope equipped with an experimental image orthicon system, an effective photo multiplier.

In the train to Newark. Tuesday 14 May 1974.

Jesus Casanova is a great name for a New York cab driver. This fellow just drove me like a madman across dirty Manhattan streets and left me at the train station. I am on my way to visit Dr. Murray Turoff at the New Jersey Institute of Technology, the first man who ever used a computer for serious conferencing **(18)** just as I was first to use a network for the same reason, so we have much to talk about.

After lunch with him I'll be on my way to Washington: The thought depresses me after the light and spirit of New Mexico. On Sunday, when Allen finished reading the revised manuscript, we drove out across the border to Juarez, enchanted by the Latin rhythms, the bright eyes of the kids, the smiles of the women, all so vibrant. We visited a small museum and had lunch at the El Camino hotel. Allen told me it used to be a well-known pick-up place for American women in the days of Mexican divorces.

Fig. 14. Working with Allen Hynek at Corralitos Observatory, May 1974.

Fig.15. Scientist-publisher Jacques Bergier in Paris

Belmont. Saturday 18 May 1974.

On Thursday Roy Amara and I drove over to the NSA building in Fort Meade, Maryland. They have expressed interest in buying our Forum software in support of their *Estimates of the Situation* process. We found our way to the huge square building with the high fences, the roof bristling with sharp antennas of every possible shape along with white domes from which the atmosphere and the ionosphere are being scanned for electromagnetic signals.

I spent the evening with Gerald Askevold's boss at the U.S. Geological Survey. We are close to getting support for research into network communication from several places. On the way back I met with Kit at the Dulles airport restaurant. His team remains interested in tracking down rumors but long-term research is simply not their mission, he said in response to my tirades stressing the urgency for science work. If they stumbled on hard evidence, of course they would pursue it and bring their analytical expertise upon it, but he confessed that's unlikely to happen.

"Damn it," he told me, "I've got my people looking deep within the Air Force and we can't find anybody who'll talk to us! I've spent three days with Winebrenner, and I brought up the subject as part of our work. He swore to me that FTD wasn't doing anything on UFOs any more. He said they had neither hardware nor biological data."

As a witness to all this, the irony doesn't escape me. Every ufologist including Hynek would give his right hand to find out what's really going on within CIA. Now I'm talking to the analysts most concerned with the subject there, and they spend their time trying to ferret out what's going on within the military.

"The Air Force has unfocused objectives," Kit went on."They have a shortage of scientific brains and they are weakened by the fact that their personnel rotates every two years. So where do they hide the fucking project, if there's one?"

As for Sandler, he sends proposals to the Russians, promising to take them to "the Arpa offices where George Lawrence is studying psychic phenomena and into the corridors of CIA." At the end of his documentary the public will be left speculating about a supposed "contact" with Aliens at Holloman Air Force Base. Someone is indeed manipulating American opinion. A group inside the Pentagon seems to be using the phenomenon to create the expectation of imminent contact. Contrary to what ufologists imagine, such a tactic is not at all in contradiction with an on-going coverup of real events.

Los Angeles. Friday 24 May 1974. Hollywood-Franklin Motel.

Rod, whom I saw today at Rand, gave me some news from our old team. John Borgelt has failed to take off with the Wylbur concept (**19**). Doug Engelbart's project is sinking amidst the budget debacle at Arpa. His programmers are moving over to the Xerox Palo Alto research center, known as PARC, taking with them the mouse interface, the idea of links embedded within text and his concept of an online community. He spends his time in a corner office at SRI, lamenting an ungrateful world.

Flying back from Los Angeles. Saturday 25 May 1974.

Something strange is going on at a high level. I saw Allen at Bob Emenegger's house this afternoon, where I met Bob's wife Margaret -- an agreeable woman who believes that much can be solved by "the raising of consciousness," a fashionable phrase. Too bad nobody has ever defined consciousness.

Allan Sandler said his project began with a call from DoD. He is indeed talking to George Lawrence at Arpa, at the suggestion of the Air Force Public Relations people. Initially he was hired to make routine documentaries on cancer treatment by radiation and brain-computer linkage, Licklider's pet subject. Then "the client" instructed him to include a UFO film in the series, to his astonishment.

"We started interviewing people within the military. There was one jovial fellow who followed us everywhere, a real down-to-earth friendly type. We asked him who he worked for. He laughed and told us, 'think of us as the internal spies of the Air Force.' In other words the notorious OSI, the Office of Special Investigations."

"Don't you have the feeling you're simply being used?" I asked.

"Of course, but what are they are using us for? We thought perhaps Nixon was plotting to reveal the existence of UFOs as a desperate way to stay in power in spite of Watergate," said Emenegger.

"He could declare a state of emergency," mused Sandler, "if he could sell the public on the idea that the Aliens are here."

"Pretty far-fetched," I remarked.

"Well, another theory is that Washington has decided the time has come to get closer to the Soviets, a claim of UFO news could be a convenient excuse to talk. You know, 'the planet has got to be united against the external threat,' all that *Iron Mountain* stuff." **(20)**

Allen Hynek, who didn't like the suggestion that he was being used, sat through the discussion in silence, smoking his pipe. Emenegger thinks the Holloman contact may actually have happened. He's hiring five sociologists, including Janis, to discuss the potential social situations created by a revelation of the existence of Aliens.

"Their advice to avoid panic is to emphasize the Aliens' resemblance with us humans, and to minimize our physical differences in the mind of the public," Emenegger told me.

Belmont. Monday 27 May 1974. (Memorial Day)

Yesterday Hynek and I worked hard with the editors to beat *Edge of Reality* into shape, and today I invited Pat Price and Hal Puthoff, as well as Gerald and Sally, to meet Allen at our house. The day was a delight, with a spring breeze blowing over the flower beds and the rustling leaves of the giant oak tree.

During my trip to the desert with Allen, Pat Price indeed tracked us psychically from SRI, but the transcript of the experiment is unconvincing. He "saw" a squarish building with a dome on top but missed most of the important details of our situation there.

Spring Hill. Sunday 2 June 1974.

We have spent our first night in the cabin, deep in the redwood forest. Dawn was a delight, the sun putting the first touches of gold on the rough wooden walls. Through the large window the clearing came to life out of the grayness, with ferns framed by redwoods. The nearest house, which belongs to the Daytons, is half a mile away.

Gerald and Sally came over on Saturday and drove on to Mendocino. Our only trouble came when the Jeep lost its clutch again, deep in the woods. Everything is calm now. My son is swimming, his sister chasing lizards. It has been a year since we bought the ranch. Our tenants have just told us that a neighbor had seen a strange object, the size of the full moon, land in a field near Willits: perhaps my experiments are beginning to work.

Upon our return from the ranch we got a call from Hal. He didn't want to talk over the phone, so I invited him over for coffee. "I don't know why Kit hasn't called you himself, except that technically the line of communication goes through me," he began. "He thinks you ought to know there's a group of 12 highly-placed people in the government who've decided to create a focus for the study of UFOs, with full access and funding for researchers like you (**21**). One of these people is at the deputy secretary level. He agrees with you that Hynek should be invited."

He also told me that Sandler was in fact leaving for the Soviet Union on June 8th. Their plan is to film a rocket launch and a discussion of Soviet UFOs. The sponsor for the project is Bankers Trust and Life Company of Des Moines, Iowa! I return to Washington in two weeks. Perhaps I'll meet with someone from the group of twelve (**22**). I continue to be fascinated by the fact that the so-called Black Air Force may have a secret UFO project (**23**).

Arlington, Virginia. Wednesday 12 June 1974.

Over a quick dinner with Allen at the airport, I had just time to give him our manuscript and to translate for him an article Charles Garreau had written for the French *Gendarmerie*, which Allen plans to quote in his paper for the FBI. He was exhausted after a full day of shooting with the Sandler team. By the time they finally did his interview he had been forced to walk up and down innumerable steps, in and out of elevators and back and forth along many corridors to establish the Robertson Panel scene. He was so tired that he kept missing his cues and giving wrong answers.

Sandler won't go to Moscow after all. They did shoot the Holloman sequence at the site. Joel Hynek, who served as cameraman, reported that all doors were thrown open to them.

Hubert Lipinski, the senior systems programmer on my Forum project, is in Washington with me. Tomorrow we'll give our proposal to Arpa, then we drive over to Fort Meade to install our software on NSA mainframes and train their people in conferencing.

New York, the Gotham hotel. Sunday 16 June 1974.

Wearing a colorful shirt and a vibrant tie, Kit met me at Dulles last Friday in his little yellow sports car. I was tired after a full day in the computer room at Fort Meade. Over lunch, we were told our system would be used by two different groups: first the military personnel who would be at the terminals in eight-hour shifts. In the second application, NSA intelligence analysts would indeed use Forum to prepare national "Estimates of the Situation."

Kit and I drove over to the Marriott to meet Dave M. and "Sams," who was introduced to me as a member of the new "Group of Twelve," which sounded exciting until we sat down in the bar area and I realized they were all space cadets, talking about pedestrian research worthy of the old Nicap. Sams is a 20-year veteran of the Agency, manager of a project that flies "secret vehicles often confused with UFOs." A solid fellow with brown hair and thick glasses, he said I should write a proposal with him for an ambitious effort with a big budget, but he had no answer to my questions about scientific objectives. I spoke bluntly of my disappointment.

"Sams is a development manager, not a research man," Kit answered philosophically. "He doesn't understand we need a different strategy."

Another waste of time, then. Unless it was a trap, to setup a fake research project as a cover for their newest gadgets.

Over dinner at the Lake Ann restaurant in Reston, while French students at the next table were loudly debating astrology, Kit told me about Sandler: "Yes, something's going on at the Pentagon. No, we don't want Vallee to warn Hynek. Everything's just fine," he was told when he made enquiries. More puzzle, more obfuscation.

We went over to Kit's pleasant house in the woods where I met his cheerful wife and their two sons, who made me feel at home. We spent all of Friday evening arguing, all of Saturday morning as well.

I failed to convince him that UFOs were real. He gave me the translation of Zigel's book and probed into my views of scientology, which are plainly negative.

New York. Gotham Hotel. Monday 17 June 1974.

Long dinner at the *Pen and Pencil* with Institute for the Future trustees and our chairman, Professor Henry David. We discussed artificial intelligence, notably Ken Colby's paranoid robot at Stanford (**24**), but this triggered nothing new. The Academy of Sciences can't grasp any problem before it is fully institutionalized.

Janine gave me her critique of the opening chapter of *Edge of Reality*; we spoke of love. She is in every thought, her voice calm and warm like the touch of her skin. I see our life together like those California roads where every twist and turn brings a new landscape, adding something unexpected to each mile of the trip.

My day was spent at Brookhaven National Lab, reached through the hell of New York expressways. Back in Manhattan I walked over to a publishers' bar with Bill Whitehead who gave me the final contract for *Invisible College*. The City was hot and naughty, with a parade of pretty whores along Midtown sidewalks. A woman in boots and wide hat approached a tall redhead in a miniskirt, took her firmly by the arm and walked with her into a nearby hotel while the crowd passed, blind to the raw intensity of the scene.

Indianapolis. Stouffer's Inn. Tuesday 18 June 1974.

The midwestern plains feel good after Manhattan, but I am exhausted. I arrived here after spending the day at Uniroyal in Connecticut, preaching network communications to their staff. I met the president of Computeristics on George Vila's recommendation.

Their buildings are hidden away in a forest: clean, impeccable, purposely boring, with soft colors, thick carpets, a sterile place with green potted plants, a two-hour drive from the pollution and dirt of New York where my eyes burned.

As soon as I reached the hotel I called the house. Olivier told me he'd installed his camp under the big tree. His club, which includes Chris and Spencer, our neighbors' kids, has consented to greet his sister as a member; they have even given her a big diploma.

Washington. Friday 21 June 1974.

Dr. Ruth Davis met with us this morning at the Bureau of Standards. She is the most powerful woman in computing today. Contrary to Craig Fields, she immediately understood the significance of conferencing. Next, Roy and I drove out to Reston for a presentation to the chief geologist, the director of the U.S. Geological Survey and their top staff. In the evening we had dinner with Professor Henry David and his wife at their Wyoming Avenue home. They had three other guests, including a speechwriter for Nixon.

Belmont. Sunday 30 June 1974.

Allen Hynek has been here since Thursday. He told me that Quintanilla had a fight with Colonel Friend about the reality of UFOs, which amused him. He made a big show of giving me Zigel's book, which amused me. “Perhaps you already have a copy?” he inquired. He must realize that I am not as naive as his associates think I am. Allen left on the red eye flight. I find travelling exhausting, but he seems to be rejuvenated by it.

Belmont. Sunday 7 July 1974.

On Friday, in the clearing at Spring Hill, sitting under the redwoods with the ferns around us and the cabin lit up by a kerosene lamp, Gerald told us he didn't want to go away from civilization. “And civilization is right here!” he added with his good laughter. Sally and

Janine were cooking lambchops, the full moon was rising. Olivier slept in the open with Gerry's big dog, Nicolas. The Jeep's transmission snapped again, leaving us stuck in the canyon with a carload of carpentry and lumber.

The next day we went back to see our real estate lady. She lives near Ukiah, close to the People's Temple, a big structure where buses line up every Sunday, bringing worshippers from the Bay Area. She spoke enthusiastically about the pastor, a man named Jim Jones, who is bringing together people of different races within his church.

Jean-Claude Bourret has called me with concern about some recent events: the French radio network had conducted interviews with internationally-known scientists. Now the tapes have vanished.

I've made progress in my own analysis. I think I have grasped the outline of the control system. The next step is to get closer, to interact. I do know this: the group of 12 is wasting its time. If I were in Paris tonight I would walk aimlessly in heart-rending streets that smell of dirt, like Rue Vivienne where Maldoror lingered.

Belmont. Friday 19 July 1974.

Je t'aime. (Janine's handwriting on my manuscript).

Belmont. Saturday 20 July 1974.

Peter Schwarz, a clever futurist who works for Willis Harman at SRI, is excited about recent leaks concerning the Sandler documentary: "If we're really visited by ETs," he points out, "the social implications will be enormous! We shouldn't let Nixon and the Pentagon control this. We have to tell the truth to the public."

The humanistic counter-culture is caught in a trap: "It's to us that the duty falls, to tell the world about these weighty events..." A few weeks ago the same intellectuals were laughing at crazy farmers who saw things in their fields. All of a sudden, because Hollywood happens to be making a movie (bought and paid for by the same Pentagon that is covering up real sightings) they jump on the bandwagon. Real research wasn't deemed necessary when they thought UFOs didn't exist, and it isn't necessary now that their opinion has been reversed. The solution seems so obvious...

Belmont. Sunday 21 July 1974.

Kit just left, along with Hal, Russell and two of his kids. We had a long discussion after a demo of my landing catalogue. Kit has dropped out of Sams' covert "Group of Twelve."

Emenegger tells me that Colonel Bill Coleman, who represented the Air Force in the film, had been retired for three weeks when he got the job. For nine years he'd served as the Air Force's spokesman and had been intimately linked to the UFO question. More games: One of his men, a Captain Horner, confiscated the Holloman movie just before Sandler could get his hands on it.

The Holloman sequence is based on a bluff by Emenegger. He couldn't find anyone on the Base who recalled such an event. There was only a rumor that in 1971 a helicopter had filmed three objects, one of which landed. Three occupants had supposedly come out. They had Assyrian noses, a rope twisted on their head for a hat, blue-green skin, eyes like ping-pong balls with a hole in the middle. One of them had a wire in one ear and carried a vertical staff with a spiral antenna. The Aliens were taken to Building 830, then to building 930 on Mars Avenue. They remained there two or three years, allegedly "helping the United States decode space messages from another Alien civilization." A biologist named Alfred Lorenzo is supposed to have worked with them. None of this makes any sense.

When Allen was here I asked him if he still had his clearance. He said yes, theoretically he did, but he didn't think it was active, yet Kit has found Allen's clearances active. "Do you know there are 800 reports of foreign UFOs in the CIRCOL files?" he asked. "Why didn't Hynek ever look into that?"

He warned me that a new experimental device was being tested. It is known lovingly as a "flying bathtub." It is a flying triangle with a rounded front, but it could look strikingly like a saucer when seen from the side, and will surely be mistaken for one.

Belmont. Wednesday 24 July 1974.

Allen Hynek called from Blind River, upset about an irate letter from Regnery reminding him of an earlier contract giving them the right to publish *Edge of Reality* and threatening to sue him.

John Whitmore ("Sir John") also called today. He's working with Puharich in his post-Uri period **(25)**. They're studying a healer who serves as a medium between Puharich and a mysterious *Encore* group, picking up where Uri left. *Encore* is supposed to be linked to Spectra, Hoova, the Nine and something called Rhombus 4D. They're all going crazy.

12

Paris. Rue de la Clef. Saturday 27 July 1974.

Olivier and I landed yesterday at the futuristic Charles De Gaulle airport at Roissy. We had been at the apartment less than an hour when a distinguished silver-haired gentleman arrived. He introduced himself as Professor Meyer, dean at the *Université de Provence* and a friend of Aimé Michel. A specialist in the analysis of global development, Meyer has contradicted the dominant hypotheses on population growth by showing that a positive feedback exists between technology and human survival. One of the consequences is that development follows a hyperbolic curve, not an exponential one.

He concludes that we are headed for a major geopolitical discontinuity, which his equations place some time between 2010 and 2030. He doesn't speculate about its nature. Given the close-minded attitude of French science he hasn't been able to get his results published. He wants me to collaborate with him by extending his research to information technology, then by seeking publication in America. We spent a pleasant couple of hours together. **(26)**

Today I have lunch with Jean-Claude Bourret and tomorrow I leave for the Alps. There is sweet sunshine everywhere, petunias in bloom all along my mother's windows. I have ordered a telephone for her.

Marseille. Hotel Nautique. Wednesday 31 July 1974.

Bourret is a dynamic, solid fellow, about my age. He told me the director of CNES had refused to read the UFO files offered by the Defense Minister, which made Poher mad.

Now it is four o'clock in the afternoon. Marseille is dirty and noisy. I just spent two days in the Alps with Aimé Michel and Lagarde, finally seeing Aimé's magnificent house. We went to La Javie together on a dizzying mountain road that stopped a few miles from a point Pat Price had indicated to me, by remote viewing from SRI, as a possible location for a UFO base, but local people scoff at the idea of an undiscovered cave in the vicinity. Aimé's family owns a little stone house in the village, where Lagarde and I spent two nights. We spoke of his experiences in dowsing.

The expressway between Aix and Marseille is ugly. Hundreds of motorbikes thunder along the boulevards amidst hundreds of trucks, thick pollution rises from it all and the statue of Notre-Dame de la Garde is barely visible through the smog. I have yet to visit my French editor Georges Gallet in Cassis before going on to see Poher in Toulouse. I write to Janine every day and dream of Spring Hill.

Paris. Rue de la Clef. Saturday 3 August 1974.

My mother did get a telephone, but it will take another three months to obtain the dial tone! As a result I have to go to the Post office to call Olivier in Normandy, Jean-Claude Bourret on the other side of Paris and Roy Amara in California, the latter to confirm that we will meet in Stockholm at the IFIPS conference (**27**).

On Thursday I woke up with the noises of the *Vieux Port* and left for Cassis after breakfast. I found Georges Gallet in a poorly-furnished apartment. He was kind with me, jolly, full of enthusiasm for *Invisible College* and life in general. We had lunch at *Roches*

Blanches, the bay at our feet. A cool wind rose from the Mediterranean. I regretted not having Janine with me. Gallet enjoyed discussing America. He was full of stories about the early days of science-fiction. He told me that Roland Villeneuve, a former executive at Crédit Lyonnais and leading French expert on the Devil, was among my mother's neighbors on *Rue Monge*.

From Cassis I drove to Nîmes and on to Toulouse. I fell in love with Arles as I saw the little medieval town, its white houses squeezed together. The historical depth of the region is wonderful, but hideous modern creations make it increasingly hard to grasp. Protesting farmers were blocking the road to Spain, creating a 20-mile traffic jam. Prices are rising; small companies are going bankrupt at an alarming rate.

Over lunch, Poher talked on and on about Ummo, which continues to fascinate him, and about his research. He had no doubt about his funding. "I feel secure because I'm protected at a very high level", he told me, adding that even a change in government wouldn't affect him. This means that his budget is approved at the very top.

I experience no pull towards a return to France in spite of all the friends and memories I have here. Now it is past midnight and I cannot find sleep. I think of love, the responsibility that comes with it. My day was spent in bookstores: several interesting discoveries, notably a *Theology of the Angels* which is nothing if not a treatise in parapsychology. At *Mandragore* I ran into Gerard Klein who now heads up a science-fiction collection; he would like me to write new books in French. Tomorrow Maman and I will have dinner with Roy Amara and his wife.

You are in my very depth, Janine, and that is the only thing of which I am certain in this world, that I cannot love you more than I do, and that I always will.

Paris. Rue de la Clef. Tuesday 6 August 1974.

I had lunch with Jean-Claude Bourret again, along with Rémy Chauvin and Campagnac, an interesting industrialist who heads up a private research group called Gepa. Chauvin is a great scientist with a subtle sense of humor. Later I went to see Denoël, my former publishers. They had "lost my address," they said, hence the lack of royalty checks. But their accountant had not tried very hard to find me, and acknowledged they owed me money. *Dark Satellite*, my science-fiction novel of 12 years ago, was reprinted several times.

Stockholm. Friday 9 August 1974.

Ironically I find myself again in an American hotel, with piped-in music and a plastic atmosphere, but I have time to translate *Invisible College* into French. I saw Bill Olle, with whom I had a friendly chat, and Murray Turoff. Roy Amara told me how impressed he had been with my mother's lively conversation over dinner.

Practically all the participants in this convention are men -- busy, serious, concerned men. Why so few women in computer science? The answer seems to lie in the absurd conditioning that comes with social roles in business. This morning I gave a paper about Forum which was well received. I listened to Ted Codd of IBM, who spoke about relational databases, the hot new topic.

The Swedes are turning morose at the thought of winter, its early signs already in the air. New ideas are discouraged by a social system that creates an idiotic equalization of the good with the bad: Mediocrity is the result. But an endless pink sunset lights up my room, the streets feel alive.

Stockholm. Wednesday 14 August 1974.

Christopher Evans is a clever psychologist from the National Physical Laboratory in England. Gordon Thomson, who inspired many innovations in electronic communications is here too, and Larry Day from Bell Canada, and Elizabeth Feinler, whom everybody calls Jake. She now runs the network information center for Engelbart, using the software I developed for the first NIC on Arpanet before leaving SRI.

Our group meets in little bars and coffee shops; we argue long into the night, and stay in touch through e-mail. There are few emotions in that intellectual atmosphere, no reference to anything other than technology. Even discussions of social impacts remain abstract and dry, occupied with issues of response time and performance. Then what good is that technology?

Last night Chris Evans made the observation that the information centers in our brains were biological beings that sacrificed mobility in return for information, as opposed to insects, which did the opposite. Human beings have succeeded in combining increased mobility with increased information, he pointed out.

French newspapers increasingly mention Lopez Rega, about whom Jacques Bergier had warned me so sternly last December. A former law enforcement official, Rega has succeeded in convincing his followers that subterranean ectoplasms were living under Buenos Aires and that he was in contact with them: shades of the Shaver Mystery! He is erecting monuments shaped like crystal balls, and has been nicknamed the Argentine Rasputin (**28**).

More ominously, the themes promoted by Rega's band of neo-Nazi occultists in Argentina resonate with contact beliefs that are being spread in the U.S., stories of crashed disks and underground facilities where the military is said to conduct autopsies of alien bodies.

Treated as harmless delusions by the media, these rumors do infect public consciousness at a deep level. Is there a conspiracy to use the genuine mystery of aerial phenomena to promote extremist political themes?

Paris. Rue de la Clef. Thursday 15 August 1974.

The shortness of the trip from Stockholm is striking compared to American distances. It brings into focus the wasted opportunities of Europe, the density of its brilliant intertwined civilizations. Olivier has brought back from Normandy some of my late uncle's technical devices, to be used in his experiments in Belmont. He packed it all up carefully: a magnifying lens, some test tubes, dozens of resistors. He will become an incorrigible tinkerer like me if he's not careful.

Olivier, my mother and I went for a walk in the botanical gardens under the stifling heat. The seals had wisely retired into the shade.

We went on along the quays to St. Michel, after which I continued alone towards Notre-Dame where a crowd had assembled. Today was the Feast of the Assumption. I went into the cathedral in time to listen to the last canticles of Vespers, after which I heard an organ recital before a crowd of tourists in T-shirts, the nave cut in two by an altar with a horrible crucifix and an ugly dais. There were spotlights throughout, as if the setting sun streaming through the *Rosaces* was not enough. That summed up my trip: we may have great technology, but the wisdom of the past is forgotten.

Belmont. Saturday 24 August 1974.

On Monday evening the house nearly burned down. Janine had been kept on the phone while a pot filled with oil bubbled on the stove. She heard a crackling noise, opened the door, saw flames and called out. Rushing over, I grabbed the burning container by the handles and carried it to the sink as the flimsy curtains above me were vaporized by the fire. I ran for the phone, my daughter started screaming, Janine threw water into the wooden cabinets the flames were attacking. The oil itself had stopped burning by then, but the fire reached the attic. Help arrived just as the power blew up. The house was full of the smell of grease and burning wood.

Now, five days later, scary images are still with us, of firemen in full gear running through my son's room (knocked down by jet lag, he went on sleeping through the ordeal), of the acrid smoke, of leaping flames in the heavy pot. What precipitated the accident was the tension of our return, Janine's weariness, a tear in our existence. I had to force her to rest on Tuesday, take a day off. I am lucky to come out with only a few burns, a scab on my nose and a lingering, nauseous feeling that I have trouble shaking off.

Belmont. Saturday 31 August 1974.

A symposium on UFOs and radioastronomy organized at Stanford University by Peter Sturrock and Ron Bracewell (**29**) has gathered a select group of specialists for the last three days. Allen, who attended it, left early this afternoon, after which Janine and I drove down to the scientology church in Palo Alto to attend Hal's wedding with his girlfriend Adrienne Kennedy. Janine was so stunning in a white dress, tall hairdo and high-heel white shoes that our daughter burst into tears when she saw her, thinking her own parents were going to get married, and neglected to take her along! Brendan and Kit were there, each surprised to discover that I knew them both rather well. We ended up talking about Sandler while a woman in a long dress played the harpsichord on the lawn.

Last night we went to San Francisco to see a movie, after which we met Don Hanlon, who now calls himself Brian, and his girlfriend Mande for dinner at Coffee Cantata on Union Street. I found some of our old friendship rekindled.

New York. Friday 13 September 1974.

At the offices of Instinet I spent the morning watching stock market transactions on the terminals. Prices were tumbling down. People feared the index would fall under 631, the lowest value in the darkest days of 1970. Tonight we are well below, and at the lowest point since 1962. Perhaps because of my pragmatic Norman roots I have always regarded Wall Street with mistrust. Tonight Americans realize there is no such thing as miraculous economic growth, and that the price of a share doesn't reflect an objective fact, only a fragile collective belief about future performance. (**30**)

I spent the rest of the day walking through this ant-hill, watching human determination displayed in the face of adversity. A tired waitress poured coffee into my cup in the basement coffee-shop of the Time-Life building without a smile: bad food, high noise; never a glimpse of blue sky.

Last night I spent several hours with Bill Whitehead editing the *Invisible College* manuscript. *Passport to Magonia* is displayed in several bookstores on Broadway.

Roy Amara and I have spent three days in the corridors of NSF. Over dinner with Alvin Weinberg, who was director of Oak Ridge during Project Manhattan, in his apartment at the Watergate, I found him a disappointed man, reflecting on past hopes of atomic energy: "We thought we were ushering in a golden age," he told us. "Nearly free energy, a few cents per kilowatt-hour -- clean industry for a change, with high moral standards. Instead look at what it has become... And the disposal of radioactive wastes, an unsolved problem. Can we put the genie back into the bottle?" **(31)**

Weinberg has just been named director of the U.S. Office of Energy Research and Development.

On the return flight to California. Saturday 14 September 1974.

Futurist Herman Kahn invited me to lunch today, so I took the train at Grand Central, in itself an interesting time trip back to the days of Metropolis, with tunnels lit up by yellow light bulbs that may well have been manufactured by Edison himself and seem designed to cast their eerie glow over some diabolical crypt. Chappaqua looked like an anachronistic English village. It even had a little fair, where Kahn was supposed to come and sign his book after his lunch with me. His house was large but unpretentious, at the end of a cul-de-sac, every room filled with books from floor to ceiling. The man himself was so large that I was surprised he could actually move. The atmosphere was peculiar. His 16-year old son started out by announcing in an aggressive tone that he didn't believe in UFOs. I had brought some slides but Kahn's projector didn't work. His wife snatched control of the conversation from him and never relinquished it. I liked Herman Kahn, and I thought he must have had some reason for wanting to be briefed about the phenomenon, but I never found out what it was.

Belmont. Saturday 28 September 1974.

My colleagues at the Institute wished me a happy birthday over the network on Tuesday. Our children had prepared a celebration. I am 35. "Do you feel old?" asked Janine laughingly. Not really. But I don't feel any wiser.

Olivier and I drove away to Spring Hill overnight. We unloaded the

Jeep, full of shingles for a second cabin. The air smelled of fresh leaves and wet redwood bark. Janine joined us, bringing coffee, sandwiches, and dessert. We visited the real estate lady. Her husband told us about his psychic experiences in bilocation and clairvoyance. He's had visions of a place where he believes Patty Hearst is sequestered (**32**). They also told us of their growing admiration for the People's Temple, located further up their road. Every Sunday dozens of buses bring its members up from the Bay Area.

Belmont. Saturday 5 October 1974.

Mid-morning; still in bed. Hynek calls: Regnery is sending a contract for *Edge of Reality*. At the Institute we're starting a new computer program named Planet, for "Planning Network." Using improved software for group interaction combining instant messaging with long-term communication, we hope to get support from both NSF and the USGS to demonstrate group interaction among experts in disciplines ranging from geology and aerospace to art and the Humanities. We will also be able to move the system from the shaky environment of Arpanet to a more stable commercial network.

With several hundred users of Forum across the world, it is time to recalibrate our work. Research money is tight. The economy is still in a disastrous state, the Dow under 600.

On Thursday night I went over to the Veterans Auditorium with Trixie and her husband to listen to a Buddhist guru who has a large following in America. He was so fat he could barely walk. Visibly drunk, he spoke incoherently for twenty minutes. The crowd of 3,000 was calm, young, patient, very nice, lost, and confused.

Belmont. Saturday 12 October 1974.

Holding a press conference in Florida, a professor named Robert Powers has stated that the Air Force had recovered two extraterrestrial vehicles and three occupants - one in bad shape, the other one healthy - and that they were kept at Wright-Patterson Air Force Base. The beings were three feet tall. "An announcement will soon be made by the DoD," he added on a radio news program.

This evening we met Don/Brian and Mande again to attend a celebration of Aleister Crowley's birthday: he would have been 99 on October 12th. The event took place in Berkeley, in a student house where one of the best-known residents is Robert Anton Wilson. In attendance were intellectual witches, stoned hippies, one insane fellow and the always pleasant Grady McMurtry alias Hymenaeus Alpha, Grand Khalif of the O.T.O.

Belmont. Wednesday 16 October 1974.

The analysis of the Delphos material confirms it's an agaric fungus that sends out mycellia. They radiate in a circle and the fruiting bodies occasionally can appear as a phosphorescent foxfire under certain conditions. This particular fungus is *Nocardia Albus*, an actinomycete. There's no question that's what caused the ring. But why did it fluoresce on that particular night, after the UFO was seen? That remains a mystery. Did an external anomalous source trigger the luminous reaction?

On Friday I leave alone for Chicago, then Zurich and Vienna where I'll join a panel on computer networking at the International Institute for Applied Systems Analysis. I return through Paris at the end of the month. The weather is hot, heavy; the air smells of smog.

Baden-Vienna. Sunday 20 October 1974.

The front desk claims it is half past five in the evening but I am still on Chicago time, across a gulf of uncertain sleep. So weird and yet simple is time when one is far from love, when the brain is nothing but a great cavern of tiredness, when the rain pounds the windowpanes, the wind a Wagnerian tune. I slept intensely, my 30-hour stubble scratchy against the pillow. In Zurich, as I was waiting to change planes, computer scientist Vint Cerf came and sat next to me. He told me a new research institute was looking for a director, and would I be interested? All I think of is California.

On Friday night, in Evanston, Fred and I met Hynek at the new

LARC observatory. His assistant Elaine, researcher Alan Hendry's wife, is putting the Air Force files back in order. I wish her luck. Allen paid no attention when I told him that the fungal organism responsible for the Delphos traces had been identified. He was far more interested in gossip about little Aliens at Wright-Patterson.

I went back to Chicago with Fred and spent the night in the 27th floor apartment he occupies near the University of Chicago with Sandra and a big dog. An exact opposite of Fred the epicurian esthete, musicologist, expert on fine oriental carpets and complex sauces, the dog is an ugly brute that takes a sick pleasure in hitting Fred's Chinese gongs out of rhythm, tearing the precious rugs and defecating in the kitchen. I slept well, in a bedroom which doubled as a study, from which I could see most of Chicago. The next day we spoke about the book. With his usual keen logic Fred recommended some thoughtful changes. We drove up to Evanston again. At Hynek's place I found my old friend psychologist Bob O'Keefe and a visitor from NASA, Dr. Richard Haines, with whom I spoke for a while, until Fred drove me back to O'Hare.

Laxenburg, Austria. Tuesday 22 October 1974.

I won't see Vienna tonight. I felt so sleepy this afternoon that I left the meeting and went to bed. The Institute for Applied Systems Analysis (IIASA) was created three years ago to serve as a link between East and West. Dr. Raiffa is the American director while a young Soviet scientist, Sacha Butrimenko, heads up computer research. They've succeeded in creating a fragile feeling of cooperation, but it would be foolish to believe that any of the world's problems will be solved in this pretty castle of the Blue Court, built as a playground for princesses.

It is raining in Austria. Through the tall window panes I see roads covered with the fallen leaves of chestnut trees. This is Europe. One waits half an hour for a phone line, but on the way to lunch I noticed a fine pastry shop. I am happy to contemplate my own life from an unknown city. Such is happiness: to think quietly of Janine, of picking up Catherine when she stretches her arms to me, and of

Olivier who studies hard, gets mad, breaks everything -- then comes over to be cuddled like a kitten afraid of the storm.

Baden-Vienna. Thursday 24 October 1974.

Finally I hired a taxi and went to Vienna alone. The Danube is not blue, it is grayish and muddy. A subway is being dug up. The fine squares and avenues of this city have been eviscerated, as in Paris.

My presentation of Forum was greeted with interest but when we tried to run a demo it turned out it would take an hour to obtain a line to Tymshare in Paris, after which the technicians realized that their terminal was inoperative. Our whole group ran over to a temporary building where computer scientists are housed. They had terminals in working order, but their phone was dead.

The weather is cold again tonight. The wind screams as it whirls around the hotel.

Paris. Rue de la Clef. Monday 28 October 1974.

The French economy is in turmoil; everyone expects another crisis. The Post Office is on strike, unemployment is rising as well as prices (up 1.1% in the single month of September, which *France-Soir* has the gall to term “a slight increase”). There is much animation around *Les Halles*. The Fountain of the Innocents, where Nicolas Flamel painted the principles of the spagyric art, is now supported by scaffolding on top of an excavation half a mile wide. Bulldozers drive into this abyss along a curving path. At the bottom, cement trucks mold huge tunnels for future sewer collectors and storm drains. Underground rivers burst into new canals.

I have a cold. I spent the day in bed, sorting out my Uncle Maurice's documents. Some letters date back to wartime. I was only a baby then, my mother had taken me away to Normandy. My brother Gabriel was writing to my father, still in Pontoise:

> My little Daddy, We now know where we stand with regard to the fire at the house. Already, last Tuesday, half-an-hour after

> you left, a letter from madame Stolz dispelled any hope of recovering anything. Every instant we think of something we would have liked to see once more and that, by some worthless person's fault, we will never find again. (Written from Villedieu, 28 July 1940)

One letter, in August 1943, speaks about their precarious lives. We had gone back to Pontoise, while my brother remained in Normandy:

> Thanks to Michel, we chanced upon two beautiful things like those Maurice had gotten at the Fair last week. My uncle paid for them. I took care of transportation to Villedieu without incident. Now we need to get them to you one by one.

He was referring to fine hams, disguised to fool the German post. Another time he remarked there was no opportunity to use the bread tickets: "All we find around here are small saccharine pancakes."

On November 10 my brother wrote again:

> I hope that Uncle was not hit day before yesterday. He must have been at work and probably was under the bombs. We are very poorly informed here. People inflate meaningless details and they don't pay attention to huge events. Yesterday 150 birds passed in a southerly direction. I was able to see and count them. When I got back into town I was told there were a thousand!

Those "birds" were Allied bombers, on their way to Germany.

The Queen Mary, Long Beach. Saturday 9 November 1974.

Twelve years ago to the day we were aboard this ship in mid-Atlantic, in a lower cabin. This time we enjoy greater luxury, walls of acajou, a huge bed, and two portholes. Adding greatly to our comfort, the Queen has become a hotel and doesn't move a bit.

Twelve years. We were alone then. Today our children give meaning to our lives, laughing as we play with them.

We spent the day with professor Price-Williams of the psychiatry department at UCLA. We reviewed the 3-hour videotape of Herb Schirmer's interview under hypnosis. Schirmer is the typical solid country cop. On 3 December 1967 he saw a big object that made his car slide around. He found himself paralyzed. Two humanoids, three and a half feet tall, came out. The first one held a box in both hands, emitting a green flash. The second one applied an object to the base of his neck, hurting him. During his subsequent tour inside the object he remembers receiving instructions: “Watchman, some day you'll see the universe.” They told him they'd come back 14 years later.

There are several interesting things to note in connection with the case. First, there had been a knock on Schirmer's door at 10:45 a.m. that day. The dog rushed to the door and Schirmer opened it: there was no one there. In another curious detail, he never felt his body after the green flash. Price-Williams asked him under hypnosis if he felt his feet touching the ground, and he said no. He “woke up” near his car, feeling hot and sick.

Over lunch Price-Williams told us that in his opinion Cufos had no plan and did nothing. He is concerned, as I am, about the new contactee movements because they could sweep all rationality aside.

Parapsychologist Thelma Moss keeps getting visitors from the government who want to see her psychic lab. They come from the CIA, AEC, FBI... All these visits began in the spring of 1971.

Belmont. Sunday 10 November 1974.

This morning we left the Queen Mary, driving to Bob and Margaret Emenegger's fine house in Hollywood for lunch. Bob confirmed that his involvement with the Pentagon started when Jack Verona, who told him how to set up the program, wrote the first letter and gave him access to Holloman. He has been transferred to Greenland.

Bob knows Haldeman, a former assistant of Nixon deeply involved in Watergate. He tried to find out what Nixon knew about UFOs. Apparently the answer is: nothing. Yet Bob still speculates that their movie might be part of a political plot leading to a state of emergency. He got nowhere with this hypothesis when he tried it on Coleman. As he was pestering him, the wily Colonel told him: “Look, we can play; I'll let you propose 10 hypotheses about UFOs. You won't come close to the truth.”

Bob took up the challenge: “Does it have to do with aliens?” No, said Coleman, who also said no to the other questions. He only hesitated when asked, “could we be dealing with people having peculiar abilities, used by the military for special assignments?” Coleman added, “In 10 years, I'll take you out on my boat off the coast of Florida and I'll whisper the answer into your ear.”

Emenegger shows little patience with ufological zealots. When one fellow found mysterious balls in a pasture, he was astonished to see Hynek devote energy to what Jim Harder regarded as a big mystery. Bob told his secretary: “Find all the companies that manufacture spheres like this!”

Hollywood secretaries are notoriously efficient. It took less than an hour to locate the Chicago Float Corporation. Their hollow steel balls come in eight, ten and twelve-inch diameter, and are used by merchant and fishing vessels.

“Three weeks later Hynek and Harder were still trying to do scientific analyses of the damned balls!”

“You didn't tell them you knew the answer?” I asked in surprise.

“I didn't have the heart! They were so excited!”

Belmont. Wednesday 13 November 1974.

We ran a telepathy experiment over Forum today with Puthoff, Targ and Ingo Swann online at various terminals, asking them to describe remote targets. According to a Navy friend of theirs a SAC plane was approached by a UFO on 15 October. A jet fighter was scrambled, was forced into a dogfight and crashed.

On Monday Janine and I stayed with the kids in San Diego. We had a pleasant dinner with physicist Jack Sarfatti, his Viennese girlfriend Uta, and Charles Musès.

Belmont. Sunday 24 November 1974.

I have been working on critical future topics for the Rockefeller Foundation. I have proposed to include frontiers of physics, parapsychology and extraterrestrial intelligence for consideration, to the dismay of my colleagues who stick to safe topics.

Pursuing a new statistical study of close encounters, taking into account the time of day distribution (**33**), I was surprised to find that if one assumed that landings were independent of the presence of witnesses -- as they would have to if we are dealing with visitors surveying the Earth -- then the peak would take place about 3 A.M. The number of landings would have to be in the millions, an outrageous result, especially if one remembers that landings occur more frequently in areas of lower population density.

Belmont. Friday 6 December 1974.

I am about to leave for Chicago to attend a meeting of the new board of Cufos before going on to Washington to present our information technology research to various agencies.

I've finished reading Burton Wolfe's book about Anton, *The Devil's Avenger*, a fair portrait. Wolfe argues we must reform society to make man happy, but Anton believes it is up to individuals to take destiny into their hands. Inside the puppet of the Devil that moves on the stage of history is hidden the same hand that moves the Bishop with his mitre, the Pope with his cross, the Gendarme with his stick. It is to the puppetmaster that one should speak. He may be the same individual who makes the saucers fly. He may be the *Maker of Unavoidable Events* of my own little tale (**34**).

Evanston. Saturday 7 December 1974.

From the small bedroom in Allen's house, that looks out over naked trees, I see the dead lawn and a few heaps of dirty snow. The streets are clear and so is the sky, but more snow is on the way. Fred proposed a brainstorming session to the board, but there was no structure for it. Sturrock, Price-Williams and Haines feel as isolated as Fred and I do. Yet we worked hard today. Allen inspires the group but it runs on a shoestring. Two businessmen who support Allen seem serious but I couldn't get any answer from them about breakeven revenue. Allen guessed it would be about $12,000 a year.

When Allen gave me the floor to introduce the "scientific" part of the meeting I urged that research proposals be solicited from all qualified members. I stressed the need to publish the reported cases in various amateur journals: who cares who gets the credit?

Dave Saunders assured us everything was about to change: secrecy in high places was breaking down; the government was on the verge of telling the truth. I remained skeptical, we've heard that before.

Sherman Larsen, an insurance agent and president of Cufos raised administrative matters: the Center had reserves of $16,300, he said, of which $6,000 came from 300 individual donors. There was a grant of $4,500 from the Research Corporation, proceeds of $3,000 from Allen's lectures, revenues of $1,000 from document sales, $800 in books and reports, and a $1,000 gift from the *National Enquirer*. At lunchtime we were joined by Dr. Mitchell, a Chicago hypnotist. Also present were Dr. Edward Zeller, Irv Anderson, Patrick Donnelly, Mark Bates and Mimi Hynek.

I was surprised to find out that Allen was not the Center's president, only its scientific director. Cufos is actually an outgrowth of an earlier group presided by Sherman Larsen, who co-founded it with another man. This fellow acted strange after his investigation of the Schirmer case: he started hearing "clicks" inside his head. One day he loaded the files into his car to burn them because UFOs were "the work of the Devil." Larsen had to fight him physically to save his own papers.

Arlington, Virginia. Monday 9 December 1974.

The day was spent training NSA analysts at Fort Meade. There was a funny moment: sitting at a classified terminal to demonstrate Planet over the Arpanet, I caught a live user online. He turned out to be Hugh Collins of the British Post Office research unit.

He was in London, demonstrating the system to the *Times*. Our chat went on quietly under the suspicious eyes of the Fort Meade people. Surely we were breaching security!

Arlington, Virginia. Tuesday 10 December 1974.

Over lunch Kit told me he'd been able to reconstruct all the data alluded to by Emenegger. "Everything checks out, but I can't find out if the Holloman movie actually exists." He confessed, "When I got to that office I bumped into a short fellow, less than five feet tall, with a bulbous nose. I thought, I've been in this job too long!"

Kit reluctantly confirmed there was a group of 15 engineers in the Midwest (I assumed it was McDonnell in St.Louis) secretly doing UFO research for CIA under cover of "aeronautical research." They're getting data through leaks from Cufos and other amateurs. I congratulated myself for working alone, keeping my own counsel.

I spent two fine hours in the office of Tom Belden, a legendary analyst at the Institute for Defense Analyses. He came to pick me up in Kit's office and said with a chuckle, as he guided me down the wide corridors of the CIA at Langley, "Do you realize that I have to use this bloody Agency as my cover?"

He told me stories about the early use of conferencing in the Intelligence community. We discussed crisis simulation games on computer networks, a subject on which I was eager to have his wisdom. He explained why multilingual computer conferences should use interpreters rather than translators, and told me about the ingenious research games he had invented to create standardized conflict simulations within dispersed groups.

Today Ehrlichman cried on television over his dismissal by Nixon.

Belmont. Saturday 21 December 1974.

In the current *Air Force Physics Manual* Janine and I are cited in a section about UFOs. Two of the illustrations are drawn from *Challenge to Science*. Uri Geller is in Germany, trying to sell a record of syrupy love songs. Progress on the professional front: I have new hopes of obtaining research funds from the computer science section at NSF.

The FBI has sent a kind-looking gentleman to see me. He wanted to talk about the Russians. "There's a full-fledged Soviet consulate in San Francisco now," he said, "scientists like you at the Institute are a target. The topics they're interested in are economic and military."

My joint article with Meyer has been accepted in *Technological Forecasting and Social Change*. *Science* magazine had turned it down, arguing against any discontinuity: growth simply must always follow a well-behaved curve, they said. Yet the envelope doesn't!

Belmont. Sunday 22 December 1974.

Janine is putting the house in order for her mother's arrival tomorrow. The kids play under the oak tree. The other day the FBI man found Olivier in front of our home. He asked him for our phone number, which I thought pretty sneaky, and then inquired if he was excited by Christmas. Olivier told him he was a lot more excited by the upcoming dedication of his tree house.

Now the rains have washed the landscape clean and life is vibrant. Janine is going to take a full-time software development job in Santa Clara County. She doesn't want to go back to research or management. As for education, she says it's nothing but politics: "The issues these people solve are false problems," she observes, "the school system is set up on a skewed basis, nobody wants to face reality." One could say the same about science.

Belmont. Saturday 28 December 1974.

Janine's mother joined us before Christmas. My daughter painted a colorful plate for us; Olivier gave me a lighthouse made of wood. Today we played with an electric train, watched movies. It was the kind of holiday I wanted, detached from the flow of time. Janine and her mother have gone out to the harbor to visit the French Navy training ship *Jeanne d'Arc*. I built a wooden airplane for my little girl. Another busy year ends. I wonder who runs the world.

13

Belmont. Sunday 5 January 1975.

Allen prepares a paper for the upcoming AIAA conference where Poher will be my co-author. I am reading a convoluted novel by David St. John, actually E. Howard Hunt of Watergate fame, entitled *Diabolus*: a group of satanists led by a French industrialist who is manipulated by the Chinese (!) is trying to implicate the wife of a French cabinet member in a sex scandal. The story combines the Markovic affair (**35**) with voodoo. The hero ends up in Pontoise...

I have trouble working, sick with an intestinal disease that gives me dark worries.

Belmont. Monday 6 January 1975.

Invisible College proposes the notion that UFOs don't necessarily come from space but serve as elements in a control system. If I am right, it seems unlikely to me that governments would know the answer. Their own investigators, like Kit, either belong to services that keep looking for the wrong thing, or get sidetracked by the first weird claim that comes along. As for academic scientists, they remain blind to the subject.

It is hard to change the direction of an organization that has acquired its own culture. Arthur Young recently explained to me how he'd invented the rotor for Bell helicopters. It took a major battle to get an airplane company to understand what he wanted.

"Didn't they have all the engineers, the manufacturing plants, the test pilots?" I mused.

"That's true," he said, "but all those resources were harnessed to produce devices that took off horizontally, not vertically..."

I have the same problem with the folks in Washington, always looking for an enemy. Since UFOs are not an obvious adversary, and the best data doesn't come through intelligence channels, they are lost. The notion that we might be dealing with phenomena more subtle than politics is a tough one.

Main lesson for me: don't belong to anything.

So, where do UFOs come from? The link between the phenomenon and the occult must be explored cautiously. Twentieth-century science is based on truths that esoteric tradition articulated centuries ago, as the SRI research in parapsychology keeps reminding us. Techniques for the projection of consciousness are slowly finding their place in experimental science. I disagree with Aimé Michel regarding the inability of the human mind to grasp truth at that level. If we allowed our consciousness to develop, who knows what we could accomplish?

As for the "higher aliens" theory, it doesn't explain the facts. Why would gods from the cosmos waste their time scaring airline pilots? *Something else is involved.* Yet none of the occult groups I have studied knows anything new or interesting about the subject. If I were to assess the results of my meetings with Manly Hall, Serge Hutin, the Amorc staff, Pauwels and Bergier, Abellio, Anton LaVey, Hanlon and his sorcerer friends, Ken Anger, Israel Regardie and even Hymenaeus Alpha, I would have to conclude that they were as confused about the problem as the man in the street or the average scientist. My search, so far, has been a failure. If I ever lose everything, I hope to keep one thing longest, namely the ability to doubt my own theories, question my own beliefs.

Belmont. Tuesday 7 January 1975.

Still in bed, medication knocks me out. I did some work at the terminal, exchanging electronic mail with Brookhaven and Connie, who gave me the latest Arpa scuttlebutt: Steve Lukasik has taken a job at Xerox, leaving the agency in disarray.

I've refined my principles: 1. Keep my distance from all groups, including the spooks: I will not become a pawn in somebody's game, even as I study the chessboard. 2. Never rely on paranormal research for financial support. 3. Only devote my skills to this work when a serious effort gets organized by people I trust (we're a long way from this) 4. Turn away disciples and groupies. I'm a good leader but shouldn't let the illusion of power fool me. 5. Define my own standards and stick to them; grow through the human adventure, apply the lessons of childhood, don't betray youthful ideals.

Belmont. Friday 10 January 1975.

The doctor thinks I have some sort of dysentery. All meetings cancelled for the week, I survive on tea and Coca-Cola. I managed to finish a proposal for the Atomic Energy Commission. Allen puts final touches on our *Edge of Reality*. I'll soon see him in Pasadena, at the AIAA meeting. He mentioned with some rancor that Mimi was "becoming a politician," running for city office in Chicago.

Peter Rogerson, an astute observer of English ufology, has sent me his investigations of an area vibrant with poltergeist, ghosts, witches and alien craft: "There's a depressing atmosphere here, hard to explain; it forms the focus of a number of Magonia cults." He sees the Geller myth as classic fairy-tale: an amoral hero breaks the rules of the techno-scientific structure. The ultimate irony resides in the observation that the New Age hero is himself nothing but an instrument of Hoova, a mindless computer in the sky. Its key for the universe turns out to be a meaningless formula.

Pasadena, Saga Motel. Later the same day.

Sandler's house is a beautiful little castle. After breakfast there we went to researcher Idabel Epperson's place. We stayed at her party long enough to shake hands and re-establish a few contacts among local ufologists. Sturrock and I drove together to the restaurant where the scientific board of Cufos was reunited. Allen read the formal agenda while Mimi, across the table from me, took notes: the group is one year old, let's review its publications, nominees for the board, fund raising campaigns, research proposals. Someone asked if there would be a report about the decisions made at the meeting we held last March, but nothing had been done. Peter Sturrock quietly asked, "What's the purpose of the scientific board?" Allen answered that this would be discussed later. First he was going to suggest new members. Davies jumped in, repeating Sturrock's question: "Why should we add new members, if we don't know the purpose of having a science board in the first place?"

We never got an answer, because the restaurant was too noisy, so we left and crowded into Peter Sturrock's room at the Saga. Allen started reading comments sent by Cufos members. One of the questions had to do with computer catalogues. Saunders said he was converting Ufocat for an IBM 370 that Standard Oil was letting him use. The system had reached 40,000 cases, but no one has seen any statistical output yet, perhaps because it's an assemblage of apples and carrots. The excuse for not releasing the catalogue was that Nicap didn't allow publication of its cases. These groups clamor against government censorship, demand openness, invite the public to submit sightings, and then they quickly lock them up. (**36**)

A radar engineer named Eugene Epstein tried to build a case for instrumenting UFO research by putting pressure on NORAD and NASA. A girl with a round face and round glasses jumped into the discussion with a passionate speech about the benefits of gas chromatography! Nobody seemed to know who she was, why she was there, or why gas chromatography was suddenly on our agenda.

The high point of the evening was a statement by Bob Nathan of JPL. He was going to take Hynek to a NASA meeting about the future of space research, after which they would meet Professor Pickering. Nathan mentioned that someone at NASA now had responsibility for UFOs. Pickering is supposed to have told Nathan he could spend as much time as he wanted on UFOs as long as nothing was public and nobody asked for money. I had the feeling that NASA, following CNES, would dip a timid toe into the mud. Kuettner, looking very much the great scientist with his silver hair and formal gray suit, warned that he was going to ask fundamental questions. ("That's about time," I thought.)

"The science community isn't moving, because they don't believe there's a real problem here. You haven't established its basic reality yet. Your best chance is to start with statistics, as we do in climate

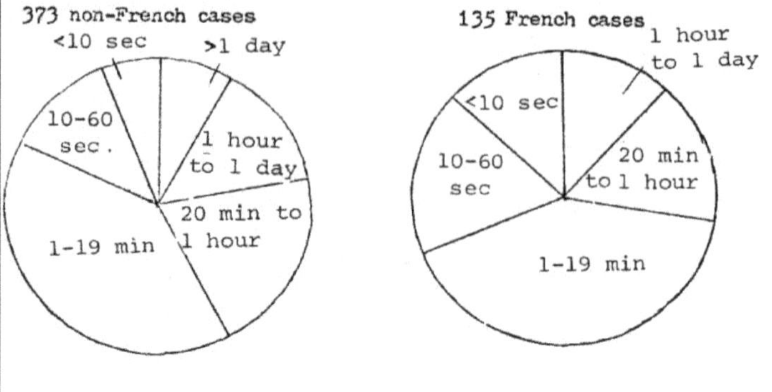

Figure 4. Sighting duration

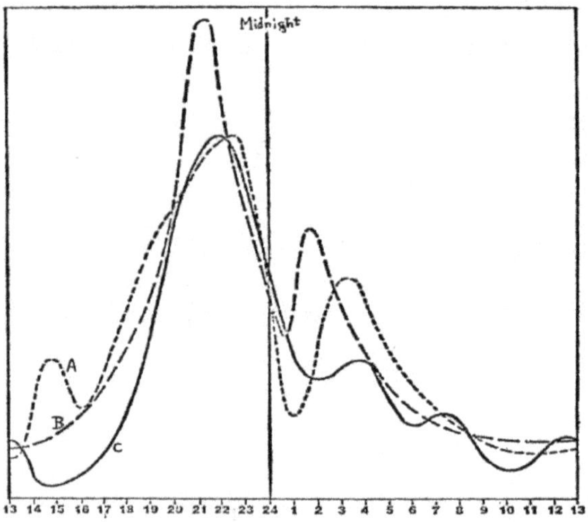

Figure 7. Frequency of type-I reports as a function of time of day

A: 362 cases prior to 1963, all countries
B: 375 cases in 1963-1970, all countries
C: 100 cases from Spain and Portugal

Fig. 16. Statistical Patterns behind the UFO Phenomenon.

I presented these findings with Poher before the 1975 AIAA meeting in Pasadena. The top graph shows the stable patterns in sighting duration, the bottom one shows the "Law of the Times" demonstrating that close encounters are not randomly distributed during a typical day but follow a fixed pattern.

studies. But you'll need the support of major scientific institutions. Vallee's work with Poher is exactly the kind of thing we need." In the ensuing discussion Allen mentioned that in one year Cufos had received 74 reports of close encounters. So where are they? Why didn't he keep his promise to make them available?

In the plane to San Francisco. Monday 20 January 1975.

Ted Phillips joined me this morning at the coffee shop. The avenue was filled with girls in short pants, convertibles cruising with the top down, a carefree scene that contrasted with his anger. Ted is intelligent and direct. For years he has been doing field investigations of physical trace cases. Last night we both heard Hynek talking about the fact that we should replace amateur investigators with "real" researchers, meaning professors, people with Ph.Ds. One physicist's idea of scientific progress was to replace the term "UFO" by "atmospheric phenomena."

"I'm gonna drop everything," said Ted. "I'm tired of talking about "investigations." We don't have any analysis, you see. I break my back digging up evidence, I send the stuff out and nothing ever comes back. I feel like a fool when the witnesses ask me what the scientists have found out. They spend their time trying to impress their colleagues instead of studying the phenomenon."

At the AIAA presentation Saunders read his paper in a monotone. I followed him with a series of slides showing the correlations between my statistics and those of Poher (figure 16). Fred gave a good summary of photographic cases.

Ted Phillips did speak, convincingly as usual. Kuettner drew lessons from our presentations in a conciliatory tone. But I don't expect anything new to come of it.

Belmont. Saturday 25 January 1975.

This prolonged illness scares me, I feel weak with lack of sleep. Janine, her mother and the kids have gone off to Spring Hill. I survive on tea and toasts, steadily losing weight. Our doctor found no bacteria. I am touching the bottom, and perhaps it is better for me to be alone now, to question my life. For a year I have been fighting the Washington windmills. Evidently Kit is an honest, intellectually rigorous analyst, but he doesn't have the right access and is biased by his own training. Perhaps it's time to leave this behind.

Yesterday I met with Ray Williams and gave him a plan for the creation of a company called InfoMedia, which would take our conferencing system to the real world. The *Financial Times* has just published an excellent article about our system.

Belmont. Tuesday 4 February 1975.

We've just returned from a short snow vacation in the Sierra, in a chalet Janine and two of her colleagues had rented out. We had six laughing kids with us, and Mamie, with whom I get along well. But I am still suffering from sharp intestinal cramps. I try to survive on pasta and heavy medication.

We have been lovers for 16 years, Janine and I. Work is as intense as ever. Price-Williams called me last night, asking me to record my dreams during his experiments with Carlos Castaneda, who is sending us psychic images of the entities he calls his “Allies” (**37**).

Belmont. Friday 7 February 1975.

I had lunch with Hal and Russell, whose project is dying for lack of support. With them was Hella Hammid, a remote viewer. I took them all to Alain's new place, the Little Store in Woodside, where his waitress Missie served them onion soup, pâté and Napoléons. I deplored that, in their rush to apply remote viewing to specific missions, they hadn't studied the information angle that seems to me of greater scientific interest, the “addressing scheme” of human perception I had suggested to Ingo as a topic of exploration.

It was that conversation two years ago that led Ingo to the idea of coordinate remote viewing, but that research never went deeper into the implications about energy and information, entropy and the linkage between mind and reality. It never developed into the systematic testing of hypotheses we had envisioned.

I gave Hal a copy of the *Invisible College* manuscript. As a physicist he'll grasp the idea of the control system but he still has trouble thinking of close encounters in terms other than nuts-and-bolts craft, in spite of his own references to esoteric teachings.

Olivier called me at the office this afternoon, very upset. Someone at school had stolen his lunch. He found the brown bag in a trash can, his sandwich still in it, but whoever had taken it kept an $18 check intended for the girl who drives him back every afternoon.

Belmont. Sunday 16 February 1975.

The doctors have finally diagnosed amoebic dysentery. I must have picked up contaminated water on a plane from some faraway land.

Friday was spent at the University of California in Santa Barbara, where the Political Science department is running communications experiments that parallel ours. In the afternoon I met with John Griffin, a friendly fellow interested in consciousness and martial arts. He is in contact with George Hunt Williamson alias Michel d'Obrenovic, alleged witness to George Adamski's famous contact.

Janine and I went to Charles Musès' house for dinner. An enigmatic figure, Musès is something of a recluse. We spent the night and the next day in his white house with the green door, hidden behind luxurious trees, a veritable museum: 35,000 books (most of them in boxes in the garage), hundreds of art objects, the home of a true collector of the strange, magical and esoteric. Charles lives in simple style among pictures, statues, instruments piled up wherever the hand has abandoned them. Christiane Musès, who is French, was warmly hospitable. The guest room, too, was filled with books, correspondence, a generator of negative ions, African masks. The bed was barely accessible through this marvellous chaos.

Belmont. Monday 17 February 1975.

Today is a holiday. I have time to design a landscape for Olivier's electric train, to go buy a lilac tree with Janine, and to reflect on our visit to Musès, a remarkable scholar, a gifted mathematician and scholar of magic. Unfortunately Charles had nothing to say about UFOs. Esoteric philosophy is an operational body of rules and skills. This led us to discuss control systems. Sade observed that, if one gave pleasure to another human being, one could not be certain of being the source of that pleasure, while the reverse situation was true for pain. Both Charles and I think this notion absurd. Anton once made this subtle remark that in a sado-masochistic relationship it was always the slave who had true power, another fact that had escaped the attention of the Divine Marquis.

A weak point in Charles' makeup is his desire to be recognized by the fools who rule the establishment. I can see this weakness because I am a victim of it myself. It comes from pride, the worst sin -- perhaps the only sin. Man's fundamental need and weakness is to belong to a group, to be accepted, recognized, nurtured and loved.

Belmont. Wednesday 19 February 1975.

On Monday night we had a memorable dinner *en famille*. Alain, Mamie and Janine did the cooking, Missie helped set the table, Kit came over for a long talk about Lopez Rega, the cults of California and my theories of control systems. He was flying up from Los Angeles where he'd met Sandler and was thrilled.

Meanwhile Hal and Russell, whom I met by chance today in a Menlo Park restaurant, confirmed they were running out of funds, their salaries had been cut. Mamie flew back to France today. I'm still weak from dysentery.

Belmont. Saturday 8 March 1975.

The Institute for the Future is trying to keep me in an academic role. Roy came into my office and told me that I would be wrong to leave. "You may be in a cage here," he said, "but the cage has no locked door. Why don't you stay? You won't be happy with the stress of day-to-day business on your shoulders." I love the Institute, but I do need to tackle new challenges not found in academia.

The day was spent playing with my children, the happy life of the suburban father. Tonight we are all going to a concert at Nueva School. We needed such a quiet time: Janine's car was hit by a truck two days ago. Fortunately she was unhurt.

Charles Musès and Claudio Naranjo came over to our house last week, with a charming sculptress. They spoke of Buddhism, consciousness, training the Soul. Berkeley is filling up with mystics from every corner of the world, especially Tibetan "Rimpoches" who mumble aphorisms. What they do find here is booze, big cars, wealthy Americans who long to be saved from the emptiness that has followed the Hippie revolution, and armies of adoring girls, more than willing to sit on their lap to get closer to enlightenment.

Musès has come closer to grasping basic principles, witness his article on *The Real Revolution* (**38**):

> The function of a State in practice is to deny or suppress the creative development of the individuals subject to that State (...) No course in our universities is given in the psychology of deception which actually governs the lives of people today. Most people's lives are lived in circles, not evolutionary spirals. Only in rare instances is this effect of cultural hypnotism overcome.

Belmont. Sunday 9 March 1975.

On Friday I had lunch with Colonel "First Class" Floryan, who brought me fresh news of his friend Manuel the abductee. We drove over to the Little Store in his old blue car, a Chrysler in a poor state of maintenance, with a medal of the Virgin Mary hanging on the driver's side. In the opening months of WWII Floryan was in charge of counter-espionage for the east coast shoreline from Long Island to Atlantic City. "What was striking was the large number of observations of German ships reported by sincere witnesses, which were without any foundation whatsoever. In Intelligence you quickly learn that the social milieu and the respectability of the witness don't amount to much."

My magistrate father had often made the same remark.

"How are we going to find out what's going on, then?" I asked.

"It's a question of method. Hynek and you have been trained as scientists, with processes that work best in the lab. Pictures and tape recordings, witness testimony, that's fine, but it doesn't necessarily mean anything. Think about it: the phenomena are under the control of the other side, don't you see? It can always mask reality by using appropriate cutouts; it provides you with what it wants you to get. In science, if you have 95% of the data you're happy; you can make excellent inferences about the phenomenon, can't you?"

He took a big spoonful of Alain's rich onion soup, wiped the melted cheese from his chin and went on. "In my business, if I have 95% of the data I must suspect it's the wrong 95%, namely those facts my opposition wanted me to have! My job is to go out in search of the missing 5%. Only, it's going to be more expensive, the cost curve is much steeper. That's the difference between me and you, between espionage and science. The only way to get to the truth is to talk to a lot of people, looking for tiny absurd indications."

Colonel Floryan is cheerful. He looks like my old uncle Maurice: A big face with lively eyes, a good sense of humor. He is stocky, squeezed into a three-piece suit too small for him. Floryan is not a bigot. He has his own language to speak of people who study paranormal phenomena. He says we are "in the Work."

"Somebody should concentrate on the Gestapo archives," he added. Jacques Bergier had spoken to me in the same way, with a sense of painful foreboding. "Those Nazi thugs knew a lot of things. They had electromagnetic devices that affected both the physical and the psychic. Look up *Zodiac and Swastika*, many names in that book (**39**). Talk to your friends in France, don't do the research alone. Find a retired librarian or a military archivist to guide you. The Germans were *in the Work* a long time before the War."

Belmont. Saturday 22 March 1975.

On Sunday night I had dinner in New York with Professor Henry David and Roy Amara, after a session of editing with Bill Whitehead in the bar of the Gotham. The next day I presented the concept of InfoMedia to the Institute Trustees. On Monday I was in Washington for meetings at NSF and Army Matériel Command. On Tuesday, in Texas for a presentation on networking before a group of skeptical educators. The fiery sky reminded me of our first arrival there. The astronomy department has relocated into a new building, and De Vaucouleurs is off to McDonald observatory. Part of Hynek's old team has moved from Evanston to Austin: Karl Henize with his well-financed work, along with Jim Wray and Lazenby, the photographer who kindly helped me in the Sixties. On Thursday night I landed in El Paso and waited for Hynek's plane. We spent the next two days at Corralitos observatory, going over the final draft of *Edge of Reality*.

Belmont. Sunday 23 March 1975.

Physicists who conduct experiments with Uri Geller at Lawrence Livermore report paranormal apparitions of their own - globes of light in their bedrooms, materialized objects. Infrared pictures taken during Geller's metal-bending show two shadows for every object, as if two intense infrared beams had converged. The primary source of this news is Ron Hawke: Geller has convinced him that he was part of an elite group destined to uncover the ultimate truth! (**40**)

A couple of weeks ago Kit met in Virginia with Russell in Hal's hotel room. They had started to discuss a case in which a mysterious mechanical arm appeared out of thin air in the bedroom of a Livermore engineer when the three of them suddenly heard a key turning in the door. Hal and Kit positioned themselves on either side and jumped on the intruder as soon as he pushed the door in, grabbing a little fellow with only one arm! The poor man swore he had been given the wrong key. They called the front desk. Indeed he had gone to the wrong room, but why did his key open Hal's door?

Spring Hill. Sunday 30 March 1975.

My daughter just came into my room: “When someone I love dies, like Papy, I make a feeling song...”

Spring Hill is magnificent today. The three waterfalls that converge at the head of our canyon drop down over 60 feet of rock to tumble into the gorge. The Russian river is flooding, mud swirls in eddies. A canoe has overturned in Cloverdale, a man drowned.

Olivier got mad at me because I was taking his picture. In a sulking mood, he went to lean against the wall of our old barn. The scene struck me: his anger and solitude in the midst of towering trees, the explosion of Mendocino Springtime, millions of joyful colors from tender green to ochre, and all the gold in the willow that embraced him like a great nurturing giant. He saw none of that, mad as he was against me, the world.

I plan another trip to Santa Barbara to talk to John Griffin who promised to introduce me to George Hunt Williamson. I read his *Other Tongues, Other Flesh* with puzzlement. I can't decide if Williamson is sincere or pulling our leg when he describes the symbols on the shoes of the Venusian who greeted George Adamski in the desert, a scene he claims to have witnessed, thus helping turn Adamski's fanciful books into international best-sellers.

In the willow near our barn a swarm of bees hum in the sunshine, but in Southeast Asia people are dying. Pnom Penh is surrounded. Refugees are fighting one another in Danang for a place aboard the last American helicopters.

Montecito. Saturday 5 April 1975.

John Griffin, a gentle bearded giant, introduced me to George Hunt Williamson today. *Prince d'Obrenovic van Lazar, Duke of Sumadya*, (as he likes to call himself, although the last male descendant of the d'Obrenovic line was assassinated in Yugoslavia in 1903) is a dynamic and likeable man, his voice clear and assured. “The Prince,” who lives in the chic section of Montecito, says he supports himself through lectures and royalties, which is difficult to believe. I was told that he was more prosaically employed by a local private school. His interest in UFOs had been aroused when he read one of Keyhoe's early books while studying the local Indians. Later he served as marketing manager for an NBC affiliate in Arizona (he obtained a degree in anthropology along the way) when he met a radio ham who got messages from space.

I asked Williamson what he believed about George Adamski.

"I don't believe a single word of his second book," he answered. "But there were times when George was sincere, even if his public statements were often absurd." When I pointed out that this attitude made no sense, he didn't defend Adamski, but insisted that he had seen a saucer on the day of the famous 1952 contact, even though he never saw any being, Venusian or otherwise.

"Adamski had gone forward behind a dune by himself. I couldn't see what was going on. I did find the imprints in the sand where Adamski showed them to me. I got carried away by all the enthusiasm," he confessed. He went on to tell us of purple letters floating in the air in his bathroom, which reminded me of Ray Stanford's tale of hawk feathers seen with Geller.

After Williamson's departure I met Bob Morris, current president of the Parapsychology Association. He wears round spectacles and short hair, in contrast with current California fashion. He's a classic product of the Duke University School, a student of Rhine. We listened to a tape Wilbert Smith had sent Williamson 20 years ago. Smith talked about a "time field" that he theorized should be orthogonal to the electric and magnetic fields. As an explanation for UFOs it's a bit simple-minded. Smith's Alien friends had instructed him to build a device by winding a wire around a ferrite cylinder eight inches long, one inch in diameter. It was supposed to emit a time field and telekinetic effects.

Belmont. Saturday 12 April 1975.

Hal tells me that he thinks Musès is one of the most intelligent men he's ever met. Janine and I spent the day in Santa Cruz with the children, playing in the sand, running up the levee to watch the boats in the channel, stopping for ice cream on the way.

There are some curious things in Williamson's book. He cites a case that is supposed to have happened early in 1954 near March Field, in California. Several young men saw a saucer on the ground. They came close to it, but a man suddenly appeared in front of them, raised his arm and threw a fireball at their car. When they described the man to the sheriff, *they said he was wearing a half-mask made of metal*, which reminds me of the Lead Mask case in Niteroi, near Rio. Williamson notes the similarity with a 1953 case in Italy: a man saw two occupants of a saucer who also wore half masks made of metal.

Williamson believes that the U.S. government has had a contact with occupants and that a secret project, called NQ-707, is under way at Edwards Air Force Base to establish a radio link with the saucers, inviting them to come down near the Salton Sea. Similarly, the phenomenon of self-erasing magnetic tapes, which I thought was peculiar to Puharich, allegedly plagued Williamson for years. He also told me that two amateur investigators named Karl Hunrath and Wilbur Wilkinson took off from Gardena airport to track down a UFO case on 11 November 1953 and were never heard from again.

Belmont. Sunday 13 April 1975.

Hynek has gone to see Donald Rumsfeld at the White House. Everybody was gloomy there because Nixon had just made a rather poor speech. Allen described the work of the Center, putting it at the disposal of the government. He "had a responsibility before the scientific community," and didn't want to waste his time tracking down false reports, he insisted. Therefore he had the need to know if there was a secret study somehere. Rumsfeld replied abruptly: "You do NOT have a need to know." Now Allen wonders if the man was reacting purely as a bureaucrat, or if he really knew something.

At the Institute, Roy Amara has confided to me that four months ago he was contacted by an FBI agent who wanted to know about our research: the Soviets were buying all our publications. We're on their hot list. That explains the visit I had in December.

Belmont. Saturday 19 April 1975.

Most of my efforts now go towards providing my team with funds to continue its work after I leave to run my own company. I have sent

NSF a new proposal. This week we had Gerry and Sally for dinner, as well as Thad Wilson and a cable television entrepreneur named Aaron Katz who wants to explore the potential of computer conferencing in connection with his news programs.

Belmont. Saturday 26 April 1975.

Jack Sarfatti called. He is researching a movie on extraterrestrial contact with scientist Fred Wolf. They told Francis Ford Coppola that Aliens were in the process of contacting humans, to which the filmmaker replied: "Oh yeah? Then why don't they contact me?"

Sarfatti, witty and quick, answered: "But they do! They're contacting you by sending me." The upshot of all this is that we're all invited for dinner at Coppola's house.

Kit is now talking to every ufologist worth his salt. Last night he told me that the Holloman film that Sandler was trying so hard to locate had been withdrawn from the library by a Captain Harner who has since been transferred! But he can't find any trace of any Harner, or any such film at the Pentagon.

I spent the afternoon with Paul Moller, a professor of aeronautical engineering at U.C. Davis who's built a saucer-shaped vehicle that flies a few feet off the ground, using a series of propellers powered by snowmobile engines. He is a young fellow in blue jeans, interested in UFOs. Moller's research contradicts Claude Poher's statements about the aerodynamic properties of a disk. Poher concluded that disks were aerodynamically poor. "That's only true as a gross generalization," Moller told me. "The situation changes if you take into account the properties of the interface between the object and the air."

Last night I had a discussion with Don Hanlon as we walked near the Cliff House. A full moon threw an eerie light on the tormented landscape of the rugged shore with the waves of the Pacific breaking on Seal Rock in bursts of silver spray. He conceded that connections were possible between Crowley's O.T.O. and the Nazis. But has the relationship continued? (**41**) Witchcraft groups are using the latest techniques in brainwashing and hypnosis, often in connection with nitrous oxide, leading to amnesia and irreversible post-hypnotic suggestions. The gas itself is undetectable; the only sign is a slight prickling of the extremities. So there may well be an occult organization that uses the UFO phenomenon for its own ends, and it could reach into higher levels of the military or Intelligence community. My concern is that a conversion to the belief in Aliens may become a convenient lever for any group with strong ambition.

On Thursday evening we had a poltergeist. At 8:30 p.m., as Janine was loading plates into the dishwasher, an electric clock hanging from a nail on the wall leapt out to the center of the kitchen where it landed without breaking, still attached to its wire!

Belmont. Wednesday 30 April 1975.

This is the night of Walpurgis. In Vietnam the last few helicopters have painfully taken off with the last few Marines, a scene of chaos. News cameras show overloaded copters crashing on the deck of ships or hitting the sides. Those that landed safely were immediately unloaded and pushed into the sea to make room for more. The communications fiasco was only equal to the political upheaval. General Ky, after condemning those who left, gave orders to "defend Saigon to the death" and ran to the nearest American helicopter to get away from the inferno he had contributed to creating.

Last night Janine and I had dinner with Francis Ford Coppola and his quiet wife Eleanor at their big white house on Broadway: high ceilings, Miro paintings, precious wood, leather furniture, enclosed garden, large windows framing the Golden Gate Bridge. We met Jack Sarfatti there, along with Fred Wolf and Bob Tobin (their book *Space, Time and Beyond* has just been published by Bill Whitehead). Jeff Mishlove had come from Berkeley, serious and well organized.

Sarfatti and Wolf summarized their theory: "We're all contactees..." Sarfatti's interest in the paranormal dates from a series of childhood incidents: a computer-like voice kept calling him over the phone, he claims, feeding him advanced physical formulas. He read quotes of Wheeler and Einstein that he pulled out of a briefcase while Wolf spoke of the Kabala, Geller and quantum mechanics.

Belmont. Monday 5 May 1975.

Fred has just come back from France, where he got into an argument with Aimé about mysticism: he wouldn't believe that nuns could survive without eating. When Aimé, teasing him, cited the case of a saintly woman who hadn't urinated for years, Fred accused him of believing every silly claim made by fanatical Catholic doctors. Aimé walked out and slammed the door, but he came back an hour later and resumed the conversation as if nothing had happened.

Poher continues to study UFO physics but he confesses that it hasn't taken him far. Following my advice he is putting all the cases on his computer, and he's met Commandant Tizané whose stories of hauntings have shaken his rationalistic underpinnings. Poher told Fred he would make one more attempt at a strict physical approach and that he would give up if he didn't succeed. Guérin behaved in typical fashion. Irate at first, he refused to see Fred, then told him abruptly to come at 10 A.M. for an hour; they were still talking at five in the evening. All of them said they liked *Invisible College* but that my Control System theory was "too speculative." Time will tell.

"Allen has given up the post of chairman; he's determined to go wherever his fantasy will take him. The Center is very important to him," Fred said. "Yet when I attended the latest meeting I found myself in a roomful of strangers, housewives, nice folks with little understanding of science. David Saunders was there, but he went upstairs to work on the files. Peter Sturrock has declined to join the scientific board. Allen is afraid others will leave."

Belmont. Sunday 11 May 1975.

My illness finally over, I feel stronger, ready to change my life. I must be available to my children, without ever giving them the impression they're interfering with my work. They are more important than any trip, any book. We spent yesterday on the laguna near Pescadero, playing in the sand, exploring the creek in a rubber raft that threw us laughing into the waves of the ocean.

Hal and Russell, with whom I had lunch on Thursday, were

depressed: Bart Cox, their manager, has told them they had to find new financing or close the door. Yet they have just completed a series of four successful experiments with Hella Hammid.

Belmont. Tuesday 20 May 1975.

Louis Pouzin, a French networking expert, came over for lunch yesterday. He told me the sad story of the French government turning its back on Europe one more time. The C2I Company that manufactures the machines of the *Plan Calcul* will enter into an alliance with Honeywell, which will pick up a number of contracts guaranteed by the State.

Jim Hurtak, who now wears a béret coquettishly set on the side of his head, wants me to take part in a television documentary (I said no). He promised to give me a copy of his Enochian keys, alien information he says he received through a beam of light. His conversation was peppered with muddled esoteric references: "The Fraternity is coming to earth, in accordance with the Council of Nine, twelve and one hundred and forty-four..."

Belmont. Sunday 25 May 1975.

Our daughter was seven on Wednesday. We had a big cake for her; the neighbor's kids joined us. We went to Nueva school to attend a concert given by ten-year old Dimitri Cogan and yesterday morning we drove up to Spring Hill where we cleaned up the redwood cabins, watched the lunar eclipse and setup Olivier's tent in the pasture.

I mentioned the theory that earthquakes often coincided with the full moon; sure enough we felt the cabins shake this morning, fortunately without damage; the children were impressed.

After leaving the ranch we drove up to Willits along Black Bart road, which quickly turns into a dusty trail. We had to ford the little river half a dozen times, to the joy of the children who played in pools of water where we could see catfish and eels.

Aaron Katz has agreed to sponsor the world's first psychic network conference, as I had suggested in response to his offer to research the capabilities of the new software. Over lunch with Arthur Hastings we discussed the project and ended up joining Hal at SRI. He had a visitor: Richard Bach, author of *Jonathan Livingston Seagull,* a best-seller derived from a personal vision. Richard is giving money to help Puthoff continue his work. He fell in love with the idea of staying in touch with all of us through the computer.

Washington, D.C. Sunday 1 June 1975.

Roy Amara, Bob Johansen and I have travelled to Washington together to attend a World Future Society conference. I soon got tired of the gossip about which pundit was sleeping with which politician, and who would get the next fat grant to research the environmental needs of poor countries, so I excused myself as soon as I could. I spent the morning at the CIA in Langley with Tom Belden, who gave me a demonstration of his conferencing system.

Over lunch Kit said that a friend of his recently attended a witchcraft session in San Francisco, where he actually saw the Devil. Later he was shown a tiny pipe connected to the central cauldron. It gave off a gas which made the participants susceptible to suggestion, after which they were programmed to agree on features of the apparition. Some of their adepts swear they have received communications from higher beings.

I went back to the hotel after a visit to the Pentagon, where Roy and I tried to explain networking research to a colonel who didn't understand the first word we said.

Belmont. Saturday 7 June 1975.

My daughter parades around wearing an armband she earned in school (it reads “gerbil expert”) and a Planetary Citizen button I brought back for her from the World Future Society conference.

Roy Amara and I have started to look for funding for InfoMedia. On Wednesday we visited General Electric in Rockville, Maryland. Their network is the largest one in existence, but they are scared of the legal implications of communication: could the postal authorities outlaw our proposed system?

I spent the afternon with Don Hanlon at his flat. He said Regardie was furious at occultist Kenneth Grant who aspired at Crowley's spiritual succession. Regardie even wrote a bitter review in *Gnostica,* taking issue with what he called Grant's obsessions. Don and I are intrigued by the symbol of the winged disk: "Aiwass" appeared to Crowley in Egypt as an Assyrian. The Holloman beings in Sandler's movie are Assyrian too, and wear a classic turban.

Don and I spoke of sorcery and nitrous oxide. He confirmed that his occultist friends did use it, not just to induce "astral" travel but as a recreational drug. As for its use in hypnosis, Don hadn't heard of it. We discussed similarities with abduction reports in terms of amnesia and impressions of astral trips. Don believes that Crowley once took a disciple on such a trip by using the gas. Don himself once participated in such a ritual that ended in confusion.

Another topic than Don continues researching is the connection between Crowley and Parsons: "Don't forget that in 1945 Jack Parsons, who belonged to the *Agapè* Lodge of the O.T.O along with Hubbard, went into the Mojave desert where he met a spiritual being he regarded as a Venusian, an incarnation of Babalon that anticipates Adamski by seven years!" He said. "Following this meeting Parsons wrote a science-fiction novel that was burned by his wife after his death. She said Jack's ghost instructed her to do it!"

Jimmy Page, of Led Zeppelin fame, multi-millionaire friend of Anger and John Michell, has bought Crowley's Boleskine Castle on the shore of Loch Ness. In an interview with William Burroughs he recently mentioned the special effects of trance music, creating hypnotic impressions in the audience. Burroughs makes reference to infra-sounds (below 16 Hertz, with greatest impact around 7 Hertz) once investigated for the military by a Frenchman named Gavreau.

Belmont. Sunday 15 June 1975.

Father's Day. Olivier and I went canoeing on Stevens Creek reservoir, after which we all had dinner at Alain's restaurant. Olivier gave me a painting of his and his sister improvised a magic show.

We're going to see *Les Visiteurs du Soir* with Gerald and Sally. Tomorrow I fly to New York. Everything else is moving forward: our psychic conference, the first such experiment over a computer network, is under way. It includes Ingo in Manhattan, Richard Bach in Florida, Jean Baudot in Montréal, and a group of other participants that includes Brendan O'Regan and Gerald Askevold. The latter has supplied me with a series of unique geological samples from the USGS collections that will serve as targets for remote-viewing experiments.

Galleys of *Edge of Reality* and *Invisible College* have arrived, the latter in excellent shape, the former full of errors.

Belmont. Saturday 21 June 1975.

Tonight Arthur Hastings will test our software from his home in Mountain View over the conferencing network, along with me and Ingo Swann, who will take part from a terminal I have installed at his flat in Greenwich Village.

In New York, business tycoon George Vila, chairman of Uniroyal, drove us to IBM headquarters in his little red car. Vila is a big forceful man who drives like a mexican cabbie, going through red lights and frequently commenting on the varied sex appeal of passing women, to the horror of the more dignified Roy Amara.

The headquarters of IBM are a big white castle on a grassy green hilltop. We met their executive VP for industrial relations and his two assistants. When I plugged in my portable computer terminal under his desk and borrowed his phone to call the network he became visibly confused. And when I started exchanging messages with Thad Wilson in California he thought the demo was canned. The meeting concluded with a suggestion that they "study" our system, taking apart our source code, so we declined.

The next day I went to Arpa and USGS and chaired a session on computer conferencing at the Bureau of Standards. The weather was unbearably muggy. The economic crisis has thrown into the streets a diverse subpopulation of unemployed people and idle young toughs. Broken refrigerators rust away in dilapidated houses a few blocks from the White House.

A few hours later I was back in New York, which didn't look much better. The city is bankrupt, thousands of employees are about to be laid off. At my hotel a few gloomy Italian waiters seemed about to collapse with tiredness and old age. George Vila came back, this time to take us to Western Union headquarters in New Jersey -- another castle on another green hilltop, where he walked in as if he owned the place. We met Johnny Johnson there, a former Air Force Brigadier General who saw our demonstration, was impressed and told us they would have to do a market study before giving us an answer: Another impossible six-month delay!

The manager who drove us back to La Guardia lived in Wanaque. He was surprised when I told him why I knew the area. "I've seen some unexplained lights over the lake myself," he said, "I didn't tell anyone, of course." A member of a volunteer rescue team, he'd heard a police message about three high-altitude UFOs. The Air Force was sending a jet. He came out in time to watch the plane and saw the three lights vanish. When the jet went away they reappeared.

Roy and I flew on to Dallas, where we met with top managers from Texas Instruments.

Belmont. Tuesday 24 June 1975.

Allen, to whom I spoke on Monday, railed against Regnery because of mistakes in the galleys of *Edge of Reality*. Allen has spoken to one of the directors of Nicap, General Richardson, who offered him the chairman's role. He countered with the suggestion of a joint research agreement where Cufos would put its scientific talent behind Nicap in exchange for money. I am skeptical of this scheme, for the simple reason that Cufos has no scientific talent and Nicap no money.

In her latest letter Maman tells me about her recent trip to Darmstadt and Heidelberg, where she found memories of the Passavant family. In the museum at Frankfurt hangs a portrait of Johann David Passavant, the friend of Goethe who went to Italy with him. He was the uncle of my grandfather. The curator of the sculpture museum in Frankfurt is a Passavant as well.

Belmont. Wednesday 2 July 1975.

A busy week of conferencing. We performed a preliminary telepathy experiment over the net last Friday, and over the weekend we began formal tests with the rock samples selected by Gerry, which participants were asked to describe by remote viewing. They type their impression directly into the system for everone to read.

I have insisted to base the experiments on rock samples rather than abstract symbols like cards or drawings because I feel parapsychology should address the physical world in all its diversity. Our samples have unique beauty. They include gold ore, silver, magnetite, and a block of europium that can only come from one place on earth, a mine in Death Valley. It will be interesting to see which parameters come through, either in the telepathy tests (when an experimenter holds the sample in hand at a particular time of day) or in the remote viewing tests, which use double-blind, sealed bags.

At an SRI meeting this past week I had a chance to talk to Saul Paul as well as Hal, Russell and Arthur Hastings. I heard that Tim Leary (recently visited in jail by Carl Sagan and Drake to discuss non-human intelligence) had recorded a series of statements. So Janine and I drove up to Cotati to listen to these tapes. Sarfatti began expounding about physics while one of his barefoot acolytes made a beeline for the potato chips, sat in a corner and went to sleep. Saul Paul Sirag came with Elizabeth Rauscher. A lively crowd assembled.

Leary's tapes are brillant, controversial, hard-hitting. He points out that evolution is simply too complicated to be explained by Darwinism. He believes in a higher form of intelligence that communicates with us in a latent way, through the nervous system it has given us to decode. “I'm bored with the body people,” he says of the hippies, solely concerned with physical well-being, massages... He doesn't believe in “mushy hindu heavens” either, he states, adding that he thinks like a scientist, in terms of reproducible, localisable phenomena. He mistrusts humanists, Buddhists, flying saucer believers. None of that seemed to disturb the assembled hippies, humanists and flying-saucer believers... They held hands, formed a “circle of energy.” One girl fell into a trance.

Belmont. Saturday 19 July 1975.

American and Russian astronauts have docked Soyuz with Apollo and shook hands in orbit, truly an exploit. Olivier is at a camp in Utah. Catherine flew off to Paris by herself, in her dark purple suit with embroided flowers. Now we enjoy life without kids, getting up voluptuously at any hour we want. Allen is elated because he'd received an invitation to Brazil that includes an opportunity to address the Brazilian Congress next month.

As we proceed with the judging of our psychic experiments, the correlations between descriptions of the samples (particularly those containing salt crystal or opal) and the actual targets are striking. Ingo and Richard Bach produced the most consistent matches, with the rest of us at the noise level. Some of the properties, like magnetism or unique geographic features, were missed. It is notable that there is no difference in results between the telepathy tests and remote viewing, as if the human intermediary was irrelevant in the transmission of information.

Belmont. Tuesday 5 August 1975.

Last Wednesday we drove off on a holiday trip, stopping in Auburn in the Sierra foothills. The next day we went through Reno and Ely where we spent the night. I wanted to visit the site where, in February last year, two men driving a truck had the classic encounter with a luminous object that Allen and I relate in our book (**42**).

We drove along the same road at night, looking for any features that could explain their sighting. We found none. The landscape is a desert tapestry of faraway mountains, short bushes, dry grass, occasional marshes. As we drove along we spoke softly, stopping once to roam around the ghost town of Frisco: 6,000 inhabitants a century ago, none today. The silver mine is still there, its rusty machines scattered around crumbled walls.

As we approached Utah the scale became grandiose. It took hours to reach the first of three mountain ranges that separated us from Olivier's camp. There was water now, a trout stream, cottonwood with trembling leaves. The road turned to a dirt trail, bordering a precipice that reminded me of my drive in the Alps, chasing the elusive Ummites.

As the climbing got tougher the Volvo started coughing, the transmission gave up; a stench of burning oil replaced the scents of the mountain. The car reluctantly took us to a paradise, a blue lake in the forest, deer grazing among log cabins.

We slept in Cedar City, left the car with a mechanic, and drove back in a rented Chevy, in a stunning landscape of cliffs and ravines. We finally reached Navajo Trails, following the river that comes down from the Aquarius plateau, plunging into wild colors of tumbling rocks.

We found our boy there, his nose scorched by the sun, walking around bare chested. He showed us the fish he had caught, the belt he made out of a piece of leather. He told us about his week-long horseback excursion. We drove back in second gear, through Las Vegas and Barstow along the road that stretches between Edwards AFB and Death Valley. I'll never buy another Volvo.

Belmont. Monday 11 August 1975.

The development of computer networks moves forward in California while the rest of the planet sinks in old conflicts rooted in ancient cultures. Will the two worlds, the American technical vision on one side and the old stumbling planetary reality on the other, ever comfort each other? Or are we going to witness a battle among two dreamers who fight because, having abruptly fallen from the same bed, they discover that they were not having the same nightmare?

The annual convention of amateur astronomers was held over the week-end in San Francisco. I was a guest on a panel with Barney Oliver (vice-president for technology at H-P) and John Billingham, head biologist at NASA-Ames, both strong skeptics about UFOs. Harold Weaver, the Berkeley astronomer, was our chairman. I was able to measure once again the huge distance between the discourse of the scientists and the intellectual interests of the public.

Belmont. Sunday 17 August 1975.

We are trying to chase away the dark memory of a disastrous trip to Spring Hill, where local kids trashed our cabins, throwing our clothes into the creek, tearing down bushes and polluting the spring. We spent a rough night in a motel and swore we'd sell the place, where we keep sinking what little spare money we should be saving. The next day, of course, we were seduced once again by the sheer magnificence of the site. As soon as we came home the phone started ringing. Sightings are starting up again. Unknown flying objets have been reported two days in a row near San Jose.

Dick Haines, who went to see one of the witnesses, found him being interviewed by a private detective.

On Wednesday night I attended a meeting of contactees at the Bechtel International center on the Stanford campus. Eight serious people said they had abandoned everything in life to follow a middled-aged couple, "the Two", Marshall Applewhite and Bonnie Nettles, who believe they will soon leave the earth, transcending death in the process, transforming themselves from caterpillar to butterfly, becoming eternal.

The surprising fact to me was the feverish feeling that spread through the audience. Some 40 people swarmed over "the Two", begging them to reveal how to transcend reality, to reach a higher level.

Someone asked about any fees for those who joined.

"It only costs your life!" they answered cheerfully. (**43**)

I was amazed at people's willingness to become converts.

Santa Barbara. Saturday 23 August 1975.

The Parapsychology Association is meeting in this town, an opportunity for me to see Williamson again. He is married to the daughter of an actor from the Thirties who belongs to Montecito high society. He made some horrible coffee for us, or rather boiled it. We sat on the lawn to discuss his adventures at an esoteric monastery of the Seven Rays in central Peru, whose "external" existence is supposed to have come to an end about 1965. Dr. Laughead (pronounced "Low-head") was with the group. When they arrived in Lima he claimed that he had a contact with extraterrestrials. He was eventually pushed out, according to Williamson.

The parapsychology conference is a boring affair, attended by many of my friends: Arthur Hastings, Brendan O'Regan, Stanley Krippner, Targ and Puthoff, Charles Tart, Jean Mayo, Hella Hammid, Bob and Joanna Morris, Jule Eisenbud, Alan Vaughan and of course Madame Mathey.

I also met Charles Honorton and an extraordinary explorer, geologist and journalist named Pamela de Maigret, who told me many personal stories about South American UFOs.

Belmont. Sunday 24 August 1975.

To taste real freedom one must drive along the Pacific Coast highway as I did yesterday, with the mountains on the left still shrouded in morning fog. I was going to L.A. to pick up my daughter. Along the way I thought about the inspiring but idealistic speech Willis Harman had given about impending social changes to be precipitated by recognition of man's psychic abilities.

Pamela de Maigret, more realistic, told me about her observations in Brazil, where she did geological research and operated several mines. Levy-Strauss had understood nothing about the "savages" of the Amazon and their legends about mankind coming down from the stars in silver birds, she said.

Pamela used to belong to a spiritualist group headed up by a Brazilian woman. Most of what they did was white magic, except when they cast a spell on a man who had run away from the woman's daughter and her child. He fell sick but did not return, so a final spell was cast. He died shortly therafter. Pamela used her influence around the city to order an autopsy. The pathologist found his stomach inexplicably ruptured.

After the conference I went to LAX to meet my daughter, who jumped to kiss me as she came out of Customs. We drove back to San Francisco, singing "*Meunier, tu dors*" at the top of our lungs.

Belmont. Wednesday 27 August 1975.

On Monday morning I was flying again, to Chicago this time, so I rented a car to go see Allen in Evanston. I found him at the old observatory, which looked rundown. He had two French visitors: Alain Boudier, who has a consulting office near Nantes (**44**) and Sabine de la Panouse, a woman from Winetka who served as Boudier's interpreter. Boudier wants to organize a lecture tour for Allen and influence the French government, where he claims to have high level friends.

In contact with Boudier's enthusiasm Allen caught fire, launching into a dozen plans, ignoring my more sedate research proposal. After dinner we picked up the galleys of *Edge of Reality*. Allen mentioned that Saunders was making a gift of his Ufocat computer file to Cufos to justify a deduction from his taxes, adding there was little prospect of getting useful statistics out of Ufocat, where good and bad cases are mixed together and blurred by an obscure coding system.

Allen had an early flight to Youngstown (Ohio) to interview policemen who had seen a UFO. I don't understand how he can cover so much ground with such zest and energy, and have so little to show for it in terms of tangible results. I got up at seven and went to Chicago, where I took a nostalgic drive through Bryn Mawr. I had to see the old subway station where I had waited for Janine on so many evenings of snow and rain. Later in the day, at the annual meeting of the Chemistry Society at the LaSalle Hotel, I gave a presentation on the use of computer networks for science research (**45**), after which I walked through the Loop. There was high ozone content in the air. A pollution alert had been declared. I left without regrets.

Belmont. Saturday 30 August 1975.

Reading Williamson's first book, *The Saucers Speak!* published in 1954, I find some puzzling things that force me to reconsider my view of the early West Coast believers. They may have been naive, but they were experiencing something odd. For instance, they were puzzled by shortwave communications from "Affa," the same mystery source that would tantalize the CIA and Art Lundahl five years later. The result was to push them into the arms of Adamski: they started believing anything without discrimination. Here we are 20 years later, Williamson is pennyless and broken, and he regrets his credulity of the early years. He has severed connections with the field, so effectively that even Jerome Clark thinks him dead, calling him "the late George Williamson".

Allen still says we should compile our "twenty best cases", which makes me laugh because in 1963 we used to talk about compiling our "one hundred best cases."

Yesterday I met an abductee named Helen. She had never heard of me but found the Institute in the phone book and called up under pretense of looking for a job. She was actually looking for a sponsor for a revolutionary energy source, an idea that came from a flying saucer encounter. During the summer of 1968 she was in a car with her boyfriend John. She was sitting behind the driver, a fellow named Don. They were returning to L.A. from a concert in Lompoc where Don and John had performed. They'd driven for about 15 minutes when they saw a bright white object detach itself from the hills. It maneuvered for half an hour, approaching less than 200 feet from them, in her estimation. Four beams of light reportedly came out of the object and focused on the passengers. Caught in the beam, she felt her body extend into space, beyond the car. The light followed them until Burbank, she claimed.

Hal and Russell were at the same restaurant where I was talking to Helen. After she left I joined them to discuss their research. Their situation was improving, with the Navy now funding their EEG experiments. They said Kit had left Washington to go through an accelerated medical education program.

Belmont. Sunday 31 August 1975.

Ron Westrum, a Michigan sociologist, met with me on Friday. He was back from Europe, where he saw Ballester Olmos and Aimé Michel. I introduced him to Peter Sturrock. Another academic researcher who has walked studiously close to the heart of the problem is David Jacobs, a historian who has recently published a *History of the UFO Controversy in America* (**46**). The book is heavy on "scholarly" dates and figures but light on insight and often sloppy. Thus he puts me among "the scientists who became interested in the question at the time of the Condon Committee!"

Jacobs never bothered to interview those, like Fred Beckman and me, who could have told him about the hidden years, the facts that happened before and during the time of Condon.

The failure to recognize and document underground currents is the curse of historical research. Fred tells me that Jacobs' omission is deliberate: he is leery of my research on UFO occupants. He doesn't think this aspect of the phenomenon should be mentioned, because the issue of landings is too controversial for him. (**47**)

Belmont. Monday 1 September 1975.

Labor Day: I cannot imagine anything more perfect than these long hours of work, writing at home, close to Janine. Our intimacy is a treasure, in contrast with the world around us. Last night, we were at a typical San Francisco party at Katz's Victorian house on Broadway, among a jungle of huge potted plants. The main topic of conversation among the guests: their sport cars.

On a flight to Hollywood. Friday 26 September 1975.

Helen has come over to our house with Arthur Hastings. We discussed the advisability of using hypnosis, not a safe procedure to use with abductees. Wisely, he cautioned against the power of suggestion. Allen will be at Sandler's house tonight, and tomorrow we make a historic presentation together before the AIAA. McCampbell and Stanton Friedman will be there.

I should also note a recent business conversation: A Frenchman with the unlikely name of Jacques Johnson called me from Minneapolis to discuss UFOs. As an executive with Control Data, he came to see my project at the Institute, asked pertinent questions about computer conferencing and promised me free machine time.

Hollywood. Saturday 27 September 1975.

The day was a success, starting from the discussion of UFOs as psychical phenomena and ending with a brillant reception at the home of Idabel Epperson. I met Reverend Crutwell and Stan Friedman and learned some new facts about the phenomenon in Brazil and Indonesia. Allen Hynek was in rare form. Emenegger arrived: the supposed Holloman footage has not been found.

The conversation moved on to the cattle mutilation episodes in the Midwest. Allen got up for one of his theatrical announcements, telling us, 'It's all been solved! Don Flickinger, who's a Treasury agent with the ATF, says it was all done by a satanic cult. The people involved are known, under surveillance."

"Why are new mutilations still reported every day, then?" I asked: "It's too easy to blame this on practitioners of the occult." At that word, "occult," a loud crack startled us, stopping me in mid-sentence. It came from a heavy wooden dresser in the room. Sandler jumped up as if he'd seen a snake, opened all the doors and turned on all the lights. He remained nervous and disturbed all evening.

The next day over a private breakfast Allen confessed his trip to Brazil was a fiasco. General Uchoa, who invited him, had no clout. The man who managed the much advertised congress was a French journalist trying to make a quick buck. He must have lost a ton of cruzeiros, because in the end he begged Allen to give more lectures to balance his finances. As for his talk before the Brazilian Congress, that went flat: his interpreter was an enthusiastic lady who was big on ufology but short on linguistics. As for the official files, the military is keeping them under lock and key.

At the AIAA I spoke after Bob Wood, a Douglas aircraft engineer of the "nuts and bolts" school who flatly equated all psychic phenomena with hallucinations (**48**). Jim McCampbell declared he could "easily" explain all UFOs as alien spacecraft using ordinary physics. Asking these people to consider the paranormal angle was impossible. My initiation into the SRI psychic work has widened the gap between me and my colleagues in the UFO mainstream.

In the afternoon I had a couple of hours alone with Allen, who has no such illusions about physics. We went to a nearby coffee shop to work on the galleys of *Edge of Reality*. He suggested I should join the Board of the Center. "I'm not sure it serves a useful purpose, Allen," I answered. "You remember when you said we shouldn't have an organization anybody could join for ten bucks? You wanted no political bickering."

"Well, I may have been right," he said. "But we still have our Invisible College."

"The College is loyal to you. I'm not sure this loyalty can be transferred to the Center."

We went over to Mrs. Epperson's house on Citrus street. I drew aside Reverend Cruttwell who told me Papuan Aborigines had a tradition stating that mankind came from the sky. The sightings of 1959 with Father Gill have not caused significant changes in their beliefs. Goodenough Bay, where the event took place, is close to a deep marine depression where strange objects have twice been seen to emerge. One of them was a large lighted cylinder that followed a ship (as in Pascagoula?) Reports of such luminous devices in the water were common. The Aborigines have also reported at least two new cases of strange creatures on land.

"Why hasn't this been documented in the literature, Reverend?" I asked Cruttwell. He shrugged: "Probably because you're the first researcher who's bothered to ask about it."

Belmont. Thursday 2 October 1975.

Fog is spreading higher on the hill; bushes seem frozen in time, and clusters of red bays shine against the green foliage. The houses above us are already lit up, in a festive mood. The night will be damp. We haven't seen any deer for a while. I think of October nights in France, marvellous evenings of precocious shadows suggestive of magical deeds. The streets glow, fat with fog. The heart beats faster for no reason. Lovers kiss in the archways of medieval carriage doors. Near the Seine the little streets are deserted, noises stifled like the muffled sounds that rise from El Camino tonight. On *Rue de la Clef* I imagine my mother preparing a simple meal and getting ready to turn on the radio news.

Hal tells me it's impossible to believe that there isn't someone in Washington who knows more that Kit does. “He simply doesn't have the right access,” we agreed.

I am flooded with interesting mail from readers of *Invisible College*. What comes out most clearly is the deep emotion among the American public regarding the future of man, our sacred nature, the preservation of freedom. This gives me a renewed sense of confidence. I wonder if I will find the same keen anticipation in France and Spain next month.

Belmont. Sunday 5 October 1975.

On Friday Hal called me over to SRI: he had an NSA manager in his office, a physicist he wanted me to meet. I told the man the Air Force must have quite a collection of pictures, judging by all the pilots who have said they had been able to take photographs of UFOs, only to have them confiscated as soon as they landed. He assured me he knew nothing about it. Extensive searches had been made by his staff to find out if NSA was intercepting foreign messages on the subject, and if such intercepts had been ordered by the Air Force; nothing has been found, he says. I don't trust his assurances.

Yesterday evening the fog was playing spectacular tricks with the lights of San Francisco as I walked all over, watching people at work and play. At dinner time I ended up in a bohemian cafeteria at the corner of Polk and Pine. Most of the tables were taken. An American girl named Ginger who spoke French quite well came and sat next to me. In the next hour we redesigned the world on a stack of napkins.

Belmont. Tuesday 14 October 1975.

All week UFOs have been in the news. The HIM cult has become a public sensation. The Oregon police are looking for the leaders, acting on complaints filed by relatives of believers who've gone off with “The Two,” leaving their farms and kids in the expectation that flying saucers would take them away. The media love the story.

The National Science Foundation has approved our third grant for computer science research, so my team will be well funded for a couple of years: now I can start thinking about leaving the Institute.

On Sunday Arthur Hastings came back to our house to work with Helen. He induced a state of mild reverie, since we agree that hypnotizing abductees is inappropriate. In control of the process, she did recall more details than she had ever done about her experience and that of her friends.

In the evening I went to San Francisco to attend a meditation session led by Sri Chinmoy. He was surrounded with singers, Bengali musicians in sarong, and flowers in huge bouquets. The meditation oriented my thoughts towards the three enemies of enlightenment, namely intelligence, action and the flesh. Manly Hall calls them the three bandits who symbolically killed Hiram Abiff, preventing him from building the Temple.

Action is important to me, but it can't have precedence over thought: increasingly I become a silent observer. Matters of the flesh are more complicated: only the impotent win that battle easily. That leaves intelligence. The joys of the spirit would impress me a lot more if I didn't see so many adepts end up in fanaticism. My heart may not be entirely pure but it remains open, unfettered by false certainties, immune to the delusions of faith, aware of its weakness.

Belmont. Saturday 18 October 1975.

Aimé Michel worries me: he seems depressed. In his last letter he spoke of giving up everything. I can understand how he feels.

A welcome break and new friendships: Janine and I had dinner with Ginger last night, and went for a pleasant walk along the shops from the Cannery to Ghirardelli Square. The night was warm and soft, with just enough fog to create a magical backdrop.

Flying over the Midwest. Sunday 26 October 1975.

At 33,000 feet, reading Plutarque (*On the Disappearance of the Oracles*) who talks about what I think of as "meta-reality:"

> This ability is unborn in the souls but, deprived of clarity, it only provides vague images. In certains individuals, it often blossoms and shines, in dreams or at the hour of death.

Tonight I'll be in New York, trying to get publishers interested in our psychic computer conference (**49**). I watch the American night, lights spread in wide arcs along the edge of the Great Lakes. I have no intention of following in Allen's footsteps, becoming a media celebrity. The knowledge I seek is that of science, not the faith that inspires crowds. We are told by the Gallup poll that 54% of Americans believe in UFOs: a meaningless indication that we are dealing with a social issue polluted with delusions. Evangelist Billy Graham capitalizes on it, hinting at the return of the Angels.

New York. Monday 27 October 1975.

Frank Pace, a Trustee of the Institute, member of the President's Foreign Intelligence Advisory Board, received me today in his office on a high floor of a tower suspended above Manhattan. From this height the landscape dissolves into grays and delicate blues, with the silvery tones of the Hudson and a faraway bridge as a backdrop.

"Why don't you go ahead and tell me your ideas, without any preamble?" he suggested. I threw myself into a succinct exposition of the UFO subject, arguing for its gravity, its urgency: It was time to take it seriously, at an official level. I had prepared the outline of a proposal under the auspices of the Institute, but before submitting it anywhere I wanted to be sure I wouldn't look like a fool, and wouldn't bring embarrassment to the organization, I said.

"Where would you look for the money? NSF? The Air Force?" We discussed various scenarios. I mentioned the Rockefeller foundation. He was adamant: "No, you should only undertake the research under official funding, a formal government grant." He added:

"Suppose you did this research and it demonstrated the reality of an unexplainable residue. What conclusion would you draw from it?"

The strategy I would build would be designed to avoid locking into any particular hypothesis. I would assemble a set of observations such that we could test many theories rather than a single one as Condon did with predictably disastrous results.

"The governmemt will be forced to do research, if only because of public pressure. It'd be a mistake to postpone the study until emotions boil over. What I am proposing is an opportunity for a few focused scientists to conduct serious field research."

"No need to stress this point with me, Jacques. The most convincing arguments are those presented as understatements. And you understate very well." I took that as a compliment. He got up to indicate the meeting was over. He asked if he could keep the document to review it and to discuss it "with a few people." I saw warmly dedicated portraits of Eisenhower, Johnson, and Kennedy on the walls all around us. But our talk left me puzzled.

Belmont. Sunday 9 November 1975.

New meetings at NASA. The space agency had convened the directors of all the science projects that will make use of the communication technology satellite, to be launched into orbit in January. They are heavily involved in the use of Planet; we signed a follow-on contract but I am eager to do much more. First, get our network conferencing technology out of academia.

Belmont. Saturday 15 November 1975.

The news is full of stories about the disappearance of an Arizona man named Travis Walton after a sighting of a light that terrified a team of loggers. Jim Harder has gone there in secrecy at the request of the Lorenzens, who are trying to keep Hynek away because they see Cufos as competition to Apro...

I continue to track down the co-witnesses of Helen's abduction. In Los Angeles, Price-Williams has made contact with her friend John. In Denver, Jule Eisenbud promises to interview Don, the band's drummer. He does remember the strange light, and has told Eisenbud that it marked a turning point in his life.

Following an interview in *The Chronicle* (**50**) I got a letter from a

Dr. Birge, who taught physics to Ed Condon. He is over 90, an emeritus professor in Berkeley. He reminded me that his student Condon had "scientifically proven that flying saucers didn't exist!" Besides, it would take hundreds of years for ETs to reach us, he said.

Belmont. Tuesday 18 November 1975.

The science attaché to the French Consulate, Alain Déroulède, relays an inquiry from a highly-placed lady in Paris, Simonne Servais, who has read *Invisible College*. He describes her as beautiful and holding the rank of ambassador. She is a former member of De Gaulle's Cabinet and spokesperson of the Elysée, a close confidante of President Georges Pompidou **(51)**. She is interested in psychic phenomena and UFOs, he said, so she instructed the Consulate to arrange a meeting with me. This should be an interesting trip indeed.

14

Paris. Rue de la Clef. Sunday 23 November 1975.

My mother didn't expect me early, so I went to a quiet hotel, the better to savor in solitude my first night in a Paris torn by strikes and demonstrations. I got a hot dog and French fries from a street vendor and slept soundly. I dreamt that I was a curate from the country, expecting a missive from some ecclesiastic order.

The next morning Maman was eager to tell me about her travels and the art courses at the Louvre. Once settled I called Aimé Michel. He reflected that everything we knew about Contact was based on what the witnesses could tell us -- but the witnesses had experienced an altered reality manipulated by the phenomenon itself! Therefore we actually knew nothing at all, as Colonel Floryan had already told me. All we can say is that there is an undiscovered process that makes people think they have experienced what we call UFOs. I asked him the question Frank Pace had posed: Let's assume we run a full scale investigation and it proves that the phenomenon is real. What's our next step? He said we should keep any findings quiet. Jean-Claude Bourret, in contrast, is eager to launch a political crusade. We give a lecture together on Tuesday.

Paris. Rue de la Clef. Monday 24 November 1975.

Paris is calm again after much social turmoil. Inflation is high, as well as unemployment, so the peaceful interlude may be short-lived. Real estate prices keep rising. A typical apartment here costs $150,000 or about $260 per square foot (**52**). Jean-Claude Bourret told me in confidence that Minister Robert Galley had been called on the carpet by Pompidou after his statement supporting research on UFOs. The government's Delegation for Information had done a confidential study of the political leverage they could derive from the public's belief in saucers, a study criticized by the Left. There was a "Saucer" file all the way up to the Cabinet, together with a political plan to exploit the belief in UFOs to take the public's attention from other problems. The file went back into the drawer when the Leftists yelled bloody murder and unfair manipulation.

Paris. Rue de la Clef. Wednesday 26 November 1975.

Jacques Bergier works on the *Champs-Elysées*, in the same long and narrow office with a small window at the end where we met two years ago. The lack of windows in Paris bothers me. In California I have become used to wide openings to the landscape and the sky.

Bergier's world has remained a chaos of books and files in every language. An old green poster on the wall advertises a conference by "Professeur Bergier." He spoke warmly of *Invisible College* but chided me for not pursuing some of the reactions I had noted among close encounter witnesses. Many of them have felt a peculiar pain at the base of the skull: that could be an epileptic symptom, he said, referring me to a paper before the Academy of Medicine.

"Could this result from an artificial form of epilepsy?" I asked.

"Certainly," he answered. "You're on the right track. You'll find it isn't too hard to make people hear voices. I know a fellow named Klein, who built such a device."

He gave me the frequencies. We went on to discuss USOs (Unidentified Submerged Objects), Men in Black, the "Society against Sects" and the Ummo documents, which left him unimpressed. I told him of my observation that neither Anton LaVey nor the OTO knew anything important and that the Rosicrucians had forgotten what they used to know about the phenomenon. This led us to discuss black magic, a field in which he is a scholarly expert. He told me that most supposed "ancient magical texts" circulating today were fakes that had nothing to do with the real Black Order but were derived from fantasy novels.

We came back to ufology. "What conclusions can we draw?" He asked rhetorically. "First, what we call reality is far more malleable than we thought. Why is reality so malleable? Simply because it's not the real reality! We've all been hypnotizing ourselves."

Bergier's scholarship covers an extraordinary scope of the weird. He mentioned in the same sentence Victorien Sardou's astral trips to Jupiter, Frank M. Robinson's short story *The Labyrinth* in *Analog,* and an issue of *Le Masque* (no.88) that described a plot for political assassinations. He highly recommended that I become acquainted with Raymond Jones, with the *Doomsday Color Press* and *None but Lucifer,* a novel by Sprague de Camp.

When I brought up Pierre Guérin, Bergier said, "I've set up a committee with (former Prime Minister) Chaban-Delmas to look into the paranormal; this is the committee that supports Costa de Beauregard's physics work. We invited Guérin, but he only kept ranting about conspiracies, it was a waste of time."

Over dinner at a Chinese restaurant he pursued the subjects of labyrinths, learning and control systems, an idea from *Invisible College* that fascinates him. "There are two types of labyrinths, of course," I pointed out to him. "Some are closed, some are open."

"Yes, yes!" he said enthusiastically. "Take the Nazi concentration camps, a good example of a closed control system. But their true purpose has never been unraveled, there were many absurd aspects.

Close to the camp where I was held during the war, there was a smaller one. Well, one day the SS attacked it, they killed everyone including the German guards! (**53**) You ought to read *Zero* by Dr. Payne (1955) and Wells' *Inexperienced Ghost*. Also Conan Doyle's *The Horror of the Heights* written in 1911. Mind you, if you want to see an open control system you have to look at the British Establishment: You can't understand it unless you're part of it, but once you do, you're supposed to be able to run the Empire."

Most of my time in France was spent in scientific meetings at *Arts et Métiers* and UNESCO, and supervising the progress of my California group over a Planet computer conference. I have installed a Texas Instruments terminal coupled to the phone in my mother's apartment to stay in touch with my project and with Janine. I even sent Olivier a birthday cake I typed out, fat layers of equal signs for the pastry and exclamation marks for his twelve candles.

Paris. Rue de la Clef. Wednesday 3 December 1975.

As the plane followed the Spanish coast, preparing to land in Barcelona, the city was drowned in industrial smog. Any nice images of romantic Catalogna were shattered. Antonio Ribera was waiting for me at the airport with Ballester-Olmos. He drove an old bottle-green car that puffed its way through the city and climbed up to a little village, Calderas de Montbuy, overlooking a quiet square. The Roman Therms across the street, built 25 centuries ago are still in use. We drove to Sant Feliù de Codinas, the village where Antonio lives with his wife, three cats and beautiful dogs, on the second floor of an apartment building with a fine view of the mountain side. Antonio is also a translator, a journalist. Vicente-Juan was eager to discuss statistics while Antonio wanted to talk about Ummo and Bordas, two subjects Ballester called "unscientific."

The next morning I got up early, eager to walk around the ancient village with its ornate balconies and its gardens sheltered by high walls. On the main square folks were queuing up before the hot springs, carrying pails. Jacques Bordas arrived at noon with his Parisian wife Odile, a former Dior seamstress. He told us he'd recently received a message from Aliens at his cabin in Andorra. The room had filled up with flickering red tinsel; he fell into a trance. “Prepare yourself,” a voice is supposed to have said.

“You think you're in contact with Titan,” I told him, “yet I know people who claim their messages are from beings from other places, who tell them completely different things.”

“That's possible,” said Bordas unperturbed. “Perhaps these beings only tell us what they think we'll understand. There are other forces, too... which I don't understand.”

Bordas was in Barcelona to open a jewelry store. I was interested in his mention of “flickering red tinsel.” It reminded me of the Livermore episode with Geller.

On the flight back. Thursday 4 December 1975.

Antonio and Vicente-Juan drove me back to Barcelona, and two hours later I was in Paris, where the weather was icy. At Châtelet station someone had used a black marker to scribble on a wall: “The Lord is an extraterrestrial. He has come back in a flying saucer. Order of Melchizedek. 20 Rue Jules Vallès.”

I had a fever and a sore throat. Passersby ran along the walls, gray with cold, their hands in their coat pockets. The streets stank of smoke and gasoline. At *Les Halles*, the big hole of the *Square des Innocents* was being filled up with concrete. Paris goes underground, becoming a city of earth machines, tunnels, mechanical stairways that lead down into bowels with interminable white walls.

Rue Jules Vallès is located in a working class neighborhood close to the sadly notorious Charonne subway station (**54**). I climbed the stairs to the second floor and knocked on the left-hand door. A short woman wearing a wool cap and a heavy coat opened the door. I apologized for showing up unannounced.

“Not at all,” she replied, “you've come at the appointed time.”

She showed me inside two bare rooms. A fellow named Ivan stopped eating long enough to explain the cosmic situation to me: “The barbarism around us will give way before new revelations. Every government recognizes our truth. Giscard (**55**) went to see the

Pope, you realize what that means?" I tried to look impressed.

The fliers they handed out predicted that seven saucers would land at the main television facility. "The Peoples are invited to this circonvolution," they claimed.

"Will you have a glass of Champagne with us?" enquired Ivan. In spite of his old tattered shirt and his trousers spotted with grease, he was awaiting the saucers in comfort.

In late afternoon, I went to the *Quai d'Orsay* for my appointment with Madame Servais. I was escorted to the fifth floor. Amused by the contrast with my morning meeting with the Order of Melchizedek, I followed an impeccable secretary who took me to a large office, luxuriously furnished with a Minister's desk, tall bookcases and elegant lamps.

The lady herself was intense, beautiful indeed, and in control. She praised my book in few words, without flattery. Some questions were gnawing at a corner of my mind, however. It had been quite a curious coincidence for her to find a copy of the volume in an unrelated package from the publisher. She claimed she hadn't even known it existed. Her services had sent a young French doctor to India, she said; upon his return he had published a book. It seems that the publisher enclosed a complimentary copy of *Invisible College* in the same package. She insisted our contact was a coincidence...

She told me that she had extensively investigated parapsychology and was a student of the Gurdjieff tradition: "You and I are within what the Buddhists call the Red Circle, where destiny forces certain beings to meet," she added.

Belmont. Friday 5 December 1975.

When I came home last night the kids were asleep, the house was a dream and reunion with Janine an enchantment. Today I went back to work with Bob Johansen, Thad Wilson, Hubert Lipinski, clever Kathi Vian and the rest of this exceptional team. I especially enjoy working with Bob Johansen, who brings classic analytical skills to everything he does, balancing Kathi's own talent with the precise phrase, the exact word.

When I reflect on this latest trip, it is of my mother that I think first: her courage, her appetite for life. She marvels at the world, travelling with intense eagerness to observe people and things. She told me that when she was a young girl in Joinville she thought that stones could talk. Not just any stone, of course, but the bright shiny ones across the street from her house, that sang at sunrise and sunset.

Belmont. Sunday 14 December 1975.

The wide expanse of the Bay stretches from Mount Diablo to Mount Hamilton. The water reflects the purple-brown band of the marshes and the hills. I hear the faraway rumble of a truck, the barking of a dog, a child calling out. The sun splashes gold over the screen of the white sheers, the medallions on the pink curtains.

Upon my return from France I began to read Peter Reich's *Book of Dreams*. Now another coincidence: a phone call from his sister Eva Reich, who was in the Bay Area. I have no fascination with Reich. He was unjustly persecuted by the U.S. government but he was doing everything he could to attract persecution. He reminds me of Engelbart: the same "vision" they can't quite put into words, the same fanatical certainty that their complex view of the world is right. Reich, like Doug, was a true genius.

Eva Reich came over to my office wearing a green hat and an open smile. We spoke about the lawsuit she has launched to force the executors of her father's estate to release his works, so I signed her petition and will circulate it. I switched topics from psychology to UFOs, which the Reichians call EAs. I asked her if Reich had ever seen an object at close range; the answer was no. We discussed the psychic effects in evidence around Orgonon. Eva acknowledged they'd experienced a series of poltergeists, but her father flew into a rage when she used that word: "Never mention this in my presence! It's mere occultism, vulgar mysticism! This stuff has nothing to do with my research!"

Last Monday seven witnesses saw two disk-shaped lights flying at low altitude over the western side of Belmont, on the opposite side of the hill from us, near the Crystal Springs reservoir that follows the San Andreas Fault.

Belmont. Saturday 3 January 1976.

The year started on a strange note. The furnace gave up, so we spent two nights freezing. On the positive side *Invisible College* is now out in English, and my prototype teleconferencing program is up on Cybernet. I spent the afternoon dashing from the dining room, where terminal #1 is plugged in, to my basement office where I have setup terminal #2. Messages are flowing smoothly, back and forth through the main computer, which is in Rockville, Maryland.

Belmont. Saturday 10 January 1976.

We only have one car now, so we have to get up at 6:30 to drive our son to school and his sister to the bus, after which Janine drops me off at the Institute. Yesterday our son broke his wrist in a bad fall. Then on Thursday night Don Hanlon's sister called me from Chicago in a tearful voice. "I can't reach Don," she said with urgency. "I was hoping you'd know where he was. I need to tell him that his father is dead." I found Don at Mande's apartment; I had to break the sad news to him.

Belmont. Saturday 17 January 1976.

Strange moody time. The weather is mild, sunny but smoggy. No rain yet this year. Allen was in town yesterday, so we had dinner at the Marine Memorial, where Northwestern alumni held their meeting. Janine was a bright note in an otherwise boring evening, wearing an orange suit with a collar of black fur. Allen's lecture was poorly organized, marred again by ill-timed jokes.

Peter Sturrock, who came over to our house for breakfast, is preparing a UFO questionaire aimed at scientists. Cufos proposed to publish it. Peter wisely prefers his independence. "There is a need to separate this research from Cufos, which promotes a belief in

UFOs," he said. He argues that professional scientists are more likely to respond to a questionnaire from Stanford.

Allen asked me to tell him frankly what I thought of his own position. I replied that the publication of current cases should be the major role of the Center, a proactive role it currently fails to fulfill. Allen said he'd twice requested that his underlings send me copies of their landing reports as a member of their Advisory Board: They never complied. Yet the only "scientific findings" Allen was able to mention in this lecture were my statistics and those of Poher. I worry as I see the Center taking on the characteristics of all UFO groups. As Ted Phillips remarked, nobody does the actual research.

Belmont. Thursday 22 January 1976.

Brendan is recovering from a series of unhappy events. His father died, he went off to Ireland, fell ill and had to stay in the hospital for a month. When he came back he bought a used Porsche but someone broke into it, stole $3,000 worth of jewels that belonged to his friend, Paul Getty's daughter. They also stole family papers and his father's will. Among the stolen objects he had brought back from Ireland was a first edition of *Paradise Lost*.

"Do you work for the CIA?" I asked him directly. He swore to me that he did not, although he had been indeed "approached," as I had surmised. Brendan and I share the same reaction to the Intelligence community: Some fascination, mixed with disgust. "These guys are unreliable, their contacts can't be trusted," I said.

"Not only that, but they keep playing games," he replied. "You're right to stay away."

Belmont. Sunday 25 January 1976.

Jacques Johnson is late. He's supposed to bring a contract with Control Data that might enable us to launch InfoMedia in earnest.

Yesterday Janine and I went on an expedition into the Mojave Desert with journalist Peter Gutilla who claimed to know about a "bridge between realities" somewhere near Edwards and China

Lake. I loaded my Olympus with infrared film. Gerald Askevold lent me some fine crystals from the USGS collections and he gave me a prospector's map of the area. During the two-hour drive North of Burbank Peter told me Sandler's company was in financial distress when the government offered a contract for a UFO documentary.

Our vehicles rumbled and rolled, passing the ghost town of Gerlach, entering a region filled with old mines. The desert was magnificent, even if it didn't open up to reveal a parallel universe. I did take infrared pictures, some through the crystal. All they showed were heat spots. I think that Trevor James Constable's pictures of “amoebas” in the sky, which he believes to be living UFOs, are similar artifacts. The most interesting person we met on the trip was a Hollywood engineer I’ll call “Jim Irish.” He used to be part of a special NSA group dedicated to research on aerial phenomena. He had been given special equipment by the government and was sent all over the land in search of data. It was an impossible life, said Jim, so he quit and now heads up a recording studio.

In the plane to New York. Wednesday 28 January 1976.

Flying over Wyoming, I think of Janine. I am headed for Brookhaven again, squeezed against the window. Down there the ground is covered with snow. I can barely see the boundaries of the fields. I unwind behind me the long trusted thread of your love.

Belmont. Saturday 31 January 1976.

This was my second trip to the atomic center. Bob Johansen and I slept in the visitors’ quarters. The weather was icy, the surroundings silent. After the science meeting we drove back to New York and I flew on to Dayton, where Kent Collins, an executive of the Kettering Foundation, was awaiting me: They support some of our work. When I asked Collins how the SRI report on “Images of Man” (authored by Willis Harman with the help of Brendan and Arthur Hastings) had been received, he told me it had polarized the Foundation. Some Kettering managers were intrigued by the dissertations about the human potential; others regarded them simply as airy-fairy stuff from California. The hard fact is that neither meditation, nor Esalen, nor Werner Ehrhart, nor psychic research has seriously addressed the social and economic problems of the world.

This morning, snow had turned Dayton into a scene of delight. Kent drove around the expensive section of town to show me the mansions of the rich and the estate of the Wright Brothers: a white structure on a hilltop. Others are more subdued, hiding among trees.

Belmont. Tuesday 17 February 1976.

Jacques Johnson wants me to fly to Minneapolis to brief Control Data executives about computer conferencing. He said the French Atomic Energy Commission had a file of UFO cases reported by French law enforcement agencies, including an incident in which two gendarmes fired on a landed saucer and found themselves lying on the ground, with no trace of the UFO, in Nancy five years ago.

Belmont. Monday 23 February 1976.

Last night I came back from Los Angeles, where I met with "Jim Irish." His studio stands in a dilapidated section of Hollywood haunted by drunks and drug heads. When it comes to electronics this fellow with a boyish face, a beer belly and black hair neatly pulled over his skull knows what he is talking about. He is equally astute when it comes to photography: I showed him the pictures I had taken in the desert, and was treated to a lecture on infrared film and its artefacts. One dark object I caught must be the result of heat bubbles in the developer. He added that over years in the field he had recorded a dozen actual photographs of real UFOs on infrared film.

"I spent a lot of time trying to get hard data for the NSA... I ended up withdrawing from the project."

"What made you decide to leave?"

"It wasn't as exciting as you'd think. We had no freedom. When you work for those guys you don't ask questions. They give you instructions: 'go to such and such a place, investigate whatever's there.' Anytime, day or night. One of the pictures I took showed a large convex object that went inside a mountain! They sent soldiers in to find traces. They never figured out what it was."

"So why did you quit?" I asked again. Nervously, he told me: "One day, in the desert near Barstow, there had been sightings. The team we sent never came back. We found two bodies, reduced to ashes, near a burned-out car. Two guys from our group, one of them a close friend of mine." His voice trailed off.

"What did the two men die of?" I thought of the Lead Mask case.

"The official report said they burned to death because the car had a gasoline leak and they lit up a cigarette! In the first place, in this business you don't smoke on the job."

"How many investigations did you do?"

"Dozens. The Highway Patrol is given a confidential number to report sightings. Higher-ups decide if it's worth following up. An investigator goes to the spot with his equipment, makes a report. That's the end of it, I'd never hear about it again."

"How many teams like yours are there?"

"In the whole country? There must be three or four hundred guys, maybe fewer since Watergate, although the NSA budget hasn't been cut as much as CIA."

I left the studio in puzzlement, but the weirdness was just beginning. I walked over to the Roosevelt Hotel, caught a taxi at random in a stream of traffic. The cabbie was a buxom blonde who drove erratically. When we reached KABC she gave me a receipt for the fare. I pulled it again while preparing my expense report, and I had a shock when I saw *it was signed Melchizedek*. There is only one entry under this name in the L.A. phone book.

Is this another intersign? For weeks I've been spending much spare time researching Melchizedek. I have sent my secretary to the library to dig up references, and I have read every possible book in search of clues, from the Urantia cosmogony to the work of Frater Achad. And when I leave all this behind for a week-end in Los Angeles I have to catch the only cab in town driven by Melchizedek!

During a radio interview with Carol Hemingway a man named Andrew Isaacs said he had a brother, an Air Force colonel, who once saw the bodies of several humanoids. We also had an interesting call from a witness named Brian Scott, who was plagued with strange balls of light. I put him in touch with "Jim Irish" who may be able to document any physical effects that take place.

At 11 o'clock I called Hynek, who had just arrived from Florida and was hungry. We found an open coffee shop on Wilshire. He was in fine shape, smoking an odorous pipe and carrying piles of papers. Allen told me things were looking up at Cufos, so I asked what had happened to their commitment to send me landing data. "We're not getting close encounter cases right now," he said flatly. Yet Brian Scott had just told me he'd sent Allen a report and expected his visit. This threw cold water on our conversation.

On Sunday we met with Leo Sprinkle, a tall balding fellow with a fine mustache who reminds me of my brother. He has a charming smile and impeccable intellectual credentials. He teaches psychology at the University of Wyoming. An expert on contactees, he has hypnotized 100 witnesses or so. Frank Salisbury, always reserved but open-minded, was with him. We met with Herbert Schirmer for two hours, reliving every detail of his abduction, after which Schirmer took me aside, gave me his private address and a detailed drawing of the entity he recalled seeing aboard the object that abducted him. He said he was fed up with the UFO groups, wanted nothing more to do with believers. Since his meeting with the beings he has been awaiting "their" return, living alone in a little house that looks out towards the ocean.

Now I am packing my suitcase again, for a trip to Minnesota. I just learned of the death of Bob Low, killed three months ago in a light plane crash.

Belmont. Tuesday 2 March 1976.

There was ice on the ground in Minneapolis but the snowfall had stopped. We had a fine champagne dinner at the home of Gérard Beaugonin, amateur astrologer and trumpet player, associate of legendary tycoon Bill Norris and manager of *Technotech*, a database subsidiary. CDC Headquarters form a rectangle of steel and gold colored glass, a striking sight against the white sky. From the eleventh floor I could see the frozen river, black trees sticking out of the snow as in Eisenstein's films, and an endless dance of snowplows. When I finished my presentation Beaugonin took me aside and said I must work for them, name my terms. But I am not looking to leave California.

Back in L.A. "Jim Irish" has gone to see Brian Scott, taking his sensitive electronic equipment along. Curiously, his tape recorder signal was extinguished although batteries and the electronics remained in working condition. Jim also reported strong headaches. Other things are going on, complicating the picture: animal mutilations are on the rise, although it is such a disconcerting and ugly subject that neither the media nor the ufologists want to discuss it. These bizarre killings are radically different from the simple sacrifice of chickens or goats that is part of cult rituals.

Belmont. Friday 26 March 1976.

During a meeting with Muktananda on Sunday afternoon (**56**), I spent an hour and a half at his ashram, discussing kundalini and UFOs. Today I witnessed a meeting of Urantia, another silly, colorful church inspired by alleged extraterrestrial spirits (**57**).

Allen's entourage is jealous of our friendship. They didn't even tell me about Flickinger's report on cattle mutilations. According to Allen it terrified them. I got my own copy through Brendan: Flickinger claims he's tracked down individuals who took part in satanic rites and executions of animals and humans. Unfortunately he is misinformed about occultism, mixing together groups that have nothing in common. His report is sloppy, as when he speaks of some individuals as "members of the Occult," as if there was an organization by that name! Allen finds reasurance in the report because it places the burden for mutilations on a few hypothetical satanists, thus pushing the topic away from ufology.

Things are not so simple. From my own analysis, which runs contrary to Kit's conclusions, only a small number of cattle mutilations can be attributed to cults or predators.

Brendan told me that Puharich had money from Sir John Whitmore for a study of medium Phillis Schlemmer, who charges ahead where Geller stopped, and for a new project with Jim Hurtak.

Belmont. Friday 2 April 1976.

Lunch in Woodside with Puharich and Hurtak. Andrija, more excited than ever, claimed he was getting coded extraterrestrial messages on his watch; the fine chronometer he was wearing would suddenly stop, and the position of the hands could be decoded to get specific warnings. Both Hurtak and Puharich are convinced that a mass alien invasion is imminent. Their willingness to jump to conclusions leaves me breathless.

Belmont. Monday 5 April 1976.

Allen stayed here on Friday night and took back with him my letter of resignation from his science board. I asked: 1. In what way does Cufos differ from other groups? 2. Who are its directors and officers? 3. What is expected from the board, which has no power?

Allen took it well. "I've always regarded the Center as being composed of you and me, Fred Beckman and only two or three others," he said. "But it's drifted in a different direction. I like your letter. It'll help me set a few things straight. You're the only one who's had the guts to pose these questions."

I argued for pursuing the physical implications of observations like Webb's sighting in Arizona. This scientist looked at an object through polarizing glasses and saw concentric rings. If the object was 100 meters away it may have generated a field of one million gauss. My files are replete with cases where witnesses said they were "paralyzed" in the presence of UFO entities. Allen agrees that academic researchers like David Jacobs who refuse to study close encounter cases are missing an important point.

In reality, as my brother the doctor has pointed out to me, the witnesses only lost muscular control and were not truly paralyzed in a physiological sense. One way to induce such loss of control would be to create an electromagnetic field at a frequency of 3,300 Mhz or so (at a wavelength of about 9.2 cm) with most of the energy contained in a 20 degree main lobe. Such a beam wouldn't burn any tissue because of its rapid pulsing. Very little energy would be absorbed by the body, but if one could deliver 10 milliwatts per square centimeter that might be enough to stimulate the nerves and decrease their reaction threshold.

Belmont. Wednesday 7 April 1976.

On Monday night I went to Oakland to meet a witness of psychic surgery, a black nurse at Kaiser Hospital who is a friend of architect Bill Calvert. They spent much time in Brazil, where they knew Donna Maria, a remarkable healer, intensely religious who was 20 at the time and lived in utter poverty among the local people. Bill's friend saw her open up patients in an apparent trance state. She extracted diseased tissue in their presence from these people's open abdomens, eliminating any sleight-of-hand such as the trickery of "Dr. Toni" in the Philippines. All patients were local people.

Donna Maria never sought publicity, didn't try to attract wealthy foreigners; she died in the arms of the church at age 25, convinced that her information came from an order of superior beings.

Belmont. Friday 9 April 1976.

Cufos had a meeting on Monday night, attended by Mimi and the publicity person. Fred told the group he agreed with my letter. He recommended closing down Cufos unless its mission of scientific information could be restated. As for public relations, he said they had no place in the Center's work. Yet Allen wanted to continue.

"Where will the money come from?" asked Fred.

"We have research ideas..." Allen answered vaguely.

"Anybody can write a proposal on a piece of paper," Fred pointed out. "That doesn't mean anything. If you can't face reality, I'm driving back down to Chicago."

Belmont. Friday 16 April 1976.

"Allen finally takes your letter seriously," Fred told me as we discussed Cufos. Peter Sturrock, who is quietly setting up a real scientific group as a committee of the AIAA, sought my advice about the agenda. I said I would stress physical effect cases and avoid pointless quarrels with Menzel or Klass.

On Thursday Bill Norris, CEO of Control Data, invited me to a private dinner with him in San Jose. I summarized my plan for network communities. He liked it and again offered to hire me. But at CDC I'd be mired in bureaucracy, since the Plato staff is already trying to implement conferencing as a simple form of "chat," and is not getting anywhere.

Belmont. Sunday 25 April 1976.

I've confronted Anton with the Flickinger report on mutilations, which specifically mentions his group. He tried to tell me it was a fabrication by the hippies at the *Berkeley Barb* (**58**). I laughed at this: Flickinger is a Federal Agent with the Treasury Department, not a bearded leftist. So Anton, his back to the wall, pulled out his wallet and showed me his badge of the San Francisco Police Department:

"I'd have known about it, if the SFPD had uncovered serious evidence. I work closely with their Intelligence unit. They call on me when they have a crime that involves witchcraft or cults, like the murder in Daly City a year ago..."

The idea that Anton had such connections makes sense. He thinks that the government will eventually "land" a fake saucer somewhere, behind barbed wire, to generate speculation and demands "for the release of the data people think the government must be covering up." Writer Bernard Newman had proposed such a deception scenario as early as 1950 in his novel, *The Flying Saucer* (**59**).

"Come on, Jacques, it's an old magician's trick," he added, intensely serious now. "They've got to take attention away from real problems. The government's right hand does something spectacular to capture people's eyes while their left hand goes on with the real work."

Philadelphia. Friday 7 May 1976.

Judging by Fred's assessment of the "scientific" ufologists who recently gathered in Chicago I didn't miss much by staying away. "The presentations were worthless. McCampbell's paper was especially bad. Poher and Petit left in disgust."

"What about the Scientific Board?"

"Evaporated. There were only six of us. Fred Winterberg kept making long speeches; Berthold Schwarz was there. Robert Hall, the sociologist said Cufos had turned into another Nicap; they're broke again. We didn't have a business meeting, just a quick breakfast."

New cases keep coming up in California. Last week I interviewed the wife of a Berkeley professor, a mother of four, who called me about an apparition at her house: two luminous, undulating objects. She observed something as clear as a hologram: a dove against a black background, soon replaced by a golden flower **(60)**.

The theory I am forming is that (1) there exists another reality level with which humans can relate symbolically and (2) entities endowed with consciousness operate in that plane. This is the core knowledge, the basic fact. The consciousness in question may or may not be related to us. As for the notion that saucers represent extraterrestrial visitors, I now regard it as a misleading sidetrack.

Philadelphia. Saturday 8 May 1976.

Tears came to my eyes, to my vast surprise, as I sat quietly in the deserted hotel coffee shop, reading the *Epic of Gilgamesh.* I am in Philadelphia to meet a group of businessmen who have hired Ira Einhorn as their consultant to revise the positioning of their company. And here I am in this plastic room, with the noise of the street and all the bustle of Philadelphia, crying over the oldest text in man's history. I was shocked to realize how much power these ancient images still held.

The long road as we drove in the Poconos reminded me of France, its pretty country villages and pine-covered hills. Our meeting was held in a chalet owned by an executive of the company for which Ira was consulting. I spoke about the medium-term business future as a backdrop to their decisions: demographics, needs and opportunities for new industrial products, the predictable impact of the fast-developing computer industry, with the erasing of management hierarchies to the benefit of networks. Ira had also invited Shel Gordon, president of the investment division of Lehman Brothers to speak about capital markets. He saw a deterioration of economic conditions after a brief period of growth. He believed inflation may reach a level of 18 to 19 points, accompanied by a rise in rates.

It was fascinating to see Ira operate among the nine executives who were listening to us, dynamic business types, facing both a crisis and an opportunity. The key was a drastic reorganization which meant firing their own CEO. Ira was an unlikely catalyst for such a decision: a radical leader from the Sixties, he sat there with his long hair, bushy beard, bare feet, yet he proceeded to give them a brillant, lucid analysis of their problems, from the reshaping of their offices to the modernization of accounting methods, an appraisal of new European markets and the streamlining of product lines.

After the meeting we got back to Ira's apartment, sitting on the floor around a game of GO, discussing Uri, publishers and books. He showed me his poems entitled *7818-7880*. Ira has a unique lifestyle: no television set, no car, no radio. He doesn't own a tape recorder or a record player, hasn't owed taxes for 10 years since he has no significant income. He's about to spend three months on an island in Nova Scotia, so he plans to buy a used car to drive to Canada, selling it when he comes back. We dropped in on a party given by artists in a Chestnut street hangar and spent the evening talking about women. “I lived with Holly for three years,” Ira said, “but things became impossible. Now we only see each other once in a while.” The mainstream and the counter-culture are curiously parallel when it comes to defining relationships in terms of personal convenience. In the latter setting this translates into a life of anonymous encounters, free sex and one-night stands. In the former it means expensive weddings followed by even more expensive divorces, a cycle of guilt-ridden affairs, analysis on the shrink's couch. Both lifestyles seem irrelevant to me. I am proud of the way Janine and I conduct our life. My delusion is that I can change those I meet, especially when I love them. I have trouble reconciling extremes: it is so hard to influence another person's life, so easy to upset it!

Belmont. Tuesday 11 May 1976.

The day was spent in Los Angeles, where I walked over to see “Jim Irish” again. He thinks his audio recorders may isolate the voice of an entity that speaks through Brian’s throat; he also caught electrical effects and a low frequency vibration that permeates the house. Brian witnessed lightning bolts criss-crossing his room, after which they focused on the wall heater, burning the panel. Jim did verify the phenomena on the four-channel recorder: Statics started on the highest channel before the witness perceived anything. On the second channel one could hear a television program and Brian's voice suddenly saying: “What's that?” In the meantime the fourth channel only recorded the low frequency vibration.

I have brought back Brian's drawings and notes. Allen has a complete set but never mentioned them to me, possibly because they scare him: Jim Irish and his wife recalled his visit to their home, stressing how impressed they were by his gentleness. He came to the conclusion that they were dealing with occult phenomena, so he recommended that the family contact the Catholic Church. Jim's wife called up the bishop: an exorcism was conducted. Everything returned to normal, but that hardly meets my idea of research.

Last night Janine and I founded the InfoMedia Corporation with Ray Williams. The company now has the official status necessary to receive and fulfill the contract from Control Data.

Belmont. Saturday 15 May 1976.

More travel: This week I twice went back to Los Angeles and on Wednesday I leave for New York and Paris.

I got an interesting call from a vice-president with Environmental Systems in Van Nuys who'd read *Invisible College*. As early as 1955 he belonged to a UFO group at Douglas Aircraft in Santa Monica.

He worked there with Wheaten (now at Lockheed, in the submarine division), Ted Gordon, Klemperer and Dave Crook. They were asked by Douglas management to assess cases from Blue Book, complete with photos and films. Their conclusion, which they were asked to "forget," was that the objects used multi-dimensional physics.

He now claims they found no less than 2,000 sites in Owens Valley alone, including places where objects seem to go in and out of the solid ground. All this encourages me in a direction that takes me farther away from the ufologists, who really know nothing and understand nothing, but it also leaves me puzzled, and a little apprehensive about the next steps in my fragile research.

15

Westbury, New York. Wednesday 19 May 1976.

A strong cold wind was blowing when I landed at Kennedy. I rented a car and managed to get away from the metropolis. I stopped at a non-descript motel next to the expressway. Tomorrow I will go on to Brookhaven again, to interview the scientists who use our system in network conferencing trials with colleagues at other national labs.

Flying back to California. Saturday 22 May 1976.

Sunset behind Manhattan, the plane climbing through grayness, and suddenly a higher world of light.

I met Marcel Vogel today. He is a massive block of a man, a jovial fellow, an expert at IBM where he studies plant telepathy and other paranormal topics. He made so many millions for them with his discoveries in magnetic recording that they leave him alone, with a fat salary and his own lab.

He was anxious for me to examine what he called a piece of a UFO found in the Santa Cruz Mountains, so we went to his room. It was a silvery fragment, light and plastic in appearance. No evidence of melting. Vogel also showed me two beautiful quartz samples he was using for "projection experiments."

Belmont. Sunday 6 June 1976.

I just flew back from Minneapolis with a check for InfoMedia signed by Control Data: advanced payment towards our conferencing system. I spent the day studying their technology and watching demonstrations of Plato. **(61)** While in Minnesota I also interviewed federal agent Flickinger. He no longer believed in his own report on cattle mutilations: the two convicts who confessed to him do appear to have had contacts with a cult in Texas, but they never had the resources to perpetrate the operations described by the veterinarians and were indeed lying, as I had concluded, about satanists being implicated. The technique that was used to remove the organs of the animals consisted in inserting a scalpel through the rectum to cut internal ligaments. This was the work of a human surgeon, hardly what would happen if the mutilations were performed by cult members staggering through the darkness. This also eliminates animal predators. No link to UFOs, either.

TWA 800 Flight to Paris. Thursday 10 June 1976.

Anton has written a curious article filled with laudatory comments for Marcello Truzzi's new *Zetetic Scholar*, a skeptical magazine. Sociologist Truzzi is a member of Anton's inner circle. Philip Klass, James Randi, Carl Sagan and a few other *beaux esprits* are expected to write for his new publication.

Paris. Rue de la Clef. Sunday 13 June 1976.

Jean-Claude Bourret assures me that every ufologist in France will be with us at the Poitiers Congress on Tuesday, except for Aimé Michel, who doesn't leave his mountain: "I don't know what to say anymore," Aimé told me, "Every time I say something, I feel like saying the opposite."

Writer Jean Sendy lives in the attic of the Pompadour's former mansion and is proud of it. "As you can see, even the servants' stairs sported carved woodwork; they've remained intact since the 17th century. These aristocrats weren't swines; a big difference with today's wealthy folks." He lives with a pleasant young woman from Normandy. He says nobody takes Poher's theories seriously.

Paris. Rue de la Clef. Monday 14 June 1976.

Georges Gallet, my old publisher and friend, was waiting for me to discuss our contract for *Edge of Reality*, after which publisher Francis Monnier passed on a confidence from a friend, a highly-placed diplomat formerly with the French secret service: a special Gendarmerie unit in Lyon is investigating UFOs, working with the Air Police to predict future sightings… This left me unconvinced.

Earlier I had spent an hour in a bistro near Denfert with Guérin, who chastized me for not paying enough attention to physical models. I tried to explain why we need a whole new approach, one that accounts for psychic phenomena as well. He refused to listen. He added that Poher and Petit had come back from Chicago telling everybody that Cufos was scientifically worthless, and that no serious research was going on in the U.S.

On the train to Poitiers. Tuesday 15 June 1976.

It hasn't rained in France for two months. The heat is unbearable, pollution ugly. Distant buildings drown in bluish haze. The Seine is suffering; fish float toward Le Havre, their shiny white bellies sadly exposed to the sky. I woke up in the middle of the night and began reading Pauwels' excellent book about Gurdjieff.

Now the train is going through Ablon; I can see cottages on the hill. We might be living there now if we'd stayed in France. In Juvisy there are flowers in front of every house and green shutters on the windows, but local developers couldn't refrain from erecting concrete towers high above everything. After Brétigny come the plains. The Loire is dry, with exposed sand. My mind is slipping, I find myself pleasantly lost in eternity. The castle of Blois rises before us. I have never been in this region, where I now "find myself". To find oneself: that is what Gurdjieff was trying to teach.

Pauwels says it clearly:

> Sometimes, as if by chance, in spite of us, the true consciousness comes to the surface. At once, everything around us takes on a weight, a smell, a taste that was unknown before. Our memory fixes itself on it forever. Or rather, I should say that, in the rare instants when we are in this state of true consciousness, we live what we live forever; we live it while escaping out of time.

Poitiers. Later the same day.

A large bedroom with three beds. Poitiers is clean; it has integrity and character, perched on a hill, with streets full of little shops and helpful people. Yet nobody was able to tell me where *Notre-Dame-La-Grande* was, until I found a dignified gentleman coming out of the Hall of Justice, the Legion of Honor at his buttonhole. He pointed it out to me politely. It's an eleventh century marvel, its polychrome columns painted in bright colors, evidence of sophisticated Arab influence. I walked around the altar admiring the *lutrin*, a carved piece where a huge eagle with widely open wings held the heavy book of prayers. The beautiful Roman Vesperal was open at the Feast of the Holy Sacrament. I read the page:

> Sacerdos in aeternum Christos Dominus *secundum ordinem Melchisedech*, panem et vinum obtulit.

Melchizedek again... Simonne Servais calls such coincidences "Tom Thumb's little white pebbles." Colonel Floryan refers to them as "tiny absurd indications." I think of them as intersigns. Sitting down in the nave feeling very humble, I sent out love to those dear to me, and thought of Janine.

Paris. Rue de la Clef. Friday 18 June 1976.

Jean-Claude Bourret drove me back to Paris at three in the morning in his BMW. The Poitiers meeting was a success, with lots of laughs, excellent food and hearty arguments, the ingredients of any good French conference. Professor Maessens from the Belgian group Sobeps, a theoretical physicist, level-headed and pleasant, told me that my *Invisible College* went too far, that it wasn't prudent to tell the public about the weirdness of the phenomenon and that I shouldn't mention the psychic angle, "too shaky."

The problem is that Europe only knows of psychic research through mediums, charlatans, tabloid tales or skeptical exposés disguised as "rationalism." The notion of a psychic component with physical characteristics makes them uncomfortable.

Poher was friendly as usual. Guérin, Poher and I were all in tan suits, so I hinted at a conspiracy of "the three men in beige." Then Captain Cochereau arrived in his beige Gendarmerie uniform, and wondered why we started laughing as soon as we saw him.

The conference attracted some 300 people. Poher opened the session, introduced by Bourret. He gave a thoroughly scientific talk where bi-logarithmic graphs followed histograms amidst a few classic photographs, some cartoons and a reference to the Betty Hill star map. He argued that the number of sightings rose in proportion to population density and to the lack of cloud cover, which tends to show that we are dealing with real objects. (I have found that landing cases, on the other hand, varied in inverse proportion to population density). The number of cases varies like the cube of the visibility index and sounds are only reported for objects seen at less than a 150 meters, all of which could be interpreted by a skeptic as proof that the objects are conventional craft.

Poher advocates monitoring stations, but if they built 2,000 of them in France they would only expect one sighting every 10 years. Instead, he decided to use diffraction gratings that could be widely distributed in the hope that someone within the Armed Forces or the Gendarmerie will be able to catch a UFO spectrum. This reminded me of the failed Videon project the Air Force had launched in 1947.

Speaking after Poher, Cochereau had these nice words: “As Gendarmes, we were at the service of Justice; now we are also at the service of Science.” My turn came. I stressed American statistics and only alluded briefly to paranormal aspects, because Bourret insisted we had to present a “rational” approach to impress the media.

It is with Maessens that I had the most useful talks. He didn't agree with my “Hillside Curve,” which states that the probability of a case being reported rises with its strangeness, goes through a peak for sightings that are truly unusual, and decreases again as the cases become frankly weird, because witnesses are terrified by the spiritual implications of what they've seen (**62**). Instead he'd draw the curve with three distinct peaks, respectively for UFOs, paranormal phenomena and “miracles”: A devout Catholic, he has set up a model in which these three categories are separated.

Gendarmerie officer Kervandal made it clear that Poher's project at CNES was little more than a French version of Blue Book. Claude only gets civilian cases, not those that originate with Air Force or Navy intelligence. And there is indeed a man in Lyon who heads up an investigative effort on behalf of the *Gendarmerie de l'Air*.

On Thursday Guérin railed against “rationalist blockheads” and Jean-Pierre Petit, looking like a bright young student with his unruly black hair, gave a terrific presentation on magneto-hydrodynamic (MHD) propulsion illustrated with photographs of a disk-shaped model. Patrick Aimedieu spoke about parapsychology.

Bourret was furious as he read an Agence France-Presse dispatch about our conference, entitled “UFO = Hallucinations,” a piece written in Paris by people who had not bothered to get any information on what we had presented. The curtain of silence will fall back in spite of Bourret's visibility and clout. That answers my question about the suppression of data in the U.S.: the same manipulation is happening here.

Paris. Rue de la Clef. Saturday 19 June 1976.

My impression is that Cochereau simply serves as a mailbox for Kervandal, who is of higher rank. He said they had kept few reports from the 1954-73 period, a hole of 20 years in their records! After Minister Robert Gallet's decision it took months to setup a process. They only began sending data to CNES in July 1975.

Poher acknowleged that once the reports were on tape nobody was doing the follow-on research, a classic fallacy with databases: a big mass of data doesn't constitute information. Military cases don't go to the Gendarmes and never get to Toulouse: thus Poher never found out about a UFO that recently flew over a French aircraft carrier and a submarine anchored in the harbor at Douarnenez. **(63)**

Petit's work is interesting. In his experiments one can actually see the saucer surrounded with a halo, and the electrodes shine like portholes. However his propulsion theory would only work in salt water or in the atmosphere, since it requires an ionizable medium. In the U.S. this is met with skepticism: it can't be applied to space propulsion and requires a source of energy as powerful as a small nuclear plant. This does make sense in a submarine but nothing like this will fly until miniature reactors can be made reliably, as both Hal Puthoff and Paul Moller pointed out to me years ago.

Back in Paris Maman has fitted her apartment with a reinforced steel door and multiple locks. She has been burglarized twice, with the ugly feeling of violation such crimes leave behind. In the first incident neighbors heard blows when intruders broke down her flimsy door but they didn't bother to intervene or call police. The second incident took place on a Sunday while she was away at lunch with my brother. She found her door busted open, all the lights on. Fearing that the burglars were still inside, she called for help... "and the only noise I heard was the sound of deadbolts turning in my neighbor's flats," she said. The cops came over casually. They said, "These days in Paris, it's everybody for himself."

Life is hard here, while the more fortunate accumulate obscene wealth. France is being turned over to careless promoters.

Bayeux. Later the same day.

At last I have made my long-anticipated visit to Tilly-sur-Seulles, a site of ancient miracles where the 19th century visionary Vintras created one of the strangest sects of that troubled period. We found the Chapel of the Rosary at the end of a field where Marian apparitions were reported in 1897. We saw a young girl sitting there alone, crying before a lifesize statue of the Virgin. On the wall was a statement by Reverend Lasserteur, dated August 1902:

> At the site of the Apparitions that lasted three years there were visions, ecstasies, graces of every kind, including graces of conversions and miraculous cures (...) On 8 September 1897 the ecstasy lasted 55 minutes. Rain kept falling. It was noted with surprise that the clothes and the shoes of the visionary woman were perfectly dry.

Vintras may have been a scoundrel, but he was right to call this "a land of honey and roses." Now I think about Janine. For people like us life is a simple passage, a river crossing we make hand in hand, jumping from one stone to another, laughing at the water splashing around our feet. What does it matter if one shore is called birth, the other death? I believe less and less in time's vaunted tyranny. Midnight rings in this ancient farmhouse loaded with rich objects, precious memories. I shudder as I think of you.

Paris. Rue de la Clef. Monday 21 June 1976.

The year's shortest night: I took advantage of it to walk through the fields, with some disappointment at not finding lutins or sylphides -- or even those mischievious Norman *goublins* -- along the way. I try to place myself in conditions where witnesses have experienced phenomena. I try to recognize situations conducive to illusions.

We came back from Caen by train. All along the way my son was making notes of technical ideas in his journal. Olivier, now twelve and a half, has taken a remarkable turn: serious, studious, focused, an excellent observer. In Bayeux he struck people by his ability to isolate himself in the rich universe of his own thoughts.

Our daughter is in Normandy, playing with the goat Mirliflore, the dog Ullia, the rabbits and the peacocks that can be heard all around the farm. In Paris it was good to meet my brother Gabriel at the isotope department of Necker Hospital, which he's been directing for several years. We were able to speak quietly in Montparnasse.

Belmont. Friday 25 June 1976.

Back in California, the patio is filled with flowers; the horizon barely holds the wide blue Bay. I have piled up the books I brought back, sorted out the mail.

When I met Aimé Michel in Paris he was just returning from London, where he had visited Arthur Koestler.

"I'm trying to get him to write a book about the UFO issue," Aimé said. "Such a book would unlock public opinion. What you need to do is send him lots of documentation."

I promised to do it, but things are not that simple: "Public opinion only has two positions with respect to UFOs: if you dislodge the popular mind from the idea they are hallucinations, it'll fall into the idea that they are simply extraterrestrials," I said.

Aimé doesn't see anything wrong with it. He still believes the extraterrestrial theory is the best one. I asked:

"Don't you see that a technology that can create local deformations of spacetime topology could not only produce UFOs, but all sorts of other miraculous phenomena?"

"I agree," he said, "but that's already implicit in the extraterrestrial hypothesis."

"No, it's implicit in the control system theory, of which the extraterrestrial hypothesis is only one possible branch, among many others. The actors of the spacetime deformation in question don't have to be from another planet."

Perhaps we're both right. The question of the possible origin of UFOs also came up in my long discussions with Simonne Servais in her Neuilly apartment near the Bois de Boulogne. We spent two evenings arguing about the politics of the paranormal. I told her Gepan was nothing more than a French Blue Book. "The real work has to be somewhere else," I concluded. I thought it was time to brief serious people, thinking of de Marenches (**64**).

She looked out at the faraway trees of the park and sighed: "Believe me, those people don't understand anything about this..." Well, neither do their American counterparts, I thought to myself, recalling my pointless talks in Washington. But what if some UFOs were a human manipulation?

She had a strong reaction: "Look, I've had a long, rich political life," she said. "I was a Cabinet member while France had riots and barricades in 1968. I know first-hand about man's appetite for power. If you turn out to be right I'll jump into the Seine."

My own working hypothesis is that there exists a parallel reality to which some individuals have access. Whether such access is accidental, deliberate or "by invitation only," I'm not able to decide. The phenomenon provides evidence that our own world is influenced by a higher force acting from that other reality.

Belmont. Thursday 22 July 1976.

On Monday I had lunch with Sir John Whitmore who spoke of his adventures with Andrija Puharich and medium Phyllis Schlemmer. He swears she's the third medium sent over by "Spectra." The second one was a Florida healer who tried to commit suicide.

John follows Phyllis' instructions on behalf of *The Nine*. Whenever her "voices" tell her he should be in Cairo, Tel-Aviv, Warsaw, Helsinki or Moscow this group rushes to buy airplane tickets (with Whitmore's money), and off they go!

Belmont. Saturday 24 July 1976.

Last night I flew back from Los Angeles with my two children who returned from France with songs and stories. I had been recording interviews in L.A. about *Invisible College* but my mind was at Spring Hill. On planet Mars the Viking robot is taking photographs and will soon start digging in search of organic life.

Last Monday I met Ken Shoulders, a dynamic inventor dressed in light blue clothes that matched his blue eyes. He had white hair, a balding head. "I've been asked to do a survey on psychical research," he told me. I gave him a transcript of our computer conference.

Now Catherine has opened her suitcase, extracting many treasures, song books and toys. Her brother brought pictures from the Riviera and an interesting clipping sent by my mother: It seems that the French TV recently held a debate about UFOs where my old Paris observatory boss Paul Muller was invited.

"Those alleged sightings would be very different if the witnesses had used binoculars," he said. "To begin with, they'd realize many saucers are simply weather balloons. I must say that none of us has ever seen anything, and no photograph has ever shown anything other than satellites, shooting stars or planes." A bundle of lies, but the French public swallows it.

Belmont. Monday 26 July 1976.

Allen called me last night using the new phone line paid for by his backers. He was eager to convince me that he had taken a serious turn. He's hired a competent fellow named Allan Hendry and will publish a magazine. "We need to sell 5,000 copies to recover our costs, but beyond that we split the profit 50/50 with our backers."

"What about the actual cases? Will you make them available? As you know, UFO magazines only print polemics and not data."

"You can be sure we'll publish all our cases; the information will build up in every issue."

Belmont. Sunday 1 August 1976.

Emenegger believes that Alfonso Lorenzo is back at Wright Field under a new name.

Yesterday we took the kids to the Pinnacles, a picturesque park with a volcanic lake amidst a jumble of huge dark rocks. The whole day would have been delightful if I had not allowed myself to get mad at my son. I was even angrier at myself. At thirteen Olivier is tough and creates much tension. That was no reason for my over-reaction, which tells much about my insecurities. I swore I would control my nerves in the future. I feel terrible and ashamed.

Belmont. Sunday 8 August 1976.

At Spring Hill water is still flowing nicely from the well in spite of the dry weather. We went to the cabins in the redwood forest, where I drafted my letter of resignation from the Institute, a difficult step because I am caught between my respect for Roy, Bob Johansen and other colleagues, and the desire to take conferencing technology into the business world. Our "business angel," Ray Williams is helping us financially; we're renting a small office in Palo Alto.

Fred called me, utterly disenchanted: "Allen mistakes for glory what's sheer exploitation," he observed. "He went to Puerto Rico. They told him they had 50 mutilation cases, with surgical techniques in evidence, which excludes predators, so now he tends to agree with you this is serious stuff. But he isn't going to pursue it, because it scares him. He'd rather spend time in Hollywood; there's a rumor Stephen Spielberg is making a UFO movie."

On the way back from the ranch yesterday we stopped by the shore of the Russian river at Healdsburg. Olivier and I happily paddled a canoe along the river to pick blackberries from overhanging bushes. My son is growing up to be tough-minded, independent. I must not interfere with this. In the world that is coming, those will be important strengths.

Flying back from Minneapolis. Wednesday 18 August 1976.

I spent last Friday at SRI where Kit was on a site visit to the psychic project. Now a visit to Control Data headquarters has left me angry and puzzled. After a good demonstration of the teleconferencing prototype I've developed with Bob Beebe I had a confrontation with an attorney who talked of rewriting our contract, taking all the rights to our system for a small lump sum, and leaving us with no royalties.

Belmont. Wednesday 25 August 1976.

We took another trip up north, starting in Healdsburg where we rented canoes again to harvest juicy blackberries along the river. We slept in Ukiah and drove on to Willits, a region caught in an uneasy transition between the horse and the motorcycle, between quiet retired folks and ebullient hippies, between struggling loggers and millionaire pot growing gangsters.

The landscape is tortured, sometimes grandiose, with pines and redwoods at the edge of mossy precipices; white fog lingers among dense ferns. We went on to Fort Bragg, walked to the beach, scaled the rocks, and built sand castles. We drove to Mendocino at a leisurely pace. The wind from the Pacific rose with the tide, beating against the old wooden towers and the savage beauty of the Coast.

At Gualala we played with a raft bobbing up in the waves, went to Bodega Bay for more sand castles. Gray fog rushed up the estuary, and we only saw the sun again when we reached Point Reyes near the primeval seascape of Inverness, then an abrupt transition into the City, the rush hour as office workers drove en masse over the bridge, and the explosion of noise and color they call San Francisco.

Coming home I found a letter from Peter Rogerson, a knowledgeable analyst. He made astute comments about similarities between the Ummo stories and tales by Jorge Luis Borges. He called my attention to the connections contactees like Adamski and Williamson had with neo-Nazi American organizations such as William Dudley Pelley's Silver Shirts. Williamson even worked for Pelley's Soulcraft group. The links between him and the Stanford brothers deserve further study, he wrote. Oddly enough they are resurfacing as "scientific parapsychologists," surely a step backward for people who used to enjoy close contact with extraterrestrials.

"Contactee ideology derives from the populist-fascist-occultist matrix of the thirties," Rogerson went on.

Belmont. Friday 27 August 1976.

This summer has transformed our children. There's nothing left of the little child in our daughter, now a mixture of Parisian *aplomb* and California sophistication, while Olivier crosses the last bridge towards adolescence with energy, quick to jump with both feet on the sand castles he still condescends to build to humor his father.

Allen called me last night, cheerful; the old magic came back into our dialogue. It was past midnight in Evanston. He said we had sold the Japanese rights of *Edge of Reality*. Dell is sending two writers to help him with a hurriedly-compiled paperback about Project Blue Book (**65**). As for the Spielberg movie, he will indeed have a silent role in it, making his way to the front of a crowd of technical people who surround the first landed saucer. I'd love to see the out-takes: They shot a sequence where Aliens surrounded him, pulled on his beard, took his pipe and poked it into their nose.

Belmont. Tuesday 31 August 1976.

Science Magazine has again distinguished itself by publishing the announcement that the Air Force was turning over its UFO files to the National Archives, giving its readers the misleading impression that all secrets were now revealed, the data in the open.

On Sunday night Janine saw two green rays when the sun set over the Pacific South of Fort Bragg. There was a curious coincidence as we had dinner in a Gualala restaurant: we were waiting for the food with two restless kids after a long day. Around us elegant couples stared at us with disapproval. I started drawing funny cartoons on a napkin to keep the kids occupied. We had watched the fishing fleet in the harbor at Fort Bragg, so I drew a trawler at sea, the crew pulling their nets, surprised to find a cursing sailor in them, and next to this, the periscope of a trapped submarine.

Today's *Chronicle* carries an article from Associated Press, filed in Tokyo: “Mystery sub snags nets, drags fishing boat.” It must have happened last week-end. Why do such psychic impressions often come to us when the mind is upset, or ill at ease, caught in unfamiliar, socially uncomfortable situations? Why is there no signal that tells us when those fleeting images are significant?

On the plane to Washington. Thursday 9 September 1976.

Dr. Erich Fromm remarks that many so-called “normal people” only seem well-adjusted to our mode of existence because their voice has been reduced to silence. They don't fight any more, don't feel pain or sorrow; they don't even develop neuroses. Citing these words, Huxley observes (in *Brave New World Revisited*) that these people are only "normal" by reference to an abnormal society. "Their perfect adjustment to this abnormal society is a measure of their illness... they only cherish the illusion of their individuality."

I had dinner with Aaron Katz on Union Street, the current center of San Francisco snobbishness. Aaron is devoured by the rage of creation. His bald head reflected candlelight and his eyes burned when he described his plans. As we left the *Coffee Cantata* I saw Don's friend Mande working as a waitress next door. She rushed out to kiss me. "What eyes! What style! Are you a dancer?" Aaron gushed. She said Don was penniless, living in a decrepit hotel.

New York. Sunday 12 September 1976.

A powerful dream lingers in my mind, of a circle of witches, forked branches held high. Later I was at Spring Hill, adjusting a ladder that led to a skylight cut into the roof (**67**).

Jeane Dixon predicts that beings from space will be landing here before next August. Her Aliens, as usual, will help us wipe out cancer, heart disease, famine and war. If only they could also wipe out superstition! The same issue of the *National Enquirer* also mentioned, more discreetly, a statement by Arthur Lundahl (**66**), the nation's top photo-analysis expert. He said that the Newhouse movie, shot at Tremonton in Utah, was authentic. Lundahl, at 61, retired from the Intelligence world three years ago.

New York. The University Club. Monday 13 September 1976.

The launching of InfoMedia came up today before the Trustees of the Institute for the Future. Roy expressed regrets at my leaving. One trustee applauded my initiative but cautioned that our company shouldn't step on the Institute's domain. He was rebuffed by George Vila, the Uniroyal President, who said that they "shouldn't put any restrictions on anyone who had the guts to venture into new fields."

A motion was passed to allow the Institute to take a small position in the company in return for a license for our Planet system.

Belmont. Sunday 26 September 1976.

Books and letters accumulate, including another batch of notes by Peter Rogerson about the links between contactee groups and Nazi philosophy, as expressed by the I-AM movement of Guy Ballard and William Dudley Pelley's *Silver Shirts* (**68**). Why isn't anybody studying these groups? Academic research is paying no attention to the new religious movements that are growing around their feet.

Our children are playing, listening to records. I read Casanova's *Memoirs* again, impressed by the difference in intellectual and emotional contact, cultural diversity and richness between his society (1750) and ours. The comparison is not to our advantage. They were managing quite well, thank you, without computers and phones, cars and radios, airplanes and electric blankets. We're limited by the obstacles we put in our own path.

Belmont. Tuesday 28 September 1976.

Last night I went back to *Coffee Cantata*, this time for dinner with Brendan O'Regan. He was shaken by a recent experience while on a panel at a psychic conference in Miami, along with Bill Tiller, Alan Vaughan, old Professor Rhine and Evan Harris Walker, an Army researcher from Aberdeen Proving Grounds.

"I started talking about certains things I should've kept confidential," he told me. "I'd recently heard from a classified source about extended psychic experiments done by soviet cosmonauts, and I spilled out the story. It's not like me to be indiscreet."

Other strange things happened at that conference. Walker took polaroid pictures of the audience. Brendan looked at the photos with him. But an hour later both the camera and the pictures had been stolen. The next day Brendan was relaxing on the beach when Walker joined him. He was worried because of recent security breaches at Aberdeen.

"They have a classified library there, holding a description of every U.S. weapon system. A few months ago the guard was found dead, killed with his own gun. The Army called it a suicide. Did someone wander around freely inside for five hours?"

Sir John Whitmore is indeed providing funds for Puharich's futile chase. When Puharich slept at the Great Pyramid following Hoova's psychic instructions, he was awakened by a peculiar noise, turned on his flashlight, and saw he was sharing the sacred spot with a mouse!

Belmont. Sunday 10 October 1976.

Allen has assured me again that his wild travels were over. "From now on I'll only follow up on critical cases," he said, "I won't give any more free lectures for Northwestern."

Indeed the University has been exploiting him. When he requested permission to seek private funds to support Corralitos Observatory, they asked: "You're not going to use it for your UFO stuff now, will you?" But whenever the Alumni have another dinner they beg him to address them, because he always draws a crowd.

Allen has high hopes for his magazine and for police reports, yet statistics are disappointing: Based on the first 35 calls from law enforcement, no less than 33 were misidentified stars or planets.

Arthur Koestler, whose attention I called to Dr. Lindner's *Fifty Minute Hour,* has written back. On to the topic of contactees, he points out their tales sound to him like "poorly told dirty stories," embarrassing for everybody. Last month I met Ed Krupp at UCLA (**69**), an interesting writer on astronomy.

I've received another letter from Allen, excited about a new trip: "I'm about to go on a world tour: Indonesia through London, Tokyo in December..." So much for his promise to cut down on travel.

Belmont. Monday 1 November 1976.

We spent a magical Halloween night, the city mad with fantasy. Janine wore a stately black cape and black mask, while I had a silver robot head. As the night progressed we found ourselves drinking wine with Ginger and her friends: an elephant, a camel, a few crazy Martians and a fat girl in pink with cat whiskers.

The real fun was on Polk Street. The police had halted traffic to turn over the pavement to revellers in every state of wild dress or undress. The crowd was well-behaved, cheerfully controlled by miniskirted boys. It felt good to laugh at the world. A chemist in a white smock walked around, shaking a bottle where a pink liquid swirled. There were Frankensteins, graceful elves and an alien who inspected us with bug eyes and said: “How strange you people are!”

Around midnight we found our dancer friends, Enjil and Vernon in their North Beach dressing room. He borrowed my robot mask. Their last dance of the evening was a ceremony, Vernon wearing robot attire he improvised to go along with my mask. After the show we joined their friends at a warehouse South of Market where The Tubes had a colorful party. We stayed until four in the morning, when cocaine began circulating and we saw it was time to leave.

The evening was a welcome diversion: in a few days I leave on business for the East Coast.

Charlotte, North Carolina. Sunday 14 November 1976.

In New Jersey I had a series of meetings with Murray Turoff and Richard Wilcox, a pioneer of teleconferencing at the State Department, which sharpened my view of the field. Their ideas have stagnated like the New Jersey landscape, identical to what I knew seven years ago. From New York I flew on to Philadelphia to meet with Einhorn. I spent the night at the home of Ira's friends Tom and Christine Bissinger, in a pleasant loft with a thick carpet.

I had breakfast with Ira and Holly, who is sweet and self-effacing. Ira is one of the few intellectuals who understand what network technology means. We discussed parapsychology, the works of Charles Musès and Tom Bearden. He told me about advanced communications research at Bell, where he was consulting.

The Bissingers live on Lethgrow Street, in a dilapidated area that local artists are skillfully rehabilitating. Old brick houses that can be bought for a song are turning into pretty little castles.

Belmont. Saturday 4 December 1976.

Douglass Price-Williams is the latest researcher to resign from Cufos, tired of seeing his name on the masthead of their newsletter: "There's no real research in anything they do," he told me.

Fred Beckman, who met Allen for dinner recently, found him with a lady from Indonesia. "He finally shook her off and pulled out two suitcases. I asked him what they contained and he told me, 'things you should look at while you eat!' As you know, if there is one thing I detest, it is looking at something other than food when I eat. So I told him I much preferred talking to him; he merely grunted. He mumbled that some people like to sit on their butt while others do all the work!"

During the filming of *Close Encounters* Allen had breakfast every morning with "some French actor." **(70)** It was François Truffaut!

Last night I went to the Jack Tar Hotel to listen to Claude Vorilhon, the French contactee. He was furious because the local media hadn't greeted him with appropriate awe. His lecture was boring, for a man who thought he was Jesus Christ reincarnated. When I shook his hand he reproached me for not coming to see him at his Brantôme headquarters: "Your room was ready," he told me in a friendly way.

Dayton, Ohio. Sunday 19 December 1976.

With regret I flew away from our tall Christmas tree covered with white flocking and lights, a log burning in the fireplace. I'm on another trip with Bob Johansen to present our work to the Kettering Foundation. I'm also working on geological databases with Gerald who is now in Idaho. We communicate through the net, editing our joint article through our terminals. Some day everybody will be able to do this: the world of communications may change at last. **(71)**

Anton LaVey has discovered a musical similarity between "Yes we have no bananas!" and Haendel's *Messiah*, so he composed a tune blending the two together. Now he does not know whether to call it "Allelluya Banana" or "Yes, we have no Messiah!"

It's cold in Ohio, with bright snow on the ground. I thought about my first trip there with Allen (**72**). Bob and I walked along in our gray overcoats between concrete walls, arguing about electronic media that won't exist for years.

Flying back from Tucson. Wednesday 22 December 1976.

Jim Lorenzen has just told me about a witness who "lost" several hours while driving in the mountains near Tucson. Jim, who met me at Tucson airport, cultivates a resemblance with Allen, even growing a gray goatie. As we drove away he said he worked for a company doing organ and piano repair. We stopped by the shop to meet his boss, on the way to the Apro offices, a converted garage with a leaky roof. Later we went to their house and I finally met Coral.

Jim and Coral are in poor health. Jim has already suffered a heart attack, and she complains of back pains. They are sincere, hard working, and direct in their lucid assessment of their research.

Back at the airport I invited Jim for lunch. We found we agreed about many things, even though he remains faithfully attached to the first-level extraterrestrial hypothesis, nuts and bolt spacecraft. Jim worried about Hynek, always distracted, except when he dances with Jim's daughter, "and always cheek to cheek," he added with a wink.

Belmont Saturday 25 December 1976.

The weather has turned gray and wet; the fog seems to lift our house into the sky. Janine reads the notes from my trip. It is maddening not to know, she said: "The government's keeping too many things from us. We're already in ignorance about life, about why we're here, on this earth. And all these secrets..."

We spent a sweet holiday. Catherine played Noëls for us on the violin. Santa Claus brought us two guinea pigs, and a chameleon.

Part Eight

CLOSE ENCOUNTERS

16

Belmont. Sunday 2 January 1977.

Alone: Janine has driven up north with her brother and Olivier. Our daughter is staying with our friend Maud. Many families have gone off to the snow of the Sierra; those who stay are safely huddled before their televisions sets. The rain has come; the storm goes on with horizontal bands of gray sky I see through the window soaking the hills of Alameda, drawing darker stratas over the lighter tones of the Bay and the swamps of Redwood City.

I have been reading Aleister Crowley's magical Journal, magnificently edited by Symonds and Grant **(1)**. It is filled with remarkable observations, notably this passage dated 1 February 1920, where he comments upon the Society for Psychical Research:

> All their work only proves that there are extra-human forces. We knew about them all along, the universe is full of obscure and subtle manifestations of Energy (...) But what nobody else before me has done is to prove the existence of extra-human Intelligence, and my Magical Record does this. *I err in the interpretation, of course* (my emphasis --JV) but it is impossible to doubt that there is Somebody there, a Somebody capable of combining events as a Napoléon forms his plans of campaign, and possessed of those powers unthinkably vast, by which to direct the actions of people whom he has chosen to play a part in the execution of his purpose.

This is important, even if Crowley wasn't the first to claim this proof: Facius Cardan, John Dee, the *Comte de Gabalis* and other hermetists had seen it before. It brings us back to a psychophysical control system. There's a secondary human impact, easier to analyze, the undercurrent working through groups using the alien mythology to propagate their own agenda. Examples: the Ummo hoax, the cults, the shadowy military folks who promote the Holloman affair. But I still don't understand the connection between these two aspects.

This relates to my own evolution within the field. As I started going deeper I found facts and theories becoming simpler, clearer. I reached a point when it was encompassed by just a few hypotheses. But when I kept digging the landscape became confused again.

Belmont. Saturday 8 January 1977.

Sitting at the computer, I am putting the files of our InfoMedia startup in order. Curious impression of the office on the first day: no receptionist, silent telephone, the old terminal, not even any supplies. If I want a pencil, I'll have to go out and buy a pencil: This is better entrepreneurial training than any Business school. Bob Beebe and I tested out the program we're developing for Control Data. Their third payment has arrived.

Belmont. Sunday 9 January 1977.

Allen called me up last night. Returning from Indonesia, he's been ill with the flu. His trip began with a three-hour lunch with Koestler in London, thanks to an introduction by Aimé Michel. "Unfortunately Charles Gibbs-Smith was there, the old blabbermouth from *Flying Saucer Review*. I couldn't get into any serious issue," Allen said.

"What did Koestler ask you?"

"He was bothered by the cartoon-like humanoids."

Allen left for Jakarta. They lost his suitcase for four days.

"I was embarrassed at the luxurious way they greeted me in Indonesia: chauffeured limousine, official receptions, and ten-course banquets. I gave lectures everywhere. I even spoke before the Indonesian Air Force staff. The local culture accepts the notion of invisible, multi-dimensional entities."

"How much do they know, at Government level?" I asked.

"They rely on Air Marshall Yakov Salatun, who's written on the subject, but his book isn't very good. We both had an audience with

Malik, their foreign affairs Minister."

Back home Allen said he found a "troubling, almost insulting" letter from Poher telling him that publishing a magazine was a bad idea, that none of it constituted good research. Faced with such criticism from friends Allen keeps restating, with some justification, that "the Center has a mission to educate the public. We must publish carefully-filtered facts. Look at Apro's mistakes, Jacques, taking common weather balloons for flying saucers. They discredit themselves. We've got to learn from such errors."

Belmont. Thursday 13 January 1977.

Our company is getting off the ground, although we just had a setback at the Geological Survey who declined to install our software. Their systems people feel their power threatened by the concept of conferencing: the network would give local and State geologists straight access to Washington, bypassing regional bureaucracies. Next week I'm going to New York for a meeting of futurists, where I hope to find new support. We've already demonstrated that computer networks could be used for more than computing, that they were a new medium of group communication with exceptional features.

I saw Hal and Russell today. Their book *MindReach* is out **(2)**. They've moved their research to the SRI Radiophysics lab, more quiet and secure than the old office.

New York. Essex House. Monday 17 January 1977.

The temperature will drop to zero tonight. The airport was covered with snow and ice when I landed. The wind was so strong that people were rushing awkwardly, grasping for precarious support from lamp post to lamp post. I don't see clearly within myself. Yesterday I worked in my library, dealing with correspondence, an article for an information science journal, messages over the net. We went to Nueva School to hear an admirable medieval concert. We came back holding hands, more in love than ever.

New York. Essex House. Tuesday 18 January 1977.

Breakfast with Wes Thomas, a futurist who works with Barbara Marx Hubbard **(3)** and a group of technocrats. The day was spent listening to speeches full of undefined words like "legitimacy" and to a lecture by Orville Freeman, former Secretary of something, whose only novel idea was to "change the image of business."

La Guardia Airport. Friday 21 January 1977.

New York's stridence weighs down on me, grotesque and foul. Consider this word "foul"... "Foule" means "crowd" in French. I had never put these two words next to each other, because I love crowds, animated streets, and the psychic stimulation of other humans. But here in New York it often turns to a feeling of evil pressures over one's thoughts.

I wait for a plane to Washington for a one-day trip to the Space Institute. My mind goes back to those winter mornings in Pontoise, when I used to walk down *rue de l'Eperon* to the train station, math books under my arm. The town was asleep, its houses in quiet rows, the stars bright. The noisy train stopped everywhere, jumping over increasingly dense junctions as it got close to Paris. The sun rose over the smoke of greasy suburbs.

Last night Ingo and I spoke of psychic research. He confided to me that his SRI work now went beyond what Targ and Puthoff's *MindReach*: "I have free rein to run my own experiments, while the skeptics keep harping on minor statistical arguments," he told me as he reclined over a mound of cushions among the white statues and the large paintings in his Greenwich Village studio, "but we should remain vigilant. These people are motivated to derail humanity's attempt to become spiritually emancipated."

New York. Essex House. Later the same day.

I returned from Washington in time to catch Allen's lecture. He was coughing, still in the grips of his Indonesian flu. Jim Moseley was there, and Rita Livingston. Researcher Ted Bloecher, whose hair has turned white, came to dinner with us afterwards. He's left his theater career and now works with a company that processes inventories for major stores but spends his spare time patiently cataloging UFO landings. He knows the field as well as anyone.

In a confusing lecture, Allen mixed together drawings of creatures reported by witnesses with comical cartoons. This had the effect of denying credibility to the genuine sightings even as he described them with eager precision. Whenever the audience asked questions he retreated into a conservative stand, yet the next minute he was taunting them again with slides of astral paintings.

As soon as he stepped off the stage his amazing energy bounced back. We went to his room for a while. He opened his briefcase and pulled out the latest copy of his newsletter, showed me a photo of his Mexican representative and spoke about the "progress" made. After dinner he went off to a disco with his son Joel, who has just gotten married. His brother-in-law owns a night club called Infinity.

New York. Saturday 22 January 1977.

The conference of the Space Institute was held at the Statler-Hilton in Washington. Gerry O'Neil's presentation on space colonies left me unimpressed. Timothy Leary told me he counted on the new wave of space enthusiasm among the public to bring him back to national prominence. He looked buoyant in a blue flight jacket. When I described computer conferencing he understood it right away. I found this refreshing after all my difficulties with fellow scientists.

Astronaut "Rusty" Schweikart joined us. We discussed the prospects for space exploration. Once I was alone again with Leary I asked him if he considered himself to be a contactee. "I'm just a reporter broadcasting messages from KDNA," he told me. "The genetic code is the closest instance we have of higher intelligence; it knows how to assemble our brains!"

Leary projected an image of easy-going, intense amusement, but his carefree behavior didn't seem genuine. It reminded me of Puharich's pretense of kindness and cosmic joy.

Belmont. Monday 24 January 1977.

Elmer keeps calling today, his pasty voice slurring revelations. Allen called, too: he had dismissed Elmer but worried that the fellow might do something extreme if we refused to take part in a four-hour phone séance with his astral guide "Shining Face."

Fed up, I told him I just didn't believe in drugs as a source of wisdom. "Shining Face demands to speak to you!" he insisted. "If he's so powerful, surely he can find me," I said.

Later the same day.

Allen was right: Elmer is in trouble. Barricaded in his garage in Palo Alto, he tells the police he's in psychic contact with extraterrestrials and threatens to kill himself if the cops come close. After Allen refused to take his drug-induced messages seriously, Elmer called a woman who became so alarmed at his delusion that she called his doctor, who alerted police. An officer was trying to reach me, Janine said when she paged me. I called back, telling him about Elmer's earlier history. I said he was harmless, and I hoped they wouldn't send the SWAT team crashing into his little garage.

Belmont. Tuesday 25 January 1977.

The Palo Alto police did keep their cool. They waited for four hours while Elmer threatened to kill anyone who came close to his place. They evacuated ten houses, cordoned off several blocks and eventually talked him into surrender. He had no gun.

Allen called me after a "fairly rational" conversation with Elmer, who was in the hospital. He gave police a tape recorded statement intended for Hynek, but had no recollection of their morning talk.

Belmont. Thursday 3 Febuary 1977.

We delight in our children. Last night we built a clock together; Olivier told us he'd passed his exams, would go to Menlo School next year. I marvel at these precious moments. Our daughter sings old French songs for us, changing the words to her own fancy (**4**).

On Sunday night I saw Aaron Katz again in his jungle-like apartment. His two boys were watching two separate color television sets that yelled constantly, tuned to different channels. Aaron was about to leave for Philadelphia to launch a new venture. Someone approached him with an offer: Would he take money from the CIA? He said yes. What happened afterwards was interesting.

"They sent a woman to interview me, a *vacuum-cleaner.* She told me to spill out everything. That went fine until I described your computer conferencing system. They didn't believe what I told her. They couldn't decide whether I was a crook or a visionary. They said nobody could run such international conferences by computer, that it was far beyond the state of the art. Do you know what these idiots told me?" he added with a chuckle, "they said, if such software existed, surely the Agency would've known it before me! And it would be classified!"

The idea that such fools could ever solve the UFO problem is ludicrous.

Belmont. Friday 11 February 1977.

Elmer has been released. He speaks in a calmer mood but his New Age delusions are still with him: he gives demonstrations of automatic writing to his landlady.

Doug Engelbart is caught in a disintegrating spiral. The management of SRI is turning over his project to another department, where the staff had a champagne party to celebrate the news, even as Doug was holding another long soul-searching meeting of the few remaining faithful "to clarify his future role."

Belmont. Saturday 12 February 1977.

Janine tells me she loves me, that I am her treasure. "But like anyone who has a treasure, I don't know what to do with it: Should I lock you up, give you to someone else, bury you?" she asks. Just keep me in your heart, and I'll be happy.

We're going to live through a crazy year. I am barely surviving on a half-salary, yet we have to travel more than ever. I am flying to Denver in ten days, then to Mexico for a conference in Acapulco. A month later, Germany and France for professional meetings, and a short vacation with Janine in Morocco.

Belmont. Sunday 13 February 1977.

This is what I relish: A sky busy with the fragrance of spring; a Tartini record on the stereo; the accacia in bright yellow bloom; the sun playing over a pile of firewood; our long silence. It brings back the smell of the rain on the cobblestones of Pontoise. I could extend my hand to touch the Middle Ages, scratch the earth to rediscover Caesar's roads, catch a glimpse of Nicolas Flamel.

Last night Charles and Christiane Musès came over for dinner. He once met a policeman who had unsuccessfully tried to infiltrate satanic groups. The man was certain they were responsible for cattle mutilations. They took the skin and made amulets out of them, he thought. None of these theories, unfortunately, can explain the facts: it is rare for the skin to be removed in mutilations. The cops just repeat rumors they haven't checked.

We spent the rest of the evening discussing hypernumbers (**5**) and deploring the way parapsychology was becoming institutionalized. "These so-called researchers who pontificate about psychic science are like boxing managers who take the spectator's money but never get any of the blows. The true researchers are the subjects themselves, not the scientists!" Said Charles.

Denver. Tuesday 22 February 1977.

Murray Turoff and Roxanne Hiltz are attending this meeting on teleconferencing (**6**) where panelists argue endlessly about the Delphi technique of forecasting. I spent the evening with Richard Sigismond, the prospector and psychologist who once went into Professor Condon's office and challenged him to focus on UFO landings. His experiences are those that Lee Sanella has catalogued for the awakening of the Kundalini (7). It is tempting to believe Richard, yet he hasn't found the precious minerals towards which he was supposed to be "guided."

As I came out of a session where Turoff was a speaker, I found myself face to face with Bill Powers stepping out of another meeting. We were happy to see each other after all these years. He wore a graying beard that made him look like Allen. Conversation turned to research on higher consciousness under his feedback system of behavior. "The only way to study a control system is to introduce perturbations into it," he advised.

Belmont. Wednesday 23 February 1977.

On the way back, flying over the magnificent landscape of Utah, I read Jacques Duchaussoy's book *La Parole Perdue,* raising issues of human history. I don't believe the human race was created by extraterrestrials, as some ufologists claim. There's no indication that Man is an experiment by other beings. But the possibility that primitive man and another form of consciousness were in contact centuries ago must be examined, unlikely as it may be.

Traces of such early contact may exist in the epics of Antiquity, in Sumerian cylinders and basic myths. For the Greeks it is Demeter sending over "some Gods whose names must remain undisclosed" (Plato, *Laws*) who proceed to direct human agriculture and urban planning. She provided Triptodemus with winged chariots to spread civilization. The same theme applies to Osiris in Egypt, to Partholon in Ireland -- like the angels of Judeo-Christian folklore, represented as luminous wheels in medieval iconography. *The Tibetan Book of the Dead* speaks of them as spinning wheels.

Belmont. Thursday 3 March 1977.

Spring is bursting through the stained glass, books glow richly in the red shades. Birds sing, perched on the windowsill. Last night we went to hear Jean-Pierre Rampal with friends from Woodside. Today

Ira Einhorn called me, eager to follow-up on rumors that Jessup's death was an assassination. Why is he falling for these silly rumors? He assured me the Russians had discovered the secret of bilocation, and that SRI was working along the same lines. (**8**) Like the ufologists, he loses sight of the real mystery in a fog of false rumors.

Anton LaVey is interesting when he discusses the nature of secrecy (**9**). He points out that people are most thrilled by the impression of "discovery." Therefore if you want the masses to accept your claims, you should never try to reveal anything but you should arrange for them to "discover" it.

The best process to achieve this is what he calls the Easter Egg Formula: (i) The magician gets up before everybody else, scattering brightly colored eggs for others to find. (ii) He hides them in such a way that they can be discovered with relatively little work. (iii) The secret of the existence of the eggs is leaked out. (iv) The crowd rushes out and finds them, delighted with this revelation. (v) Congratulations follow. (vi) Real secrets are safe and the magician's prestige is enhanced. Is this how the belief in UFOs works? Is the undercurrent built on the Easter Egg Formula?

The saucers are indeed like Easter eggs. Someone got up early and scattered them around for us to discover. Then he leaked out the notion that they were extraterrestrial. I'm not interested in discussing the eggs, nor do I care about the scientists who "explain" them away. Let's find out who makes them, and why. Actually I think I know "why." The target is human mythology, the most powerful force on Earth. And there is no question that the phenomenon also functions on the material, physical level.

Belmont. Friday 4 March 1977.

Skeptic Bob Schaeffer (who has just published a scathing review of my *Invisible College* in *Zetetic*) unfairly ridicules Rhine and his "famous transparent cards" for telepathy. As if Rhine' tests were not pathetic enough with cards that are perfectly opaque.

Hynek sounded dejected when he called last night. Fred told me the real issue: "Alan Hendry, a solid researcher who was the key editor and secretary for the Center, has just resigned," he said. To Hendry's credit, he pursued hundreds of cases that turned out to have natural explanations. He courageously published his results. This is good research, a rare commodity in ufology, but it's bad for an organization that promotes a mystery. They have only collected 1,600 subscriptions instead of the 10,000 they were seeking.

Belmont. Sunday 13 March 1977.

Gérard de Nerval, a Freemason, wrote an interesting account of the death of Adoniram, in his *Journey to the Orient*. He quotes an Arab legend in which Tubal-Kain makes a prediction to Adoniram and goes on to describe how Adinoram gets killed. His body is found by nine disciples who take as their new password MAKBENACH, which is supposed to mean "the flesh leaves the bones." An ugly rumor among occultists claims this was the password for the Kennedy assassination, ordered by J. Edgar Hoover, head of a secret group... One more unverifiable rumor.

Belmont. Saturday 19 March 1977.

At the Institute for the Future, where I have reduced my involvement to a half-time basis, a recent seminar brought together thinkers like Peter Schwartz and Bill Harman of SRI. They reviewed a study undertaken for the science adviser to the President, an intellectual exercise that views the national destiny in terms of "problems" to be solved: the Problem of Women, the Problem of Blacks, the Problem of Childhood... Not to mention the Problem of the Water, the Air, the Trees, the Housing Problem, the Crime Problem.

I feel increasingly estranged from that field; I am incapable to see women, children, Blacks and trees as problems to be "solved."

On the plane to Washington. Sunday 20 March 1977.

On the way to the Capital, and from there to New Orleans for another conference about computer conferencing. I plan to come home through El Paso where I'll meet with Dr. Green, still in medical school. I expect we will argue again about the reality of UFOs and mutilations, both of which he keeps denying.

My ingenious son and my mischievious daughter are a delight. To be a good father I must pay attention to my own anxieties, even as I attend to material needs. If I was told I could have complete knowledge of any mystery provided I left behind those I love, I would certainly turn away from the knowledge. As for money, it doesn't interest me for itself, only as a tool to remove obstacles that hamper creativity. I must stay on the narrow path, walk to my own drumbeat. I am unimpressed by people with secret clearances. UFOs and psychic phenomena are best studied in the field, not in the secrecy of Washington circles. Kit's colleagues make mistakes like everybody else. In fact, they are probably easier to fool, compartmentalized as they are. They can even fool themselves.

Now the plane is flying over Colorado. The cabin is filled with bored businessmen. I read Raymond Bernard's curious book *Secret Houses of the Rose+Croix*, which I had almost set aside after scanning its esoteric platitudes. What prompted me to pick it up again was Bernard's suspicious description of his interaction with a man he calls Maha, who exercised mind control over the Grand Master of the French Branch of Amorc. The organization teaches rudiments of the Kabala and a great deal about self-hypnosis. The actual knowledge comes from an older organization created in France by Péladan and de Guaita circa 1890.

Bernard claims he was contacted by an emissary from a "High Council" who told him mankind was in transition to a one-world economy. Who has a vested interest in spreading such a message through occult groups?

Last night we went to see *Demon*, a movie that links UFOs to the occult in funny and ominous ways. In *Passport to Magonia* I had mentioned the case of a Moscow contactee whose voice inspired the killing of a scientist in the subway. In *Demon* the son of a woman who had been abducted by a saucer in 1951 inspired people around him to kill in the name of the Lord: Christ as ancient astronaut?

Flying over Arizona. Thursday 24 March 1977.

In Washington I only had the time for one brief investigation of the case of a woman who felt she was "outside time" during the remarkable wave of sightings that took place in Vernal, Utah and was analyzed by Frank Salisbury.

When I saw him in El Paso Kit was bothered by John Wilhelm, the *Time Magazine* journalist who wrote *Search for Superman* and is now hot on his trail. Kit has started to study cases of unexplained deaths and comas that have struck parapsychology researchers. Over dinner in Juarez he told me that the SRI work, which he follows on behalf of the CIA, was at a critical point again.

I am disappointed that my suggestion to analyze the "addressing scheme" in remote viewing hasn't been picked up. Theoretical implications in terms of entropy are obvious. Parapsychologists research Psi functioning as if they studied electricity or optics, but it doesn't occur to them to apply it seriously. They analyze Psi as if it existed, but go on living as if it didn't.

Belmont. Tuesday 29 March 1977.

Ira Einhorn has just sent around his network a report on psychic methodology in the Soviet block, where Pavlita is supposed to have performed convincing experiments under a Czech research program on psychotronics. Pavlita is also said to be working on a weapon that generates loss of muscle control, leaving people paralyzed. This effect is familiar to all those who have investigated UFOs. The military is interested. Yet Ira told me that his contacts, dissident Czech scientists, didn't want to pass on their information to the U.S. because they were sure the KGB had a mole inside the CIA and used the Zetetic movement in an effort to derail psi research in the West.

Belmont. Thursday 14 April 1977.

The other evening I met Gerry O'Neil again at KQED and heard the details of his plans for space colonies. The future that rolls towards us, full of violence and contradictions, doesn't resemble his smooth, rational space cities. On Sunday Timothy Leary and Eldrige Cleaver will be in Berkeley for a benefit in memory of Luna, the daughter of Robert Anton Wilson. The poor girl was 15 when she was assassinated. Berkeley, once a symbol for enlightened love, great music and free spirit, has turned into a nasty center of drugs and death. I'm tired of losing my friends to drugs. I welcome my next trip with Janine, our visit to Mexico, a change of pace.

Acapulco. Sunday 17 April 1977.

The first person we met at the Mexico City airport was Bill Spaulding of *Ground Saucer Watch* and his wife, strikingly dressed in a transparent outfit. We breezed through customs and bumped into Jim Lorenzen. The Spauldings pretended not to know him. How typical of ufological quarrels! They became enemies over the Travis Walton case (**10**).

We were joined by Hynek and his entourage. He introduced us to Sir Eric Gairy, a tall black man, Prime Minister of the tiny Caribbean island of Grenada. He recently gave a speech at the U.N., praising Christ and flying saucers in the same breath, pushing for an official research commission. Together, we boarded the flight to Acapulco.

Our arrival was high comedy. A fellow named Guillermo Bravo greeted us. He took Hynek, Sir Eric and me aside and forced us to sit in a little room where we had to listen to a welcoming speech by a delegate of the Mayor of Acapulco. His wife was with him, wearing bandages over one eye. "Do you think he beat her up?" Allen asked me in hushed tones while I stifled a chuckle. Two unfortunate tourists locked up with us in the VIP room by mistake didn't dare raise a complaint. They just shook hands with everybody as if they knew us, adding to the eeriness of the situation.

Several cars and an impressive police escort were waiting for us. Pedro Ferriz, an ebullient television personality, joined us as confusion increased. Janine was put into one car, Allen in another and me in a third with Mimi. The drivers kept arguing among themselves over the radio while policemen retrieved our suitcases. In

Spanish I spoke to our driver, a member of a group of 300 who thought they were in contact with Martians. They had their own medical centers and "transcendental" technology. We ended up in a villa in Pie de la Cuesta, overlooking a fine beach. Our room is rustic, with a ceiling fan but no hot water. We were introduced to many people whose names came from the dusty past of ufology, like Ian Norrie from England and Hans Petersen from Denmark. A fellow from the U.S. Navy took me aside to talk about God. I was saved from this confusion by Antonio Ribera. We fell in each other's arms and started telling funny stories.

Acapulco. Monday 18 April 1977.

It didn't take long for discord to spread. Over breakfast Ray Stanford complained that his wife had been bitten by a spider and that the Congress has no schedule. Others brought up various gripes. Yet there is interest for UFOs among high-ranking Mexicans. The wife of President Lopez-Portillo herself is said to be close to Geller.

We suffered through a long speech by Gairy. There were barely 400 people in attendance, many of them speakers or reporters, so the affair promises to be a financial fiasco for the organizers. The atmosphere got heavy as the time for the banquet arrived. Three women journalists fortunately offered us to skip this formal event and to dine with them and Eric Von Daniken. We gladly accepted their invitation and soon found ourselves in a colorful Arab restaurant downtown. Second-rate "rationalists" make a name for themselves by attacking Von Daniken, and it is obvious that he's no scientist: he doesn't claim to be. But we found him alive and buoyant; we enjoyed the evening thoroughly.

Acapulco. Wednesday 20 April 1977.

"Are all these people just going to talk about their own little chapels?" one of the journalists asked me, bored to tears. "They keep arguing about who has more equipment, who has the Truth... When do we get to hear about the phenomenon?" Janine and I have met

Hynek's backers, Dave Baldwin and Carl Deutsch, and saw a brief "teaser" for Spielberg's forthcoming *Close Encounters.*

We heard Padre Freixedo this morning, followed by John Keel. They offered the first original notes in this quarrelsome assembly. As a former Jesuit Salvador Freixedo has a tendency to preach, but his fiery sermons are interesting. He argues that some saucers are projections from the collective unconscious. He echoed my own thoughts when he argued that the UFO phenomenon was essential to an understanding of religion.

Janine was impressed by John Keel. Although I do like his ideas and his recent writings, I find he keeps contradicting himself. Typical of his style was a casual, throw-away comment that there were live dinosaurs in Texas.

At the break Allen and I interviewed a young man named Carlos de los Santos, a pilot who had a close encounter with a UFO in flight and later was intimidated by "men in black." We were both impressed with his story. We had lunch with a close associate of Jim Hurtak, a man named Adrian Ness who said he was "retired" from the Air Force's Office of Special Investigations, the notorious OSI. They show up everywhere and are much more likely than the CIA to be the true manipulators behind the scenes.

After lunch I made my presentation and Allen gave a longish astronomy lesson. We managed to escape a reception given by Eric Gairy, who had planned to harangue us in a private session where wives were not invited. Then a local amateur proposed to start a worldwide "research" organization which he would head up: All of us should go live in the desert under his leadership. Instead, Antonio, Fabio Zerpa, Janine and I went away for another fun-filled Latin evening, laughed at jokes and told stories.

Acapulco. Thursday 21 April 1977.

With journalist Marcia Seligson, of *New West* magazine, we shared a friendly meal with John Keel. In the evening Allen and Mimi gave a party in the magnificent villa where they were guests of Dave Baldwin. The residence had been built by the Rothschilds before they decided they preferred the Riviera. It included lodgings for servants and a private beach. The party was attended by numerous people associated with Cufos, notably Brad Ayers, a Minneapolis-based investigator and former CIA operative. He said he'd seen a UFO and the experience had changed his life.

Belmont. Saturday 7 May 1977.

Marcia Seligson called to say that Steven Spielberg wanted to have lunch with me on Thursday in L.A. The UFO subject is growing in popularity in anticipation of the release of *Close Encounters*. The public relations people at Columbia Pictures are adroitly spreading tidbits of UFO news through the media, capitalizing on President Carter's statement that he saw an unexplained light in the sky years ago in Georgia. Steven Spielberg at 27 has an impeccable record, since he was responsible for the $400 million *Jaws*. He came to our lunch in a sweater and blue cap, and spoke of his project.

"I already made this movie once," he told me. "Nobody saw it. I made it in eight millimeter, as a teenager."

He has long been fascinated by the subject. He said the essential scenes came to him in a series of dreams. He supports the extraterrestrial theory, as he reminded me with a laugh:

"When *Jaws* came out, many Americans stayed away from their own swimming pools!" However he isn't certain that CE3K will be equally successful: "*Jaws* could have been a failure. The *Godfather* could've bombed. Nothing's sure in this business."

Marcia Seligson, working on her *New West* article, asked him about the character of the French scientist played by Truffaut.

"Of course it's based on Jacques. I've read your books. The idea of a Frenchman doing research on UFOs in the States struck me as interesting. In one of the scenes we're unfortunately going to cut, Truffaut is sleeping at some Holiday Inn in the country; he's got a tape recorder on the bedside table, softly speaking in English. He's constantly trying to learn the language in order to communicate better with the military guys. But he bought his training tape in France, so the voice on the tape has a heavy French accent!"

We went on to talk about the section in the movie when the mothership is about to land; a part of the script that was bothering him, a key transition was missing. He was looking for a way to describe the moment when human experts would decipher the first message from the approaching mother-ship. Their laboratory was filled with computers, but somehow they had to transform the signals from space into meaningful patterns.

"I've spent useless hours over at the Jet Propulsion Lab," he said with frustration in his voice. "I've listened to all their explanations, all those long-haired guys with multi-million dollar machines and lots of blinking lights, but I couldn't make any sense out of their jargon. The scene's got to be graphic, visual."

I came up with a proposal for a sort of triangulation process that could logically lead the scientists on the ground to pinpoint the landing site: "They could be getting numbers and reading them as angles," I said. "You'd see the lines intersecting on a screen. Is that visual enough?"

"Yeah, it's visual," he said, "but it's too long. And it's not funny."

I remembered something: "You know, if such a momentous event did take place, it probably would mean chaos, the same confusion the first *Sputnik* created," I said. "It would be unlikely for so-called experts to be ready for it. In Allen Hynek's office at Northwestern there's a funny photograph of three astronomers climbing up ladders to fit a piece of string around a big globe. That took place in the middle of the night, at the Smithsonian Observatory. They were trying to find out where *Sputnik* was going, using the globe of the Earth in the public lobby as their way of mapping its orbit! In the meantime their programmers were frantically trying to come up with a computerized solution... You see, nobody had expected the Soviets would be the ones to launch the first artificial object into space."

"That's it!" Spielberg said, "they'll be getting a bunch of numbers, and somebody'll figure out they're just coordinates, longitude and latitude, only nobody's got a map! And the project leader says, 'you mean you've got a zillion bucks worth of classified electronics in this joint, and nobody thought of bringing a map of Wyoming?' (**11**)"

Flying to Washington. Wednesday 18 May 1977.

Columbia continues its promotion of CE3K with a $19 million advertising budget. *Playboy* plans books and articles to capitalize on it. George Leonard has written a novel for them, *The Alien.*

UFOs were with us long before World War Two and Arnold. We're dealing with a real phenomenon with powerful psychic aspects. This could point to an extraterrestrial origin. But other facts lead beyond this idea: *UFOs might be something far more interesting than spacecraft!* I mentioned this to Spielberg. He replied that Hollywood couldn't give the U.S. public something it couldn't visualize: "People out there expect extraterrestrials; I have to give them extra-terrestrials."

Flying to London. Saturday 28 May 1977.

Mount Shasta looms in proud majesty ahead of our plane, a bit of passing magic that will turn into a white dot on the horizon before we sink into the great polar dusk. Then Heathrow airport, Hamburg and Berlin, where the International Communications conference takes place this year. From Germany I'll fly back to Paris. Janine will meet me there with the kids in a week.

For my daughter's ninth birthday we suspended a piñada over the patio. Her friends came to hit the hairy cardboard dog, bright candy spilling out. My son has a good year, extending healthy roots in Belmont. His latest invention is a pinball machine adorned with dragons, filled with electrical relays, which spits out colored lights.

Later the same night.

Now we hover in the beams of hazy dawn, somewhere between Iceland and Scotland. I can't sleep, uneasy when I think about my research. One of the most troubling UFO cases I have recently studied took place in Iran. Although I don't want to use this diary as a record of events I research, this one is a remarkable exception. Only know half the story is known publicly. The press hasn't been told that the Shah personally called Jimmy Carter after the sighting: The United States had just sold some AWACs to Iran. The planes were equipped with radar equipment impervious to jamming.

"What is going on?" the Shah asked Carter. "What's wrong with your equipment? This object jammed those radars you sold me!"

Now the U.S Air Force is compiling a thick analysis of the case. So is Soviet Air Force Intelligence. So is French Air Force Intelligence. Their agents are tripping all over one another, trying to find out what could have jammed the AWACs.

I think of the UFO phenomenon as a kaleidoscope with three levels: a purely physical, technological level; a sociological level; and finally a personal, subliminal level playing on the subleties of the human psyche. The first aspect could spell out an extraterrestrial origin; the second one, if taken by itself, would point to human mythology and anthropology: that is the explanation favored by Kit and sophisticated skeptics, as opposed to Menzel and Klass, who flatly deny everything. The third aspect is ominous: it provides a hint of a darker, terrestrial origin, earthly manipulation.

Berlin. Schweizerhof Hotel. Monday 30 May 1977.

Up at 4 A.M. Pastel sky filled with pink clouds. When I was a boy in Pontoise my mother used to predict rain the next day, whenever the clouds were pink as they are now.

Janine wouldn't mind leaving California to spend a year in Paris. We are weary of San Francisco, its trendy researchers, their drugs. Yet I won't find the key I want in France or in morose Berlin, which looks like any other big city, an assemblage of massive blocks.

Paris. Hotel de France. Wednesday 1 June 1977.

They've cleaned up the old *Halles* and filled up the huge excavations under the *Place des Innocents*. I saw Beaubourg and liked it, to my surprise: I am not fond of museums. I walked along the darkening streets, had dinner at the corner bistro. An old woman was yelling into the ear of a tired fellow who was trying to fill out some papers for her, official forms she didn't understand. An Arab walked around the tables, peddling sticks that lit up. Paris will remain vibrant, warm and surprising, as long as there are poor people around. It is the wealthy sections of the city that have no spirit.

Paris. Rue de la Clef. Thursday 2 June 1977.

My mother and I went back to Beaubourg. We found the computers. I proposed the use of Planet, our new system, to link major museums together. The attendants listened to me as if I came from Mars: How could computers communicate? And assist artistic work?

My skepticism about this beautiful country returned. The French are missing something important about the world. *L'Express* has just published an asinine analysis of *Close Encounters*, which they translate as *Brèves Rencontres* ("Brief Meetings!") It leaves the reader with the absurd notion that Spielberg believes that Little Green Men come from India.

Paris. Rue de la Clef. Wednesday 8 June 1977.

Again, I asked Simonne Servais if it would make sense for me to make contact with someone in the French government. She shrugged and said wearily: "If you knew how incompetent they are... It's hopeless." She fears a disintegration of the régime. Aimé Michel lives in fear of a soviet invasion. Nobody seems to realize that France could simply rot in place, without changing very much.

I met Janine and the children at the airport. Olivier came out of Customs brandishing his year-end grades for me to see. Our daughter was poised and elegant. The rain had cleaned up the streets. Janine, who hadn't come back to France in three years, saw the city in all its beauty. We caught the movie *Zardoz* near the Sorbonne and walked happily in the rain as if we'd never left. Today we had lunch with the Gauquelins, still working hard. Their research remains under bitter attack from both skeptics and astrologers! From the window of their apartment on *rue Amyot* we watched sadly as a bulldozer destroyed the last wall of an old Benedictine convent across the street.

Paris. Rue de la Clef. Thursday 9 June 1977.

When I met him at Necker Hospital my brother looked serene and mischievious under his big mustache, but when we talked over lunch at a nearby brasserie I found his views of the future disheartening. At 52 he has concluded that creativity was always overtaken by "the system," run by people on power trips. I think he's wrong when he generalizes to humanity at large, which he describes as primarily motivated by the urge to crush one's neighbor. I see a different aspect of man, more hopeful solutions.

Aimé Michel told me that Poher had an official UFO project within CNES. "It's a stupid idea," he commented. "When you're paid to do research you have to find something, and what can you find, in this field? Poher is turning into a combination of Hynek and Condon, wasting his time. Do you know I've discovered a wave of sightings in Belgium, around 1930?" he said. **(12)** "I'll come to see you in Paris on the 21st," he said happily.

"Good, we'll celebrate the Solstice together..."

"Yes, like Druids!" he said, now laughing like a kid.

"We'll go into the woods of Meudon. As in olden days, wearing white robes," I joked.

"And false eyelashes," he added as we both cracked up.

Last night Janine and I met Simonne in her office and went off to dinner. She had received pseudo-science trash from Bearden, who claims that UFOs and cattle mutilations are the precursor signs of a massive psychotronic attack by the Soviets. This doesn't fool her: she believes the U.S. is trying to sow confusion by flooding French researchers with this crazy stuff. (*) Simonne pointed out that since the death of Georges Pompidou, "Important people don't care about the country. They only want to know whether it's an Independant Republican or a Central Radical who'll be elected in Cantal!"

(*) Much later it came to light that U.S. services had a vast program called *actives measures*, using true information subtly taken out of context, in order to manipulate opinion. The belief in UFOs was often used in this program, occasionally with disastrous "blowback."

Paris. Rue de la Clef. Saturday 11 June 1977.

We attended an elegant dinner last night, at the home of Marie de Castéja. She is the wife of the former French Consul in San Francisco who now serves as Chief of Protocol at the Elysée. Brendan was there with Pamela de Maigret, Rémy Chauvin, Costa de Beauregard, four other scientists and psychic Jean-Pierre Girard who sported a bow tie. Supposedly described a rough fellow of rustic origins, Girard seemed remarkably sure of himself as he expounded about his experiments in the salon of the Countess, while the setting sun put a touch of orange and pink magic over the gold of the dome of the Invalides across the square. It was a fine Parisian evening.

Chairs had been arranged in rows in the hallway so we all could watch a movie where Girard was seen twisting metal bars and displacing small objects on a table top. It was interesting but scientifically unconvincing, given the poorly-chosen camera angles.

Dinner was announced. We asked many questions but learned little, except for the disclosure that members of the *Académie des Sciences* had bent metal bars themselves in his presence, a fact they were not eager to discuss. Another interesting idea by metallurgical expert Crussard, was to ask Girard not to bend the metal but simply to alter its properties. We were told they worked with an alloy which became magnetic under certain conditions. He's also tried to harden metal samples without deforming them (**13**).

This afternoon we spent an hour with Bourret, his blonde wife Monique and their cat at his apartment in the 15th *arrondissement*. He told us the French military was eager to pursue Petit's research -- without Petit. Everything is classified now. I didn't tell him that Petit's ideas were old hat at SRI, where magneto-hydrodynamic (MHD) propulsion of submarines was a hot topic back in the 60s. Bourret has had a brief conversation with Giscard d'Estaing: "Now that it is known that Carter has seen an UFO, what do you think of the question?" he asked.

The President answered: He used to have a keen interest in astronomy in his youth, but he was "not familiar" with the UFO file!

Tomorrow we leave all that behind, for our trip to Morocco.

17

Rabat. Hotel Rex. Monday 13 June 1977.

As soon as the plane touched down, Arab women on board donned embroidened robes over their western clothes. Children with big black eyes clinged to them and looked around with anticipation. Customs officers scrutinized our faces. This is a land of deep, meaningful, hungry eyes: women in the Medina practically make love to you from behind layers of veils; at every street corner young men devour Janine's silhouette like hungry wolves tracking a gazelle.

Moroccan development froze when the French left, with an odd sense of being suspended between two eras. One can feel the ancient opulence underneath the hotel's dirty wallpaper. Telephones work but the plumbing leaks. Someone tried to stop the rot by gluing tape over the worst spots. Only the mosques are impeccably maintained, with a concession to modern electronics: The Muezzin doesn't bother to call out prayers from the four corners of the tower anymore. Loudspeakers carry recorded texts to the faithful below.

All day Janine has led our promenade through places she remembered well. On *rue de Bruxelles* she found the building where she lived as a child. The shops where she bought food and sundries are still there, making a brisk business. Her school still stands behind white walls, with views of a beach, blue sky, dark trees, a California look. In the Medina, the ancient Arab city protected by its medieval walls is filled with hundreds of small shops with mysterious smells, jewelry, fine fabrics, pewter utensils, shiny gadgets.

Fez. Hotel Excelsior. later the same day.

In the small lounge with the blue tile walls we rested on red cushions and watched people go by. Moroccan pastries would be our dinner. We drove to Meknès earlier today, stopped for lunch. Janine knows these cities; they haven't changed much since the war; she needs no guide. The art is in the mosques, and in the velvety eyes of carefully made-up women, behind traditional veils which hide only their shapes, not their thoughts.

We found the *Gendarmerie* in Fez, the swimming pool Janine recalled. She was three years old when her father, who served as a Gendarme in France, applied for a post in Morocco and moved the family for a two-year assignment. The war began: they couldn't go home. They were sent to Missour, and to Rabat, which they didn't leave until March 1945. Janine remembers well the train ride to Oran, the rough sailing to Port-Vendre aboard an old steamer, the *Gouverneur Général Lépine*. They arrived in Paris exhausted, disoriented, dragging heavy suitcases. That same year Janine passed her *Certificat d'Etudes* and was sent to a boarding school for girls in Normandy where life was harder than anything she had known.

It is to recapture these impressions that she has come here, and for me to learn them. Some symbols have changed. The *Gendarmerie* has become “Royale.” It now stands behind ugly barbed wire. Photographs are forbidden. The military are everywhere. On the road to Meknès police stopped traffic by the side of the road. Suddenly there were helicopters above us, green trucks all over the pavement, rifles behind every tree. The King and his entourage drove by.

It was market day in Kemisset. Women riding donkeys converged towards the central square, carrying baskets. Kids played in the dust. Stately storks rested atop every chimney. Tomorrow we drive south, towards the Sahara.

Ifrane. Grand Hotel. Tuesday 14 June 1977.

The luxury of a warm bath greeted us after a long day, travelling through Sefrou and up towards Boulemane where the hills are green and the pastures full of black sheep. As one goes further South the road winds up, nature takes on an arid look with only a few green springs. Eventually one reaches a forlorn spot. A cement marker rising out of a mound of gravel gives the traveller a choice between Missour, 73 kilometers away and Midelt, 86 kilometers: two straight roads in an infinity of beige and gray, no tree in sight.

At the intersection an Arab sat against the marker, a wooden crate at his feet. He got up when he saw our rented Fiat and gesticulated wildly. We picked him up. He spoke no French but Janine remembered enough Arabic to determine he'd arrived from Midelt on the morning bus. He was quietly waiting for the 5 p.m. bus to Missour. Just before that town he motioned for us to stop. He picked up his crate and thanked us deeply, hand over his heart. He disappeared behind a mound of stones.

Janine was moved to rediscover the place that had marked her childhood. The house where her brother Alain was born no longer stands, but her teacher's old home is still there, the school too. The square is not visited by caravans from the deep desert anymore. New structures are being built around it. Little by little we have left civilization behind, yet there is no room here for ecological enthusiasm: people simply throw their trash on the road, cars stink with burning oil. Even the desolate road to Missour is punctuated with thick black smoke from heavy construction trucks.

Janine showed me the pool where she had learned to swim and a house people feared during the war because its occupants were *Pétainistes*, while the Gendarmes were for De Gaulle and the *Résistance*. The infirmary where Janine's father used to assist the local doctor on those frequent occasions when two Arabs slashed each other's bellies with their knives in a bloody quarrel, had turned into a dilapidated ghost of a structure, but the park was still green and the main street was filled with neatly dressed kids who ran after us, eager to be photographed. The sky was empty. There was no sound. Nothing moved outside the town, except for the lazy smoke that rose from a nomad's tent.

Fez. Holiday Inn. Wednesday 15 June 1977.

Ifrane was cold and deserted, a winter resort that slept through the off-season in a site full of cascading rivers and luscious woods. The hotel staff seemed astonished to see customers arrive. One waiter had to go down the basement to retrieve the butter while another one pulled out an old dance record from the 50s and played it on the ancient gramophone. They brought us some instant soup. It chased away the chill. We found the heat again as soon as we drove down the mountain. We re-entered Fez with its clutter, its buses that seemed to drive at random, its *fatmas* embarrassed in their veils.

Rabat. Tour Hassan. Friday 17 June 1977.

We'll fly back to Paris from Rabat tomorrow. We would enjoy spending more time in stately Fez, safe behind its fine battlements. Ghost-women glide among the crowd, vanishing into side alleys, mere slits in a maze of shadows. The *Oued Salé* swells noisily along a medieval channel that rushes into underground vortices below the old stone towers. Patient donkeys stare with sad eyes. The Medina is a jumble of smells and desires, colors and shapes that seem to issue from some alchemist's delirium. Narrow streets become hallways, turn into houses, sites of worship, cool fountains, as in a dream.

You get lost easily in such a setting, but a heady thrill comes along with the disorientation. You find yourself passing a door that reveals stranges machines at work; the next moment you're confronted with young girls who carry water and bread, talking gaily, laughing in easy high notes. The next door leads to an ugly place that reeks of urine. It opens into a courtyard covered with fine mosaic, behind which you do not find the stately home you expected, but yet another courtyard, more donkeys, and cloth merchants.

There is water everywhere, waterfalls in tumult around the wheels of ancient mills. Older, grizzled gentlemen in sober grey robes and red hats politely salute merchants as they pass by the shops. Everything is civilized here, with a strong underlying order in the apparent chaos. We felt like simpletons lost in an intensely complex world. For a few coins, a kid guided us out of the maze to the Jamai Palace where we stopped for tea.

Yesterday another kid took us to the booksellers. We saw some admirable Corans, and a Torah that was a true museum piece. There were alleged "magical" texts too, derived from Koranic commentaries but they were only the Arabic equivalent of our *grimoires*, silly superstitious recipes for chasing evil spirits.

Paris. Rue de la Clef. Sunday 19 June 1977.

Walking along the Seine with Olivier this afternoon I browsed through the bookstalls and stumbled on an edition of *Sub-Espace* I had never seen. I had to shell out four francs to buy my own book! When I called my publisher and complained, he told me that science-fiction was enjoying a fresh burst of recognition, just as Hachette was getting out of the business, bad timing. Other publishers are reprinting all his titles. He feels vindicated but sad. Reluctantly, he will send me a little money.

Pamela de Maigret and Brendan had a project to fly Girard to the Noetics Institute in California. It has been upset by mysterious forces: the French are not eager to see their psychic subjects exported. Brendan threatens to tell the media that he "hasn't seen any evidence of French parapsychology work." It is hard to blame Crussard: the international parapsychology scene is increasingly poisoned by secrecy. The work done by Targ and Puthoff at SRI remains classified. The Soviets have arrested an *L.A. Times* journalist, Robert Toth, after he was reportedly handed a parapsychology document by a Moscow biologist named Petukov. Held for espionage, Toth was eventually extradited.

Paris. Rue de la Clef. Tuesday 21 June 1977.

Another long meeting with Bergier erupted into a fountain of citations: he recommended Colin Wilson's *Enigmas and Mysteries* as well as *Beyond Baker Street*. I brought the discussion back to the topic of the Nazi occult experiments.

"The kind of documents you're looking for is pratically impossible to find," Bergier said immediately. He astounded me again by his prodigious memory. "The Germans used to have a psychical review, *The Orchids Garden*, which the Nazi suppressed. Fritz Lang tried to get copies; he offered crazy sums in vain. There was a fellow named Stephan George who ran "Cosmic Circles." It is said that Stauffenberg who, like Adolph Hitler, was a genuine medium, had developed his gift under George's guidance. There were a "white"

Germany as well as a "black" Germany, you know. We tend to forget it. Perhaps you'd find something of interest in *Alchemy and Medicine*, by Alexander von Bernus. Also you should read *The Nine Unknown Men* by Talbot Mundy."

"What about the Russians?" I mentioned Ira's claims about their microwave weapons aimed at the U.S. Embassy in Moscow.

"Einhorn is plainly wrong; I don't think their psychotronic research is offensive in this case. The beam may be designed to resonate with the water molecule, which could help them locate people within the U.S. Embassy building. The human body is mostly water. We're nothing but walking water bags. That's the answer I gave the French secret service." (**14**)

"What do you think the Soviets are doing along occult lines?"

"All I know is what I learn through a group of émigrés in Paraguay. By the way, you should read *VIG* by Gogol. Look up *La Russie Illustrée*, 1935. I wonder if Steiner's Goethenaum wasn't destroyed by a Communist commando, rather than by the Nazi."

"What makes you say that?" I asked in astonishment.

"I've noticed that about the same period, the years 1922-23, Steiner disciples in the Soviet Union were all herded together and sent off to die in the Gulag."

He added that he reproached himself for not having paid attention to his father's ideas about Russia and Germany after 1917.

"He presented everything in such an extreme anti-marxist framework that I rejected the whole thing," he said. "At that age it's common to reject your parents' ideas. My father kept insisting there was an occult group lurking behind the soviet régime. People who knew about it died in curious car accidents."

He paused and laughed. "You know, in order to be hit by a car in the USSR in the thirties, you had to do it on purpose. Or someone wanted to kill you real bad!"

Bergier also told me that a crazy man had tried to kill Jean-Claude Bourret. The fellow was getting messages from extraterrestrials, which sent a chill through me because it reminded me of Elmer's threats. "As soon as he was released from the institution where he'd been sent for treatment, he got himself a rifle and fifty bullets, and went straight to the television station, demanding to see Bourret."

Aimé told me he was staying away from the public scene. He was even reluctant to see Brendan when I offered to set up a meeting. He did tell me he was getting a lot of documents from Einhorn. Albin Michel has just published *Chasseur d'Ovni* by a former French intelligence officer, Henri Jullien, under the name François Gardes.

This is my last night in Paris for a while. Janine is off to Normandy with our son. This building pulses with secret life, each apartment a cell filled with its own drama, aches and pains, the infirmities of its occupants, their conflicts. On the top floor students and drifters rent the old servant rooms, occasionally hiding some petty crook on the run. Earlier this month the police came and arrested several people who kept weapons there.

Flying to Chicago. Wednesday 22 June 1977.

Aimé Michel suspects that General Ailleret's death in March 1968 was an assassination (**15**). Was it triggered by his statement, a few days before, that he would go public with the UFO files? Or was it a settling of political accounts with some enemy of the régime, a fascist group, or a foreign power?

Paris is full of cops. Blue buses of the riot police are parked everywhere. Dressed in battle gear and helmets, with shields and sticks, they stand and watch the crowd. Brezhnev is in town, a few rightists have burned a red flag. Under its mild democratic appearance France is one of the most heavily policed and militarized countries on earth; it exports twice as much weaponry per capita as the U.S., five times as much as the USSR. French intellectuals, secure in their hypocrisy, ignore these statistics.

The Postal authorities here feel threatened by the current expansion of computer networks and the prospect of electronic mail terrifies the bureaucrats. As a result they are changing their tariffs to discourage international links. They are doing the same thing as the British Post Office, demanding that all networks go through a single entry point, so messages will be taxed in transit and tapped by French spooks. The decision clearly shows the feudal character of the European

PTTs: consumers pay them for a privilege. The notion of "public service" remains a joke in Europe.

Aimé sees all this philosophically. "In medieval times the serf gave most of his harvest to the lord of the castle and was rewarded by a boot in the *derrière.* The PTTs operate on the same principle, even if they must strangle the French telecommunications industry in the process, while Americans plunge freely ahead into the world of office automation, network mail and teleconferencing."

The PTTs also raise the cost of doing business for any company established in France by creating another heavy telecommunication tax, hidden within their tariff structure.

When it comes to the paranormal Bergier is a formidable source. Twice he played a historical role: First as a member of the Intelligence network that found the Nazi rocket base at Peenemunde (His old nemesis Werner von Braun, has just died) and later when he saved De Gaulle from a diplomatic mistake about Pierrelatte. American spy planes were flying over this nuclear plant, taking reconnaissance photographs. Furious, De Gaulle wanted the planes shot down. Bergier argued they were only interested in Pierrelatte because the Chinese were building a plant on the same model.

Aimé encourages me to pursue my theory of the associative universe. I have pointed out to him that since Energy and Information were two sides of the same coin we should really have two kinds of physics. Why do we only teach the physics of energy? What happened to its twin sister, the physics of information?

It may exist in rudimentary form in magic. It begins where her academic sister stops, at the level of psi phenomena. While the universe of energy is a swamp cluttered with the concepts of space-time coordinates and linguistic artefacts like "force" and "field," the information universe I envision would look like a collection of events where space and time are illusions, mere consequence of consciousness traversing associations. This would validate remote viewing and provide a framework for radically novel experiments.

Now I am on the way to Chicago, where a conference is supposed to celebrate 30 years of ufology. But the hippies may be right, "you can't trust anyone over 30..."

Chicago. Thursday 23 June 1977.

In the lobby of the Pick hotel I bumped into Jule Eisenbud followed by Ted Serios, utterly drunk. Jule gave him money to get home. In the process he forgot to pay for his own lunch. Are these the people who are going to turn parapsychology into real science?

Fate Magazine holds a private seminar for a few researchers. Thus I met Ray Palmer, Kenneth Arnold and Berthold Schwartz for the first time, as well as Frank Jamison, a mathematician who became interested in the subject after reading *Anatomy*.

Chicago. Saturday 25 June 1977.

Hynek introduced me to Margaret Mead yesterday in his room at the Pick. He's trying to recruit her for his Center but she won't commit herself. She spoke kindly of my research. Margaret Mead is a short, energetic woman who stomps around the conference floor with her forked walking stick, wearing a bright red coat. She told me how she had managed to get the Parapsychology Association accepted as an affiliate by the AAAS.

"It happened for irrational reasons, as so often takes place in so-called "rational science." I had prepared a resolution for their annual congress in Texas but the day before the meeting there was a terrible blizzard, most members didn't show up. The local Texans defeated my proposal. The following year the meeting was in Boston, among Protestant intellectuals. I made a passionate speech about Galileo and the stupidity of the Pope. My motion in favor of parapsychology was summarily approved!"

A reporter who said he worked for the ABC network affiliate introduced himself and requested an interview. When I asked him what he would do with the tape he became confused and confessed he wasn't working for ABC at all but for Cufos, which was preparing a record they were hoping to sell. Is Allen aware of this little trick?

Yesterday was the 30th anniversary of the Kenneth Arnold sighting. A press conference included Leo Sprinkle, Betty Hill, Curtis Fuller, Arnold himself, Allen and me. Betty was holding a bust of her extraterrestrial abductor, tenderly caressing his bald head.

Arnold impressed me as a solid citizen. He gave a sober, fact-filled presentation, speaking without embellishment. A nice touch: when asked to show his movies in a side room in conflict with my lecture, he refused.

Arnold also told me he'd just met Hynek for the first time. I found it astonishing that they had never spoken face-to-face before.

"His official evaluation of what I saw back in 1947 is all wrong," Arnold told me. "If I allowed myself to believe in mirages I'd have crashed my plane a long time ago. I found out today that he'd never read the original report the Air Force had asked me to write. The Blue Book folks gave him a file that didn't contain my actual statements."

Harold Sherman, a true American pioneer of psychic science, has now invited Allen and me to a conference he has organized in St.Louis to discuss UFOs and consciousness. Many "sensitives" are also invited, along with actress Gloria Swanson.

Flying to San Francisco. Sunday 26 June 1977.

My last evening in Chicago was spent with Cliff Linedecker, his delightful Korean wife Junko and their friends, a fun-loving collection of occultists and magicians.

When we met at their home in New Town, Cliff showed me his study and we spoke about his books (**16**). One of his friends told me of a personal UFO incident during which his car stalled and the crystals of his radio transmitter got cracked.

He also told me of an amusing episode when a magician, a prominent skeptic, proposed to be locked up inside a bank safe in Toronto, with great fanfare, to demonstrate his powers of escape. But he found himself unabled to get out, and had to be rescued by giggling colleagues.

"This incident is known among the trade as *Houdini's Revenge*, because the guy had pretended to be in touch with Houdini's ghost. His colleagues thought that was tacky, so we deprived him of the tools he needed to get out of that vault," said Cliff's friend.

Saint Louis. Friday 5 August 1977. (17)

When Allen and I had dinner with his son Paul last night, all he talked about was the Center.

"When will you release Ufocat to outside researchers?" I asked.

"Well... he began, embarrassed, "I don't think I'll be able to do that. I know the catalogue started with your data, but my assistants... They're volunteers, you see. They've worked hard on this catalogue."

"So what? It'd be a credit for them to publish it."

"They don't see it that way," he continued sadly. "They fantasize they're going to get breakthroughs, incredible discoveries out of it."

Ed May and Russ Targ were so disappointed with Allen's presentation they got up and left the auditorium, saying Allen was "out of focus."

After my talk, a woman named Barbara Bartholic asked if I believed that certains individuals had a special role to play. She went on to ask whether contact with the phenomenon was always a good thing. I told her that for some people it was disastrous. What about her? She'd never seen a UFO, she said, but she had interviewed "The Two," founders of the H.I.M. group, so we spoke of the folly and the hope that surrounded their movement. She offered to help me investigate their whereabouts. She said her boss would probably let me see the interview if I came to the TV station where she worked. Our conversation left me puzzled and moved.

The most notable fact was a breakfast invitation from Trammell Crow, a friend of "Mr. Mac," McDonnell the aerospace tycoon. Seven of us attended this private meeting: Anne Gehman, Harold Sherman, Al Pollard, Ingo Swann, Allen Hynek and me, as well as Stephen Schwartz, who tries to apply psychic research to archeology. Mr. Crow asked me to come to Dallas in one month to repeat my lecture before "a few of his friends."

Belmont. Thursday 11 August 1977.

Kit and I spent two hours arguing yesterday at The Little Store in Woodside, closed for the afternoon. Alain gave us two *Napoléons*, a pot of coffee and left us alone. I proposed to attack the UFO system by moving upstream along its own feedback loop. I explained to Kit how the topology of a control system worked and why we could try to affect it, even if we didn't yet know the nature of the actual agent (extraterrestrial, ultra-dimensional, collective unconscious, human manipulation, etc...)

Something bothers me about such conversations with Kit: We speak past each other. I try to make him see the reality of the phenomenon because he's one of the few people in a position to bring the subject up before decision-makers, but he continues to deny it, in academic terms that don't take the facts into account.

Fred just called me from Chicago, concerned about Allen's health. When I saw him in St Louis last week he complained of headaches. Fred tells me that Allen fainted on the way back, something which has happened before, because he has low blood pressure. An added source of stress is the financial state of Cufos. The printer hasn't been paid for two months.

Belmont. Sunday 14 August 1977.

A magazine has recently published an interview of Margaret Mead, who recommended our *Challenge to Science*. Admiral Turner, current director of the CIA, has answered a recent article on psychic spying by John Wilhelm with a tongue-in-cheek statement: indeed, he said, about 1972, some experiments had been conducted with a subject who could reliably describe distant scenes (Pat Price, note *), but he died and "no contact had been made since then!"

Note (*) Actually Pat died in mysterious circumstances in a Las Vegas hotel room. His body was buried before an autopsy could be conducted, yet another suspicious death of a psychic researcher. According to Ryan Dube, an independent researcher (quoting a 1977 report by Kenneth Kress, the project manager of Dr. Puthoff's project at OTS/CIA) Price's summer 1973 exposure of an intelligence facility near Washington triggered an intense investigation of the SRI researchers. After a raid against the offices of the Church of Scientology in Los Angeles, the FBI came to believe (falsely?) that Price was used by the scientologists as a spy against the CIA.

Belmont. Sunday 28 August 1977.

Everything was clean this weekend at Spring Hill. Plenty of water from the creek and our well, and how generous the land is, with pears and grapes and juicy blackberries, apples and figs and quince, while the woods are filled with moss and fern. Olivier and I opened a path with hatchets, all the way to the cabins. We imagine what life would be if we were to use the place as our retreat. But my work is still precarious, with reduced income as I phase out of the Institute.

We drove up Black Bart Trail in the truck, climbing along the unpaved road, fording the rivers until we reached Willits, where we visited a witness who'd seen a lighted disk south of Laytonville.

Belmont. Wednesday 31 August 1977.

Don Hanlon called. He's moved again, and met the daughter of contactee Howard Menger in a cabin on Mt. Shasta. In Los Angeles he's met John Wilhelm, on the track of scientology.

A colleague from SRI has gone to Washington to see Stanley Schneider, assistant director of the Office of Scientific and Technology Policy under Carter. He said Schneider told him that Robert Frosch, of NASA, was planning to setup a UFO office.

Belmont. Tuesday 6 September 1977.

This was Olivier's first day in High School, and my first presentation before venture capitalists in search of startup money for InfoMedia.

Over lunch in Healdsburg, Trixie told us that low-flying objects had been reported. The military claimed that the witnesses had seen the lights of aircraft over the coast, which is highly improbable.

Belmont. Sunday 11 September 1977.

One of the most intriguing UFO cases of all time is the "Lead Mask Mystery" in which two men died on a hillside near Rio. I have new information about the case through my friend Bill Calvert who recently spent several hours in Brazil with General Uchoa.

In Brazil General Uchoa plays the same role as Allen Hynek in the States. Bill, who used to live in Brasilia, brought me a tape recorded at my intention by the General, with instructions on how to contact extraterrestrials. He assured Bill that he'd succeeded in doing it himself. They manifested in the form of balls of light, as in the Aveyron case I know well; or the objects I described in *Sub-Space*.

Bill's primary goal on this trip was to continue his research on Donna Maria, the young healer. He returned with details of her operations. This girl from the Interior of Brazil (**18**), a devout catholic, always prescribed modern medicine, contrary to most Brazilian psychics who rely on plants. At the age of four she saw a globe of light. A lady came out of it, holding a rosary and a golden book from which drops of blood were falling. After this vision she started to perform operations, first on animals and later on humans.

The Virgin was supposed to be her guide, but she saw other beings too, with large hairless heads, in a machine that floated in mid-air.

Belmont. Wednesday 14 September 1977.

Another crisis at InfoMedia. Our financial backer, on whose advice we rely, is busy with Magnuson, a new computer company (**19**).

Peter Sturrock has heard confirmation from NASA solar physicist Harold Glaser that Administrator Frosch had received a formal request from OSTP for an evaluation of the UFO problem by NASA. Peter sent a letter to Frank Press to say he'd be happy to serve as consultant. He is in touch with Dick Henry in Frosch's office. Peter's move has frayed some egos but it shows serious academic interest.

Belmont. Saturday 17 September 1977.

It turns out that Press and his assistant Stanley Schneider at OSTP report to the Domestic Council, headed by Stuart Eisenstadt and Nancy Dorman. It is at the Council's request that they've asked NASA's administrator Frosch to undertake a study.

Belmont. Tuesday 20 September 1977.

Steven Spielberg called me this morning. He said he had just finished reading *Invisible College*, regarded it as the best book on UFOs and wanted to quote it in the promotion for CE3K.

Sturrock had made some progress: he determined that Frosch has been asked (i) to provide a central point at NASA for all public inquiries and (ii) to conduct a thorough assessment, followed by real action. Frosch said yes on the first point but he requested more time to address the second one, which he delegated to Hennize, of the science division, who in turn passed it on to Dick Henry, of the section on astrophysics. Thus the bureaucracy is grinding away, trying to digest the President's request and do nothing ("a flurry of alarmed paralysis," a journalist calls it).

The issue sank further into an administrative quagmire when Dick Henry tried to solicit the opinion of his colleagues, which triggered premature publicity.

More rumors come out of Brazil about the Lead Mask Case. This event continues to fascinate me because it illustrates the double nature (part public, part secret) of the mystery. In France and the U.S. an effort is ostensibly being made to setup "open" UFO studies under the auspices of the space agencies: Carter has been putting pressure on NASA while CNES is creating its study group.

"They even requested my collaboration," wrote Aimé Michel, "with a tone of respect I'm not used to. Next time you're in Paris we should take Guérin with us and go piss on Danjon's grave (**20**) in celebration of this new era."

Flying to Chicago. Tuesday 27 September 1977.

Fred Beckman offered to pick me up at O'Hare, suggesting that I stay at his apartment while attending the computer science meeting in Chicago. I have little new information for him. Allen Stern, scientific consultant to the Domestic Council, has rejected any study of "unusual atmospheric phenomena." Dick Henry is in an unfortunate position as pointman for the project at NASA. A good astrophysicist

and head of Seti, he is too committed to extraterrestrial life to be viewed as unbiased by his colleagues.
Yesterday Helen called me up to retrieve the tape recording of her regression. She thanked me for the positive role she said I'd played in her life. She added she now understood the symbolic nature of her abduction. "Many people believe I'm crazy," she said touchingly, "but I'm not crazy. I am waiting for them to pick me up, to take me home..." Jim Lorenzen has told me that many abductees were orphans. That's the case of Helen, born on Christmas Day.

Chicago. Wednesday 28 September 1977.

It's not a pretty sight, this meeting of computer scientists. The rooms of the Conrad Hilton are filled with frail geeks with shrill voices and fat librarians in shapeless gray dresses: "The virtual file holds the abstracts," they whisper to one another in hoary confidence, "The keys are processed separately. We balance the trees and we print a monthly catalog, by inverting on specific parameters." This will go on for two days.

I like Chicago but I don't believe what Fred says about any decrease in pollution. He showed me the place where he saw his UFO. Like Aimé Michel, Fred doesn't believe the problem is ready for a solution. It isn't even mature enough to be studied scientifically, he argues. He likes *Invisible College* but leans towards a government-led conspiracy hiding the data. Both could be right. We spent the evening talking about music, about Julian Jaynes' book on the bicameral mind (**21**) and psychology in general.

This morning we went to see Allen. Mimi was there with Father Gill, the church official who had witnessed a large hovering object over the ocean from his mission in Papua in 1959. (Gill and many natives in his group had waved at the occupants of the craft, who apparently waved back). Over lunch Allen asked me cheerfully if my commitment was still good, to drop everything and come work with him if a genuine study got started. I told him yes, assuming that the study was serious, not the passing fancy of some wealthy patron. Where would the support come from?

Allen's renewed hopes are based on Jimmy Carter's instructions for a new study. He says NASA has been asked to study the evolution of the problem over the last ten years, the period elapsed since the Condon study. In other words, the conclusions of the University of Colorado won't be challenged. This is politically right and scientifically wrong, as usual. Allen is counting on the Spielberg movie to give new impetus to his research.

Father Gill was kind enough to answer some questions from me.

"Do you ever dream about the 1959 incident?" I asked him over coffee.

"Yes," he answered simply.

"Anything unusual about those dreams?" I went on.

"Funny you should ask that. Few people inquire about these details. I dream about something that happened *an hour after the object flew away*."

He heard an explosion just outside the Mission building, in Boainai: his hair stood up. That's the moment that always comes back in his dreams, he told me, rather than the sighting itself. We had a long conversation, after which this excellent man got up and said "if Heaven isn't equipped with good armchairs and good coffee so we can have this kind of talk, I don't want any part of Heaven!"

Allen went off to teach a class. At 67 he is spending his last year as a Northwestern professor, after which they will only keep him, he says, as an ornament. Fred took me to see the Center, three rooms in a non-descript house next to a vacuum-cleaner shop. Men walked on the sidewalk, carrying old machines they were bringing over to be fixed. A skylight made a sunny spot over the stairs. A cardboard sign on the door spelled out the Center's identity. A small lobby served as a library filled with boxes and two bookcases with volumes from all over the world. A door led to the secretary's office, another to the file room. The secretary's office was adorned with photographs of Sherman Larsen, President Carter and some cartoons, and flyers promoting Allen's lectures enlivened with little flying saucers. A dusty window gave onto the avenue. The buzz of an air conditioner completed the scene.

The next room was larger. It held several tables and the file cabinets I bought when I reorganized Hynek's files ten years ago. They should have been kept locked, if only to protect witnesses' names, but the secretary told me she didn't know which key worked, so if she locked them she might never open them again.

"Don't you think you need better precautions?" I asked.

"Probably. I've found out we were missing some cases. Especially foreign ones."

"You mean, they got lost?"

"No, intruders, after office hours... One day we came in unannounced, we found the landlord in here with a bunch of people. We never found out who they were."

Washington. Friday 30 September 1977.

Stanley Schneider, who received me on the third floor of the New Executive Building across the street from the White House, was a short grayish man with folds around eyes that never looked quite straight at me. He confirmed NASA had the task to centralize UFO information. The Carter Administration didn't want another Condon fiasco, and it didn't want to turn the problem back to the Air Force that did such a bad job in the past.

"Will NASA actually conduct investigations?" I asked him. "Or will they simply respond to information requests?"

"That's one of the things we just don't know yet. We're only beginning. Administrator Frosch has until Christmas to decide."

"As you know, scientific opinion is divided. Some people believe the problem isn't mature enough for valid research," I pointed out, thinking of my conversation with Fred Beckman the day before. "But others are eager to go ahead, both here and in other countries."

"True, but we're in a politically impossible situation. It's not surprising that the military folks swept UFOs under he rug. The President could never announce on television that the phenomenon is real without triggering uncontrollable reactions..." **(22)**

After my conversation with Schneider I spoke to Kit at Dulles. We ended up at the coffee shop of the Marriott, where we had once met with "Smith."

"Whatever happened to that guy, anyway?" I asked, "And his Group of Twelve?"

"We never found out why he wanted to know you, did we?" he said, evading me. I have my own idea that "Smith" wanted to make his own assessement, for whatever purpose. Kit was skeptical that NASA could study UFOs.

"They don't have the resources to do a good job," he argued. "They don't have the right psychologists, medical experts, analysts. We're the only ones with those resources."

"What are you waiting for, then?" I challenged him.

"We can't do it until the Executive tells us to study the problem."

Yet Schneider had just told me he'd never trust the CIA to do a reliable study: "The information that the Air Force and the CIA collect never sees the light of day again," he had said angrily, confirming my own impressions. "They twist everything to suit their own political schemes. Even when the White House asks for it, it's like pulling teeth to get them to release anything, and you never know if those guys tell the truth or make up false data." I think Kit is a bright scientist with an open mind but he is the exception in a bureaucratic empire that smothers research. Even if he did know something he couldn't use it, so what good is that?

Flying to Tulsa. Saturday 8 October 1977.

The plane banks over Mt. Whitney, a magnificent sight, with the mountain plunging into Death Valley. The beauty of the American West always catches you off-guard, forcing you to look at life in stark, solemn terms.

Stanley Schneider told me he'd received numerous offers for help, including a proposal to deploy sophisticated equipment to detect UFOs. Allen Hynek called him just the day before my visit, but he had not told me about it, which was childish. It could have been an opportunity to strengthen our common cause by presenting a credible team. Instead Sturrock, Hynek and a few others are acting on their own, pushing their own agenda. People see conspiracies everywhere. The most extreme theories pale before reality. I had a proof of it in

Livermore. I went there at the invitation of an engineer with the atomic weapons lab. After dinner with his family we were joined by his colleagues. They closed the door, loaded a tray of slides, turned off the lights and told me their story. It appears that Uri Geller was invited to do a series of hush-hush experiments at the Livermore lab while he was in California for the SRI work. They asked him to bend metal samples that he couldn't touch, as Crussard had done in the French experiments with Girard. They rigged up an infrared camera with appropriate filters. The metal was indeed bent as a result, but that was not the main effect. The big surprise was in the photographs. They showed Uri and everything around him bathed in coherent light of greater intensity than any laser we can make today at that wavelength.

The engineers believed there were two sources of illumination. They tried everything to reproduce the effect, in vain. It was as if at that particular time Uri had found himself at the intersection of two large infrared lasers. Coming from where? The intensity varies from one picture to the next. Another piece of equipment recorded the phenomenon independently. And the metal was bent at the lowest point of the light's intensity, not at the highest. None of this makes sense. None of the data will be published, so this is another paranomal experiment the scientific world will ignore.

In the meantime cults are filling the vacuum. Bo and Peep expect to leave the earth soon in a flying saucer. Their videotaped message to the world is supposed to remain secret until they actually go away, but I will see it tonight at the TV station that recorded it. I am told it is a long, boring theological dissertation. Bo is the son of a preacher, and Peep, a former nurse, is a short plump woman who is supposed to represent the "advanced consciousness of the higher level." What a confusing word, "consciousness!" It is becoming associated it with every kind of intellectual garbage.

Dallas. Tuesday 11 October 1977.

I can't help it if I like Texas. It's not the landscape, or the city that give me such a great feeling, although Texans are the salt of the earth. It's a force that seems to emanate from the ground and the sky. I've always felt oddly at home there. This time I have travelled to Dallas in response to Mr. Trammell Crow's personal invitation. His chauffeur came to pick me up at the airport. He didn't have much to say. It was a good thing that I happened to know that the University of Texas football team, the Longhorns, had just beaten Oklahoma; otherwise we wouldn't have spoken two words before I got to the hotel where a reservation had been made under my name. Mr. Crow's business is real estate on a grand scale: hotels, shopping centers, merchandise marts, warehousing.

"Let me show you the list of people I've invited to your lecture," he told me genially. "You just relax, hear? It's a small group of friends."

The intimate reunion would include the mayor of Dallas, the Hunts, the CEO of a financial empire, the general counsel for GE, a vice-president of IBM and a vice-president of Xerox. My lecture was scheduled for four o'clock: Would these busy people actually drop their work in the middle of the afternoon to come and listen to me? I had lunch with Mr. Crow, after which I gathered my thoughts in his open office, watching the grayness of the Texas sky from the 32nd floor. The city is growing too fast. The buildings erected in the Fifties are now in the way of the new skyscapers. They will have to be blown up one by one. I scanned the well-known faces in frames along the walls: "*To Trammell and Margaret, thank you for your kindness, Betty and Gerald Ford.*"

People began arriving at a quarter to four. As Trammell had announced, the atmosphere was easy, convivial, and informal:

"Hi Mary, how was Japan?"

"Good to see you, Mister Mayor."

"Hello Bill, I saw that deal of yours in the Wall Street Journal."

I kept my lecture sober and square. I called attention to the need for research, stressing hard data, avoiding the extraterrestrial pitfall: We know that the witnesses have observed a real, unexplained phenomenon, I said. We suspect it is caused by a technology. It isn't certain that it represents a visitation from outer space, although that remains one of the most interesting hypotheses.

"What else could it be?" someone asked, predictably.

"A technology that used a revolutionary understanding of the topology of spacetime," I answered. An animated debate followed. The IBM executive took me aside: "Have you discussed this with Watson?" As if I could pick up the phone and call the chairman of the largest computer company on Earth to discuss flying saucers?

Trammell Crow is an impressive man. I am not in awe of his wealth or lifestyle, even if he can park his Mercedes with impunity in the red zone in front of the tallest building in Dallas. The World Trade Center is harmoniously designed around an inner courtyard animated by glass elevators. "What a beautiful building," I said sincerely, staring up in awe at tapestries that floated down from the 20th floor. "Thank you," he replied. It took me a few seconds to realize he had built the complex and supplied the art himself.

Atlanta. Sheraton Hotel. Wednesday 12 October 1977.

In the hotel lobby I bumped into Larry Roberts, the architect of Arpanet. We shook hands. I told him about my new software company. He invited me to join him for lunch. General Gavin was giving a speech about the early days of the space program. He told a funny story: in 1957 he was in charge of the missile program at the Pentagon. A frequent topic of discussion with von Braun was the idea of an Earth satellite. Unfortunately they were constantly denied an adequate budget, because "experts" kept telling Congress that satellites had no practical applications.

One day a producer came into Gavin's office. He was making a film for the Pentagon, about rockets.

"You know what would be great, General?" he asked. "It'd be to show the launching of a satellite that would orbit the Earth. Is that technically possible?"

"It's been possible for years," said Gavin with a sigh of frustration.

"How much would it cost?"

"Von Braun could do it for a million dollars, but we don't have the money."

"I'll fix that," said the producer, who flew back to California intent on raising the additional capital and including the satellite in his film.

Three weeks later the Russians launched Sputnik, narrowly beating Hollywood to the punch.

Belmont. Sunday 16 October 1977

Over the last five years we have watched the little town of Ukiah evolve from a tiny rural center, sleepy with local government bureaucrats and retirees, into a community that is attracting dreamers from all over California -- people fleeing big cities, anxious to raise kids in the cleaner air. The region wants no industry, in part for fear of pollution and in part because it might disturb the local underground economy, based on cannabis and illegal drugs, and the exploitation of the labor of Mexican immigrants. These unstable compromises keep the town away from the real world and prevent it from realizing its potential.

Belmont. Monday 31 October 1977.

Over a Japanese dinner I met with Don Hanlon and found him changed again. The relaxed calm of the old days was gone. He no longer glided through life with the grace of a young hungry tiger, certain to find juicy preys and docile females. He was stoned. He poured tea all over the tablecloth, missing his cup.

NASA is not making much progress either. Peter Sturrock has seen the letter sent by Frank Press to Dr. Frosch. It said that the White House was besieged with requests for information on UFOs and that it was time for NASA to "do something." Why not establish a study, under a scientist "such as Carl Sagan?" The mention of Sagan's name is a clear signal that the White House is only pursuing a public relation track.

Belmont. Saturday 5 November 1977.

I spent Thurday afternoon pleasantly installed at Alain's place, drinking coffee and listening to my friends Tom Gates and Mark Uriarte describing several sightings in Northern California that people haven't wanted to report to the media. The latest case is so remarkable that it's worth noting here. It came through the Sheriff's office in Colusa, where a local Indian man named Amos claims to be regularly visited by a strange being. The police heard about it through a local rancher. It turned out Amos had been seeing his visitor since the Fifties. The scenario was constant: an object landed near the cabin and a little man came out, wearing a suit and mask that gave the appearance of a trunk in front of his face. He had cylindrical legs and could levitate by twisting a knob on his belt. He wore mittens and could go through walls: when the saucer arrived the cabin just started vibrating and the wall "got erased" while the entity glided in.

Amos is illiterate. One of the last surviving members of a local tribe, he lives in a wooden cabin with no electricity. He intensely dislikes the little man, who "smells bad and takes away all the meat in the house," the product of Amos' hunting. They don't communicate. Occasionally the being points to the bed, as if ordering Amos to lie down, and he says "Airfield, airfield, airfield."

Belmont. Sunday 6 November 1977.

Mark and I drove up to see Amos today in the foothills of the Cortina chain, which wealthy American farmers abandoned long ago because the land was too poor to grow wheat or even rye. The Indian lives with his brother Clifford and their horses. Amos explained to me in bad English how the "airplane" landed next to the cabin and what it looked like. He drew it for me -- a dome on four round legs, with a horizontal propeller on top, an absurd detail. At first he refused to draw the little man, saying it was "too hard." But he often dreamed about him, he said. In the dream the being always asked for water as in the famous Joe Simonton case at Eagle River. **(23)**

We went to the top of the grassy hill, but we could find no traces. From there one couldn't see any town, not even a farmhouse; only the dark hills to the West and the ghostly outline of the Sierra Nevada to the East. Between us and the Sierra, nothing but the weird shape of Sutter's Buttes, a pustule of lava rising incongruously from the flat expanse of the plain.

We walked back to the cabin, impeccably kept. I asked Amos about his interaction with the being, his reactions. He told me he always felt weak the day after he saw him. However he didn't exactly regard him as an enemy.

"Do you think he's your friend?" asked Mark.

"No, of course not!" Amos answered, piqued.

Mark tried to trip him: "The little man, didn't he ask you to fly with him?"

"No! And me, I wouldn't have agreed."

Belmont. Monday 7 November 1977.

In his book *Cosmic Trigger*, Robert Anton Wilson makes the interesting observation that the lies and deceptions commonly engineered by Governments promote a paranoid atmosphere which permeates the public mistrust of science.

Any form of collective thought is subject to influence and suggestion, and blind on fundamentals. Free individual thought, the reflective work of a solitary researcher, is the best path to discovery. It is subject to mistakes but those are easier to correct, provided one stays close to key facts and seeks the advice of independent thinkers. That ingredient -- critical thought -- is the most difficult one to find.

Belmont. Tuesday 8 November 1977.

I had another absurd premonitory dream on Sunday night. It was disarmingly funny: I had been chosen to head up the sewer department in Palo Alto. Thrilled at the opportunity, I had in mind innovative reforms, notably the creation of special lanes for canoes, similar to special bike lanes recently instituted near Stanford! The dream, as usual when special meaning is present, woke me up in the middle of the night, so I remembered well looking down into the sewers. I wondered about its absurd content. I didn't have long to wait for results. The plumbing along our street backed up that evening. City services were alerted. At one o'clock in the morning I found myself peering into a sewer hole with workers from Public Works, helping pull out tree roots that had grown into the pipes.

Why are such episodes so silly and striking at the same time? As in my earlier dream preceding my son's dog bite, my mind had added Freudian luxuries to the text. How could we ever sift through such bizarre details to extract relevant information?

Belmont. Saturday 12 November 1977.

On Thursday night Janine and I flew down to Hollywood for the Première of *Close Encounters* as guests of Columbia Pictures. A limo picked us up with Allen, so we had a chance to talk before the screening. He was in superb shape and told us he had the highest hope for the NASA study. During the press conference, Spielberg cleverly declined to explain the holes that critics exposed in the script. It should be viewed as a work of art, he said, all aspects of which he didn't claim to understand. He didn't want to debase it by a personal interpretation! He was superb in his handling of the press.

The boy in the movie, five years of age, couldn't hide his personal interpretation: “I've seen myself in the movie,” he said confidently. “And I liked it... I thought it was rather good.”

Charged up by Hollywood, Allen was ready for the big time when we had dinner with him. The tiredness of Saint Louis was gone. Columbia has mentioned his Center in the press book, although Allen was given no screen credit. They've bought 2,000 subscriptions to his newsletter, a $20,000 total.

“Margaret Mead has agreed to join the science board,” Allen said with a wink in my direction. “By the way, how did your meeting with Schneider go?” he enquired.

“I wanted to find out if his office was going to remain involved. Evidently the answer is no; they've washed their hands of it.”

Janine and I fled before another press conference. We went looking for old books. Frank Salisbury has dropped his own study of UFOs under pressure from the Mormon Church and the University of Utah. He sent Allen a letter filled with anguish.

Belmont. Thursday 17 November 1977.

Rumors are piling up like the wet pages of old newspapers caught by a storm. I called Allen this morning, asking him simply if he could contact Regnery to retrieve the illustrations of our book for the French publisher. This touched a raw nerve.

"I'm not in good terms with them," he said with disgust. "They've sued Colombia for the use of *Close Encounters* as the title, claiming they own the copyright, because I first used the term in *UFO Experience*." The suit has ruined Allen's honeymoon with Colombia.

Stanton Friedman called me last night, mad at Allen and the film, citing "inaccuracies." I ascribed his reaction to envy of Hynek's newfound celebrity. Stanton told me about an incident in Cuba, where a MiG was allegedly destroyed in an incident with a UFO. All the information recorded by civilians in Florida was confiscated by the NSA. This made me think of the Intelligence boys I have met. Either they don't know about such incidents, in which case they are poor analysts, or they do know and they've never shared the information, in which case they're playing games. Kit keeps explaining away the sightings by a combination of witness unreliability, fugue states, paraphrenia, or unspecified "anthropological" factors; none of which accounts for the hard core data. As for cattle mutilation cases, which may or may not be related to UFOs at all, he dismisses them as the simple work of predators.

Toronto. Tuesday 22 November 1977.

A series of computer science meetings at IBM-Canada have brought me to Toronto for one night. I keep thinking about UFOs and the role of the secret services. I don't envy those who have more power than I do, more access to secret things, more wealth. My favorite movie is *The Tall Blond Man with one Black Shoe* (**24**), a French comedy in which an innocent violinist is mistaken for a superagent by an accident of fate and the bumbling of official spooks.

I keep pondering what Stanley Schneider told me in Washington: Even if the CIA came out with an official statement that the UFO phenomenon was real, how would we know it's not another one of their lies, designed to hide a bureaucratic bungle, fool the Russians, or protect some esoteric weapon system?

Belmont. Friday 25 November 1977.

The promotion of *Close Encounters* is reaching saturation while the proposed NASA study remains enmeshed in bureaucratic absurdity. On Wednesday I called Fred from O'Hare during a change of planes. He told me that Allen was inaccessible, absorbed by his newfound celebrity, photo opportunities, a new book and the nasty lawsuit.

"Allen was furious against you when he learned that you'd gone to Washington, to Frank Press' office," Fred warned me. He had calmed down when we met in Hollywood.

A woman named Ann Shapiro has published an article in *Annual UFO,* claiming that I was none other than the *Comte de Saint Germain!* (**25**).

She doesn't seem deterred by the fact that the Count is known to have died a couple of centuries ago at a castle in Hessen "in the arms of two chambermaids," a fate I find enviable.

Belmont. Sunday 4 December 1977.

Another week-end spent editing *Messengers of Deception.* I argued with Janine about what space, if any, should be devoted to cattle mutilations: she believes they are unrelated to our main research.

On Friday we went to hear Maurice André in concert, after which we joined a group of parapsychologists in San Francisco. Russell Targ was presiding. He pulled a batch of papers from his briefcase and reported about an Iceland psychic conference and his trip to England, after which part of the group had gone off to France.

We were told that an English professor named Hasted places detection instruments in his lab, recording mysterious forces. Bits of metal get twisted in the presence of psychic kids supposedly inspired by Uri Geller's performances.

Belmont. Wednesday 7 December 1977.

Aimé Michel now claims, "No progress can be made in our knowledge of UFOs without changing man's brain. And I'm talking about a biological change, not just a spiritual or psychic change."

He may be right. He also reported on his meeting with the American parapsychology group in Paris, the same group Russell Targ had mentioned. He saw Walker, Elizabeth Rauscher, and Puharich, "all terribly marginal, impotent, repeating the same tired things." He doesn't think much of Gepan either, writing that no good comes from it. Pierre Guérin is more sanguine. He tells me that Poher's project is now under the control of a council that comprises one third pro-UFO scientists, one third neutrals and one third skeptics. This council is scheduled to review case investigations conducted by a team comprising a Sorbonne psychologist and a judge. They examine statistics conducted "with modern means, to look serious," as Pierre says. He adds that if a majority of the council remains unconvinced, the staff will resign *en masse*, and Poher will go sailing around the world on his boat. Pierre's letter goes on:

"I must say that Hubert Curien's decision, as head of CNES, to create Gepan at the urging of the military has aroused the hatred of all his dear colleagues. They were forced to let him proceed, but they're determined to destroy Poher at the first opportunity."

The sad fact is that, even in their most daring moments, Poher and friends recoil before the evidence that the phenomenon displays paranormal components. This dooms their study to failure, in my opinion: The paranormal factors are key to the solution. Another problem for Poher is the behavior of the ufological groups, newly excited at the prospect of official recognition. The fight between those who like aliens and those who hold for a psychic explanation results in unending backbiting and character assassination. It doesn't occur to them that the two hypotheses are compatible.

On Monday I flew back to Hollywood for dinner with Spielberg and Marcia Seligson; they had picked a restaurant so exclusive that it wasn't listed in the phone book. Omar Sharif was seated at the next table; all the women wore exquisite furs. Spielberg came in with his old leather jacket but he had left his legendary baseball cap in his car. He still thought that Columbia was going ahead with the funding of a network of observing stations to look for UFOs under Allen's coordination. (**26**)

I got back to my hotel after a slow, sickening drive in the densest fog I'd ever seen. It turned the L.A. freeway network into a nightmare landscape worthy of any horror film.

Belmont. Saturday 10 December 1977.

On Friday I took Marie de Castéja to SRI, where I introduced her to Ingo Swann and the psi research team. She told me there were unsolved animal mutilations in the South of France. The countess is an extraordinary woman, in appearance a superficial socialite, but the next second she skewers us with lucid remarks that take everyone by surprise. After seeing our Planet system, she gave a remarkable analysis of the information economy and the impact of computer conferencing: "The first country that understands this new medium of communication will have an enormous advantage," she said.

Belmont. Sunday 11 December 1977.

New contact with a group in Washington with an interest in computer conferencing (**27**).

When Kit got back to his office after his stay in Texas he was angry to discover that the UFO files he had collected had been scattered by Agency attorneys in answer to FOIA requests. He had difficulty gathering them again. His boss called him on the carpet: "You're supposed to cover life sciences," he told him, "this stuff has nothing to do with it."

The Agency allowed him to pursue the topic privately. He told me that something curious was happening in Mexico, with rumors of multiple UFOs seen on the ground and mysterious deaths of animals. One of the objects is said to have remained on the ground for two and a half days, surrounded with tanks and Mexican troops.

"Unfortunately we don't have any real facts," he went on. "Puharich went there but the *milicia* stopped him before he got to the site. He couldn't get anything out of Lopez Portillo, with whom he believes he has a friendly relationship."

Belmont. Friday 23 December 1977.

Guérin has sent me a long letter with his candid appraisal of Poher's efforts and the recent meeting of the scientific advisory committee of Gepan: "They started out cleverly, by showering us with flowers for the quality and quantity of the work, and so on," his letter reports. "They praised our seriousness and the fact we had secured the assistance of a real psychologist and of a genuine magistrate."

The committee then went on to review statistics, noting "they had been taken as far as they could." Guérin did agree reluctantly. After all, purely psychological or hallucinatory phenomena, too, would present some sort of internal structure under the same statistical treatment. As for any "proof" of the phenomenon, it was still eluding them. In other words, they remained unconvinced.

"Poher was depressed," Guérin goes on in his letter, "he had assured us he'd resign if they still wanted more proof, after everything we've given them. Nothing will change a year from now."

Every day, during these school holidays, I have had the pleasure to take my children to my office with me. We go to lunch at Marcel's restaurant, where Rich Miller often joins us. We are happy. Our only sadness this year was to see so many of our friends absurdly falling victim to drugs or the stress of life. The tragedy is that we could only witness their downward spiral -- unable to help.

18

Belmont. Thursday 5 January 1978.

For the last two weeks a fierce storm howls around our roof and rattles the garden gate. A nasty rumor has started within NASA. It claims that CNES only created Gepan because Poher's boss had no "real scientific" assignment, nothing for him to do. Allen wrote to Poher so he could dispell this lie, but he got no response.

Yesterday I received a phone call from a fellow who works with McDonnell-Douglas Astronautics. He told me that, "on a private basis," he was compiling a new close encounter database. I am not stupid enough to believe that his company has no corporate interest in the matter. They have an on-going secret project, well-funded, with the blessing and official monitoring of the CIA and they're discreetly connected with major UFO groups, all of which love the secret intrigue of a link to the spooks even as they vilify "the government coverup" in their public pronouncements. I am not playing that game; let others do it.

Belmont. Sunday 8 January 1978.

Elmer Burns came out of the wind and the rain like a devil in a long black coat and a mariner's cap. With his beard, his tape recorder and his tall bald forehead he looked like an evangelist for some cult out of Lovecraft. He insisted I had to listen to the voice of a "Doctor Z" who now speaks directly through him in a heavy Italian accent. Dr. Z has given Elmer a "clearance" to show me technical data: I must study the spectrum of Alpha Lyrae. Elmer also wanted me to listen to his latest conversation with Hynek, which lasted an hour. Instead I pushed him to the door and he melted again in the storm, taking with him his tapes, his Dr. Z and his glossolalia. We have more serious concerns. Janine has to take tests for a growth in one breast; we are intensely worried about it.

Red Bluff. Friday 13 January 1978.

It's raining all over Northern California, with great slabs of water that shake the motel room door and slam the window frames. Tomorrow I meet Bill Murphy for breakfast to investigate the *Copper Medic* case (**28**). He is among a dozen correspondents, like Barbara Bartholic in Oklahoma, Mark Uriarte in California and John Williams in Texas, who keep me informed about current events in the field. I stopped here for the night, 20 miles away from Redding. We'll go to the site together.

Two nights ago I had dinner with Allen, who was giving a lecture in Santa Clara. It's hard to remain angry at a man like Allen for long.

Belmont. Wednesday 18 January 1978.

Alone in my lair, I hear the steady rain pounding the house. Janine is spending the night at the hospital, with exploratory surgery tomorrow afternoon. Sensing the seriousness of the situation, the children are quiet, doing their homework after a peaceful dinner.

Paul Cerny, local Mufon ufocrat, is mad at me for going to Redding without him. He gave me a lecture about the dangers I was going to run into in Northern California: The woods are full of crazy hippies, he said, and the old miners are quick with the trigger finger. I should let him "keep control of his witnesses!"

Flying to New York. Saturday 21 January 1978.

Janine has come back from the hospital, reassured after the removal of a benign cyst. Olivier, when I brought him back from school in the evening, managed to hide his emotions. Yet when we visited her in the hospital the previous evening, he had to leave the room when we found her tense, her skin a pale white, a needle in her arm. Catherine asked me at once, "is Janine back?" Yes, she's back. Life has re-entered the house.

Some of the theoretical papers I'd sent Kit have disappeared from his home study, just like Poher's photographs vanished from

Bourret's apartment. And my letter from Russia.

In ancient Egypt people were controlled by a religious order supported by prodigies. Only the top priests knew how they were manipulated. One could speculate that society still runs that way. Is someone trying to provide humanity with a renewed Pantheon? The new Gods could only come from the sky. Is that why so much attention is directed at the notion that UFOs must be spacecraft while the more fruitful theories are discouraged or censored?

New York. Roosevelt Hotel. Monday 23 January 1978.

Another tiring conference on office automation is spinning a boring tale. This happens to be the latest technology frontier. Experts drone on, their gray transparencies covered with jargon.

I am shocked at prices in New York. An omelet costs $4, a bad sandwich $7. Carter came before Congress today with a 500 billion dollar budget. Kennedy had caused a scandal 15 years ago with the first American budget over 100 billion: the expenses of the government have been multiplied by five!

Messengers of Deception is giving me some concerns. I don't like the material I am dealing with. I have trouble organizing it in a coherent way. The book may be too far ahead of its time.

New York. Wednesday 25 January 1978.

Yesterday I had breakfast on Wall Street at Lehman Brothers and visited publishers. Ballantine tells me they have reprinted *Anatomy* and *Challenge* in mass paperback, both selling well. The snow melts in Manhattan, the city looks like a swamp. The environmental bureau lies that air quality is "acceptable."

Travel sleep, filled with sharp light, sudden darkness rough as a lunar crater. Over dinner Bill Whitehead told me he liked *Messengers* and would like to publish it in the fall but he has a conflict with his director of distribution. "He's an old guy, very conservative," he said. "We don't get along. Dutton hasn't done a good job with *Invisible College.* We treated John Keel even worse."

We went on to discuss Puharich. Bill, who'd published his book *Uri*, asked me what I frankly thought of him. "Andrija puzzles me," I said, telling the bizarre episode when he was receiving coded messages in Hebrew on his wristwatch.

"Well, his latest manuscript is a disaster, long extracts of wishy-washy messages from Hoova and Spectra... a total mess."

We said goodbye at Grand Central Station. He said again that *Messengers* was an important book. I would have liked to celebrate, but I didn't know anyone in New York with whom to celebrate, so I went back to my hotel, sloshing through pools of black mud. Tomorrow I am taking the train to meet with Ira in Philadelphia.

In the "Senator" train to Washington.
Thursday 26 January 1978.

Ira Einhorn's enthusiasm chased away my melancholy, although I was tired of dragging my 25-pound Texas Instruments terminal to demonstrate our conferencing system to his friends. He took me to Bell of Pennsylvania to meet with Ray Smith, the president, for whom he acts as consultant. Going up to the executive offices of Bell with Ira is quite an experience, because he knows everyone by first name, from the janitor to the CEO. Unwashed, in sandals and long hair, he gets people to resonate with him and raises the level of any room when he crosses the threshold, whether it's a student meeting, a Union protest, a board room or a fashionable café. We gave a scintillating demonstration of *Planet* to Ray Smith, after which Ira had arranged a dinner with the director of the Franklin Museum. Puharich's name came up.

"We haven't spoken to each other in a while," Ira said. "We had a falling out. Andrija's gone nuts, but the phenomena around him are real."

"What about Tom Bearden?"

"Tom's onto something. We ought to pay more attention to the scary psychotronic stuff the Soviets are doing. The French are years behind on that. You ought to straighten them out. Aimé Michel and Jacques Bergier are dealing with obsolete data."

"What makes you say that?"

"Bergier's three books on espionage don't tackle the current stuff. Take the space hardware: A soviet satellite crashed in Canada recently, did you know that? The damn thing was radioactive, uranium on board, more than necessary to power the transmitter or the experiments. What were they trying to do? Nobody seems to know. That's what Bergier should investigate. The British Minister of Defence has asked Tom and me to fly to London to brief him."

Belmont. Saturday 28 January 1978.

Kit and I met at Dulles airport on Thursday. Again we spent the evening arguing. I asked him what he thought of the Soviet psychotronic work, of Tom Bearden's contention that they are seeking offensive use of psychic techniques. He said that Bergier was mistaken when he argued the Soviets had a defensive approach.

"We began our first really serious analysis of Soviet parapsychology work about 1970," he said. "Other agencies thought we were crazy, but they've now changed their tune. They even went beyond what we did. There've been four independent analyses, all classified. I was only responsible for our own study. The Garrett Airesearch report that's circulating represents only a tenth of the findings. We found a dozen centers for psychotronic research in the Soviet Union."

"What do they do?"

"Their work focuses on gifted subjects. They look for them in systematic fashion, throughout their population. Not like our own research work, at SRI and other places, which is theoretical and aims at defining abilities like PK and remote viewing in the lab. But we think they've only had limited success, with few practical applications. DIA and others went farther than we did. I can't tell you more, but they speculated that the Russians had offensive labs where they were trying to blow up people's heads at a distance and break their spinal columns by PK."

"What about the Foreign Technology Division?

"Their conclusions came in between these two extremes."

Belmont. Sunday 29 January 1978.

Allen Hynek was back in San Francisco yesterday. I was busy with computer work but he insisted to get a faithful translation of Poher's latest letter, stating the conclusions of the Gepan scientific committee. It didn't add much to what I already knew from Guérin. The members seem obsessed with the desire to remain anonymous.

We invited Peter and Marilyn Sturrock for dinner with Allen. The consensus was that Poher had gotten himself into a vulnerable situation. In his letter Poher practically demands that Hynek send him a 500-page report on his best cases. He requests 60 copies! He expects our investigations to be reviewed and signed by “great scientists.” He adds that, given the situation, any exchange of funds would be “inappropriate.” Not only does Allen feel insulted, but he concludes that Poher just doesn't understand the situation.

Peter Sturrock pointed out smartly that the military was still keeping the best data, both in France and in the U.S. Allen is urging Fred to fly to France to see Poher: “Is it really true that he's spent over a million dollars in his investigations?” That amount, which Poher mentions in his letter, is purely theoretical: he has access to government labs for which he isn't paying from his own funds, so the final accounting figure is fiction.

A similar situation exists in Washington. Kit has been told that the Agency didn't have a mission to monitor the subject. His personal notes and files have been returned to him with instructions to take them home. Which brings us back to the big question: If those guys actually know nothing, who the hell is in charge?

Flying to Tulsa. Sunday 5 February 1978.

The audience of a recent sci-fi conference in Oakland came to hear Hynek, who turned them over to Paul Cerny, who spilled the story of the supposedly “confidential” Redding case. Details are splattered in the Sunday paper although the investigation has barely started. So much for Paul’s ability to protect witnesses and work discreetly.

I've now met Colonel Coleman, who still works at the Pentagon.

He's the man who organized the Sandler documentary and told Emenegger: "Some day I'll take you out on my boat, we'll sail off the coast of Florida, and I will whisper the answer in your ear." Coleman is a white-haired man with a white beard, jovial, sturdy. He works on "Project UFO," a television series that glorifies Blue Book.

None of the speakers at the conference dealt with the real problem, the physical nature of the phenomenon. Why are the objects capable of appearing and vanishing out of nowhere? Why is their surface so different from that of metallic objects? How can they change shape dynamically? Why do they sometimes appear as flat surfaces?

Discussing this with Hal the other day, I was able to convince him that these phenomena could be accounted for if the objects manipulated another dimension. He reluctantly agreed that the same processes applied to the psychic experiments his team was conducting at SRI. Esoteric traditions flow from that same idea. Why do I imagine, in fugitive glimpses and treasured moments, that we can have access to that knowledge?

Hal told me of an observation he made at SRI, that his subjects have an easier time finding a hidden thing than an open target, and an emotionally loaded object rather that an inert one. Is it for that reason that religious and occult rites use color, sound vibrations, secrecy, and flickering flames? Are these designed to operate subtly on another physical plane? Allen never understood this, but he came very close when he worked with Manly Hall.

Dallas. Wednesday 8 February 1978.

A blizzard hit central Texas last night, wreaking havoc with the roads. Cars rolled into the ditches, trucks veered at odd angles, intersections were crowded with stranded vehicles. My correspondent John Williams took me to visit Bill Daniel, a crippled man with a brilliant mind, like Ray Palmer and Aimé Michel, who may own the world's most complete collection of UFO books. We found him in a wheelchair, whirling around a room furnished with a piano, a sofa and extraordinary bookshelves. He keeps binders full of clippings and catalogues dating back well before 1952. One of his sources, Elliott Rockmore of Brooklyn, was already publishing a *Saucer Review* in 1951. "He had to stop the following year," Bill told us with a guffaw, "he couldn't keep up with all the data!"

He showed me his great treasure, a copy of the Varo edition of Jessup's book. He agreed that the book's value resided purely in its rarity, because the contents, which started the ludicrous myth of the *Philadelphia Experiment*, were worthless, even with the famous marginal annotations supposedly made by Aliens!

I spoke at the planetarium before the Texas Society for Psychical Research and spent the rest of the evening reviewing the Hyattsville case with John Williams. He showed me the infrared photos of the site and gave me some bark samples from the burnt trees. The energy emitted by the object was in the range of half a million kilowatts.

Belmont. Monday 13 February 1978.

Guérin and Aimé Michel have both written to me last week, commenting on Poher's decisions. Guérin is surprised that Gepan is still active, given the high degree of antagonism among French scientists. Poher has even succeeded in getting more money. He runs his operation with an iron hand, pushing aside Petit who won't acknowledge his authority. The new director of the Astrophysics Institute is a skeptic. He comes from a politicized level that "makes" and destroys researchers. Pierre concludes his letter with acerbic comments about *Close Encounters*.

Aimé Michel sends new details about the death of General Ailleret.

> The circumstances were the following: (i) His pilot was a well respected ace. (ii) When he took off from La Réunion airport, where everybody knows you have to turn towards the sea because of the mountain, the pilot stubbornly turned the other way, resulting in a loud "boom" and a need to find a new chief of staff for the French Air Force. (iii) The statements in question said that the Air Force had reached the conclusion that the UFO phenomenon was serious and that he, General Ailleret, was going to setup a commission to study it.

The next chief of staff has done nothing of the kind. Aimé adds that in 1976 French higher-ups re-examined the "pilot error" theory and blamed the accident on sabotage.

Aimé's opinion of CE3K is the same as Guérin's, namely that the film is childish. Finally he recommends that I read *Ten Problems Concerning Providence* by Proclus (*De Decem Dubitationibus circa Providentia*), just translated into French.

Belmont. Saturday 18 February 1978.

Allen refuses to send me any information about the "confidential" case I am studying in Redding because Paul Cerny, on behalf of Cufos, insists to keep the data to himself. When Peter Sturrock assembled a meeting with David Fryberger (a warm, clever physicist), Tom Gates, Paul Cerny, Dick Haines and me, Cerny told us he was sure he would soon find a flying saucer, "kicking the tires" and perhaps going away with the crew: "If I vanish some day, fellows, you'll know I have succeeded!" he told us dramatically.

Peter gave me credit for inspiring him to start the Society for Scientific Exploration, and to publish a journal as a source of verified, peer-reviewed UFO data. (**29**)

Bill Murphy called me last night. The Redding witnesses, Mr. and Mrs. Chapin, are fed up with ufologists in general and Cerny in particular. They've requested to meet with me and will take me up to their mine to show me the actual place where the object landed, and tell me the real story.

Belmont. Sunday 12 March 1978.

This afternoon I flew back from L.A. after meeting with Jay Levey and Timothy Leary, Robert Anton Wilson, Esfandiary and Barbara Marx Hubbard, among a motley group of space enthusiasts and immortality researchers. On Saturday I was able to spend an hour with Jim Irish in his sound lab. It was an opportunity to learn about ELF (Extremely Low Frequency) radiations and their effects.

Belmont. Thursday 23 March 1978.

Peter Beren at And/or Press in Berkeley sends me a contract for *Messengers* and Tchou has agreed to publish the French version. I hear that Jim Harder is now convinced that I am a contactee! On Tuesday afternoon Sturrock and I had another meeting at Stanford with Harder. Dick Haines, Bruce Maccabee and Brad Sparks were there, all a bit too serious.

At the moment I am alone, without courage to write. Janine is away at the snow with the kids. This beautiful house is empty and sad without her.

Belmont. Sunday 26 March 1978.

Yesterday in Healdsburg, Mark Uriarte and I interviewed the Cray family, terrified by a low-flying object over a vineyard (**30**). I came back carrying two bottles of Colombard 1977, whose grapes had been bathed briefly in the light from the UFO. Perhaps Fred Beckman will be able to taste a distinctive extraterrestrial *bouquet*? At least the incident will provide us with an excuse for opening another bottle together.

Cherry trees were blooming in Healdsburg. The little town, sleeping as it does in a loop of the Russian River, was idyllic and serene. It seems lost in the nineteenth century, and there's softness in the air. On the way Mark gave me some impressions from his work at the FBI. One of his colleagues recently commented, "Here goes another flying saucer file!" as he put a thick document on a table where they were sorting papers to be reviewed and destroyed. The file contained letters, clippings, and a letter from J. Edgar Hoover, dated 1949, requesting that any information on UFOs be sent to him.

Our children are happy, their faces touched with the light of peaceful spring. Flowers are blooming everywhere, putting heavy, syrupy nectar into the atmosphere. Even in California I have never seen such luxury in every moment of simple living. The hills are like reclining goddesses, their curves clad in soft green fur.

Fig. 17. Prelude to "Heaven's Gate": This picture of "The Two" (Marshall Applewhite and Bonnie Nettles) was taken at a Stanford meeting where they told their followers: "You only risk your life!" My 1979 book *Messengers of Deception* tried to alert believers against such sects but the warning went unheeded. The "Heaven's Gate" cult committed mass suicide in 1997. (credit: G. Askevold)

Fig. 18. Meeting in Dr. Sturrock's office at Stanford, March 1978. From left: Jim Harder, Dick Haines, Brad Sparks, J.Vallée, Bruce Maccabee, Peter Sturrock.

Belmont. Thursday 30 March 1978.

My daughter has drawn a flying saucer for me, with a ladder underneath. All the rungs are slanted because, as she puts it, “those Martians, they're weird.” Next, on an impulse, she drew a rainbow on another page. I stepped out to the living room, which overlooks the Bay, and there was a rainbow in the sky. I called her to watch it with me. Who could say what mankind would be able to do, if education and culture did not extinguish such spontaneous abilities in children?

Belmont. Sunday 9 April 1978.

Elmer, slurring his words, called me again with news from the Aliens. He's applied for a patent for a process to “extract energy from the gravitational field.” He claims Cufos has made a deal with him, 20% of profits in exchange for legal and financial support. “I've gone through a conditioning process,” he said in his convoluted jargon. “I realized that these transformational maneuvers, with their profond logic, came both from myself and from outside -- You see what I mean?” Everything Elmer observes is always “profound” and “transformational.” An eager disciple, he spends long hours on the phone with Allen.

Flying to Washington. Saturday 15 April 1978.

Elmer called us in the middle of the night on Monday, his voice pasty. He threatened Janine, yelling, “I've taken so many drugs I'll be dead tomorrow morning! If Jacques doesn't talk to me I'm gonna come over with a gun and blow out your windows.”

When she told him to get lost he threatened to kill us all, so she hung up. I have other fish to fry, working hard to get my company going. We have just hired a marketing vice-president, and won two contracts. Trammell Crow is now financing Hal Puthoff's work, according to Ed May. I offered to hire Ed at InfoMedia but he's sure a breakthrough is imminent at SRI, so he decided to stay there.

Reston, Virginia. Sunday 16 April 1978.

Some brave researchers are trying to extract UFO data from the government through the FOIA. “All they'll get is a lot of garbage,” Kit told me. “The government no longer files anything under the UFO label. All personnel have been told to drop any research, direct or indirect, about the subject. I got mad at this. I told them they had no right to tell analysts what they could and couldn't look at.”

Government attorneys will be able to swear truthfully before the Courts that there are no files on UFOs and no work on the subject.

“What do you know about Wilbur Franklin?” Kit asked. The name was familiar.

“He's a physicist, I saw him once at SRI. He looked a bit wrinkled and sad, like someone who had been kept in somebody's cellar for a long time...” Kit was not amused. “The poor guy died last week, in rather strange circumstances,” he told me, wiping the smile from my face. “It's the fifth or sixth death of a parapsychologist in 18 months.”

“What happened?” I asked in astonishment.

“Several people saw him very healthy two weeks ago. He went home for the weekend. He was in his forties, mind you, not an old man. On Monday he didn't show up at Kent State, where he chaired the Physics Department. His colleagues alerted the police. They found him at home in a coma, took him to the hospital. Attending physicians found nothing abnormal in the tests: X-rays of his brain, other tests, all normal. On Wednesday his brain waves go flat. On Thursday he is dead.” **(31)**

“I suppose there was an autopsy?' I asked.

“That's were it get weirder. They found something but the coroner in Cayoga County won't say what it is, except that his conclusions contradict those of the attending physician. Apparently the body had burn marks.”

“What was Franklin working on?”

“Nothing big, apparently. He wasn't briefed on classified psi research. He was doing work on the physical characteristics of some spoons Uri Geller had bent, harmless stuff. He was also working on a book attempting to gather in one place everything that's known in parapsychology."

"It's frustrating to see all this research stalling," I said, "people working more or less at random, with no resources."

"That's what Mr. McDonnell said recently at the CIA. He came over to see the director, and told him point blank that he thought this was the most important area of research; he wanted a full briefing on our classified work in psi. Mr. Mac has just given a million and a half to the University of Washington School of Medicine to advance the state of the art in parapsychology, and he's also paying for a 7-million dollar building."

"What did the Director say to that?"

"He asked him if he wasn't kept busy enough by the recent contracts he got from the government. As you may know, the U.S. has decided to sell lots of aircraft to Middle Eastern countries. McDonnell said he found time for parapsychology because that had the highest priority in his mind. As a result the Agency sent me to Kansas City to brief Mr. Mac for three days, on all American and Soviet work."

We spent the rest of the evening arguing about close encounters.

When we spoke again this morning after breakfast Kit told me he had spent most of the night reading my analyses.

"I've drawn a number of lessons from this," he said. "For one, all the physiological effects you describe appear to belong to the autonomous sympathetic nervous system which relates to the rhinencephalon in terms of smells and feelings of nausea. Those are two features often noted by your witnesses."

"Does that lead you to look for psychiatric explanations, then?" I asked, already on the defensive. "Psychiatric explanations won't explain these cases, you know."

"No, I've become skeptical about psychiatric hypotheses," he answered to my relief. "Psychiatric effects are present, but there may be a physiological cause that triggers them."

We went on to discuss the recent deaths, a suspicious concentration. All subjects were studying parapsychology on a private basis, part-time, with their own funds, in the same way I'm working on UFOs. All were regarded as serious people, but they were outside the circle of government funded research. One of them was Ron Hubbard's own son. Wilbur Franklin is death number five.

In the case of Price, too, the circumstances are suspicious. Both Hal and Price's wife saw the body, so there is no question about its identity, but an unidentified ambulance driver had taken the corpse away and it disappeared for 24 hours before reappearing at a local hospital, equally mysteriously. An ailing heart was blamed for Price's death, but he had told his daughter some time before that he thought the KGB might try to kill him.

Belmont. Tuesday 2 May 1978.

Tonight Elmer called again with more revelations. I told him that after his threats of the other night I wanted nothing more to do with him, even though he now is an official Cufos representative.

"It wasn't me, the other night!" He protested. "That's the second time it happens. Somebody takes over my voice to call people. I'd never threaten your family."

"It was you alright, Elmer, you were stoned to your ears," I said.

"That doesn't matter," he insisted, "I always remain normal when I'm stoned."

"Sure, Elmer. Still, I don't want anything more to do with you."

He got mad at me and started yelling.

"If you ignore what I have to say, you'll be missing a big research opportunity..." He looked for something momentous to say: "You'll be a historical asshole!" he blurted out.

I laughed. "I'll take that chance, Elmer," I said as I hung up.

Los Angeles. Thursday 18 May 1978.

I finally took Kit over to Jim Irish's lab. As we drove through the L.A. traffic Kit told me about his meeting with Bob Beck, who researches brainwave entraining. I think Beck managed to convince him that entraining was possible, but he remains skeptical of Bearden's notion that the Russians are using it as a weapon. In this sense he's rather on the side of Jacques Bergier. Beck is even more afraid of scientologists than of the soviets, in terms of psychotronics. Beck also told him he knew Jim Irish, whom he considered as a solid fellow with a good technical mind.

Jim proudly showed us his facility. We sat down in his dubbing studio and spoke of his days working with the military. It seems they hired him as a specialist in infrared photography. They would call him up at 2 A.M. to send him to the hills and take pictures of a certain region of the sky at a specific time.

"I think the fellow is exactly who he says he is," Kit told me once we were back in the car, driving along Sunset. "He must have worked as a private contractor for ASA, and later for NSA. They paid fairly well, as he said."

"What do you think they were doing?"

"I suspect NSA wanted to find out if it was possible to detect specific systems aboard satellites. If Jim Irish could pick them up with his polaroid plates, it's likely that the Russians could do it too."

"So you think it all had to do with radioactivity?" I asked, recalling a recent conversation with Jacques Bergier. He had told me I might find a key in the correlation of the sightings with atmospheric radioactivity, but most of that data was secret. Jim Irish also told us about the time when they sent him to the coast of Alaska to photograph a Liberian cargo ship that had run aground. It carried radioactive stuff. Behind his reconnaissance plane they sent bombers to sink the ship before the Russians could get to it.

"That wasn't in the *New York Times* the next morning!" he said.

Another remark by Jim Irish struck us both: He was never called by his intelligence bosses during periods of high UFO activity in civilian areas. But if there was the slightest UFO incident near a military base, they launched a thorough investigation, even if the report came from a drunken cowboy.

About 1956 in San Luis Obispo there was a rumor about a UFO having crashed near the seashore. The Army was said to have hidden its remains under a geodesic dome which could be seen from highway One. Camp Roberts was evacuated and overflight of the area was forbidden. The incident had nothing to do with a UFO, but a nuclear bomb may have fallen off from a strategic bomber and the dome was put there to prevent debris from being scattered.

We finally discussed cattle mutilations, which left him fairly stumped. Kit leans towards the theory that witches are responsible. I don't find that convincing. It doesn't match occult practices. Nor does it account for the technical details.

Belmont. Friday 19 May 1978.

Upon my return from Los Angeles I met with Ira Einhorn at his hotel. We spent several hours discussing Bob Beck, Puharich and Valerie Ransone, a contactee who has worked in Washington for Nixon's WIN (anti-inflation) campaign. She is active in high-level circles, organizing trips to the desert in hopes of watching UFOs.

Confirming what I'd heard from Kit, Ira told me that Valerie and Puharich had gone over to see Beck in March or April 1977. Beck claims he can take his ELF generator to a coffee shop, turn on the device and cause every child in the place to start crying; conversely he'll tune it to a frequency that induces euphoria... Some German executives are said to have a device that shields a person against such waves (**32**). In a letter to Ira, Beck writes that "competent authorities" have asked him not to reveal the frequencies in question.

Flying to Pittsburgh. Monday 22 May 1978.

Kit remains skeptical about mutilations. A bright scientist with all the pragmatic attitudes of a good physician, he's impressed by the Flickinger report, but the skill demonstrated by the perpetrators is yet to be explained, so we argue endlessly. Kit points out that a cut made with a butcher's knife (or a rat's front teeth) is just as "surgical" as a scalpel's cut, but what about the cases where instruments were introduced through the rectum to sever internal ligaments and remove abdominal organs?

Kit is in close contact with most of the UFO groups, so his interest is only confidential among the uninformed. Right now he is on his way to Houston, where Valerie Ransone and a group of contactees have promised he would witness materializations. But what are his true intentions? He belongs to a small cadre of very bright Intelligence types who are looking for elements of truth. There is no way to know what really goes on, and who pulls the strings. And even the bright ones can easily be fooled by their own system or fool themselves. It is becoming obvious to both of us that some of the rumors about extraterrestrials have been planted, perhaps as a cover to esoteric weapons systems, or as part of psychological warfare exercises in which ufologists are a convenient test bed.

Flying back to San Francisco. Wednesday 24 May 1978.

I am watching a faraway storm through the plane's window. Next to me is a Styrofoam container filled with ice. When I didn't let the stewardess put it away in the luggage compartment we almost had an argument, yet I couldn't tell her it contained a section of a calf's heart, its liver, a test tube filled with blood and the flesh that surrounded an unexplained incision. I also bring back photographs of primitive witches altars found in the same area, although there doesn't seem to be any correlation between the two. My intent is to study this without fanfare; to get the hard data, as I've tried to do in every mutilation case I have investigated.

We have driven all over the area from Tulsa to Eureka Springs. In Bentonville, where the weather was hot and humid, we sat in the sheriff's office studying maps, pictures, reports of autopsies compiled by his men. Last night, in the mountains, I grilled witnesses who had seen a large UFO fly over. Among them was a physicist who had worked on the Manhattan project at Oak Ridge. This is a case that Alan Hendry had "explained," but without going to the actual site. Hendry generally does good investigative work but in this case his explanation doesn't hold.

Flying to Milwaukee. Sunday 11 June 1978.

Valerie Ransone is setting up a company to disseminate messages she believes to be of extraterrestrial origin. Since networks are now at the cutting edge of information science, she's also building up a Center for Advanced Technology that plans to use conferencing. The whole thing is reportedly financed by *Security around the Globe,* an industrial protection and private detective firm.

Valerie is an attractive 28-year old woman with a brilliant mind. She's being helped by high-powered executives, captains of industry, impeccable business leaders she calls her “silver foxes.” One of them arranged for her to meet the director of the Scripps Institute and Gordon Cooper, who's made curious statements lately about witnessing the retrieval of crashed saucers. She's also in touch with a fellow who owns a lot of real estate in San Francisco.

Journalist Wes Thomas, who heads up Valerie's computing center, has called from her office to enlist my help. Valerie got on the line to assure me of the seriousness of her project. I declined to become involved, bothered by all their pseudo-science.

Flying back from Chicago. Tuesday 13 June 1978.

Fred Beckman and I met at a Chicago restaurant after I changed my flight plan in hopes of seeing him and Allen. I was told the latter was in a meeting. I tried to connect with him on the phone but the Cufos secretary wouldn't let me through.

“I don't blame you for not driving all the way to Evanston just to sit on a chair outside his office,” Fred said with a sigh. Still, I am sad not to see Allen, who has just given his last University lecture and retires from Northwestern this month.

“Something curious happened in Las Vegas,” said Fred. A 35-year old nightwatchman, who was out walking around with his wife and dog, had a close encounter. The dog died during the incident. Allen asked for the dog's internal organs to be shipped to Evanston.”

“What did they find out?” I asked.

“They never got anything. When they went to see the veterinarian he told them that two white men in business suits had come and taken the dog away. They came back later, but the nightwatchman pulled out his gun and there was a scuffle.”

Fred thinks the scenario may have been a test of the Center's ability to do genuine research. This seems unlikely. More simply, it appears as just another bungled investigation in a sea of unverified rumors.

Belmont. Wednesday 14 June 1978.

Evidently the CIA has a contact inside Cufos, as it does among most UFO groups: Someone close to Allen in Chicago has leaked a pile of internal documents to Dave M. Another curious episode: as soon as Dave got the Cufos papers his secure phone rang; a Colonel requested to see them. Now Kit himself is wondering who could be watching them, as in a bad drama, or a good comedy. It reinforces my impression that working with these folks is a waste of time. They keep looking for the wrong things.

Belmont. Tuesday 27 June 1978.

Upon my return from an investigation trip to Happy Camp in Northern California Allen told me that a meeting with the Secretary General of the U.N was being setup for us in two weeks. On Thursday, local UFO researchers will pay a visit to San Francisco attorney Melvin Belli to determine if the government can be sued in connection with its mishandling of UFO incidents.

This morning both of our children flew away to France for the summer. Janine and I found ourselves alone again, with delight.

Belmont. Sunday 2 July 1978.

I relished the flamboyant ambiance of Melvin Belli's brick house located between the lofty skyscrapers of the Financial Center and the fleshpots of Barbary Coast. A guard was at the door, revolver in a holster. We met with the King of Torts, Stanton Friedman and I, along with Shlomo Arno, Tom Gates and Paul Cerny.

Stan spoke first, sure of himself, his eyes shining, his beard moving forward provocatively. Tom Gates was more subdued. Paul Cerny, in a brown shirt and dark glasses, looked like a comic actor playing a Nazi. He kept rummaging through his briefcase, looking for newspaper clippings as if he was about to extract sensational items from its depths, never finding them. The crafty lawyer watched our group with amusement.

With his back to his smiling skeleton (Erasmus) and his photographic gallery of *causes célèbres*, Melvin Belli explained that he wasn't concerned by money or glory. I found it hard not to smile. We discussed UFO cases in which the witnesses might have a reason to claim damages against the government, but none of it was within the statute of limitation, so nothing came of the discussion.

Belmont. Saturday 8 July 1978.

Aimé Michel writes that the Poher group has compiled a five-volume report devoted to ten cases, systematically analyzed. In every case, he said, the conclusion pointed to an unknown craft.

When Brendan O'Regan came over to InfoMedia yesterday he brought me the State Department document about the Iranian case and told me that the Navy was concerned about the loss of several helicopters that had overflown Soviet trawlers. The rotors became caught in a sort of luminous halo and the copters fell into the sea.

He wonders if this was the result of some novel technology. The Navy has allegedly classified the accidents as being UFO-related to create a diversion about their true nature.

Rye Town, New York. Sunday 9 July 1978.

Wes Thomas was waiting for me at Kennedy. He spoke about Valerie. He's known her for several years, having met her when she was the public relations person for an energy information group. Her family came from the Chicago area, and she studied journalism at Northwestern. Wes introduced her to Puharich two years ago. She spent several months with him, exploring every site where ELF research was going on. This particular topic of extremely low frequency seems to fascinate her.

"I think Puharich convinced her that she was a contactee," said Wes. "I'd never heard her mention it before she met him."

Washington. Wednesday 12 July 1978.

Kit was waiting for me at Dulles, driving a Volvo full of kids, so we were not able to talk seriously until after dinner. Once we were alone I brought up my concerns: "It's obvious there's a secret project somewhere," I insisted. "Take a case like Tehran… someone must be working on it, even if you guys don't. Also, I've been thinking back about our discussion with Jim Irish. He evaded all our questions about the death of his colleagues near Barstow, didn't he?"

"You may be right," Kit finally said, "about a secret project."

"What about *Security Around the Globe*? Where does Valerie come into all this?"

"SAG is owned by a lady and her two sons. They've had a private detective agency in Nevada for 15 years. She has lots of contacts."

Belmont. Sunday 6 August 1978.

Richard Sigismond and Barbara have come over to San Francisco, the latter bringing her data, her humor, her enthusiasm. Janine and I met with them last Saturday. We ended up at the Cliff House, where the waves broke over the rocks, a magical time, music and laughter.

On Friday I set up a computer conference with Valerie Ransone in Houston, Wes Thomas on Long Island and Brendan O'Regan in San Francisco. It took a curious turn when Valerie announced that her purpose was to select 13 individuals who would be invited to her "Signs of the Spirit" conference in Washington next December. She said: "My goal is to establish a foundation for those who will meet space people in December." I reminded her that two years ago Puharich had already predicted massive landing "within 18 months." Later on he revealed that "The Direction" had decided to land invisibly! Always the same absurd stories.

Belmont. Sunday 13 August 1978.

I visited Douglass Price-Williams this week to consult him about the anthropological aspects of the complex Arkansas mutilation cases and on a Belgian abduction I'm studying. Next I paid a visit to Israel Regardie, again in search of clues about ritual mutilations. If anyone knows about cult practices, he'd have the information.

"Do you know that a major schism has taken place in LaVey's group?" asked Crowley's former secretary. "Michael Aquino, who was his lieutenant and a member of his Council of Nine, has founded his own church, the Temple of Set." Regardie gave me a biography of Aquino and showed me his commentary on Crowley's *Book of the Law*: "One more commentary!" he said sadly, putting it back on his well-stocked occult shelves.

"I don't like LaVey but I don't think his group has anything to do with the mutilations you're describing," he said after examining the symbols, the color photographs and the detailed accounts of the scenes I had brought back from my latest field trip.

The next morning I went back to see Jim Irish. This time he gave me the location of his sightings and told me details of his former operations that he hadn't revealed to Kit. We discussed my plans for continuing investigations in the Redding area. A colleague of his had three old surveillance cameras, which I bought on the spot.

Jay Levey, Bob Emenegger and Alan Sandler have asked me to help them in the updating of "UFOs: Past, Present and Future," to be re-issued under a new title: *UFOs: It has begun*. They wanted me to narrate the new footage, and were looking for unpublished data. I recommended adding a section about cattle mutilations.

I arrived at LAX as my children's plane touched the runway. At the airport restaurant they recalled their latest adventures. They made me wish I were back in France for a while. But research is dead in France. This is where everything is happening, here in California.

Flying to Oklahoma. Saturday 9 September 1978.

Someone has firebombed the house of Puharich in Ossining, in the Hudson Valley, North of New York City. Andrija was in Mexico, but the house was full of kids, psychic subjects he had collected.

I have been reading Albert Speer's *Journal*, written in Spandau. I find it stunning, even if I detest the régime this man served.

InfoMedia gives me a lot of trouble. Software development is going very well, but we look in vain for a small amount of startup capital, to buy the computer we need.

Allen Hynek won't go back to Northwestern this year. He's leaving for Canada, on a spiritual retreat for two weeks. Allen has the limpid mysticism of true Bohemians; contact with nature and the sky come easily to him. He loves travelling. As my plane hovers above Bryce Canyon and the Painted Desert I feel close to him in spirit. Now I am on the way to Arkansas again, to study several mutilation sites with Barbara and the Sheriff of Benton County. There was no trace of drug in the tissue samples I'd brought back last time. On Monday I will also visit Phillips Petroleum in Bartlesville: They've signed a contract with us for computer conferencing software.

Flying home to San Francisco. Wednesday 13 September 1978.

The sheriff of Bentonville received us in his office cluttered with seized cannabis bundles and piles of cattle autopsy reports. He told us that recent mutilations had taken place in Picher, Oklahoma. He suspected ordinary criminals because the victims were primarily dogs and cats, so we drove off and there, a few miles North of Miami, Oklahoma, we entered another world.

The geological survey map simply shows an area of mine tailings. It doesn't prepare the visitor who suddenly finds himself among desolate mounds of gravel drowning the trees, covering up the prairie: One hundred miles square of gravel dunes. I stopped the car near stone cliffs with a feeling of sacred horror; the humid weather hit us as soon as we opened the doors, with holes like bomb craters on both sides of the road. Miners must have extracted millions of cubic feet of dirt and stone. I could imagine the galleries, the caverns, the crypts left behind: Picher, as in "Eagle-Picher" batteries. We were standing on top of the largest lead mine in the world.

A road is still visible in the gravel. It goes around old structures, cubical concrete masses, circular monuments of huge pillars, a satanic Stonehenge near a lake where all vegetation is dead, where birds don't sing, where only two big toads jumped into the turgid water as we approached. A few miles to the North we found Red Clay Hill. One side of its gigantic crater had collapsed. This is where sorcerers gather at night, according to the local kids we interviewed. I climbed up to the top. All I could see were gravel mounds, concrete pyramids, dark holes in the ground, and dead ponds.

We stopped in Picher. In an old saloon where a few men played pool, a jolly monster of a woman, some 400 pounds of flesh and fat, sat uncomfortably on a bar stool. The whole town has heard of the nocturnal rites. The people, the streets, the dead faces, the decrepit cabins that line the dirt roads express the misery of the land, wealth ripped out of its entrails. This dirty despair, these blind windows, radiated a Baudelairean beauty.

Belmont. Sunday 1 October 1978.

InfoMedia has made progress: Ray Williams has generously given his personal guarantee for the purchase of our computer, a DEC 20.

Yesterday morning I was alone in the forest at Spring Hill, sitting on a carpet of dead leaves, thinking of the flow of time, the frail substrate of human agitation. My plans haven't changed: I want to come here often, to run my own experiments, get closer to a view of nature which I appreciate even more since my Picher expedition. I went swimming, walked to the cabins.

When I came home I slept deeply, soundly. Then my daughter made a bad fall and broke her elbow, poor kid.

Flying to Denver. Sunday 8 October 1978.

My mother came back to Paris a week ago from Leningrad with a bad case of the flu, but when I spoke to her over the phone she had recovered somewhat. She spoke of her anxiety at seeing another winter coming over Paris. She told me about her trip in her usual limpid direct way of apprehending the world.

Allen called this morning, back in Evanston after spending two weeks at his cabin in Canada, by the fireplace, listening to the steady rain. In one sentence he assured me that he would now spend more time doing research at home, but in the next sentence he spoke of flying to New York for ABC - a TV documentary I'd just turned down. He also wanted us to spend more time together.

He has guessed, as Fred did, that I have discovered something important, and that I haven't told anyone what it was. What I have discovered can be stated simply: There is a higher level; it is accessible to human consciousness.

Spearfish, South Dakota. Monday 9 October 1978.

From my window at the Holiday Inn in the warm sun I can't see a single house: only the woods, a few haystacks, dark mounds that give their name to the Black Hills. A flag waves over a parking lot where Chevy trucks shine like red and blue toys. This is the region where Alfred Hitchcock filmed the end of *North by Northwest.*

I had another curious dream last night. I was at the hospital. Sick people were dying near me. I was ill, but I was allowed to go home from time to time. I had a stately wooden house on a street corner, partially hidden by a big tree. One of the sick people died. He was French. His first name was Alain, and I thought he was a friend of Gerald, who indeed has introduced me to a French photographer named Alain Brie. This left me confused and sad. I was seized with a huge wave of sorrow that woke me up in tears.

In the morning I heard on the television news that Jacques Brel was dead. So that was the point of my dream, and my confusion about the sad death of a Frenchman named *Brie*.

Later the same day, at Devil's Tower.

A narrow path curves around the base of the mountain. I left it behind and climbed up beyond the last trees, where the columns of volcanic rock rise vertically. It's an admirable autumn day in Wyoming. The road swerves among golden woods. I see the dark hilltops beyond. A tepid wind blows. I feel silly, wearing a jacket.

Janine called me last night, relating a call from the sheriff of Bentonville. He had just attended the autopsy of the eleventh victim there, a cow found dead yesterday morning. Neither the eyes nor the tongue had been touched, he told her. Instead the mutilators had taken the rectum, the ovaries, the uterus and part of the small intestine. The cuts were not smooth but serrated and *cauterized.* Rats and vultures don't do that.

The veterinarian has followed all the instructions I'd left. He only found a few drops of blood inside the carcass. The heart was empty. As in other incidents we've recorded in the area, this took place close to a house. Predators didn't even have time to get to the carcass.

Belmont. Saturday 14 October 1978.

Yesterday Tom Belden invited me to make a presentation on the use of networks in crisis management at the CIA Operations Center. Afterwards I was talking to Kit in his office when the phone rang. The caller was his assistant Dave, with an interesting story to tell:

"I'm reaching the conclusion that Vallee is right. Someone's manipulating us," he said.

Since Dave didn't know I was in the building Kit winked at me and asked: "What makes you think you're manipulated?"

"Well, this morning I went to see somebody at the Executive Office Building, and I lost my way," Dave said, laughing self-consciously. "I got so lost, I didn't even know which floor I was on. Suddenly a door opened up and two men came out, talking. The first one said, 'I've got a problem. I've just been asked to set up a meeting between Carter and the Prime Minister of Grenada, and I don't know how to do it.' The other guy asked, 'what'll they talk about?' The first one answered, 'unidentified flying objects.' His companion went on, 'Then you ought to go through the National Security Council.' After which they went on their way down the hall. So that's when I thought of Vallee, who's always talking about coincidences," Dave concluded.

"What would you say if I told you he's in front of me now, in my office?" Kit said, laughing. Dave was left speechless.

The Valerie Ransone saga continued. The woman who owns *Security around the Globe* became intrigued and upset when she saw the folders Valerie brought to her for safekeeping, like "Soviet Research" and "Military Intelligence." So she called the Houston office of the FBI, who went through the papers. They initiated an investigation that reached into every corner of Washington. Among the papers in question was a letter claiming that Earth was now under control of the Aliens.

During my lengthy discussion with Kit I asked him where the investigation of Wilbur Franklin's death had led him. "It's over," he told me. "The physicians said he'd suffered an unexplained break of his spinal column. The technical term is 'clinical brain stem infraction,' but the official diagnosis is listed as pneumonia. I don't know why they didn't see the pneumonia on the X-rays; it was only discovered at the autopsy."

"What was going on in his life?" I asked, too fascinated by the subject to drop it.

"He was at a critical time in his career," Kit said. "He'd decided to start conducting his research openly. He was working on a new book. He was about to go to the USSR to discuss parapsychology with people there. He felt he was under the control of an unspecified force." He went on: "James Randi, a staunch skeptic, has written somewhere that he thought Franklin had committed suicide because he couldn't stand the shame of his incursions into false science!"

On Wednesday evening I had a cup of coffee with Valerie at the Capital Hilton. She was with Jill Duvall, a level-headed woman. They've opened an office in Washington, and their "Information Network" is now registered as a California company, thanks to money invested by a friend of hers in California. Valerie told me the Aliens didn't want me to call my next book *Messengers of Deception.* I answered, "Let's see how they will stop me."

Belmont. Sunday 15 October 1978.

A great deal of activity, if not research, is indeed going on about UFOs among government organizations. Kit has a friend in Houston who is close to Poher, and I've heard that Saunders was looking for correlations among the UFO data by plotting the sighting on a sidereal time scale. Saunders works at Mathematica, a major computer contractor for the CIA. McDonnell-Douglas is continuing their quiet but well-funded study with John Schuessler, also monitored by the Agency. They seem to be looking for exotic alloys.

Who is kidding? Why is the scientific community kept in the dark about these projects? Why all the secrecy? Where do the research results go? And what about the secret work in France?

Belmont. Saturday 28 October 1978.

My French publisher requests changes in *Messengers* because Amorc refuses permission to quote "*Secret Houses of the Rose+Croix*" and the alleged experiences of their Grand-Master.

On Thursday, I went to San Francisco with my children to attend a concert of Willard van de Bogart's "Ether Ship" during which he improvised what he called a psychotronic symphony. The concert, recorded for Valerie Ransone's project, took place in a studio South of Mission, filled with electronic equipment. Willard sat at the center of his synthetizer under a neon-lit dome. The structure was shaped like a horseshoe. Willard said he visualized higher entities while he played.

I called Leo Sprinkle today to get information about abductee Sandy Larson, and I also spoke to Allen, who told me that he was in the midst of some politics: "The Nicap Board has offered me to become their President," he said. "They're launching a publicity campaign under the leadership of General Richardson. They've hired a Madison Avenue firm. What do you think I should do?"

My advice was to keep his independence, not to link his destiny with that of a discredited organization like Nicap, exploiting his name. We will have a chance to discuss the situation in more depth at the end of the month, when we are scheduled to meet in Mexico City at the invitation of a distinguished group of researchers there.

Now my mother sends me a clipping from *Le Figaro* for 14 October, which explains why Poher felt like going around the world on a boat. Unfairly, it calls him "The Frenchman who knows the most about little green men," adding, "his departure is a statement of failure." Citing a text where Poher wrote that the phenomena were "rare," the journalist unleashes a mean attack:

> When one thinks about the numerous sighting reports the Gendarmes have gathered on this delicate topic for the past ten years, one cannot help thinking that, here too, a breath analyzer should have been used for testing...

Belmont. Sunday 5 November 1978.

On Halloween night I went out for the annual revelry that has become San Francisco's version of Carnival: 150,000 people dancing and singing along Polk Street. There were red devils, young couples with babies, women bare-breasted under leather jackets; dozens of people wore masks of Richard Nixon. Ginger came in a short bright red dress, as a strumpet of the Roaring Twenties. On Thursday I saw Don Hanlon who now lives in Fairfax with a pleasant young woman. He claims he's finally writing his book. This gives me hope that he's getting wiser but his universe still boils down to Crowley's peculiar twist on the Kabala. Don worships the neo-Egyptian pictures inspired by this branch of occultism, which doesn't move me any more than plaster virgins or wooden crucifixes. His scholarship still shines, however. I was captivated by an episode he read to me, when Crowley felt his brain was taken apart by beings who examined each hemisphere in turn, as he was lying inside a large amphitheater. Don found this in *The Vision and the Voice* (**33**). Would Crowley be classified today as an abductee?

Boston. Tuesday 14 November 1978.

A pale sun ray penetrates the hotel room. Last night I gave an informal lecture at the home of some friends of Ira, who spends a few months as a Visiting Fellow at the Harvard Institute of International Politics. The house belonged to Gunther Weil and the audience included Izhtak Bentov who specializes in psychic medicine, and his Russian-born wife who seems to be one of Ira's sources about Soviet research.

Ira took me aside: the CIA had sent a man to see him, a former scientific director at IBM who asked what he knew about the soviet interest in Tesla's work. This man now serves as coordinator of advanced projects at the Pentagon. I tried without success to get Ira to tell me what he knew about the firebombing of Puharich's house.

Bentov said that he had given up studying UFOs and Uri Geller when he had understood how the whole phenomenon worked. "There's a boundary layer between the physical and the higher plane," he said. "It's child play for the entities to manifest any object they want through this layer. We look upon it as a miracle, but the ufonauts are low-level entities that play with their victims. They amuse themselves by possessing mediums like Geller."

"Have you ever encountered them yourselves?" I asked.

"Yes," he answered matter-of-factly, "but I chased them away through meditation."

Flying back to San Francisco. Wednesday 15 November 1978.

Bentov's theory is too simplistic. Speaking of a "boundary layer with the higher plane" doesn't tell us anything specific.

The dollar is in a deep crisis. America is going through a phase of false agony on the theme, "We have become a second rate country!" All one has to do to recognize the fallacy of this statement is to drive through Silicon Valley as I do every day, and to witness the unprecedented upheaval being hatched among computer companies and electronic firms. It is a revolution of information technology and knowledge power, plunging the rest of the world into social obsolescence. The cultural effect of network interaction will be huge. America is the only nation immunized against the technical innovations it creates, prepared by history to adapt to discontinuities.

In two weeks I will be back at the U.N. for the long-awaited meeting that hopes to propel UFO research to great international visibility. The statement I have prepared stresses the need for rational approach and warns against the pitfalls of contactee seduction. I keep in mind what Margaret Mead told me in Chicago:

"Why should we diminish the worth of mankind by seeking extraterrestrial precedents to every great achievement of our past?" Yet people want to hear us say that superior forces built the Pyramids. The only superior force I see in these ancient works of art and science is that of the human soul, imagination and vision, that "Daimon" Plato taught us to invoke.

As I get ready to fly to Mexico I review the parapsychology papers I have accumulated over the last few years. I am struck by the lack of vision in the field. In their efforts to appear objective and impress their sponsors, parapsychologists stifle the spark at the heart of the phenomena they claim to study. Another factor freezing open debate is the meddling of the Intelligence services into a domain of research that should be allowed, above all others, to blossom freely.

Mexico City. Saturday 18 November 1978.

The El Camino Real hotel is a fine ensemble of slanted roofs, monumental staircases, mirrors, walls of vivid colors, multiple levels. In spite of its 700 rooms it gives an intimate feeling enhanced by warm wood paneling.

I only saw Allen briefly at a reception at the home of Carlos de la Huerta. He soon ran off with the Norries and their actress daughter Sylvia while I spoke with a group of Mexican researchers and journalist Juan-Jose Benitez, who'd just received permission to publish Spanish military files.

Benitez told me that the plane that flew ahead of the royal aircraft when the queen of Spain recently went over to China had been followed by an unknown object for ten minutes. The Chinese papers mentioned the incident.

He also told me of recent mutilation cases near Malaga, where a robot-like thing was reported. The Spanish military send all their UFO reports to U.S. Air Force Intelligence, which denies all interest. An official booklet explains how to process the reports, including instructions to convince witnesses they haven't seen anything unusual.

Mexico City. Tuesday 21 Novembre 1978.

Allen and I had a long talk as we sat next to the pool this afternoon, about our common interest in Rosicrucian philosophy. Allen told me he continued to have the highest regard for the theories of Rudolph Steiner, which I find impenetrable. We agreed that contemporary groups like Amorc had become too involved in politics and had lost their founders' vision. He told me that Mimi, like me, recommended against involvement with Nicap. We prepared our strategy for the U.N. presentation in New York next week.

Janine called me from San Francisco with horrible news: 400 members of Jim Jones's People's Temple had just committed mass suicide in Guyana after gunning down a Congressman who was threatening to investigate their affairs. (**34**)

Pedro Ferriz has just sent us a discreet message, to tell us that a meeting was being arranged for Allen and me at the Presidential Palace. Officially, our appointment is with Señora Margarita Lopez Portillo, but there will be an opportunity to meet the President.

Flying back to California. Wednesday 22 November 1978.

Last night a power failure plunged our hotel into darkness: I understood that the candles in evidence in every room served more than a romantic purpose. By their flickering light I pulled a clean shirt from my suitcase to go to the presidential palace. Allen was tired and a bit inebriated after long celebrations and a press conference, so my first task was to locate some strong coffee for us.

We made it to Los Pinos, where a member of the Protocol group guided us to the suite occupied by the President's mother. We passed an antechamber filled with plants and fine portraits, reaching a small sitting room where Margarita, dressed in white, received us. She was vivacious, intelligent, and anxious to talk. We were taken to another room where about 50 cube-shaped seats were assembled. We were clearly expected to give a talk, but Allen was in no shape to lecture, so I launched into an improvised presentation while he drank more black coffee and gathered his thoughts.

General conversation followed. All the guests came forward and introduced themselves in French, English or Spanish. Dona Margarita, who had briefly left the room, returned down the stairs in the company of a heavy-set man with gray hair, wearing a brown suit. Pedro Ferriz took a few steps forward, greeted the President with some pleasantries, and introduced us with Latin hyperbole. We had a brief conversation with Lopez Portillo, who was on his way to a reception for the King and the Queen of Spain: After several centuries the Spanish crown has decided to repair a major historical oversight and to visit Mexico, a land so closely tied to its own.

After the President left I resumed my talk, stressing that the phenomenon had a psychic level as well as a physical and a social level. I didn't only mean telepathy or extrasensory perception, but all the phenomena encompassed by the relationship between consciousness and the physical world. My interpreter said: "*no hablo de la telepatia...*" I was able to catch the mistake, correcting him in Spanish: "No hablo *solamente* de la telepatia." This earned me the sympathy of the audience, and after that everything was easy.

By then Allen had recovered his usual charisma. He gave a short concluding speech, urging Mexico to support our forthcoming efforts at the United Nations. Our hosts took us to the stadium where the Spanish sovereigns and the Presidential entourage attended an emotional show. It included a remarkable performance by eight Lipizzan horses from Andalucia, after which Don Juan Carlos presented a ninth horse to the President.

I return home impressed by the warmth and nobility of our Mexican hosts and the savvy of Pedro Ferriz. While he always introduced us with flourishes, he never failed to mention Janine's contribution and our work in common whenever the subject of my research came up, a nice and too rare public homage to her own quiet efforts.

Belmont. Thursday 23 November 1978.

American reality has reasserted itself, with the heavy black headlines clamoring for an explanation of the People's Temple disaster in the heat of a Guyanese jungle, the body of our Congressman lying on a runway. Members of the sect who were left behind are afraid Jim Jones' killers will hunt them down.

Back in Mexico I had an interesting discussion with a philosopher who spoke about labyrinths. In the simplest form a central circle represents the mother, physical birth, he said. The second, wider circle is that of the family. One must leave it to find his true nature. The third wall is that of society, he argued. “It's indispensable to leave most of human society behind, too, for spiritual development to take place,” he told me. “That's why I predict that eventually you'll stop lecturing and withdraw into silence.”

Curiously, I had taken only one book on the trip, Colin Wilson's *The God of the Labyrinth*, an important book in which the key to the Control System is found in the sexual impulse.

My philosopher friend also said that the old Alchemists used to draw mazes with two solutions, a short one and a long one. The long way out is the Path of the Rich, the short one the Path of the Poor; those who own little have few material things to give up on the way to spiritual discovery.

Flying to New York. Sunday 26 November 1978.

The landscape over which we fly is a jumble of snowy peaks. Tonight I will see Allen again, along with Lee Spiegel and lieutenant-colonel Larry Coyne, the pilot of a big Army helicopter that was pulled up by a UFO over Mansfield, Ohio while he was desperately trying to make an emergency landing.

I spoke to Aimé Michel yesterday. He told me that the CNES had appointed an engineer named Alain Esterle to complete Poher's final report, which is said to conclude that unknown machines are responsible for the unexplained sightings. It is kept confidential by the French authorities, clearly embarrassed by the implications. They have even refused to release a copy to the British government.

Yesterday Olivier and I went on an excursion around the Bay aboard Ray Williams' sailboat with Rich Miller. We had a moment of excitement when we picked up a German windsurfer who had fallen into the current and was being dragged off to possible death beyond the Golden Gate Bridge.

When I read French newspapers, I recognize all the familiar names: Chirac and Giscard, Debré and Séguy. Nothing new, only institutions slowly sinking into obsolescence. Jean Sendy is dead, as well as Margaret Mead, and now I learn that Jacques Bergier passed away a few days ago. I am fortunate to have known this exceptional man who took to his grave a mountain of irreplaceable facts and many secrets from the time of the *Résistance*. **(35)**

Now Allen tells me about his latest discussions with the Nicap Board. Senator Barry Goldwater and General Williamson told him they were alarmed at Nicap's loss of prestige and imminent bankruptcy. They've asked John Acuff to leave. They hope Allen will take over to insure the continuity of members' subscriptions. I told him again that, in spite of all the good work Nicap had done in the distant past, he would be compromising his image if he joined them now. Nicap is narrowly committed as an advocacy group for the extraterrestrial cause but there's no science behind that belief.

I had a long private talk with Larry Coyne tonight, probing into neglected parts of the story. After his sighting he remained 72 hours unable to sleep. A week later he had the experience of floating out of his body. And he began some personal psychic experiments. So now we have a series of cases in which UFO observations have combined with paranormal effects that are never mentioned in the literature: Cruttwell, Father Gill, Schirmer, and now Coyne.

New York Hilton. Monday 27 November 1978.

It's snowing over Manhattan; the weather turns to freezing rain. This is the big day at the United Nations for Sir Eric Gairy. So far his initiative has only been supported by two member nations: India and the Seychelles islands.

Flying back to San Francisco. Tuesday 28 November 1978.

Sir Eric Gairy made the introductory speech, thankfully short. Hynek spoke at 11 A.M. in the stately room of the political committee filled to capacity, including the press section and the public gallery. I followed Allen. Colonel Coyne captured everyone's attention through the obvious sincerity of his testimony: he had seen an impossible object on a collision course with his helicopter. When a Committee member asked him what he'd thought he answered, "Sir, I closed my eyes and prepared to die." That wasn't the answer of a boasting hero but the humble answer of a professional soldier who has often thought about death. He positioned his machine for a crash landing, descending 2,000 feet per minute. Instead he found himself going up, apparently caught in the object's field.

After his statement the UN staff showed a short video by Lee Spiegel. When the lights were slowly turned down the room took the appearance of the inside of a spaceship, with the square windows of the interpreters high around the ceiling looking like portholes bathed in soft light. Spiegel's documentary was a disappointment, a slow enumeration of dubious UFO pictures.

If the video hadn't ruined the meeting, the press conference that followed wrecked it completely. Eric Gairy launched into a garbled apology full of esoteric mumbo-jumbo, adding that he had once seen a flying saucer as he came out of a night-club! He hadn't introduced us, so I whispered hopefully to Allen: "You don't suppose we could go away discreetly?" Allen shook his head sadly.

Later Allen and I had lunch at the UN cafeteria, where we spoke briefly to the Mexican delegate, after which we heard Stanton Friedman giving a dissertation about the size and the scope of the Universe, barely relevant to the topic of the day. Grenada officials have no doubt that their request for a serious study will be carried by consensus, but major nations scoff at the idea. When Liberia asked that our statements be printed in the Proceedings the British delegate rose in protest, arguing the expense would be too great!

Today the *New York Post* printed one of its characteristically snappy headlines, "U.S. Nix to UN on UFOs." The article said that the United Nations had experienced a close encounter with a band of resolute UFO hunters, led by Sir Eric Garry (sic). Some of the experts had expressed hope that the U.S would support the project, but American officials had told Eric Gairy they would oppose any

Fig. 19 Preliminary conference with UN Secretary General Kurt Waldheim, Nov.1978, with Claude Poher and Allen Hynek

Fig. 20. With Allen Hynek in New York on the way to the UN, 1978.

expense: "We have enough problems with the UN budget... All we need is a challenge in the Senate to denounce the use of American funds for a study of flying saucers..."

Belmont. Saturday 9 December 1978.

One of my New York editors took me to a bookstore where we found *Definitely Maybe*, a Soviet science-fiction novel by the Strugatsky brothers (**36**), the story of a group of Russian scientists trying to come to grips with paranormal happenings. They struggle with various hypotheses: Are the events controlled by the KGB? By some hidden esoteric group? These theories lead to a fact I illustrated in *Invisible College*, a control system that acts upon human consciousness, preventing it from going beyond certains limits.

On Tuesday Olivier and I went over to SRI to meet with Hal Puthoff, Ed May and Charlie Tart. They gave us advice to improve the circuit he'd designed for the *Sleeping Beauty* camera we plan to install above French Gulch to try to catch a picture of the elusive object described by the Chapins, who have now told me their whole story. We ended up discussing the epistemology of psychical research: How can one differentiate between clairvoyance and precognition? It always seems to me that the missing piece in all such debates is an adequate theory of time. Time simply cannot be represented by the "t" variable physicists use with such abandon in equations that claim to describe the universe.

Belmont. Monday 11 December 1978.

Now I'm in bed, brought down by a bout of flu. The Bay is hidden by lingering haze. Crowds are shopping in anticipation of Christmas but the atmosphere remains permeated with violence. San Francisco has experienced a riot at Halloween, the Guyana suicide, the assassination of Mayor Moscone and supervisor Harvey Milk. It is a bruised city huddling in fear behind the folds of its legendary fog.

I make vague plans for a book about computer networks. Janine is in my heart. Who will tell us the states of consciousness where love can take us, and the revelations they contain? A friend made a remark the other day, that she has never really seen Janine and me as being "married." All her married friends have gone through crises in the last few years, with separation and divorce. "The two of you have found a secret," she said, "a formula for unity that has nothing to do with social conventions. You don't wear a ring, but those who know you can feel a profound mystery between you, a deeper union."

Belmont. Tuesday 12 December 1978.

Working from home, keeping warm, I've been using the terminal and the phone to do my work. In Houston John Schuessler heads up McDonnell's operations at the Johnson spacecraft center, while another researcher, Dr. Richard Niemtzow, is doing cancer research in Galveston, one of the leading centers in the U.S. Both believe there are Alien bodies around, based on the elusive autopsy reports circulated by Len Stringfield. Until such reports can be authenticated I continue to believe they are in the same vein as the fake Philadelphia experiment, or the Ummo document that claim the Aliens come from Wolf 424, or countless other products of human fantasy, folly and greed.

Belmont. Sunday 24 December 1978.

I spent yesterday doing carpentry, building a loft in Olivier's room. Janine and I spent Friday evening touring the city with Ginger, from Ghiradelli Square where people sang Christmas carols to the Wine Cellar for good guitar playing and folksy ballads. We celebrated Janine's well-deserved promotion at Santa Clara County, where she is now in charge of a technical group running one of the most advanced government automation systems in the country.

Yesterday, while sorting through old papers, I came across a stack of copybooks from my days in school and a note penned by my father in March 1948, thirty years ago, on stationery of the *Tribunal de la Seine*. It asked my teacher for clemency in a matter of discipline. This brought back memories of Christmas with my parents, quiet little feasts around a few pine branches I would go out and cut in the nearby public park, because we didn't have money to buy a tree. We made gold stars and glittery angels out of the thin paper, carefully saved up, that wrapped chocolate bars. The nights were cold and damp, smearing street lights into wonderful glowing halos, turning the breath into a faint cloud.

Flying to Cincinnati. Wednesday 3 January 1979.

The last year of the decade begins with yet another trip, presentations at Procter & Gamble followed by a networking conference at the Office of Technology Assessement (OTA), an agency of Congress that advises legislators on long-term issues. Yesterday morning two new employees started at InfoMedia, working with Rich Miller, who will install our computer. The company is coming alive.

I spent a quiet New Year's Eve with Janine and the children. I read them the story of the *Curé de Cucugnan* and Monsieur Seguin's goat. In the current turmoil there is no greater cure for anguish than to watch my children, playing peacefully. I can only hope that those people I have touched will have felt some inspiration in proportion to the warmth they've given me. I'd like to do more: perhaps InfoMedia will put me in a position to help others, to change the world a bit, but I don't dare dream about success at a time when the company is only a fragile startup with an unproven market.

Belmont. Friday 5 January 1979.

While reading a book about the People's Temple entitled *Suicide Cult* (**37**) I was shocked to find a picture of Jim Jones engaged in friendly conversation with Sir Eric Gairy! I've confronted Kit with the fact that, according to the top-level Spanish officials I met in Mexico, the Spanish Air Force reported all their UFO data to "the Americans" -- yet another indication that a secret channel does exist. Kit denied knowledge of the sightings I recounted for him. He recently had the same conversation with John Schuessler, who thinks the secret project isn't at CIA but at NRO, whose budget is in the billions of dollars and whose initials themselves are classified. That wouldn't give scientists like us any chance to gain access to the data.

Belmont. Sunday 7 January 1979.

Progress: our computer has arrived in several large crates. It will be installed as soon as workers put the finishing touch to our machine room. My publisher tells me that *Anatomy* and *Challenge* have now gone through four editions for a total of some 400,000 copies.

Aimé Michel reports that the Russians are carefully running a "vacuum cleaner" over every piece of UFO information they can find in France. This action began after the Tehran case. The Soviet Air Force compiled a detailed analysis, after which they gathered a scientific colloquium on UFOs in Novosibirsk. They've even gone to the trouble of writing to regional journalist Charles Garreau to request a copy of an article he published in an obscure local newspaper, *La Bourgogne Républicaine*, back in 1952! The French are amazed at such thoroughness on the part of the Soviets, when their own scientists in Paris are telling them UFOs don't even exist.

Belmont. Sunday 28 January 1979.

Messsengers of Deception emerges slowly in the media (**38**), stressing the hypothesis that some UFO cases are the result of psychological manipulation by the military. On Monday I saw Allen again. He was on his way to Japan, filled with boundless energy. He is excited at the very fact of being alive. What distinguishes Allen Hynek and Aimé Michel from other researchers in this field is that there isn't a grain of meanness in them. They do have an ego, and pride, and occasionally a sarcastic thought, but they bear no ill will towards anyone, and would never act in bad faith for any price.

After 10 years Janine and I are ready to move away from Belmont. It's time to fold the tapestry of memory, to pack up books and precious images of a scintillating decade; like an alchemist who breaks his athanor to extract the refined matter after a long operation.

Belmont. Sunday 4 February 1979.

A peculiar feeling hangs over us, the forerunner of change. One looks at a familiar piece of furniture and the question arises: should it be sold? Should it remain part of our household, a treasured companion? The bookcase we bought in New Jersey 10 years ago now seems pointless, with its heavy glass doors.

Don Hanlon has written about some O.T.O secrets: Ron Hubbard did perform magical experiments with Parsons in his effort to evoke Enochian beings with a curious resemblance to Adamski's Venusians. Don has repeatedly claimed that the key references about these experiments are a series of letters from Jack Parsons to Crowley which are kept in the archives of Sir Gerald Yorke. Parsons, a rocket expert, co-founder of JPL, accused Hubbard of being a government agent who infiltrated the O.T.O to destroy the magical circle. Parsons, after whom one of the moon's craters is named (**39**), wrote a novel based on his encounter with the Venusian in the Mojave Desert, long before UFO contact had become fashionable.

Don keeps stressing that the Contact myth has occult roots that go back to pre-war days. Alice Bailey herself is said to have met with "angelic" Venusians on Hollywood hillsides. He's even found a series of texts by Aleister Crowley that form a striking parallel to Raymond Bernard's suspicious contacts with "Maha" and other so-called Unknown Superiors of Amorc.

> I am sending you an account by Crowley describing a French masonic-rosicrucian group. They may have been disciples of Pascal Beverly Randolph, whose *Hermetic Fraternity of Light* served as the prototype for the O.T.O in Austria in 1902. Crowley was initiated into this group between 1909 and 1912. You should remember that in turn, Crowley gave H. Spencer Lewis a charter to open an O.T.O type lodge in America, demanding a staggering amount of money. Amorc's literature is filled with material taken word for word from Crowley's writings, with no credit given.

Belmont. Friday 9 February 1979.

Arthur Cunningham, Dean of the Business School at UCSF, has joined the InfoMedia board with Ray Williams, our venture capital backer and "angel." My concern now is to find a businessman who could take over from me as president. Running the company takes almost all my waking time. As for ufology, it is becoming ludicrous. A man named Colman Von Keviczky, furious at "Professors J. A. Hynek and J. Vallee" (my being called 'Professor' is itself amusing) accuses us of stressing psychic aspects for the express purpose of derailing serious study of the subject: he says the Aliens are ruthlessly invading us. Another episode of high comedy took place when that august institution, the House of Lords, took up extraterrestrial intervention in Earth affairs.

Brendan O'Regan has suggested I should lead a group of legal and scientific experts to wrench the truth about UFOs away from the deep files of the government. I told him I wasn't the right man for the job. I am not even convinced the government knows much.

I have drawn two conclusions from my contacts: First, they are confused about the nature of the phenomenon, they only see the surface. Second, the best data gets lost in a black hole within the military. No group of "experts" will penetrate it. The only sensible avenue for me is not a crusade, but quiet independent research.

Belmont. Saturday 17 February 1979.

On Wednesday I flew down to Los Angeles through a storm punctured by spots of sunlight on my way to visit Tim Leary, the plane's wings burdened with luminous drops. A double rainbow followed us, bracketing a splendid view of San Francisco, as if I needed a reminder of my reasons for choosing to live here.

I showed Timothy how to use Planet. The group included George Koopman, producer Bob Weiss and Jay Levey who have founded *Future Presentations*, a lecture bureau oriented towards new technology. The notion of contact is becoming fashionable. I'm afraid that Allen and I are losing the fight for a rational UFO study.

Belmont. Saturday 24 February 1979.

We are emerging from the Belmont years. Janine is selling the dining room furniture. I have moved my technical books to the office, leaving Olivier in front of his electronic bench, building a sound generator. When we came home we were saddened to find that someone had gone through the yard and stolen a fine wooden birdhouse my son had built, his gift to me last Christmas. It's only petty theft from passing teenagers, but I felt it as a signal to us. Indeed it's time to go away.

Belmont. Saturday 3 March 1979.

Most of the day was spent with my son. I treasure those moments and wonder how he will remember this childhood he is now leaving behind, as we leave behind the Belmont years. We drove up to his school to pick up the box for the robot camera, which he'd left to dry up under a press.

On Thursday Hal Puthoff told me his research was picking up speed and support. He now gets money from "several agencies in Washington" and he's made successful presentations before the House Intelligence Committee chaired by Charlie Rose. He's scheduled to speak to the National Security Council itself. In one of their operational sessions the SRI team used remote viewing to obtain information that was only verified five years later at high cost, by conventional Intelligence techniques, so the SRI technology is now acknowledged by "the boys who run everything."

The rest of the world won't know about this for many years, although scientific opinion may be slowly swayed by such indirect evidence as may leak out. As for the public, it will continue to believe all the "New Age" garbage served up on television.

Flying to Denver. Monday 5 March 1979.

Our daughter has returned from the Sierra. She is almost as tall as Janine now, with a mischievious sense of humor in her words, her gestures, her inventions. I spent the day planning business details. Now I watch the red sky reflected in the gray mud of the Sacramento River delta. Tonight I'll sleep in Denver, tomorrow in Tulsa, Wednesday in New Jersey where I meet Rod Frederickson at Mathematica. He invited me to spend the night at his house.

I won't see Kit on this trip. Sadly, in spite of my admiration for his sharp intellect, there's a barrier between us. He's cleared for all kinds of secrets to which I have no access. It's pointless to talk, and I can't trust his bosses with my information. I carry my notes for *Network Revolution*. There is much to say about the world of computers we are building, the “solid-state society” on the distant horizon.

Princeton, New Jersey. Friday 9 March 1979.

Dave Saunders, whose office I just left, is now director of the behavioral science section at MathTech, a branch of Mathematica whose bread and butter is the business of opinion surveys. Most of their work is directed at evaluating the impact of social aid programs, with massive compilations of questionaire responses that rely on advanced statistics, Saunders' area of expertise. I brought him up to date on my work. We spoke of Betty Hill's star map. He told me he had never said it indicated an extraterrestrial origin for UFOs, yet that was indeed how I understood his controversy with Sagan.

Dave's office was cluttered with file drawers, computer listings, reports stacked up on metal shelves, a dry environment. In confidence (“I know you're capable of keeping your mouth shut”) he gave me his personal views about various cases. We parted as friends. I should have come and seen him a long time ago. His remark about my ability to “keep my mouth shut” puzzled me until I remembered that he was part of the classified SRI psychic work.

Belmont. Sunday 18 March 1979.

Sealed in boxes, our UFO library is ready to be loaded into the truck and driven away to a rented storage place where it will spend the next few years. I feel lighter and freer now, this mass of information pushed out of my life. I haven't found out what UFOs were, but I did change the level of the problem. Too bad I can't say more in *Messengers*. As Frank Pace pointed out, I am condemned to understatements.

On January 8th, during the meeting of the American Association for the Advancement of Science, John Archibald Wheeler made a surprising speech. This brilliant physicist who has written remarkable passages about the nature of spacetime, recommended to the steering committee to sever all links with the Parapsychology Association. He said this during a symposium entitled "The role of Consciousness in Science" in which the SRI team participated. Wheeler said: "The decade of indulgence has passed. The time has come to chase the false scientists from the laboratory." The door to respectability that Margaret Mead had opened up for paranormal research may be slammed shut again. It is ironic to find that, without the Pentagon, this research would die. Psychics and the few scientists who study them shouldn't have to enter the labyrinth of politics in order to validate human abilities that belong to all of mankind.

Belmont. Sunday 25 March 1979.

In the midst of all the hard work there's happiness and laughter as we finalize the move. Once I discarded a mass of marginal data the ufological collection filled 24 big boxes, plus four boxes of essential files. The paranormal collection is in five crates, and the rest (case studies, summaries, photographs) fits into a big container. I am ready to put all that away. What have I learned? (1) The phenomenon is real but it offers multiple levels. (2) No simple extraterrestrial explanation fits the facts. (3) The governments of the U.S., Mexico and France have a keen level of interest (and the Russian and U.K. as well) but no scientific research project seems to exist. (4) Some of the brightest people in Intelligence get involved but the real data must be hidden at a different level. (5) Much of the official involvement is directed at faking data, not at discovering the truth. (6) Animal mutilations are real but probably unrelated to UFOs. (7) No solution will be found by mediocre, amateurish research.

19

Belmont. Wednesday 28 March 1979.

Janine and the children went off to see *The Wages of Fear*. I stayed behind to continue packing the library. The phone rang: George Keegan, an executive with Sun Oil who has helped start neighborhood projects with Ira, was on the line.

"Ira Einhorn has just been arrested for murder," he said flatly. "His girlfriend Holly Maddox disappeared months ago. Her family had been searching for her. They hired a private detective, a man named Pierce, who came to the conclusion that Holly had been a victim of foul play. He suspected there'd been a fight."

"Any proof of that?" I asked. "Oh, Yeah! Pierce convinced the Philadelphia police to search Ira's apartment. They found a large box in a closet containing, as they put it, 'human remains and other things.' Ira was arrested on the spot."

Keegan has spoken to Ira's mother and lawyer but hasn't been able to reach the prisoner. I felt upset by this, not only because I had regarded Ira as a colleague, but because he'd understood computer conferencing very early as an innovative form of communication.

Some hard questions have to be answered: If Ira had killed his girlfriend, would he keep her corpse in his apartment? This catches Ira just as he returns from a trip to Yugoslavia. For the last few months Ira has been telling everyone that the Soviets were getting ready to attack the West using weapons derived in part from Tesla's work. I had discounted these Tesla stories as so much New Age delusion. Now I am not so sure. Holly had other lovers than Ira. She was close to someone in the entourage of Puharich.

Belmont. Sunday 8 April 1979.

I just talked to Ira, out on bail. He was calm and spoke about business as usual. He told me I should write an article about computer conferencing for Omni. He tried to pretend that Holly's murder had never happened.

Janine has read the galleys of *Messengers*. "It's your best book," she told me. "It's clear, anyone can understand it." She is the only critic whose opinion truly counts. Not everybody agrees, of course. I hear that Jim Harder can't stop railing against the book.

Pasadena. Saturday 14 April 1979.

Janine, the children and I have flown to Pasadena for a conference ambitiously called the "World Symposium of the Foundation for Humanity." John Lilly was there, always sweet and patient; several rock groups; a children's parade.

Our panel included astronaut Rusty Schweickart and physicist Fritjof Capra. The latter, who had been described to me as a kind Taoist, sounded very dogmatic in private conversation: He spoke of the opposition between "good people" (feminists, ecologists) and "bad people", among which he placed technologists. As a computer scientist, he classified me at once among the bad guys. Rusty gave Capra a well-deserved lesson in humility, integrating the good and evil of science into a warm humanistic statement.

On Thursday I took Olivier to JPL. We spoke about satellites with Ed May's friend Ann Kahle. After lunch, we drove up to Mount Baldy to photograph the site of Jim Irish's sighting. After my lecture I was appoached by a young woman who carried a lunch box decorated with pictures from *Close Encounter*s. Her eyes betrayed a soul in pain. "People need help," she said, pushing a few blond strands of hair away from her eyes, "or else we wouldn't have been put on this planet!"

Belmont. Thursday 19 April 1979.

All my correspondence of the last several years, together with the parapsychology literature I had accumulated, has now been sorted out. I have thrown away enough old papers to stock a small museum of the paranormal, inform several doctoral dissertations or fuel an average house for a long winter. I have no regrets. The field has seen few pieces of work worthy of being preserved. Every day I hear new rumors about Ira and Holly: her father is said to be involved in rightist politics in Texas. The FBI has entered the affair.

On Tuesday over lunch with Hal, I pointed out how the secrecy around the SRI work had a discouraging impact on research at large. Our old parapsychology research group (PRG), which gave Hal and Russell the impetus and framework to start their formal effort, doesn't even meet anymore. Hal answered that he did continue to publish articles that described the broad outlines of their discoveries. That's a weak argument.

Spring has returned to our hillside. Every evening we sit together and I read aloud to my children from Casanova's escape at the prison of the Leads, as he narrates it so well in his Memoirs. I'm about to leave for France again.

Washington. Marriott Hotel. Friday 27 April 1979.

An intriguing article appeared recently in the *Chronicle* (**40**). A Quaker group, the "American Friends Services Committee," has accused the police of engaging in large-scale political surveillance through an espionage network, the Law Enforcement Intelligence Unit, whose target they claim is the American public. Some 250 law enforcement agencies are said to subscribe to it, as the U.S. slowly takes some of the characteristics of a police state.

Is it within the murky world beyond the law, the domain of private security firms, major corporations and parallel Intelligence networks, that some of the answers should be sought for the manipulation of belief systems?

At the Office of Technology Assessment, our meetings on the future of computing are over. My next series of lectures is in Germany next month, at an International Communication conference. Rain water makes a swishing sound under the tires of the cars driving under my windows. The square is bright silver; the Key Bridge vibrates with the traffic rushing across the Potomac.

Berlin. Hotel Europaischer Hof. Tuesday 8 May 1979.

It is 2:07 in the morning and I am fully awake, having had someone else's dream again. He was going to a party. He knew everybody there: the men, the women, the musicians. Nothing in common with my own life.

My window opens on a wide, deserted boulevard. The sidewalk curves away, carrying a line of streetlights to the West. To the right is the bus station.

Behind the hotel is the brand new Palace of Congresses. It looks like an aircraft carrier, or a space station, with huge glass panels and trapezoids of metal closing down over long rectangles with complicated layers.

Back in California Ray Williams assures me there is a good chance that Lehman Brothers will finance InfoMedia.

Berlin. Later the same day.

I can catch France-Inter broadcasts from here. The first voice I heard on the air was that of Aimé Michel talking about dowsing. Then came the news. The French seem amazed that California has an oil shortage. They blame it all on the Iranians... Yet part of the reason for this artificial shortage is purely financial: Price at the pump in the U.S. will become unregulated again in June. This triggers a series of obscure business vendettas.

The mayor of Berlin gave the opening speech at this Congress. Christian de Laët, the secretary of the scientific council of the Commonwealth, invited me to sit next to him. While the mayor went on with his formal statement, de Laët leaned towards me and whispered: “Ira isn't guilty, you know... It's the Tesla businesss that got him into trouble.”

When I came back for the afternoon session I met Tony Judge, another member of Ira’s vast network.

I have found a little place to eat on the Kurfürstendamm, convenient to watch the crowd walking along. People seem happy.

Paris. Saturday 12 May 1979.

I spent the night in a cheap hotel in Paris, alone, outside time. The wallpaper shows a pattern of pink flowers. Now I sit up in bed, the breakfast tray next to me. All this is familiar, warm, easy. It is hard to think that I have another life, that of an American writer, computer scientist in a startup company. I have two souls: one is the Parisian, in a world of unreal softness, like a pastel painting. Softness but no message. The other one is Californian and filled with projects. The future rises over it like haze over the pine trees at Spring Hill.

A friend of Bergier named Claudine Brelet, who lives near Parc Monceau, is editing a special issue of the magazine *Question De,* devoted to his memory. I promised to contribute to it (**41**). Claudine is a short brunette with closely-cropped hair, about 40, well connected in Paris intellectual circles. She has worked at *l'Express*, has been close to both Christian de Laët and Einhorn, and worked with Bergier until his death. Ira spent three days at her Paris apartment last summer. She showed me a letter from him, in which he states quietly that he doesn't see Holly anymore, that they are separated. That passage, sad but calm, reads like any phrase from an old lover who is beginning to forget an affair, with no hint of remorse, no violent undertone. The murder of Holly is a symbol for the end of an age that defied all conventions but failed miserably to set new standards.

Paris. Rue de la Clef. Sunday 13 May 1979.

The dominant mood in France is defeatism. Even in leading edge areas like psychic research they rehash theological generalities. Aimé himself seems confused, obsessed with the threat of terrorism to the point of paranoia.

Jacques Bergier's death happened quickly. His sister Isabelle Vichniac called Claudine when she heard the news. She rushed to his apartment. The concierge told her the body was still there, wrapped in a fabric bag. He hadn't left a will. His widow intended to burn all his papers and sell off his books. Claudine managed to take a few important documents, notably the handwritten certificate signed by General Montgomery in 1946, acknowledging Bergier's exceptional war service “in the cause of Freedom.” She lent it to Patrick Clot. Heaven knows where it is now.

I have written a piece in Bergier's honor. *Question De* has given up the idea of a special issue: most of the authors they contacted -- people whom Bergier helped in their careers -- have not bothered to respond. My contribution highlights his concept of the Multiverse which I regard as his most important idea.

Paris. Rue de la Clef. Monday 14 May 1979.

Last evening Simonne Servais confirmed my impression that French parapsychology research had stalled. She recently sent over several documents to Hubert Curien, the director of CNRS, including some of the SRI publications on psi research and my article in *Co-Evolution Quarterly* (**42**). He sent back the whole package with negative comments. Ambroise Roux, president of CGE, a large utility firm, is interested in psychic research. When he wrote a brief memorandum about the subject the reaction of his business colleagues was closed-minded: “You are bringing dishonor to this house,” they said. Now Simonne is alarmed at the expansion of the Maharishi's sect that recently organized conferences where top physicists like Costa de Beauregard and Brian Josephson agreed to speak. The Maharishi pushes for the creation of a World Government. A colleague of Costa named Vigier was also at the meeting; they challenged each other in a fight so intense they almost came to blows.

Paris. Rue de la Clef. Wednesday 16 May 1979.

Yesterday was devoted to setting up a French subsidiary of InfoMedia to develop computer conferencing here. Post Office authorities are in control of European regulations, which make everything complex, lengthy and unreasonably expensive, so our cost structure is too high. My terminal is now installed on my mother's desk. She insisted to send out the first message herself, in English. Tomorrow, when they log in on the net in California my children will find the first message from their grandmother,

May is sunny, with a soft breeze. From the building across the street, a little girl sitting on a balcony plays at sending us sunlight signals with a hand mirror. I read a book by Jacques Bergier. I miss my discussions with him.

On the roof of the *Samaritaine* department store is a restaurant from which one can see all of Paris. I had lunch there today in charming company: Claire Parenti, a young woman editor who works on *Messengers* had brought over Marie-Thérèse de Brosses, a journalist with *Paris-Match* who wore a serpent ring and a top decorated with flying saucers. Marie-Thérèse did all the talking. I relaxed, enjoying the view and following their conversation, which ranged from the rotten methods of some French publishers to psychic phenomena. Marie-Thérèse said she had witnessed séances with Maumal the Magician, a man accused of being the Anti-Christ.

Paris. Rue de la Clef. Thursday 17 May 1979.

Jean-Claude Bourret invited me for lunch today *Chez Ribe*, on Avenue de Suffren. He was in great shape. He told me that Poher had indeed given up his research, most recently sending postcards from Tahiti to his friends. As for Alain Esterle, Poher's successor, he is poorly informed, only getting a few of the Gendarmes' reports because military security intercepts the best cases, effectively preventing serious investigation. Besides, it now turns out that one of the photographs the Gepan regarded as most reliable was a hoax perpetrated by a Gendarme!

Is it the hay fever season, or fumes from the cars? I am developing painful asthma and wheezing. All evening I have been walking around Paris, thinking of Janine, haunted by a song by Aragon:

> *O mon amour, mon bel amour, ma déchirure,*
> *Je te porte dans moi comme un oiseau blessé,*
> *Et ceux-là sans savoir nous regardent passer.* **(43)**

Paris. Rue de la Clef. Friday 18 May 1979.

Every day Maman composes her messages on the terminal and sends them through *Planet* with enthusiasm. I hope I'll have as much intellectual freshness as she does when I am 80. Simonne Servais invited me to lunch with two scientist friends, Denis Renaudin and Patrick Aimedieu. French psychic research, they said, consists of little more than parochial quarrels. Once Professor Larcher and the Fouérés are mentioned, along with Chauvin and Costa, there's little more to say about French research.

Simonne gave me a copy of Ambroise Roux' lecture about parapsychology. She is amused by the fact that her American military contacts continue to send her Tom Bearden's papers that claim that the Russians are ahead of America. She recognizes this as misinformation, shielding the real stuff.

In the train to Brussels. Sunday 20 May 1979.

Last night I was awakened by asthma and the screams of a drunkard walking down the street, hitting cars and complaining about *la Bourgeoisie*. Unable to find sleep again, I read about Victor Hugo's experiments with spiritualist phenomena during his stay in Jersey (**44**). As with the research of the "Philip" group in Toronto, one touches here something akin to the software of the soul (**45**). None of this has anything to do with the dead. It is an awesome form of supra-consciousness that manifests physically through whatever convenient device can hold the poor humans' attention. Would the ghost of Shakespeare dictate verses in French, even in deference to Victor Hugo? But I am impressed with Victor Hugo's *Shadow of the Sepulchre*, who taught a sharp lesson to the experimenters.

Simonne has decided to come to Valensole with me, so I won't go to Toulouse to see Esterle. Now the train is reaching Hainaut under a low gray sky that occasionally lights up to a milky white. Churches rise heavily over the dark fields the color of spinach. They squat over the villages, as if to deny any flight of the soul.

Brussels. Hotel Mayfair. Monday 21 May 1979.

Everything was closed when I arrived in this city where Sundays are devoted to religious and family traditions. I finally discovered an old brasserie with photographs of elderly gentlemen hanging on the walls (they were the founders of a *Société d'Entraide*, circa 1929, said a yellowing sign). The atmosphere was solid, no hint of decadence, but the slice of cheese I was given was as cadaverously white as the waiter who brought it to me.

At the end of the Tomberg subway line, East of the city, I found the site where an abductee told me how she had lost her bicycle as a child, and how an object descended, with strange transparent tubes. I took pictures of it while two teams of Arab kids played soccer on the grass. Later I had a long conversation with Tony Judge (who runs the Union of International Associations) about the physics of information, which I see as the "lost sister" of the physics of energy they teach us in school. He was intrigued by the idea, adding this remark, that human beings may well have limitations in how much information they can absorb, just as we have limitations in terms of energy. We know a lot about the latter: how much we eat, how we breathe and process oxygen, how we absorb sunlight.

"On the other hand the information needs of man haven't been studied," Tony pointed out. "Is there such a thing as an information vitamin? Are there information elements without which we can't survive? Are there laws for the assimilation of information, an information metabolism?"

When it came to the sociology of UFOs, we speculated that a group (such as a paramilitary organization, an aerospace company or a secret society) could well have created illusions designed to take advantage of the genuine phenomenon. One scenario would use the creation of an artificial "crisis", the landing of a fake saucer.

Paris. Rue de la Clef. Later the same day.

The train brought me back from Belgium in time to type out a birthday cake on the terminal for my daughter's birthday: eleven exclamation marks made the candles, and alternating rows of Xs and equal signs made a fat layer cake.

Paris. Rue de la Clef. Wednesday 23 May 1979.

My publisher acknowledges he owes me about $2,000. This made me feel affluent, so I went and bought a few records and clothes on rue Mouffetard.

In the afternoon Simonne drove me to the International Metapsychic Institute to meet Dr. Larcher, a delightful man with total integrity in his approach to the paranormal. A former concentration camp inmate, he emerged, like Bergier, with a deep sense of life's meaning. He has set up several research commissions that claim to have discovered a link between the size of blood capillaries and paranormal effects.

French parapsychology is not immune to the abuses that plague the American New Age scene. Recently a man died here during a bad "group therapy" session while he was sandwiched between two mattresses, unable to breathe.

At my publisher's office I met Elizabeth Antébi, the author of *Ave Lucifer* and a descendant of the bloody Hungarian Countess Batori. This charming ancestor of hers used to shower with the blood of virgins in the hope to stay young indefinitely. Elizabeth denied, however, that her notorious relative was a vampire since, as she put it delicately, "the Countess did not suck."

We discussed true and false contemporary occultists. She told me the only genuine magician she had ever met was Julius Evola. "There isn't even any good sex among those so-called witches nowadays," she added. "They're all repressed masochists; any genuine pleasure would interfere with their cherished little frustrations."

Later I logged into Planet, where Janine had entered a scary report from home. Riots have taken place in San Francisco following the absurdly lenient verdict imposed on Dan White, the assassin of Mayor Moscone and Supervisor Harvey Milk.

Paris. Rue de la Clef. Thursday 24 May 1979.

The French celebrate the Feast of Ascension today, so nobody is working, not even the atheists. The weather is wavering between showers, thunderstorms, and sunny sky. Jazz bands play on street corners; people walk around in their finest attire. Between two editing sessions I had a cup of coffee with Claire and Elizabeth. They wanted to play a game called "famous last words." Thus Tristan Bernard died while contemplating his bedroom: "It was either me or that wallpaper," he whispered.

"And you, Jacques, what will you say when you die?" asked Elizabeth.

"I will say, *Ave Lucifer*," I replied. The title of her book. She thought that was nice.

I had dinner with Maman at the Contrescarpe Square. A guitar player was giving an approximate rendition of a song by Brassens while cool rain fell. In spite of the weather, my long walks through Paris, the cold apartment, and asthma that wakes me up early, I feel a lot of energy, jumping out to use the network at dawn. The thought of leaving for the Midi tomorrow on another field investigation trip to Valensole and on to meet "Dr. X," the witness of a remarkable series of phenomena that included alleged contact with humanoids inside his house, keeps me focused, while the net plays a major role in reducing the distance between me and Janine. This morning we had a synchronous dialogue (**46**). It was 9 A.M. for me, midnight for her. Suddenly I felt as if she was in my arms. I wonder if people had similar impression of delightful discovery in the early days of the telephone. Do emotions get channeled better through the limitations of the keyboard?

Paris. Gare de Lyon. Friday 25 May 1979.

Before meeting Simonne at the station and jumping into the train to Marseilles I have an hour or so to review the notes I took at the parapsychology conference. Held in the affluent sixteenth *arrondissement*, it was introduced by Robert Amadou who spoke about philosophy, evoking Aristotle and Schelling, whom he put in his rightful place between Hegel and Schopenhauer. He lost everybody but he droned on, drawing fine distinctions between *natura naturans* and *natura naturata*.

The session was presided by Pierre Janin, who stated his hypothesis that unpredictability constituted the primary difference between the conscious world and the inanimate world. Accordingly he is working on the construction of "parabiote" devices driven by randomness, susceptible to influence by human thought. Dice or marbles can be viewed as parabiotes. This was all very boring, so at the break I was happy to meet a dynamic UFO investigator who had analyzed the celebrated 1954 case of Marius Dewilde, the witness in Quarouble (**47**). He said the scene was geometrically impossible, but mental confusion is frequent in such close encounter situations. We both had noticed cases when the inside of the UFO was described as much larger than the outside (he drew an interesting analogy with the mother's womb) and cases when witnesses were "medically" examined in a way that made no sense biologically.

Pierre Viéroudy argues that the UFO archetype is an illusion which corresponds to the need to compensate for nuclear anguish. I disagree. My working hypothesis is that (i) UFOs do exist and they are a product of a hyper-dimensional multiverse, (ii) there is indeed official secrecy, (iii) the phenomenon is also used to camouflage classified experiments.

Janine disagrees, arguing that such a secret couldn't be kept. But it wouldn't need to be kept, because of its very structure. *It could not be assimilated by the human mind under ordinary conditions*. Skeptical rationalists are closed to the basic facts of the phenomenon while believers only look for data that confirms their preconceptions.

Gréoux. Sunday 27 May 1979.

The train took us to Marseilles shortly after midnight. Simonne has a vast store of reflexions and stories. I read to her the most striking passages from *Les Tables Tournantes de Jersey*, stressing the parallel between today's UFOs and the spiritualist phenomena of the last century. Simonne's conversation is filled with her recollections of private meetings with heads of State, travels all over the world with De Gaulle, and the affairs of government. She opens a window for me onto another social world. She lived through the Markovic affair and the May 68 riots, where she played a vital but discreet historical role that will never be documented.

I enjoyed Marseilles. My bedroom window opened over the trees of a peaceful square. I rented a Renault and we drove up toward Gréoux under a heavy sky. The little town was filled with flowers. We left our suitcases at the Villa Borghese and drove on to Valensole. The town siren was sounding the noon hour just as we reached the main square where the men played *pétanque*.

On the way Simonne first sought out Kilou the shepherd, an important element in the UFO story. The accent of the *Midi* sings on the lips, in the eyes. We went to a bistro, "Chez Dédé," for the obligatory *guignolet*. Maurice Masse, the main witness at Valensole, soon arrived like a celebrity, shaking hands with friends, speaking loudly, moving his cap back and forth over his big tanned head, moistening his lips with his tongue as if anticipating the taste of *pastis,* ready to grab the full savor of life, looking sideways at Simonne, assessing me. We spoke for two hours. He finally agreed to meet us in his field the next day. We drove up to Oraison to see the site, swept by a soft wind. Simonne showed me where the strange object had landed, near a ruined cabin. There are no lavender plants anymore: Masse has turned his land into a cornfield.

Grenoble. Monday 28 May 1979.

Masse was waiting for us in his field. I spoke to him alone, for a long time. He told me calmly, seriously, about unpublished details of his experience, and other cases in the area. The phenomenon began to look quite different from the "extraterrestrial explorer" concept most people have after reading about his experience in the UFO press.

Simonne and I decided to track down one of the silent witnesses Masse had mentioned. We found him on his tractor. He turned off the machine when he saw us, and told us his story. Before driving off we went back to the village to take leave of Madame Masse, a bourgeoise with dry pinched lips, a municipal council member.

Throughout the trip I have admired Simonne's diplomatic skill. When I thanked her for making these conversations possible, she laughed: “It's far easier to deal with visiting Heads of State at the Elysée than with Maurice Masse in Valensole!”

We next drove to the Oraison plateau and climbed the *Col de la Croix Haute*. The weather was magnificent in the mountains. Simonne took the train for Paris and I drove on to Sisteron, where I met Aimé Michel. Together we went to the house of Dr. X for lunch, enjoying the sun and the landscape, listening to music, surrounded by memories and stories that may well be true, of time travel and parallel worlds, and of contact in that same house with beings endowed with strange powers. That evening I drove back to Grenoble, a venerable town filled with beautiful women and solid, conservative fellows, but plagued with petty crime.

Grenoble. Hotel Terminus. Thursday 31 May 1979.

A fine Alpine storm is slamming the shutters against the wall and playing with my papers. The weather is heavy, hot and muggy as a Texas evening. I gave a three hour course on networking this morning. Unfortunately it will take more than one such seminar to shake the French complacency in computer usage. Routine habits and petty quarrels are ever present in this industry. I did manage to get through to Janine over *Planet*. She told me that gasoline was flowing again on the California market. Tomorrow I give one last computer lecture, then I fly back to Paris, and to the States on Sunday.

Janine has found a future home for us in Palo Alto, a small building sheltered on a quiet street among wonderful large trees.

Flying to San Francisco. Sunday 3 June 1979.

Claudine Brelet drove me to Roissy, our last chance to talk before the flight. She was back from Philadelphia where she had found Ira depressed, thinking of killing himself. “I've lived 39 years,” he told her, “I've done many things, my life is full, and perhaps it's time to leave the planet.”

“His attorney warns him he faces life in prison,” she told me tearfully. “All his friends are dropping him: Hazel Henderson, even Joyce Petzhek...”

At the airport we sat down at the restaurant. Claudine ordered some coffee. “I'm depressed, too,” she went on. “After what happened to Izhtak Bentov...”

I was startled: “Bentov? What about Bentov?”

“You haven't heard? He died in the crash of the DC-10 in Chicago last week.” (**48**)

Claudine is a funny woman with a friendly round face, like an apple that seems to be saying, “bite me!” She hides her real talent as an ethnologist and journalist behind this cheerful appearance. “I met Ira in London in 1977,” she told me. “He was there with Puharich. Holly was around too, but she looked so dejected that I didn't pay much attention to her. She didn't speak to anyone. She was practicing yoga all the time... Then I overheard her asking Ira if a certain object was in “their” bedroom. I remember thinking, well, so he sleeps with this harmless chick... How was I to know?”

The only argument for his innocence, paradoxically, is the very presence of the corpse in his apartment. Why would he keep it? (**49**)

Now the plane descends towards California. What have I learned about the UFO problem? Only that it provides a framework for the mystery of our own existence. I am left with doubt, even after meeting with Maurice Masse and Dr. X. I am convinced there is a real phenomenon that concerns the essence of our lives. A huge secret stands before us, palpable yet undeciphered, and forever beyond the cultural grasp of the few government spooks who are trying to manipulate it.

Belmont. Thursday 14 June 1979.

On Tuesday I went to Los Angeles to take my daughter to the Air France flight. I stayed at the gate even after she went on board. The plane couldn't be refueled because of a continuing gasoline shortage. After frustrating delays we were sent to a hotel where we slept only three hours. We had a whole day ahead of us until the next flight, so I took her with me to see Jay Levey and George Koopman at Future Presentations, where we spoke of computer networking. Exhausted, she was finally able to board the plane at 7 o' clock last night.

Belmont. Thursday 5 July 1979.

On Tuesday I went back to SRI with Olivier who brought along his prototype of the automated camera. Ed May suggested some improvements. We had lunch with him, Charles Tart, Hal Puthoff and Russell Targ. In eight years spent doing classified research they hadn't found the slightest trace of a credible, secret UFO project within the governement.

At Sandler's production offices Hynek and I reviewed segments of their new documentary *UFOs: It has Begun*. We will show the first accurate documentation of the cattle mutilation problem, a topic nobody has dared to touch until now. Allen was kind and funny; it felt good to work with him. As we discussed special effects that could give the audience an approximation of the close encounter experience the assembled experts warmed up to it. The technology is clearly available to simulate every detail of UFO landings, *including retractable light beams*, a fact that astonished me. The technical arguments led me to realize how easily witnesses could be fooled by today's available technology, even outside a studio environment.

Allen told us about Alain Esterle, who recently travelled in the U.S., hoping to meet leading researchers. He was frustrated after his visit to the Lorenzens: their major topic of discussion was the recent death of their dog.

"The head of the French UFO project hadn't travelled all the way to Arizona to hear Coral whining about some mutt," Allen observed with his usual humor, adding: "Esterle is a good engineer, a *Polytechnicien*, but quite naive. He's sure he'll quickly solve the problem by himself. How typically French! At least he's enthusiastic. We shouldn't discourage that."

Belmont. Tuesday 10 July 1979.

Janine and I spent most of Saturday with Colonel Stevens who told us the story of Swiss contactee Edward Meier, in great detail. This man, who lives near Winterthur, has produced a curious series of pictures that look completely fake to me (**50**). Stevens was uncritical, convinced he had the final truth at last.

Belmont. Saturday 14 July 1979.

The weather has turned hot. I spent yesterday in the city, meeting with Dean Arthur Cunningham and with Charles Crocker to discuss our financing. Last Wednesday we had a visit by Dr. X, his wife and his son Vincent, to whom I gave a cowboy hat. Last night we saw Alain who plans to buy a cattle ranch in Oregon.

I don't feel at peace. I've lost that energy I used to muster, dissolving problems. I have to hold onto every thought, muddle through every job. Perhaps the heat wave has something to do with it, or the absence of my wonderful library, or the uncertainty of our move to Palo Alto? I do trust the future but every unpaid bill at InfoMedia takes an emotional toll. We don't have the cash to stay afloat. I have to fight bouts of asthma almost every night.

Belmont. Saturday 21 July 1979.

Kate Lang visited us on Thursday for a psychic experiment with three UFO samples in my collection. We keep learning some ugly things about the seedy underside of ufology, including stories that concern Siragusa, Jim Jones, Bo and Peep. Many contemporary cult leaders claim a mysterious “contact” back in the fifties.

Jacques Johnson came over to see our company, along with a colleague of his who runs a software subsidiary of Thomson CSF. They are talking of investing in us, or even buying InfoMedia.

Aimé Michel and Price-Williams are deeply troubled by *Messengers*. The latter told me, “After reading it, I wonder if there's any real hope of doing research in this field.”

Belmont. Monday 30 July 1979.

Ingo Swann called today, bitter about the SRI work. I reminded him of our first conversation, when I suggested to research remote viewing as an addressing scheme, an idea that SRI never pursued beyond the obvious notion of using coordinates for their targets.

"I've read *Messengers*," he told me sternly, "I think you're throwing the baby out with the bath water. Although I'm not sure I can tell them apart myself," he added with a guffaw.

"What do you think is happening, then?" I asked him.

"There's a non-human system that keeps the human race under observation to make sure it doesn't develop psychically." Ingo added somberly: "You become aware of the barriers erected by this system as soon as you try to develop your psychic abilities. As we both know." The only problem is that none of this explains the actual facts of the phenomenon. I have begun a new collection of blue files to gather my personal investigations. They already fill 120 folders.

Belmont. Monday 6 August 1979.

In our future Palo Alto home we're busy repainting, changing carpets, cleaning out cupboards, fixing flaws, filling holes. In another two weeks we'll be ready to move.

The Village Voice has just published a depressing but thorough article detailing Ira's actions and his relationship to Holly. It leaves little doubt that he lied to all his friends.

On Friday Olivier and I loaded the automated camera, the computer terminal and some clothes for a two-day truck trip. He took the wheel to drive up to Redding where we met Bill Murphy and the three of us drove up into the Trinity Alps. We found a site on public land, an isolated slope overlooking the canyon where the Chapins have been observing the egg-shaped object that repeatedly lands on their claim. We buried the camera, so that now it looks like any other rock. It will take pictures from 6 A.M. to noon, every day for a month. We will come back to retrieve it.

Belmont. Wednesday 8 August 1979.

Back to L.A. on a marketing trip, I spent the night at Price-Williams' house. He described the coincidences precipitated by his experiments with Carlos Castaneda. He also gave me a quick course on hypnosis, notably Erickson's confusion technique. The next day I met my daughter's plane, returning from Paris. She came out smiling, as fresh and relaxed as if she had merely taken a stroll around the block. She deplored the loss of a frog she'd brought all the way from Bayeux. In fear of customs inspection she put it in her pocket. We're left with a glass jar that contains mud, worms, a couple of rocks. Now there is a wild Norman batracian running loose somewhere at LAX. During the flight back to San Francisco she put her head on my shoulder, told me about the castles along the Loire and trout fishing in Normandy, and fell asleep.

Palo Alto. Sunday 19 August 1979.

Annick has spent several days with us, along with her future husband Michel. Now all our energy goes into the move. The apartment is freshly painted, phone lines are going in. Yesterday was our last day in Belmont. We looked at the Bay nostalgically, drinking coffee on the deck. An observer would have been amused to watch our move in the red and white truck loaded to the roof with furniture, boxes, lampshades and cushions, followed by Alain's old white Ford.

Our new bedroom is large enough to double as a study, all white and smelling of carpet glue. Catherine threw herself on our bed to tell us how much she liked the sunlight hitting her room, filtered by venetian blinds projecting colors and shadows.

The transition feels wonderful, a sense of rebirth, fresh potential. Janine's desk in the family room faces the fireplace. Olivier will use the front bedroom, with plenty of space for his electronic workshop. We have only taken the essentials with us after 10 years in Belmont. Pratically all the UFO and parapsychology documentation is in storage, under lock and key, awaiting better days for research. Everything else has been sold or given away.

20

Boston. Saturday 25 August 1979.

New England remains alien for me, with its culture of puritanical redundancy and misplaced snobbery. Perhaps I feel this way because I've never developed lasting friendships in this area. In contrast, I felt curiously at ease in New York. The weather was mild for once, all my meetings went well. I began with breakfast downtown with Shel Gordon and spent the morning at Omni with their editor, going over an interview they plan to publish next year (**51**). The Omni formula is simple. The owner does with man's brains in *Omni* the same thing he does with women's private parts in *Penthouse*, hyping them on glossy paper with good graphics and trendy ads. They've already interviewed Skinner, O'Neil, Frank Press. Now it's my turn because they need a new approach to the paranormal, while some suspicion is building up against Allen, who suffers from overexposure after *Close Encounters*. His recent preface to Brad Ayers' book has strengthened the rumor that he's a tool of the CIA, which is absurd.

Lee Spiegel told me that Sir Eric Gairy was in San Diego, trying to recruit mercenaries to reconquer "his" island of Grenada, where the New Jewel Movement is now in power. The group took advantage of Gairy's trip abroad to seize strategic points, after which they "strongly discouraged" Sir Eric from ever coming back. (**52**)

Flying back from Washington. Sunday 26 August 1979.

Ishtak Bentov had received some threats before he boarded the DC-10 that crashed in Chicago. Yet sabotage has been eliminated as a possible cause of the accident. Bentov had a common interest with Ira, with Hubbard's son, with Pat Price and with Wilbur Franklin, but that doesn't indicate any connection between all these events.

Ira was under FBI surveillance, it turns out, because of his passport. He went to Europe in 1977, and then went back to Yugoslavia last year. It seems he flew behind the Iron Curtain regularly, so the FBI suspected him. Perhaps Ira couldn't bring the body out because of the surveillance? The police hint they have proof that he reopened the trunk, but I can't find out what it consists of. His only choice is to plead guilty, with temporary insanity. That leaves the issue of his diaries and address book. The latter is said to contain an extraordinary listing of celebrities and some exclusive private phone numbers: the Kennedy compound at Hyannis Port, the Rockefellers, many television personalities, and an exhaustive catalogue of sexual escapades. Prominent people, including someone from the *New York Times,* have called police to make sure it would never be published.

Is Ira delusional? He reported being bothered by a high-pitch sound. Yet his friends tell me that since his arrest his mind seems clearer, more analytical.

My latest discussions with Kit have left me puzzled. His well-trained mind refuses the evidence of animal mutilations. He told me that he was considering several hypotheses but wasn't able to come up with data to check them. "I'm led to the conclusion that I find no evidence for the phenomenon for the simple reason that there isn't any phenomenon," he said. It's increasingly clear to me how the perpetrators keep their secrets, since it is so easy for smart men like him to miss the obvious.

Palo Alto. Saturday 1 September 1979.

We plan to complete our move this weekend. The house in Belmont has been repainted, wall fabrics are gone along with the memories. The children live this as an adventure, awakening as they do in a new area, a town where they can ride their bikes, run to the store or go over to the Stanford campus for lunch. "We live like a real family now," Olivier says.

"Life runs so fast," Janine said last night, "We work too much, too hard, without taking the time for silly things like walking through the woods, or picking up leaves, starting a botanical collection, or just watching the clouds."

Palo Alto. Saturday 8 September 1979.

Olivier and I have just returned from another drive to Redding – twelve hours on the road and an hour with Bill Murphy who had retrieved our camera. The circuit didn't have enough power. We're making the necessary changes. We'll try again.

What's most important is the process itself: That adventure, the open road, my long talks with my son, watching the moon rise over the plains along the Sacramento River. Then I get back to work, typing invoices, calling up investors.

Palo Alto. Monday 24 September 1979.

Yesterday we drove up to the fortified crest of Fort Barry, North of the Golden Gate. We watched the big ships steaming into the Bay. The day was perfect. Over 200 years ago Father Pedro Font wrote:

> Although I have seen excellent sites and beautiful countries in my travels, I never saw one as satisfying as this. I think that if it were inhabited like Europe there would be nothing more beautiful in the world, for it has the best advantages to found a marvellous city with every possible facility by land and by sea, with such a remarkable gracious harbor.

I am 40 today. I feel confident, looking neither for glory nor wealth, having lived close enough to those who had them to discern the dangers they posed. I am preoccupied by the day-to-day concerns of my fragile company, but I will not let them overwhelm me. By the end of the year -- the decade -- it will be time to start again towards that domain of the mind where false realities vanish before the only reality, the problem that interests me, transcending the narrow world of spacetime.

Palo Alto. Monday 1 October 1979.

My daughter took the wheel of the truck and drove it yesterday, sitting on my knees, from Spring Hill to town, her eyes and mouth wide open. We love Mendocino County but we find it hard to make friends in Ukiah. I feel torn between that marvellous place in the country, where I'd never be able to make a living, and the heart of Silicon Valley where I can prosper but where my soul dries up.

Bartlesville. Monday 8 October 1979.

On the way to business meetings in Oklahoma I made a stop in Dallas, rented a car and drove to the site of a mutilation that took place two years ago, then Barbara and I went to Oklahoma City to talk to an elderly witness. His mind and memory were intact. He told us what he had seen back in 1934, as he stood in a field with his grandfather: A large saucer-shaped object landed there. The next day they found one of their pigs mutilated. He gave us the address of the farm, so we went there. Everything was exactly as he'd described it. A rancher showed us the property and mentioned recent cases, so we spent the next few hours driving from farm to farm among tractors and harvesting combines.

These people work hard and are eager to help. Everywhere they stopped what they were doing to talk to us. They were all well aware of the mystery, and deeply concerned.

Back in Tulsa I called the former sheriff of Bentonville. He was bitter: A mutilation had taken place on his own farm. Two days in a row a dark helicopter had flown low around his house before going away to the North. After nine years of service to the community he was fired because he wanted to investigate these incidents. Someone is making sure no professional investigation gets underway.

In the meantime Kit has hired Rommell, a retired FBI agent charged with a formal study. He is spending his time and much CIA money in New Mexico, pestering ranchers and sheriffs about impossible predators.

Flying back to San Francisco.

In Bartlesville it was a pleasure to visit Frank Lloyd Wright's tower, which the Price pipeline company uses as its headquarters, a copper sculpture, a beautiful piece of art. My VP of sales was with me; we signed another contract with Phillips Petroleum for the use of computer conferencing. In the evening I drove alone on the road from Nelagoney to Pawhuska. The full moon rose over the landscape; the October wind rolled tumbleweed in front of the car. I saw no flying saucers but I enjoyed the trip.

In three weeks I leave for Europe again. An election is coming, pitting a tired Jimmy Carter against the boastful attitude of Reagan supporters. All expectations point to a return to conservatism.

Palo Alto. Sunday 21 October 1979.

As I see *Messengers* in sharper perspective I understand why it antagonizes many of my friends. It's a visionary book, not a factual text. It is too far ahead and misses some of its targets.

Yesterday Olivier and I drove to Redding again. We went up the mountain with Bill Murphy in the four wheel drive truck, climbing along forest roads until lost in clouds. We found a site for the new camera but we had trouble getting the power supply to work, although it had advanced the film properly when Olivier tested it in the lab. Rather than risking a full month with no data we decided to bring the camera back to Silicon Valley and revise the design again.

I feel much attraction for Yolla Bolly - the region of wild hills and sparse population that spreads from Clear Lake to the Oregon border. Bill Murphy has lent me his copy of *The Bell Notes*, fragments from Arthur Young's diary edited by Einhorn (**53**). I miss a human dimension in this work that speaks only to the brain.

London, Hotel Russell. Monday 5 November 1979.

I attended a reception this evening at Marlborough House, in honor of the scientific secretaries of the Commonwealth. A lackey dressed in a fine red and gold habit announced my name when I came in. I had a talk with Christian de Laët and Curt Lemmon from Findhorn. After a few minutes we were discussing paranormal phenomena in telematic networks. I am happy in London, with Christian as my guide and many friends in the communications research establishment. I walked through a city washed clean by the rain.

London, Hotel Russell. Thursday 8 November 1979.

I walked all the way to the London Bridge today. The tide was low. The fast current of the Thames uncovered ugly debris strewn over the gray stones of the banks; the overcast parted away to allow the sun to filter through, leaving an occasional reflection on the wing of seagulls, then the gray returned again. I came back to the hotel through the open air market of Soho, which reminded me of Mouffetard Street in Paris, a place lost in time, *le quartier où l'on n'arrive jamais*. In Brewer and Peter Street fish sellers were yelling in their colorful slang. They took my thoughts away from California where the destiny of my little company remains suspended before potential investors.

This morning our English rep will meet me at the headquarters of Phillips Petroleum, which we have introduced to conferencing as a tool for the management of their far-flung exploration and production projects. In the afternoon I'll fly to Paris. I will miss the Londoners' quirky delight in perfection, their stubborn attention to detail. I love James Smith's boutique, where it would be easy to spend thousands for a silver walking stick but where difficult repairs to one's favorite umbrella cost no more than a few shillings. I had a pleasant dinner with Mike Tyler from the communications study group, and a private lunch at *L'Artiste Musclé* with Christian de Laët.

Paris. Saturday 10 November 1979.

The destiny of InfoMedia may be decided in a few hours when my associates present our plan to the Page Mill Group which comprises executives from H.P., Intel, Rolm and some of their key financial advisers. The strikes hadn't disabled the airport in Paris. I bought an armful of newspapers and in a few hours caught up with the recent suicide of a minister, an African scandal bothering President Giscard d'Estaing, and the mysterious death of a colonel. A legendary gangster named Mesrine who was a catalyst for the frustration of average Frenchmen fell into a trap and was promptly liquidated when the cops shot first, "for the protection of the public."

Every time I return to *Les Halles* I understand better the meaning of initiation. A few hours in these narrow streets are enough to convince me that the true meaning of existence lies in parallel worlds for which this city provides a secret metaphor.

Rue de la Clef. Sunday 11 November 1979.

A group of antique dealers have organized a show of demonological art near the Louvre. I went there with my mother. We found an admirable series of precious objects, bizarre statuettes and magnificent horrors: mummified hearts of sheep pierced with needles that reminded me of Berbiguier, sculpted canes and various power seats, including a famous armchair once owned by Anatole France. There was a group of magic mirrors gleaming with an ominous black sheen. Silver Baphomets and crystal globes completed the scene in darkness and glory.

The man who ran the show, a young fellow with a black beard, a scarf around his neck, confided to us that he had been contacted by agents of companies from Germany and Bavaria that sought to obtain "the powers" at any price. He suspected them of managing former Nazi fortunes. He added that they were offering fabulous sums for specialized libraries. Bergier would have taken notes.

Palo Alto. Monday 19 November 1979.

Catherine had decorated the car with garlands and flags for the trip back from the airport. Her brother showed me the new automatic camera under test in his room. It wakes up every morning at 6 A.M. and takes a picture every six minutes for the rest of the day.

The Diary of Anaïs Nin, which I have started to read, gives me conflicting feelings of admiration for the depth of humanity she expresses, mixed with contempt. Her life was a sequence of fancy balls, garden parties and fashionable evenings at the concert. Even in her phases of distress, the fair Anaïs spent her time between the opera and the salons of the wealthy whose doors were always open to her elegance. Reading this diary makes me want to collect the Journals of ordinary people. A diary is the record of an age, even if the author can only give a fragmentary account of it from an narrow perspective. History with a capital "H" is a set of harmonious curves, while a diary plots individual points on or around that curve, precisely. What strikes me in Anaïs Nin is her blindness and that of her friends before the events of her time.

Aimé Michel now considers that he has "wasted two thirds of his life studying UFOs." He is leery of writing another book. His last letters, in reaction to *Messengers*, were incoherent. My book has disturbed him, as it did other friends. Yet Janine encourages me to go on without looking back. We keep reinventing our life. Other couples fall into repeating patterns which soon become boring, but I have never gotten used to the fact that Janine had actually agreed to share her life with me. It's a subject of constant wonder, as if I had no memory of yesterday, of what we talked about, how we made love. I meet her again. Everything starts anew.

Palo Alto. Thursday 22 November 1979.

Thanksgiving has come, dressed up in grayish rain. I took advantage of it to stay home and to draft the outline of *Network Revolution.* I enjoy writing again, a book that doesn't discuss ufology. At Spring Hill waterfalls were cascading gaily, forest trails were covered with dead leaves, fog floated over the pasture.

Kit has come to the absurd conclusion that those mutilation reports that are not simple misinterpretations of predator actions are the product of schizophrenia in witnesses. He's impressed by the work of negative documentation done by Ken Rommel. Janine reminds me that schizophrenia is a dissociation of personality that results in the patient's inability to function in the real world. There are no such symptoms among the people I've interviewed in the field.

I have cured myself of the fascination I once felt for the Intelligence community. The realization came when I observed how easily they were fooled by others and fooled themselves.

Perhaps they are the ones who can't face the real world and have to invent their own secret games to make sense of it.

Palo Alto. Sunday 2 December 1979.

InfoMedia is broke. Our potential backers keep delaying their decision, speaking of the complexity of their "due diligence" process. I keep waking up in the middle of the night, tossing and turning.

It would be a shame to drop the company now. We are within $8,000 of breaking even on a monthly basis! Janine has told me she'd agree with whatever decision I made, even if it meant selling our house. I have concerns about the market for teleconferencing. Perhaps we are too early?

Palo Alto. Saturday 8 December 1979.

Ingo called, suggesting lunch. He came along with one of the newest SRI psychic subjects, a dynamic young man named Blue Harary.

This afternoon I went over to Berkeley for a book signing at Shambhala. A woman introduced herself, a friend of Don Hanlon named Robin Rule. *Magonia* had inspired some of her poems, which she graciously gave to me. And as the year comes to a close I am astonished to review the last 12 months: Ira accused of murder, Jacques Bergier's death, Jean Sendy's death, the crash of Bentov's plane, the passing of Chris Evans. Most importantly, I now realize how stupid I was when I hoped that the Intelligence boys could contribute to a study of the phenomenon. They have a different agenda. They make up the most absurd stories and get away with it.

There is peace in Palo Alto, and reality, in contrast to such games. We pick our own oranges and lemons. A giant tree is showering us with gold leaves. We've always lived among trees: *Auprès de mon arbre, je vivais heureux...* as Brassens used to sing. **(54)**

Palo Alto. Monday 24 December 1979.

Christmas night. My mother is with us, happy in our new place, playing with the children, meeting my colleagues. We're at the end of the decade. So what have I learned? First, the UFO phenomenon is proof that our current theories of spacetime are inadequate. I continue to hypothesize a new physics of information that would parallel the physics of energy taught in college.

Second, I believe the present is over-determined. I first felt this in the episode of the Melchizedek taxi driver, and the encounter with the griffin sculptures during my random walk with Puthoff. These events were intersigns that seemed to exude information in the form of a premonition towards which the entire day was intensely driven. Other episodes that could loosely be called “psychic” appear to confirm the hypothesis.

Third, I now know it's impossible to understand phenomena like UFOs without taking all their paranormal characteristics into account - not just the physical data. This has forced me to drift away from the mainstream of ufology. Regrettably, I have alienated some groups whose individual members I respect, like Allen's Center. They have no knowledge of psychic phenomena and no access to the ongoing research, so they see my work from the outside, as a series of disconnected hypotheses.

Palo Alto. Monday 31 December 1979.

Aimé Michel urges me to drop UFO research as he has done himself, “having achieved an *oeuvre* of which we can be justly proud!” Janine believes *Messengers* represents a chasm between obsolete views of the phenomenon (as the arrival of Aliens) and the ominous possibility of a massive social mutation. No wonder Aimé feels threatened. I do too, but here is California I don't have the luxury of ignoring the weirdness of the world, as he does on his mountain.

With the death of poor Holly we mourn our hopes for a world permeated or transfigured with new ideals of love. By his denials Ira has betrayed his friends and a whole lot of big promises: the rise of a new consciousness, freedom of the spirit, the inspiration of youth culture for which, for a short time, he'd been a symbol.

Janine is reading the *Journal* of Anaïs Nin -- "one of the least honest books" she's ever read. I read *The psychology of Anomalous Experience*, by Graham Reed, the first complete and lucid work I have found on hallucinations.

The Seventies have come to an end. We're happy to turn the page. At midnight we all kissed and drank Champagne. We'd spent the evening with my mother and little Rhea. Olivier had invited over a Chinese friend, so the house was filled with laughter around the tree and the fireplace.

The end of the year brings good news for my company: a seasoned executive has agreed to join us to help me run it. The venture capital investment we were seeking is almost assured. We'll soon start development again.

I am left with the simple prospect of human hope, and the simple warmth of your presence, which I fail to describe.

REFLECTIONS

In her book *In Search of the Light*, subtitled "The Adventures of a Parapsychologist," English researcher Susan Blackmore (**1**) laments the inability of memory to bring back the details of earlier beliefs. "I wish I could remember," she writes, "just how I felt about parapsychology all those years ago when I first began. I wish I could remember what it felt like to believe passionately in the possibility of the paranormal and to be fired with enthusiasm for tracking it down."

It is both the merit and the curse of a diary that it provides the kind of record she was calling for. It highlights the fantasies, false starts and blind alleys. In the absence of such a record my recollection of paranormal research in the seventies would be written in very different terms. I might have forgotten, or neglected, my one-time acquaintance with esoteric dreamers and alleged witnesses who turned out to be misleading or fraudulent. Yet I learned much from them, if only in calibrating my research. Equally important, I might have failed to note key events that pointed to genuine phenomena for which science is still unable to provide explanations.

What the public knows today about these subjects comes from books written by people who weren't there when the research was done. This removes nothing from their value as general presentations, but it does limit their scope. The record of computer development is an apt example. A historian of technology came to my office recently. "You can't imagine," he said, "how difficult it is to make people realize that the mouse was invented ten years before Apple's Macintosh." His reason for tracking me down was that I had written about Doug Engelbart's work while it was happening, and had a first-hand view of the SRI computer research and its impact.

Computer networking, an obscure technical discipline at the time, has become big business. Affluent corporations like Google, Apple and Microsoft hire public relations firms to write their history, but their executives have little direct knowledge of how Internet came about, or why certain behaviors evolved as they did. Some of that information is incidental, of little interest to non-specialists; other parts of it will be vital to every aspect of the future. Politicians' efforts to control the new networks or to make sense of their consequences for privacy, secrecy and the control of far-flung operations is an important case in point. All that was in gestation in the work and in the daily experiences of the few software teams that surrounded the Arpanet.

More subtle, but more sinister, is the rewriting of history that takes place in parapsychology and in the history of aerial phenomena. Many pioneers have now died or retired, leaving newcomers with every opportunity to distort the record. Raised on tabloids and television, the new wave of pundits is unconcerned with accuracy and openly contemptuous of science. They give us novel interpretations of what witnesses and experimenters have seen and done. While this isn't necessarily bad (a fresh perspective, however iconoclastic, is welcome) it is misleading in the absence of a baseline. My hope is to offer such a baseline. The appeal of consciousness development and transcendance may excuse enthusiasm, not fraud. I don't pretend to have answers to the mysteries in the field, as the book you just read must have made clear; but I must testify to omissions and deliberate lies. I was inspired in this direction by a few valuable books that did lift a corner of the veil and revealed the intricacies of the relationship between the Intelligence community and the SRI parapsychology project of which I was a part **(2)**. This work has made it possible for me to talk about matters that I had feared would remain secret.

I have not emerged from this experience with much respect for the Intelligence officials I have met, in the United States or Europe. While many are men and women of undoubted loyalty and integrity, and while they deserve full credit (alongside their equally committed adversaries in other countries) for saving us from the catastrophe of a nuclear exchange between East and West for over half a century, their performance in the manipulation of science in general, and of the belief in the paranormal in particular, has been shady, deceitful and ultimately harmful to the development of advanced technology.

While the belief in UFOs presents a convenient cover for

occasional crashes of classified prototypes, unethical medical experiments or psychological operations designed to fool enemies, much damage has been done to good research in the process.

It is difficult for a scientist who is used to the culture of open criticism and honest exchange of data to feel respect for the methods of shadowy agents who invade your personal life, listen to your phone calls, open your mail, interrogate your kids in your absence and feed you false information, all in the name of some supposed higher duty to the security of the nation they claim to serve. In my limited contacts with the agencies involved, I have met some of the brightest people I will ever know in this life, and some of the most despicable and sometimes crazy characters. There was very little between these two extremes.

From the vantage point of hindsight, it is clear that the set of manifestations known as the "UFO Phenomenon" went through remarkable periods of high activity during the seventies, with France and Brazil among the most intensely-impacted locations.

Another fact is also clear now, which we only vaguely sensed at the time: The intelligence agencies of several countries, notably the U.S., the U.K. and France (often acting in concert) encouraged a few private scientists and physicians drawn from UFO groups and aerospace companies to conduct semi-official, deniable field investigations. Some French witnesses who had been rebuffed by their local authorities were surprised to be contacted by very knowledgeable experts, including American doctors.

Presumably, the files from these investigations still linger somewhere but the follow-up was either scattered by political winds or abandoned as the field sank into the quagmire of bureaucratic neglect. As often seems the case, the superficial excitement of secret studies and boasts about "X-Files" gives way, upon scrutiny, to the realization that the data were handled distractedly by managers whose assignments and budgets came and went. The real phenomena continue to manifest under our noses, and no special access to questionable government documents is required to pursue a serious study. I tried to apply this knowledge in my own experiments during the following decade.

NOTES AND REFERENCES

Foreword

1. The first hardcover edition of Volume One of *Forbidden Science* was published by North Atlantic Books of Berkeley in 1992 and a second one by the same publisher in 1994. A trade paperback was issued by Marlowe & Co. (New York) in July 1996, with the text of the Pentacle Memorandum in Appendix. A French edition (*Science Interdite*) by Observatoire des Parasciences followed in August 1997.

2. Tilly Tansey: "Telling it like it was." *New Scientist,* 16 Dec. 1995.

3. Shortly after publication of the first volume of *Forbidden Science* I forced declassification and release of the Pentacle Memorandum, a secret document written by a Battelle Memorial Institute manager at the time of the Robertson Panel that advised the Air Force to "debunk" UFOs. It was reprinted by *UFO Magazine*, edited in Los Angeles by Vicki Cooper. See in particular her article: "Business beyond Blue Book: 1953 'Pentacle' Letter. Past, Secret UFO Study confirmed" (Vol.8, No.2, 1993, page 6).

4. Jim Schnabel's book *Remote Viewers*, subtitled "The Secret History of America's Psychic Spies", was published in February 1997 as a Dell paperback (New York).

5. Katie Hafner and Matthew Lyon, *Where Wizards Stay up Late: the Origins of the Internet.* New York: Simon & Schuster 1996.

6. Kourganoff, V. *La Recherche Scientifique*. Paris: Presses Univ. de France, 1958. Que Sais-Je? no.781.

Part Five: Computer Confessions

1. The text typed in Bayeux covered the period from 1957 to 1969. For consistency I have decided to continue numbering the parts of my journals in sequence beginning with Part Five.

2. *Spires* stood for *Stanford Physics Information Retrieval System.* It was conceived as an electronic dissemination medium for journal preprints in science. Associated with *Spires* was the *Ballots* system which aimed at complete automation of the Stanford library.

3. Edward Feigenbaum was a pioneer in artificial reasoning and expert systems. Together with his Stanford students he developed *Dendral,* a system which succeeded in identifying complex molecules. He went on to be a founder of Teknowledge Inc., one of the earliest software companies in the field.

4. The Dirac language was applied to a growing range of real-life problems, from medicine to astronomy. Among the Dirac papers that were eventually published are *Dirac and astronomical data retrieval* (ACM 1970 National Conference, New York, with a summary in the book *Computers and Crisis*, edited by R.W. Bemer, ACM, New York 1971, pp. 386-387, Sept.1970) and *Interactive computer management of clinical data, a new approach in the Blood Bank* (23rd annual meeting, American Assoc. of Blood Banks, San Francisco, Oct.1970). Two other papers are noteworthy, namely the description of the language itself published in *Dirac: an interactive retrieval language with computational interface* (Information Storage and Retrieval Journal Vol.6, No.5, pp.387-399, Dec.1970) and *La Documentation Automatique en Temps Partagé* (Revue d'Informatique et de Recherche Opérationnelle B-1, pp.3-13 Jan.1971).

5. Eric Roussel writes in his biographical book *Georges Pompidou* (Editions Jean-Claude Lattès, Paris 1984): "On 27 and 28 May, in the Latin Quarter, one could think for a moment that the turmoil of two years before is about to recur: Very serious incidents take place between the students and the police."

6. Ludwig Wittgenstein's essential work was conducted in Germany between 1920 and 1945. It is described (among many other places) in *Philosophical Investigations* (New York: Macmillan 1953).

7. See in particular *Sky and Telescope* for August 1970: "There has been no prediction of the fourth ring (of Saturn) reported here, and its discovery has been quite accidental... 'We suggest naming this the D ring. The new ring D lies inside C and is separated from it by a dark lane that is equivalent to Cassini's division between the A and B rings,' wrote Guérin, who had 'discovered' the ring in 1969 on photographs obtained at Pic du Midi observatory."

8. A prolific author born in 1930, John Keel specialized in Fortean subjects. Living in New York City, where he worked as a free-lance writer, he published such seminal books as *UFOs: Operation Trojan Horse* (NY: Putnam 1970) and *The Eighth Tower* (NY: Dutton 1975).

9. The Aveyron case has been described in summary form in *The Invisible College* (NY: Dutton 1975). The complete case was published by Fernand Lagarde in *Lumières dans la Nuit* and later in the *Flying Saucer Review*, as a result of agreements made during our meeting in Normandy.

10. Apro and Nicap were the dominant forces in civilian UFO research during the fifties and sixties. Standing respectively for Aerial Phenomena Research Organization (directed by Jim and Coral Lorenzen and based in Arizona) and National Investigations Committee on Aerial Phenomena (directed by major Donald Keyhoe and based in Washington D.C.), both groups took the position that UFOs were extraterrestrial spacecraft.

11. This barium cloud experiment over Canada and the resulting confusion when it was widely reported as a UFO and pitifully "explained" by the U.S. Air Force as the star Capella have been described in detail in *The Edge of Reality*, a book I co-authored with Allen Hynek. (Chicago: Regnery 1975, pp.171-175).

12. Maeterlinck, Maurice: *L'Hôte Inconnu* (Paris: Charpentier 1917, page 112). He also wrote such works as *Le Grand Secret* (1921) and *La Sagesse et la Destinée* (1942).

13. The horse that was found mutilated (stripped of flesh from the neck up) on 8 September 1967 in Southern Colorado was actually named *Lady*. She was the three-year old daughter of a mare named *Snippy*, who was not affected in the incident. The media made a mistake in reporting both the name and the sex of the animal and the error was never corrected.

14. Gray Barker died in 1984 at the age of 59, leaving a collection of clippings and publications now preserved in his home town of Clarksburg, West Virginia. The collection consists of some 300 books along with 75 groups of magazines, and 30 file drawers of articles and correspondence.

15. The Iowa landings resulted in an extraordinary sequence of observations involving a young farm boy and several neighbors who described close encounters and abductions over a period of months.

16. *Occasionalism* is the name of a remarkable islamic philosophy which holds that the universe is composed of events rather than material objects. On this subject see the book *Islamic Occasionalism and its Critique by Averroes and Aquinas*, by Majid Fakhry. London: Allen & Unwin, 1958.

17. Albert Szent-Gyorgyi, *The Crazy Ape* (NY: Philos. Library 1970).

18. The Arpa network, known as "Arpanet" by systems programmers everywhere, was the first true computer network and the predecessor for Internet. Developed and funded in the late sixties by the *Advanced Research Projects Agency,* its underlying communications technique was *packet-switching*, a revolutionary concept invented by Paul Baran at the Rand Corporation in the early sixties. The Arpa network suffered from many technical 'bugs' and did not come into reasonably stable use until 1972. The best summary of Arpanet's beginnings is found in the article "Casting the Net" by Katie Hafner and Matthew Lyon, *The Sciences* (published by the New York Academy of Sciences) Sept-Oct. 1996 p.32, which clarifies Paul Baran's role.

19. The Phil Klass mentioned here is a science-fiction writer, not to be confused with the Philip Klass who is senior editor at *Aviation Week*, a skeptic and "rationalist" author of books arguing against UFO reality.

20. John McCarthy is considered a pioneer of artificial intelligence.

21. *The Eye in the Triangle* was published by Israel Regardie. It contains a good summary of Crowley's magical theory.

22. Hynek's book was published by Regnery Company of Chicago two years later (1972) under the title *The UFO Experience - A Scientific inquiry*. It has remained as an important milestone in the field. Most notably, the book introduced the expression *Close Encounters*. It defined the First, Second and Third Kind of such encounters.

23. Carlos Allende was a sailor who claimed to have been a witness to a secret Navy test allegedly conducted under Einstein's supervision and aimed at making a destroyer vanish. Known as the *Philadelphia Experiment*, and popularized in a book by that title by Bill Moore and Charles Berlitz, this 1943 episode has remained a classic in UFO lore. I was able to establish that it was simply a Navy counter-measures experiment to make ships "invisible" to German magnetic torpedoes. See *Anatomy of a Hoax: The Philadelphia Experiment Fifty Years Later* for the *Journal of Scientific Exploration* (JSE Vol.8 no.1, 1994 pp.47-71.)

24. The Enochian system derived from Dr. John Dee's experiments with an alleged Angel during the reign of Queen Elizabeth the First. In this research, McMurtry would have benefited from the knowledge of his wife Phyllis Seckler (Soror Meral), herself an OTO initiate and student of Jane Wolfe, who had followed Crowley to Cefalu in Sicily.

25. This remark by Colonel McMurtry was truly prophetic. A decade later, under President Ronald Reagan, American Marines would indeed be sent to Beyrouth in an attempt to control the Lebanese civil wars. That unfortunate initiative resulted in tragedy when terrorists attacked the barracks and killed hundreds of American soldiers who, as McMurtry had forecast, could not be effectively protected.

26. Since this was written, Hubbard's life has been analyzed in detail in the book *Bare-faced Messiah* by Russell Miller (NY: Henry Holt 1987). An article by Douglas Chapman, entitled "Jack Parsons: Sorcerous Scientist" appeared in issues number 6 and 8 of *Strange Magazine* (1991), with an abundance of documentation and footnotes. In it we learn that John Whiteside Parsons (1914-1952) first approached Caltech in 1936 to experiment with a liquid propellant rocket motor. It is in 1939 that Parsons and his wife Helen came into contact with the agape Lodge of the O.T.O., which he joined in 1941. It was then under the leadership of Wilfred Talbot Smith, followed by Parsons, at Crowley's suggestion, about 1944.

27. *Voyages vers Ailleurs*, by Serge Hutin. Paris: Arthème Fayard 1962.

28. Press reports about this O.T.O. group can be found in the *Los Angeles Herald-Examiner* for 29 July 1969 and for the next day; also in the same paper for September 5th, 1969, and in the *Daily News* for 18 October, 23 October, 29 October and 7 November 1969.

29. Early in 1990 the catalogue of *Rothschild-Berlin*, a Las Vegas company specialized in erotic books and occult items, offered these mosaics for sale at $9,000 the pair, adding: "although not known as an artist, Israel Regardie was commissioned by a friend to do two large mosaics, one of Thoth and the other of Isis. The tiles are laid on a large sheet of wood, perhaps a king-size door."

30. John Symmonds: *The Great Beast, the life of Aleister Crowley*. London: Panther Books 1963.

31. Arthur Lyons: *The Second Coming, Satanism in America.* NY: Dodd, Mead 1970.

32. Alfred Elton Van Vogt was a gifted and influential science-fiction writer, the author of such classics as *The World of Non-A.* Born in Canada, he also wrote *The Voyage of the Space Beagle*, *the Great Judge*, *Slan* and many other movels and short stories.

33. "Reverse engineering" is a Silicon Valley term for the art of taking apart a given product to find out how it is built and to identify its components.

34. LARC was the Lindheimer Astronomical Research Center, a modern observatory built under Allen Hynek's leadership with funds donated to Northwestern University by the Lindheimer family.

35. Peter Sturrock's work on pulsars with the assistance of the author during this period led to several reports to the National Science Foundation and to our paper *Periodicity in the radiofrequency spectrum of the pulsar CPO328* published in the Astrophysical Journal, 171: L27-L30, Jan.1972.

36. After leaving the Center I published two more articles based on the Dirac language and its applications, namely *The organization of Research Data Banks* (Proceedings of the 34th annual meeting of the American Society for Information Science, Denver, Nov.1971, pp.387-394) and *Interactive Management of Mineral Resources, practical experience with the Alaska database*, (Proceedings of the first annual computer communications conference, San Jose State College, Jan.1972)

37. Twenty years later no system equivalent to Dirac had been developed for this use.

38. The book by Manly Hall: *Secret Teachings of all Ages* went through many successful editions. The full title was *An Encyclopedic Outline of Masonic, Hermetic, Qabbalistic and Rosicrucian Symbolical Philosophy, being an interpretation of the secret teachings concealed within the rituals, allegories and mysteries of all Ages.* Allen Hynek bought a copy of the fifth edition, published in San Francisco by Crocker in 1928. That copy is now preserved in the author's private research library.

39. Ummo is the name of an imaginary planet allegedly in orbit around the star IUMMA. Revelations about the nature of its inhabitants, along with their science and their philosophy, were contained in a series of letters mailed anonymously to researchers throughout Europe. I exposed this hoax in several books, notably *Confrontations*.

40. The book was entitled *Un Caso Perfecto*, and was published in Spain by Antonio Ribera and Rafael Farriols at Editorial Pomaire (Barcelona, 1969). See also A.Ribera: *El Misterio de Ummo* (Barcelona: Plaza y Janes, June 1979).

41. Later in 1971 I published three articles in the *Flying Saucer Review* based on computer statistics using this technique. First came a study called *UFO Activity in relation to nights-of-the-week* (May-June issue, p.8), next a major report on *Type-1 phenomena in Spain and Portugal*, co-authored with Vicente-Juan Ballester-Olmos (Special issue no.4, August 1971, pp.40-64), and a two-part article called *Researching the American landings* (Sept-Oct issue p.3 and Nov-Dec issue p.10).

42. The *Illiac IV*, conceived and built at the University of Illinois in Urbana, was transferred to NASA-Ames in 1970, in part to place it beyond the reach of radicals who might have tried to destroy it. It was the first large-scale parallel computer, but it never achieved its full theoretical power because it was plagued by numerous hardware failures.

43. Alleau, René: *Hitler et les Sociétés Secrètes*, edition unknown.

44. Gerson, Werner: *Le Nazisme, Société Secrète*, Paris: J'Ai Lu (No. A267) 1969.

45. Dr. Joseph Banks Rhine was a professor of psychology at Duke University who pioneered meticulous statistical research into many aspects of extrasensory perception. Edgar D. Mitchell is a U.S. astronaut (the sixth man on the moon while serving as lunar module pilot during the Apollo 14 flight of February 1971) who ran psychic experiments from space. He went on to be a founder of the *Institute of Noetic Sciences* in 1972.

46. *God's Man*, with spendid woodcuts by Lynd Ward. New York: Peter Smith, 1929.

47. *The King in Yellow*, novel by Robert W. Chambers. London: Chatto & Windus, 1895.

48. *The Circus of Doctor Lao*, by Charles Finney. NY: Viking 1935.

49. *Vers un Nouveau Prophétisme*, by Raymond Abellio. Paris: NRF-Gallimard 1950. The book is subtitled: Essay on the political role of the Sacred and the situation of Lucifer in the modern world.

50. This passage: "O puny man..." is quoted by Anton LaVey in his *Satanic Rituals*, see note 58 below. It was inspired by *The Hounds of Tindalos* by Frank Belknap Long (Sank City, Wisconsin: Arkham 1946).

51. About this topic, see Vallee and Ballester-Olmos, *Sociology of the Iberian landings*, in FSR 18, No.4 (July-Aug.1972) p.10.

52. "*Dites ces mots: ma vie, et retenez vos larmes...*" was a line in a George Brassens song after a poem by Aragon. "Say these words: 'my life,' and hold back your tears... There's no such thing as a happy love."

53. Dr. Carl Jung mentions Passavant on page 99 of *Memories, Dreams and Reflections* (NY: Random House Vintage, 1965). Gorres was the German author of a work translated into French as *La Mystique*, a 5-volume set which contained a complete panorama of mysticism. (Paris: Poussielgue-Rusand, 1854)

54. The *Winchester Mystery House* is a magnificent and bizarre structure erected by Sarah Winchester, the wealthy widow of the inventor of the famous rifle. It stands in the very heart of Silicon Valley.

55. In 1910 Walter Evans-Wentz had written the classic *Fairy-Faith in Celtic Countries* (reprinted by University Books, New York 1966), a book in which he courageously pointed to the possible reality of the faery realm.

56. Emile Souvestre: *An Attic Philosopher in Paris, or a Peep at the World from a Garret: The Journal of a Happy Man.* New York: A.L. Burt, the Home Library, no date given.

57. Like other early attempts I made at English-language fiction, the short story *Redeem here your Ecstasy Coupons* was never published.

58. *Satanic Rituals,* by Anton LaVey. Secaucus, NJ: University Books 1972 (hardcover) and New York: Avon, 1972 (paperback).

59. Engelbart's story was told in a *Microtimes* article by Howard Rheingold on 23 Jan.1989 ("Doug Engelbart: the Vision continues") He pursued research after the SRI group was disbanded, joining McDonnell-Douglas, when it absorbed Tymshare, which had absorbed the SRI team.

Part Six: Psychic Underground.

1. About the circumstances of my first meeting with Paul Rech see Vol.I, entry for Friday 26 July 1968.

2. Charlie Rosen was one of earliest pioneers of artificial intelligence and robotics in the United States. His SRI laboratory developed software for machine vision and language processing.

3. About psychic surgery, Dr. Hynek and claims about "Dr. Tony" see Vol. I of *Forbidden Science*. Also note 22, *infra*.

4. Maurice Garçon's book was entitled *Vintras, Hérésiarque et Prophète*. Paris: Emile Nourry, 1928.

5. The theory holds that the brain functions with two specialized halves, the right hemisphere being dedicated to nonverbal, non-linear expression as found in sculpture or painting, while the left hemisphere controls language, rational cognition and time sense. It was best popularized in *The Psychology of Consciousness* by Robert E. Ornstein (San Francisco: W.H. Freeman, 1972) and in *Using Both Sides of your Brain* by Tony Buzan (NY: Dutton 1976).

6. This remarkable passage can be found in the book by H.P. Lovecraft, *the Color out of Space*, in a short story entitled "The Call of Cthulhu".

7. As mentioned *supra* (Part Five, note 24) the Enochian language is documented in many books about magic and in Dr. Dee's biographies, notably in *The World of an Elizabethan Magus*, by Peter J. French. London: Routledge & Kegan Paul, 1972.

8. The GEPA, or Groupe d'Etude des Phénomènes Aériens, may have been the most serious civilian research organization in the field. It was founded in Paris by René and Francine Fouéré. It published an excellent *Bulletin* from issue no.1 (1963) to no.50, December 1976, when publication ceased. It was an excellent source of hard data about the sightings of that period. The GEPA furnished both the inspiration and the initial scientific staff for Claude Poher's Gepan.

9. The Fifties movie "The Ten Thousand Fingers of Dr. T." was based on a story by Dr. Seuss and directed by Roy Rowland.

10. Lieutenant Jean Plantier's theory was developed in his book "La Propulsion des Soucoupes Volantes par Action Directe sur l'Atome" (Paris: Mame 1955).

11. Commandant Tizané's book was entitled *L'Hôte Inconnu dans le Crime sans Cause*. ("The Unknown Host in the Causeless Crime") Paris: Tchou 1977.

12. Hynek, J.A. *The UFO Experience.* Chicago: Regnery 1972

(Hardcover edition.). New York: Ballantine May 1974 (Mass paperback).

13. The "Poujadistes" were members of a populist movement launched by Mr. Poujade, an extreme-rightist who advocated simplistic solutions to France's social problems, anticipating on the later slogans of the *Front National* in the eighties and nineties. Ridiculed in the media as a group of disgruntled shopowners with no political ideology, the Poujadistes were eventually marginalized and forgotten.

14. Aimé Michel was occasionally confused with publisher Albin Michel. This error was perpetuated in Blanche Barton's later book about LaVey: *The Secret Life of a Satanist*. Los Angeles: Feral House 1990.

15. Frank B. Salisbury, *The Utah UFO Display: A Biologist's Report*. Old Greenwich: Devin-Adair 1974.

16. Several chapters from *Redeem* were indeed published elsewhere, notably in *Invisible College* (the section on Ummo) and in *Messengers of Deception*.

17. In 1992 I received a letter from a man who had unusual insight into the inner workings of Nicap and its relationship to Intelligence groups. He claimed that Donald Keyhoe was a more complex character than appeared and that he was in close contact with various intelligence officers.

18. About LaVey's childhood see *The Devil's Avenger*, by Burton Wolfe. New York: Pyramid 1974.

19. René Hardy died on 12 June 1972.

20. Dr. Harold ("Hal") E. Puthoff is a theoretical physicist specializing in fundamental electrodynamics. A graduate of Stanford University in 1967, his research was in lasers and electron-beam devices. In this area he published 25 papers (including a fundamental one on the free-electron laser), holds a laser patent and is co-author of a textbook, *Fundamentals of Quantum Electronics*. His background includes engineering work at General Electric and Sperry and three years active duty as a Naval Intelligence officer with NSA, where he worked on opto-electronic computers.

21. Joseph F. Rinn, *Sixty Years of Psychical Research*. New York: The Truth Seeker Company, 1950.

22. About Dr. Hynek's interest in "thoughtography" and claims of Ted Serios and Eisenbud, see *Forbidden Science*, Vol. I, entry for 17 Dec 66.

23. Puthoff clarified this period and Targ's role in a letter to Dr.Harary: "I setup that program in the spring of 1972. (...) Russell Targ was not at SRI (he was working at Sylvania on laser projects), and did not know of my program until he happened to attend a lecture I gave at Stanford University later that year. Following that presentation, he approached me to tell me of his interest in the field and enquired as to the possibility of joining the SRI program"

24. Guilmot, Max: *The Spiritual Message of Ancient Egypt*. Paris: Hachette 1970.

25. Budge, Sir Alexander Wallis: *Amulets and Talismans*. New York: Collier 1970 (first published 1930).

26. *The Satanic Rituals*, by Anton LaVey. Secaucus NJ: University Books 1972. NY: Avon 1972.

27. Erich Von Daniken: *Chariots of the Gods*. New York: Bantam 1971 (first published in 1969)

28. This position paper I addressed to Puthoff and Targ was dated 8 January 1973. It was entitled *Alternative Scenarios for long-term research on Paranormal Phenomena*. My recommendation was for a mixed strategy that combined open and secret research in "the creation of a confidential group, secrecy being used to accomplish two practical goals: (1) shielding other scientific projects from highly-controversial areas of research and (2) allowing the acquisition of otherwise-inaccessible data elements". It was this strategy that was ultimately implemented.

29. *Croiset the Clairvoyant*, by Jack Harrison Pollack. New York: Bantam 1965.

30. That sighting by the author and two other persons is described in Volume I of *Forbidden Science*, entry for 1 September 1958.

31. James McCampbell's book was published privately in 1973 under the title *Ufology: New Insights from Science and Common Sense*.

32. *Mensa* is an organization that gathers self-selected individuals who have been tested, have recorded a high intelligence quotient and seek the company of similar personalities. Bill Powers used to joke that any intelligent persons who applied for membership to such an arrogant club should have fifty points taken off their I.Q. as a matter of principle!

33. Michael Aquino, a high official of the Church of Satan, later formed a splinter group he called the Temple of Set. It had its headquarters in San Francisco, at Aquino's house on Russian Hill.

34. It took another 20 years for Paul Baran to gain wide recognition as a founder of Arpanet, which became Internet in the early nineties. Born in 1926, he started his pioneering work on packet switching at Rand in the fifties and early sixties (see *supra*, Part Five, note 18). When he received the Marconi Award in Halifax in 1991 a Canadian newspaper noted his reputation as a modest man: "Baran appreciates the honor but calls awards 'very corrupting to the ego,' wrote an interviewer. His inventions led him to found Equatorial, Telebit, Metricom and Com21, among other high-technology companies.

35. Ingo Swann mentioned this conversation in *Report on Project SCANATE* (published 29 Dec. 1995): "I consulted a number of scientists outside of the SRI orbit, but not far away, in Silicon Valley. No one could recommend anything. But Dr. Jacques Vallee recognized the problem as one of "addresses." He said that you need an address that gets the perceptual channel to the right place, exactly as one needs a street address to find a house, or an address menu code in a computer to find and call up the desired information." This notion led him to use coordinates and became a basis of the remote viewing program.

36. *Future Shock*, by Alvin Toffler. NY: Random House 1970.

37. As noted earlier, McCampbell's book was not published under this title but as *Ufology*.

38. The article we published in *Datamation* was entitled "Network Conferencing" (May 1974, pp.85-92) Other publications from my project during this period included "Travel/Communication Relationships: Transcript of a Computer Conference" Montréal: Bell Canada Business Planning Group, July 1974. (This was the first edited transcript from a computer conference ever published). "Group Communication through Electronic Media: Fundamental Choices and Social Effects" *Educational Technology* Vol. 14, No. 8, August 1974, pp. 7-19. "The Teleconferencing System of the Institute for the Future" *Proceedings of the Meeting on Computer Networks*, International Institute for Applied Systems Analysis. Vienna, Austria, 1975. "Computer Conferencing" Letter to the Editor, *Science Magasine*, April 1975, p. 203. "Computer Conferencing: An Altered State of Comunication?" in *The Futurist*, June 1975. "Geologic Applications of Network Conferencing: Current Experiments with the FORUM System" Annual Meeting of the American Chemical Society. Chicago, August 25, 1975. Reprinted in *Computer Networking and Chemistry*, (P. Lykos, editor) Washington: ACS Symposium, Series #19, 1975. Some of these works were co-authored with Dr. Robert Johansen, Kathy Vian, Thaddeus Wilson, Dr. Arthur Hastings, and others.

39. Dr. Steve Lukasik went on be assistant secretary of Defense for Intelligence.

40. The family of Claude Poher has been prominent in French political life in several contexts. Alain Poher was president of the Senate after the death of President Pompidou. See *Les Cinquante Jours d'Alain Poher*, by Dominique Pado. Paris: Denoël 1969.

41. The Vril Movement was a secret society of Germanic inspiration aiming at the study of Man's "higher talents." The *Synarchie* was a French movement of the late thirties for an "invisible revolution" leading to a new French empire. It was inspired by the ideas of the 19th century mystic, Saint-Yves d'Alveydre. The "Cagoule" was another technological conspiracy active in the Thirties, also an extreme-right movement. All of these groups had radical objectives and were occasionally violent.

42. "L'air épais," or "the Thick Air" was an occult ritual practiced by high-level SS members in their monasteries. Anton LaVey gives a sanitized version of it in his *Satanic Rituals*.

43. A co-author of George Adamski's first contact book *Flying Saucers Have Landed* (1953), Desmond Leslie was born in Ireland in 1921. Educated at Trinity College, Dublin, he served in the Fighter Command of the RAF during the Second World War. He lived most of his life at Castle Leslie, Glaslough, Ireland. He likened the "ufonauts" to the angelic beings described by theosophists.

44. "Confravision" and video-conferencing were first tried in the mid-seventies in England, under the auspices of the British Post Office. The technology was expensive. It linked together fully-equipped television studios with control sonsoles, document cameras and various levels of equipment to attempt to re-create the feeling of a face-to-face meeting.

45. *Le Maître et Marguerite*, novel by Mikhail Boulgakov. Paris: Laffont 1968.

Part Seven: Future Networks

1. The article in question was entitled "UFOs: The Psychic Component." It appeared in the February 1974 issue of *Psychic* magazine, pp.12-17.

2. Pat Price, a scientologist and an early subject in the SRI "remote-viewing" experiments, was one of the most gifted and reliable American psychics of the century. However, as the FBI reported in 1977 after a raid on the Church of scientology office in Los Angeles, Price had served as a spy infiltrating CIA operations on behalf of scientology.

3. Charles Musès, a mathematician and scholar, received his doctorate in philosophy from Columbia University in 1951. He published studies on Jacob Boehme, Schopenhauer and the Zen Lankavatara Sutra. Musès travelled widely in Sikkim, in the Near East and the Chiapas jungles where he lived with the Lacandone Indians. He served as co-editor of the proceedings of the first international symposium (1960) on artificial intelligence. In 1968 he became editor of the Journal of bio-medical computing.

4. Allen Michael the Messiah was a colorful character who also called himself the "Comforter". His group, the One-World Family Commune, was formed in the fifties and has proven remarkably stable.

5. Puharich's book was entitled *Uri: A Journal of the Mystery of Uri Geller*. (Garden City: Doubleday Anchor Press, 1974).

6. Dr. J.C.R. Licklider was credited with establishing the basis for computer concepts like time-sharing. He died in June 1990 at age 75. In a number of papers published in the Sixties, he had outlined what he called the "man-computer symbiosis," the science of the relationship between human beings and computers, a subject of interest to the U.S. military.

7. The Pascagoula case, which took place on 11 October 1973, had two witnesses, Charles Hickson, 42, and Calvin Parker,19. It has been documented in numerous books. I must disclaim any direct knowledge of it. I never went to the site or met the witnesses myself, and I did not research the case.

8. The Lead Mask Case (Blue File No. 47) and my subsequent investigation have been described in detail in the opening section of *Confrontations,* op.cit.

9. Hoova was the name of the space entity that supposedly controlled Uri Geller's paranormal talents, according to Uri and Andrija Puharich.

10. This 1974 observation of a "bedroom visitor" is strikingly similar to descriptions given much later by Whitley Strieber in his best-selling book, *Communion*, (NY: Beech Tree - Morrow, 1987) which triggered an avalanche of reports from all over the world and gave rise to a standard image of the Aliens.

11. In a follow-up statement given in 1992 Robert Galley denied much of the significance of his statement to Bourret seventeen years earlier. Arguing that "my initial idea has been considerably amplified and changed, (...) my statements never went beyond the fact that there are certainly, at present, luminous phenomena in space that cannot be immediately explained. (...) If I had to do it again I would try to tell Jean-Claude Bourret to quote my words literally and not to wander off about UFOs."

12. The AIAA is the American Institute of Aeronautics and Astronautics, a major industry organization. Professor Kuettner had become involved with the UFO problem as a consultant to the Condon committee between 1967 and 1969.

13. These symbols or signs, which showed a double undulating form (somewhat like a letter "m" written in formal cursive) with a vertical tail at the end terminated by a cross, were carefully painted by the side of various roads in the Southern part of France. I never obtained much detail from Poher, but several of my informants in the region took this matter seriously and sent me their findings. (Blue File No. 48)

14. Georges Pompidou died of Waldenström's illness, the same disease that killed the Shah of Iran, Golda Meir and President Boumédienne. This is a curious coincidence, because this illness only touches one person out of 250,000 in the general population.

15. The U-2, a secret plane of the Fifties, was turned over to scientific missions when it was declassified and replaced by the SR-71 "Blackbird". NASA-Ames had several of the planes for research on the atmosphere, remote sensing of the earth and emergency management, as in the case of forest fires, earthquakes and volcano eruptions.

16. Our NASA report on Forum was later published by the Institute for the Future under the title "Computer-based communication in support of scientific and technical work," with Thaddeus Wilson as co-author (NASA CR 137879, March 1976). Other publications included: "Impact of a Computer-Based Communications Network on the Working Patterns of Researchers: Design for Evaluation of Effects Related to Productivity" (co-author with Robert Johansen) *American Sociological Association*, Annual Meeting, New York, August 1976. "Computer Networks and the Interactive Use of Geologic Data: Recent Experiments in Teleconferencing" *Computers & Geosciences*, Vol. 2, pp. 305-308, Pergamon Press, 1976. "The FORUM Project: Network Conferencing and its Applications" *Computer Networks*, Vol. 1, No. 1, June 1976, pp. 39-52. "Pragmatics and Dynamics of Computer Conferencing" *Proceedings of the Third International Conference on Computer Communications*, Toronto, August 1976, pp.208-213. "Distributed Management of Scientific Projects: An Analysis of Two Computer Conferencing Experiments at NASA" *Telecommunications Policy*, Vol. 1, No. 1. Dec. 1976, pp. 75-85. "The outlook for Computer Conferencing on Arpanet and PLATO" *Proceedings of the 25th Annual Meeting of the Society for General Systems Research* and the AAAS, Denver, Feb.1977, and "Modeling as a Communication Process" *Technological Forecasting and Social Change*, No. 10, 1977, pp. 391-400.

17. The so-called "Beltway Bandits" are a series of think tanks and consulting organizations such as SAIC (Science Applications, Inc.) and MITRE which occupy modern buildings near the Beltway that runs around the Western and Southern fringes of Washington. These companies survive almost entirely on contracts from government agencies.

18. Dr. Murray Turoff was an early pioneer of computer conferencing, first when he worked at the Office of Emergency Preparedness, and later at the New Jersey Institute of Technology, where he was a professor in the mid-seventies. His interest in the technique had been spurred by information scientists at the State Department and at IDA. The first system he built was called EMISSARI. It was used in the setting up of price controls under President Nixon. (See R. Johansen, *Groupware*. NY: MacMillan Free Press 1988.)

19. The Wylbur concept grew out of design work led by Rod Fredrickson at Stanford in 1968 and 1969. It was a line-oriented text-editor with powerful search, copy and replace capabilities, well-suited to the time-sharing environment. Wylbur authorized the use of powerful macros of considerable flexibility, making its use flexible both for user text files and for computer programs.

20. *Report from Iron Mountain*, anonymous text introduced by Leonard C. Lewin. Harmondsworth: Penguin Books 1968.

21. In later years this group fed the speculation about the infamous MJ-12 or "Majestic 12," a disinformation-based source of "genuine false documents" that confused so many amateur ufologists during the late eighties and beyond.

22. On 11 October 1991 an American ufologist named Dale Goudie received a statement from the CIA (reference F91-1615) under the Freedom of Information Act: "There is no organized Central Intelligence Agency effort to do research in connection with the UFO phenomena, nor has there been an organized effort to study or collect intelligence on UFOs since the 1950s." In my own experience that statement only reflects the government's perverted approach to the FOIA. (*The Confirmation Paper*, by Dale Goudie and James Klotz, Mercer Island, Washington, 19 Feb.1992, private communication).

23. In July 1992 a man calling himself Armen Victorian (whose real name is said to be Henry Azadehdel) bluntly exposed the identity and role of Dr. Christopher Green in an article published by the British *UFO Magazine* (Vol.11, no.3). Detailing his career, including his work for the CIA and later General Motors as well as his membership on various Boards, Victorian knew details of Dr. Green's background: Born in June 1940, he obtained a BA in biology at Northwestern (1962), a Ph.D. in physiology at the University of Colorado Medical School and an M.D. at El Paso Medical School in 1977. He became chief, biomedical sciences at CIA in 1971. On Armen Victorian's true identity see *Fortean Times* no.90, September 1996.

24. Psychiatrist Dr. Ken Colby developed the Parry software program at Stanford in the early Seventies to mimic the verbal behavior of a paranoid patient. Driven by an interactive English dialogue which used time-shared terminals, the program contained a model controlled by internal parameters such as fear and mistrust, which reacted to certain words in the interviewer's questions. Like humans, the model tended to take statements out of context and was prompt to lash out at the user - or to turn itself off.

25. About John Whitmore's role as the financier behind Puharich in this phase of his life, see *Prelude to the Landing on Planet Earth*, by Stuart Holroyd. London, W. H. Allen 1977.

26. Prof. Meyer's theory was developed and illustrated in our joint article "The Dynamics of Long-Term Growth" in *Technological Forecasting and Social Change*, 7, pp. 285-300, August 1975. It established the fact that technological development enhanced man's ability to survive and led to a population and resource utilisation explosion.

27. IFIPS is the International Federation of Information Processing Societies. The paper was called "FORUM: A Computer System to Support Interaction among People." *Proceedings of IFIP '74*, Stockholm, North-Holland pp. 1052-1056. August 1974.

28. José Lopez Rega is mentioned in Peter Levenda's book *Unholy Alliance* (New York: Avon 1995) as "Argentina's own version of Rudolf Hess... self-professed Rosicrucian, Peronista, mystical advisor to Isabel Peron, founder of the notorious AAA death squads... and member of Propaganda Due, P-2, the supersecret Masonic society dedicated to the overthrow of the Italian government and its replacement by a Fascist regime." (p.293).

29. Ron Bracewell was a Stanford astrophysicist specialized in radio-astronomy. Along with Frank Drake he pioneered the concept of SETI, the search for extraterrestrial intelligence. In the early sixties he had proposed the notion of a "Galactic Club" to which he speculated humanity might some day belong, if we survived long enough. He died in 2008.

30. In the five-year period that ended December 1974 stocks declined 11%, the worst five-year period since World War Two, as measured by Standard & Poor's 500-stock index, which takes into account both price changes and dividends. Stocks also declined in the five-year period ended December 1977.

31. Alvin M. Weinberg, director of the Physics division at Oak Ridge in the Forties, later served as head of the Atomic Energy Commission.

32. The daughter of press magnate Randolph Hearst, Patty Hearst was kidnapped and brainwashed by the Symbionese Liberation Army, a group of extreme-left radicals. As proof that she had rejected her bourgeois upbringing she was photographed holding a machine gun and even participated in some of the group's notorious exploits, such as bank robberies. She was eventually released, while the SLA was crushed in gun battles with police.

33. The "Law of the Times" holds that, in all regions of the globe, the frequency of UFO close encounters rises out of the noise level about 6 p.m., increases rapidly in the late evening hours and goes through a maximum about 10:30 p.m., probbaly because potential witnesses retire and go to bed. A secondary peak in frequency is seen at dawn.

34. "The Manufacturer of Unavoidable Events," which I regard as my best short story, was published in *Fiction* as *Le Fabricant d'Evènements Inéluctables* (#145, Dec.1965)

35. The Markovic Affair which marred the presidential tenure of Georges Pompidou was an attempt by his political enemies to discredit his wife, shown in doctored photographs as a participant in sexual orgies. The case profoundly affected Pompidou.

36. A tax deduction claim based on the UFOCAT catalogue was eventually challenged by the IRS, according to Allen Hynek.

37. Prof. Price-Williams was on the UCLA Faculty when Carlos Castaneda was an anthropology student there. Together they performed a number of parapsychology experiments involving dreams, Allies and Carlos' claim of a "double." The experiments led to curious coincidences during the 70s and 80s.

38. *Journal for the Study of Consciousness*, Vol.5, No.2, 1972-3.

39. *Zodiac and Swastika*, by Wilhelm Wulff. New York: Coward, McCann & Geoghegan 1973.

40. The full story of events around Uri at the top-secret Livermore lab includes visions and terrifying experiences among the scientists, such as giant birds in their yards and even at the foot of their bed, according to physicist Mike Russo and his wife. Speaking on the phone to Geller, security officer Ron Robertson once heard Uri's voice go up an octave as he described future family dramas that actually happened to the officer the following Saturday.

One of Russo's colleagues, Peter Crane, called Dr.Green who was astonighed to find the scientists sweating and weeping as they told their stories. Following Green's visit Russo received a call from a metallic voice who instructed him to stop all work with Geller. On a tape recording of the metallic voice one of the recognizable words was the codename for an unconnected top-secret project that Dr. Green happened to know about, but that was unknown at Livermore. In a later event, physicist Don Curtis and his wife observed a holographic false arm in grey fabric hovering in their living room, a prelude to the visit by a bewildered one-armed man at the

Virginia hotel room when Drs. Green, Puthoff and Targ were meeting to discuss the case!

Dr Green later reported, "To my knowledge, they all, or most of them, resigned. I don't know the details, but the information I had was that they quit from Livermore. The reason I had been meeting with them, after all, was that they wanted to quit."

41. In his later analysis of Nazi connections among United States occult groups, Peter Levenda (*Unholy Alliance*, op.cit., p.327) states that the Church of Satan was a hedonistic group ("a kind of *Playboy* fantasy with horror sound track"), too egotistical to fall into the fascist temptation: "LaVey's organization promotes fierce independence as a way of life. The slavish obedience required of a Nazi organization would be repugnant to a genuine, LaVey-style satanist (...) LaVey's feelings towards Nazi political parties are typified by his scorn of a possible satanic concordat with the National Renaissance Party." However Levenda points to Michael Aquino's spinoff, the Temple of Set, as a group fascinated with Nazi occultism. Aquino even performed a magical ritual at the SS castle of Wewelsburg in the early eighties.

42. The case of Ely was documented in *The Edge of Reality*, the book I co-authored with Allen Hynek (Chicago: Regnery 1975) on pages 34-42.

43. In 1997 a group of followers of Marshall Applewhite shocked the world by committing suicide in an expensive villa near San Diego. The HIM group had become known as Heaven's Gate.

44. Alain Boudier claimed he was a French "honorable correspondent" for the SDECE when he re-appeared in the field many years later, in the context of abduction research.

45. See *Computer Networking and Chemistry*, by Peter Lykos. Hardcover. Washington: Amer. Chemical Soc. 1975. "Proceedings of a symposium at a meeting of the American Chemical Society." Section 4 describes the geologic applications of Forum computer conferencing, by Jacques Vallee and Gerald Askevold.

46. David Jacobs' book, *The UFO Controversy in America*, was published by Indiana University Press (Bloomington, Indiana) in 1975.

47. In later life David Jacobs changed to a radical position when he became a disciple of abduction promoter Budd Hopkins in the early 1990s. In this new role he berated me again, this time for not giving enough credence to the occupants, which he saw as an extraterrestrial race on a biotechnology mission.

48. This second AIAA paper was called "The Psycho-physical Nature of UFO Reality: A speculative framework" in *Thesis/Antithesis* (Proceedings of the AIAA - World Futures Society Symposium), Los Angeles Sept. 1975, p.19. Earlier that year the same organization had published "Basic Patterns in UFO Observations" (co-authored with Dr. Claude Poher) AIAA Paper #75-42, 13th Aerospace Sciences Meeting, Pasadena, California. 20 January 1975.

49. The transcript of the Psychic Research Computer Conference was preserved (the Institute for the Future has a copy of it) but never published.

50. The *San Francisco Chronicle* interview by Ruth Stein was published on 6 November 1975.

51. See for example the numerous references to Simonne Servais's role in Eric Roussel's book *Pompidou, le Président d'avant la Crise*. Paris: Lattès Marabout 1984: "Discrete but of infinite devotion... smart, charming, totally lacking in greed, keeping cordial relations with numerous journalists, no one will do more than her for the Prime Minister's public image" (p.136).

52. By 1993, at the peak of the real estate bubble, this price had doubled to about $550 per square foot.

53. Peter Levenda (*Unholy Alliance*, op.cit., p.261) echoes this remark by Jacques Bergier when he writes "concentration camps in general must be an internationally recognized means of solving what (Rudolf) Hess calls incomprehensible riddles."

54. About the despicable actions of the French police at Charonne, see Volume I, entry for 9 February 1962. It is only in September 1996 that the former Préfet of Paris, Maurice Papon, a former pro-Nazi collaborator during the Second World War, was finally accused for allowing such criminal acts. In an earlier incident, on 17 October 1961, police repression had resulted in 60 cadavers fished out of the Seine the next day or found hanging from trees in the woods of the Paris region (*Libération* 30 Sept.1996).

55. Valéry Giscard d'Estaing, who succeeded Georges Pompidou, was the third President of the French Fifth Republic.

56. My meeting with Muktananda was later described in the book *In the Company of a Siddha, interviews and conversations with Swami Mukatananda*. South Fallsburg, NY: Syda Foundation 1985.

57. The best book about the Urantia cult was written by Martin Gardner: *Urantia*, Amherst, NY: Prometheus 1995. Gardner identified the channeler, clarified Dr. Sadler's role and beautifully de-constructed the social environment of the group, linked to some leading American industrialists.

58. The *Berkeley Barb*, an outrageously funny politico-erotic newspaper, started out as an underground student publication and became a standard in the Bay Area. It featured unconventional political views, *Zippy the Pinhead* cartoons, and many pages of erotic fantasies and sex ads of every orientation. At some point during the Eighties it transformed itself into a sex magazine known as *The Spectator*.

59. The novel *The Flying Saucer*, by Bernard Newman, was published in New York by Macmillan in 1950 (hardcover).

60. On the mystery of the "Golden Flower" see Carl Gustav Jung, *Alchemical Studies*, vol.13 of his Collected Works, Princeton University Press, Bollingen Foundation series.

61. The Plato system was first conceived by Dr. Bitzer and implemented by Control Data. The concept was to use a dedicated mainframe with up to one thousand terminals installed within the schools to deliver interactive education with quality graphics, simulations, and advanced courseware. The system was ahead of its time. It underestimated the ratio of development time to student time. The teaching community saw it as an encroachment on their prerogatives. By ignoring the emotional aspects of good teaching (to the benefit of the purely cognitive aspects) it missed an important opportunity to bring intelligent technology into the classroom.

62. The "Hillside curve" was first explained in print in *Invisible College*. It simply illustrates my observation that the probability for a witness to report an unusual occurrence rises rapidly as "strangeness" increases, but only to a certain point. When events become too bizarre for comfort the probability of reporting decreases again to a vanishing point where the conscious mind of the percipient may not even be aware of the occurrence.

63. In 2010 I learned more details: The observation, dated 7 January 1974, was made by two Gendarmes. The object was an oblong half sphere, orange in color. It circled as it rose above the aircraft carrier Foch. The French Navy denied all knowledge of it.

64. M. Alexandre de Marenches was director of the SDECE from 1970 to 1981 after serving under General Juin at the French Defense Ministry since 1946. See the book he co-authored with Christine Ockrent, *Dans le Secret des Princes*. (Paris: Stock 1986.)

65. The book was eventually published by Dell (New York) as *The Hynek UFO Report* in Dec. 1977.

66. This dream was realized when I built the Spring Hill observatory in the mid-eighties.

67. Arthur Lundahl (born in Chicago April 1, 1915) studied geography at the University of Chicago before joining the Navy in 1942 as a photographic intelligence officer. He moved to the CIA in 1953. As director of the Photographic Interpretation Center (NPIC) he played a vital role in many international crises. He reported in person to President Kennedy and to General De Gaulle when his group discovered Soviet missiles based in Cuba in 1962. Allen Dulles said of him, "he has done as much to protect the security of this nation as any man I know."

68. For the history of the Silver Shirts, Ballard and the I AM Movement, see the important book *Psychic Dictatorship in America* by Gerald B. Bryan. Los Angeles: Truth Research, 1940.

69. Ed Krupp is an astronomer, the gifted author of several excellent books on archaeo-astronomy.

70. Julia Philips, the co-producer of *Close Encounters of the Third Kind,* commented on this period in her own book *You'll Never Eat Lunch in This Town Again!* (New York: Random House 1991). She mentioned Hynek on three occasions, consistently mispelling his name as "Alan Hyneck." With a great deal of Hollywoodian arrogance she explained how they acquired the rights to the title "which had been coined by a sweet wacko named Alan Hyneck (sic) in a primer called *The UFO Experience* (...) He had broken sightings down into three oddly poetic phrases (...) The simple, elegant poetry came later, mostly as a result of cutting-and-pasting skills I had acquired in a number of publishing jobs."

71. This form of interaction through computers, which would become common through "chat" over Internet services twenty years later, was an exceptional technical achievement in the Seventies. At the time Apple was a startup, barely beginning to market its first model of a personal computer - with no communications capabilities. The idea went much farther back, however. Howard Rheingold later noted: "One of the pioneers in Computer-mediated communication, (...) Jacques Vallee, in his prophetic 1982 book *The Network Revolution*, claims that the first attempt to create a group communication medium was the Berlin crisis and airlift of 1948." (Rheingold, *The Virtual Community*, 1995).

72. I had been in Dayton with Allen Hynek 12 years earlier, for a visit to Wright-Patterson Air Force Base. Our trip had coincided with a UFO landing in Socorro, New Mexico which was never satisfactorily explained.

Part Eight: Close Encounters

1. Aleister Crowley's Journal is entitled *The Magical Record of the Beast 666.* The work quoted here was edited by John Symonds and Kenneth Grant. Montréal: Next Step 1972.

2. *Mind-Reach,* by Russell Targ and Harold Puthoff. New York: Delacorte/ Eleanor Friede 1977.

3. Barbara Marx Hubbard, noted Washington hostess, futurist and author of *The Hunger of Eve* (Harrisburg, Pa.: Stakpole Books 1976), is the heiress of the Marx toy company founded by her father.

4. My daughter sang: "J'ai descendu dans mon jardin/ pour y cueillir des sous-marins..." The ancient French children's song goes: "J'ai descendu dans mon jardin/ pour y cueillir du romarin," which translates as "I went down to my garden to gather some rosemary", not "some submarines" as she was singing.

5. Hypernumbers (such as the square root of minus one) have been studied by mathematicians like Oliver Heaviside, William Rowan Hamilton, William Kingdon Clifford and Coxeter. In the book he co-edited with Arthur Young (*Consciousness and Reality*. NY: Outerbridge & Lazard 1972) Charles Musès claimed that hypernumbers were related to "the mathematical representation of the operations of the mind."

6. Murray Turoff and Roxanne Hiltz were prominent researchers of computer conferencing in the seventies. See *supra* Part Seven, note 19. Roxanne Hiltz joined Turoff's project at the New Jersey Institute of Technology as a social researcher of group interation through computers. She co-authored a book and many articles with Murray Turoff, whom she eventually married.

7. On the properties of Kundalini see the book by Lee Sannella: *Kundalini, psychosis or transcendence?* (San Francisco: Washington Street Research Center, 1976). It describes a poorly-understood psycho-physical process characterized by sharp pains up the back and spine, roaring sounds, whistling followed by a "sunburst." Patients often report being overcome with bliss and a spiritual transformation.

8. Ira Einhorn may have confused "bilocation" (the rare claimed ability of some psychics to be in two places at the same time) with "bio-location", a more common method for finding a hidden object or determining patterns of subtle energies which is the accepted Russian term for "dowsing." The Western press commonly makes this mistake. About that time physicist Jack Sarfatti was in touch with Ira. He wrote on the "Well" in July 1996: "We stayed with my literary agent Ira Einhorn and his doomed girlfriend Holly Maddux (...) Einhorn told me he would introduce me to Stewart Brand, Michael Murphy and George Leonard when I got to San Francisco. He said he had support from the local telephone company and from the Bronfmans in Toronto to link up visionary scientists like myself. He was working with Jacques Vallee and Brendan O'Regan on a UFO database. Ira mentioned he was working with Congressman Charlie Rose of the House Select Committee on Intelligence. Rose confirmed his connection to

Einhorn in a phone conversation with me."

9. Anton LaVey's thoughtful article on secrecy was entitled "The importance of keeping a secret versus the Discovery Game" (*Cloven Hoof* Vol.IX No.2, issue 66, 1977, pp.3-4).

10. Travis Walton's abduction claim was the subject of a book and of the film *Fire in the Sky*, with a screenplay by Tracy Tormé. Philip Klass raised some important cautions about Walton's background and early brushes with the law.

11. In *Close Encounters* the French scientist's interpreter, a former geographer by profession points out that the numbers they're receiving are a longitude and latitude. Realizing that no one has a map, they decide to break into the director's office and take his globe, which they pass overhead, one of the funny moments in the movie.

12. "Une Epidémie Mentale Contemporaine," by Ladon, in *Monographies Neuro-psychiatriques*, Doin publisher, ca.1930.

13. The experiments conducted by Crussard with Jean-Pierre Girard have been documented in the article "Etude de quelques déformations et transformations apparemment anormales de métaux," by Charles Crussard and J. Bouvaist, *Mémoires Scientifiques de la Revue de Métallurgie*, Februray 1978. I also have in my files Crussard's own report dated from 1976, unpublished. The tests were also noted in *La Jaune et la Rouge*, (the magazine of the *Polytechnique* school) for June 1979. As a result of these publications C. Crussard lost his job as scientific director at Péchiney and was forced to take early retirement. Girard was also extensively tested by Zbigniew William Wolkowski of the Henri Poincaré Institute, who stopped the study after PK was successfully applied to genetic mutations in fruit flies.

14. The *New Scientist* for 28 January 1995 (p.39) noted that "humans are just big bags of saltwater containing an aqueous broth of ionic conductivity. (Scientist Neil Gershenfeld) found that it was possible to detect body movements using the oscillating fields generated at small metal antennas."

15. Only one book was written about General Ailleret's death: *Mort d'un Général*, by John Saul. Paris: Le Seuil, 1977.

16. *Un Médium Agent Secret*, by Dr. Ernesto Montgomery and Cliff L. Linedecker. Ottawa: Editions Québec/Amérique 1977.

17. I cannot find any entries I may have made for July 1977. During that month I believe that I remained in the San Francisco area.

18. The region of Brazil commonly called "the Interior" extends over the Northeast of the country, from Fortaleza to the Amazon Basin. While not exactly a jungle, it is very remote and covers much territory that is inaccessible except by boat or four-wheel drive vehicle. It contains many swamps, large rivers, banana plantations and small villages with characteristic wooden houses with thatched roofs.

19. Magnuson Computers represented one of many attempts made in the seventies to build "cluster" systems for small-to-large businesses. Magnuson, like Fortune Systems and others, disappeared rapidly. The concept was later submerged in the "client-server" architecture that used far more powerful hardware.

20. André Danjon was director of Paris Observatory in the fifties and sixties, and an outspoken "rationalist" who followed (and often defined) the academic party line.

21. See *The Origin of Consciousness in the Breakdown of the Bicameral Mind,* by Julian Jaynes. Boston: Houghton-Mifflin 1976.

22. Interview with Stanley Schneider, Washington, 30 September 1977.

23. The Joe Simonton case, which involved a lonely man in Eagle River, Wisconsin who claimed he was given three pancakes by humanoid Aliens, was described in *Passport to Magonia.*

24. *The Tall Blond Man with one Black Shoe*, a French comedy, was directed by Yves Robert, with Pierre Richard, Bernard Blier and Mireille Darc, 1972.

25. The amusing rumor mispresenting me as the Comte de Saint-Germain began with an article by Ann Shapiro ("Did this Strange Man live Forever?") in a popular magazine of the late seventies.

26. This idea was never followed upon, in part because Hynek became entangled in legal arguments between his publisher (Henry Regnery) and Columbia Pictures.

27. Tom Belden, an information expert who served as senior analyst with the Institude for Defense Analyses (IDA) was one of the pioneers in the study of group decision making. While his role on the Intelligence Community Staff in the sixties and seventies forced him to stay behind the scenes, he was instrumental in getting various government agencies to experiment with early forms of groupware, notably computer conferencing.

28. The name "Cray" is a pseudonym. To protect the privacy of the people involved when their names had not been mentioned elsewhere, I have used pseudonyms for other *dramatis personae* like Elmer Burns and Jim Irish. Our painstaking investigation of the "Copper Medic" case is discussed in chapter Twelve of *Confrontations: A Scientist's search for Alien Contact* (New York: Ballantine 1990, 1991).

29. The group of scientists assembled by Prof. Sturrock was to become the nucleus of the Society for Scientific Exploration, still in existence.

30. Our investigation of the "Winery Frog" case is described in detail in chapter Four of *Confrontations: A Scientist's search for Alien Contact* (New York: Ballantine 1990, 1991).

31. The matter of Wilbur Franklin's death later surfaced as a topic of speculation on the Internet. According to a communication from Marcello Truzzi to Jack Sarfatti on 24 July 1998, "James Randi asserted in a (Japanese) magazine interview that Wilbur Franklin had committed suicide, at least in part as a result of his depression at deciding his prior endorsement of Uri Geller's metal bending powers was discredited. Geller sued Randi and the magazine for defamation (on this and other statements by Randi) since Franklin's death certificate showed this suicide claim was untrue. The Japanese court gave Geller a financial judgment against Randi, and I believe Geller settled out of court with the magazine publisher."

32. Research on the effects of EM radiation on the brain surged in that period. Unverified (possibly disinformation) rumors stated that the CIA had an "Operation Pique" in 1978 that included bouncing electromagnetic signals off the ionosphere. It was speculated that the purpose was to affect selected areas. Scientists in a position to know have denied the existence of that operation. An interesting article on the technology studied by Beck and others is "Low-power radio-frequency and microwave effects on human electroencephalogram and behavior," by William Bise of the Pacific Northwest Center for Non-Ionizing Radiation (*Physiological Chemistry and Physics*, Vol.10, No.5, 1978.) It is typical of many studies directed at mind control on behalf of the government. The device supposedly used for shielding people's brains from such radiation was anticipated in my 1962 science-fiction novel *Dark Satellite (Le Satellite Sombre).*

33. *The Vision and the Voice*, Fifteenth Aether, page 126.

34. The People's Temple collective suicide has been documented in numerous books. Much remains mysterious, however, about the exact background of the organization and its ultimate collapse. In their book "Fifty Greatest Conspiracies of All Time," Jonathan Vankin and John Whalen note that U.S. embassy official Richard Dwyer, who was wounded in Guyana in the cult's attack against Congressman Leo Ryan, was a CIA agent. His next stop after Guyana was Grenada! Leo Ryan's aide Joseph Holsinger feared that the CIA had been running a sinister operation at the People's Temple. He cited a paper authored by a Berkeley professor claiming that the MK-Ultra mind-control program was not stopped in 1973, as the CIA had sworn before Congress, but was transferred out of public hospitals and prisons into the more secure confines of religious cults and marginal organizations like the People's Temple.

35. Bergier's secret work in the Second World War is documented (in part) in his remarkable little book, *Agents Secrets contre Armes Secrètes*. Paris: J'Ai Lu - Leur Aventure (A101) 1965.

36. *Definitely Maybe*, by Arkady and Boris Strugatsky. NY:Collier 1978.

37. *The Suicide Cult*, by Marshall Kilduff and Ron Javers. New York: Bantam 1978.

38. Notably in *Second Look* for January 1979 ("Are human programmers manipulating the UFO phenomenon?") and in *East-West Journal* for March 1979 ("Space-Age Cults: Masks of Deception")

39. The Parsons crater is located on the opposite side of the Moon, not visible from Earth. See *Sky & Telescope* no.5 Nov 70, P.262.

40. SF *Chronicle*: 17 April 1979: "Quakers claim cops have an espionage network."

41. This hommage to Bergier appeared in the magazine *Question De...* edited by Louis Pauwels, No.29. Paris: Retz 1979.

42. "The Priest, the Well and the Pendulum" in *Co-Evolution Quarterly*, Winter 1977-78, pages 80-83.

43. "O my love, my fair love tearing me apart/I carry you within myself like a wounded bird/And these people, who know nothing of it, watch us pass by..." (Aragon)

44. About Victor Hugo's remarkable experiments with table-tapping spirits in Jersey, see: *Les Tables Tournantes de Jersey*, by Gustave Simon. Paris: Louis Conard, 1923.

45. About the Philip group in Toronto, see: *Conjuring up Philip*, by Iris M. Owen and Margaret Sparrow. NY: Pocket Books 1977.

46. As early as 1973 we recognized that conferencing could take one of two forms. "Asynchronous" discussions constitute an advanced form of electronic mail. "Synchronous" dialogues, in contrast, involve multiple participants sending and reading simultaneously. Much of our early research centered on supporting all these modes together under a single framework. After the sale of InfoMedia the spread of this technology was surprisingly slow. Even as late as 1996 synchronous conferencing only reappeared in the form of elementary "chat rooms" on services such as America Online.

47. The "Quarouble" case involved a French railroad worker, Marius Dewilde, who saw a dark landed saucer and two small humanoids he described as "martians" walking on the tracks near this town in the North of France. He claimed that he was paralyzed by a beam from the object.

48. The Chicago DC-10 crash that killed Ishtak Bentov also killed the wife of E. Howard Hunt, one of the Watergate conspirators.

49. Ira Einhorn was eventually arrested and imprisoned. See "Philadelphia Murderer caught in France." Associated Press, June 17, 1997.

50. The Meier case involved a small cult in Switzerland led by Eduard Meier, an adventurer who claimed to be visited by beings from the Pleiades, notably a sexy 400-year old lady named Semjase.

51. The interview by Dr. Christopher Evans was published in *Omni Magazine*, January 1980 issue, p. 62.

52. Sir Eric Gairy died in Grenada in August 1997, at the age of 75.

53. *The Bell Notes*, by Arthur M.Young (New York: Delacorte, 1979) was edited by Ira Einhorn.Young held the patent for the rotor system of the Bell helicopter and was a close friend of Charles Lindbergh. His wife was a heiress of the Forbes steel fortune. Young financed the Institute for the Study of Consciousness in Berkeley, California.

54. The song by Brassens evokes the remorse of a man who left his family in a misguided search for novelty: "Near my tree I used to live happy... Never should I have gone away far from my tree."

Reflections

1. *In Search of the Light*, The Adventures of a Parapsychologist, by Susan Blackmore. Amherst, N.Y.: Prometheus 1996.

2. See notably the excellent book by Smith, Paul H., *Reading the Enemy's Mind*. New York: Tor, 2005.

INDEX

Lightning Source UK Ltd.
Milton Keynes UK
UKHW012112220222
399098UK00008B/277/J

9 780578 032313